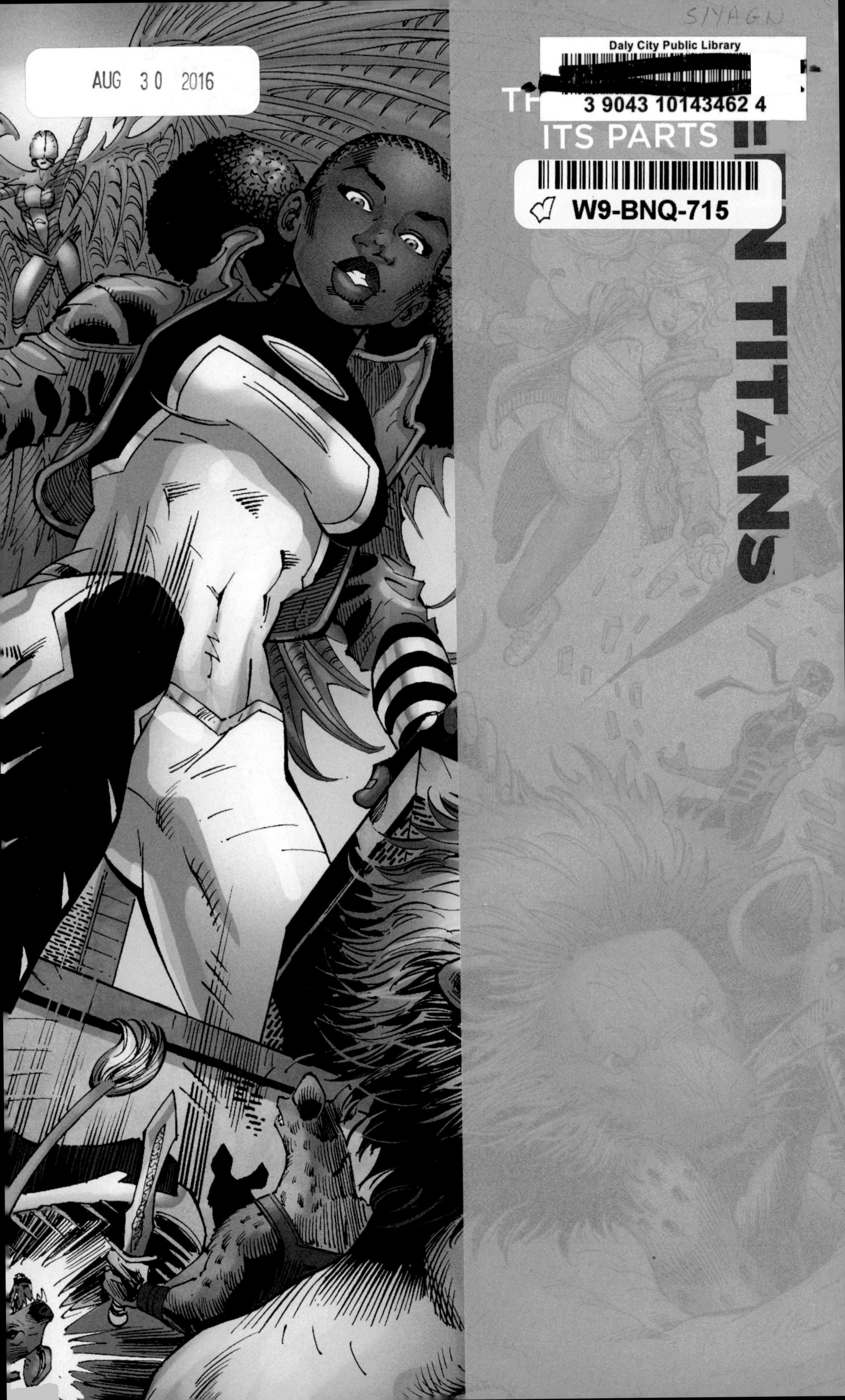
TH
ITS PARTS
N TITANS

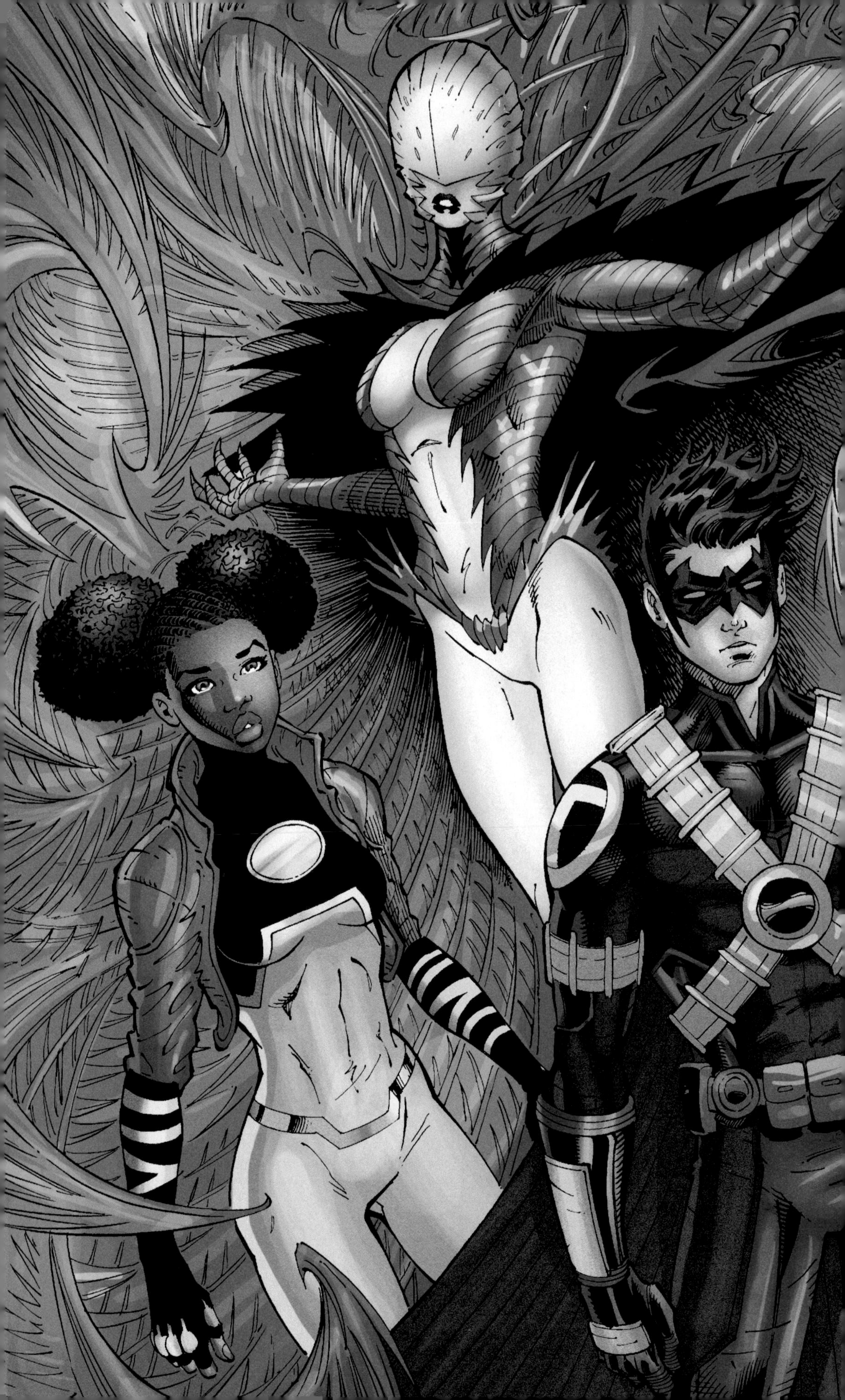

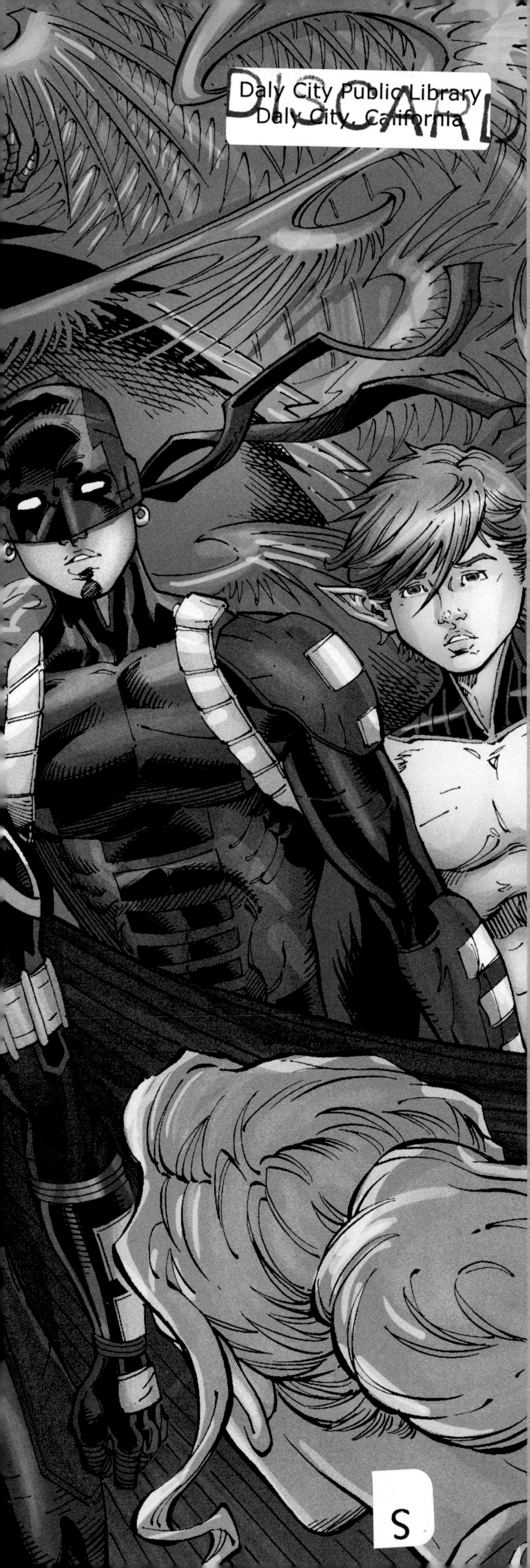

TEEN TITANS

VOLUME 3
THE SUM OF ITS PARTS

WRITTEN BY
SCOTT LOBDELL
GREG PAK
WILL PFEIFER

BREAKDOWNS BY
SCOTT McDANIEL

PENCILS BY
NOEL RODRIGUEZ
IAN CHURCHILL
MIGUEL MENDONÇA
TOM DERENICK
ALVARO MARTINEZ

INKS BY
ART THIBERT
NORM RAPMUND
DEXTER VINES
RAUL FERNANDEZ

COLOR BY
TONY AVIÑA

LETTERS BY
COREY BREEN

COLLECTION COVER ART BY
JORGE JIMÉNEZ
& ALEJANDRO SANCHEZ

SUPERBOY CREATED BY
JERRY SIEGEL
BY SPECIAL ARRANGEMENT
WITH THE JERRY SIEGEL FAMILY

WONDER WOMAN CREATED BY
WILLIAM MOULTON MARSTON

MIKE COTTON ALEX ANTONE Editors – Original Series
PAUL KAMINSKI Associate Editor – Original Series
BRITTANY HOLZHERR Assistant Editor – Original Series
JEB WOODARD Group Editor – Collected Editions
LIZ ERICKSON Editor – Collected Edition
STEVE COOK Design Director – Books
DAMIAN RYLAND Publication Design

BOB HARRAS Senior VP – Editor-in-Chief, DC Comics

DIANE NELSON President
DAN DIDIO and JIM LEE Co-Publishers
GEOFF JOHNS Chief Creative Officer
AMIT DESAI Senior VP – Marketing & Global Franchise Management
NAIRI GARDINER Senior VP – Finance
SAM ADES VP – Digital Marketing
BOBBIE CHASE VP – Talent Development
MARK CHIARELLO Senior VP – Art, Design & Collected Editions
JOHN CUNNINGHAM VP – Content Strategy
ANNE DEPIES VP – Strategy Planning & Reporting
DON FALLETTI VP – Manufacturing Operations
LAWRENCE GANEM VP – Editorial Administration & Talent Relations
ALISON GILL Senior VP – Manufacturing & Operations
HANK KANALZ Senior VP – Editorial Strategy & Administration
JAY KOGAN VP – Legal Affairs
DEREK MADDALENA Senior VP – Sales & Business Development
JACK MAHAN VP – Business Affairs
DAN MIRON VP – Sales Planning & Trade Development
NICK NAPOLITANO VP – Manufacturing Administration
CAROL ROEDER VP – Marketing
EDDIE SCANNELL VP – Mass Account & Digital Sales
COURTNEY SIMMONS Senior VP – Publicity & Communications
JIM (SKI) SOKOLOWSKI VP – Comic Book Specialty & Newsstand Sales
SANDY YI Senior VP – Global Franchise Management

TEEN TITANS VOLUME 3: THE SUM OF ITS PARTS

DC Comics, 2900 West Alameda Ave., Burbank, CA 91505
Printed by RR Donnelley, Owensville, MO, USA. 7/22/16. First Printing.
ISBN: 978-1-4012-6520-5

Library of Congress Cataloging-in-Publication Data is Available.

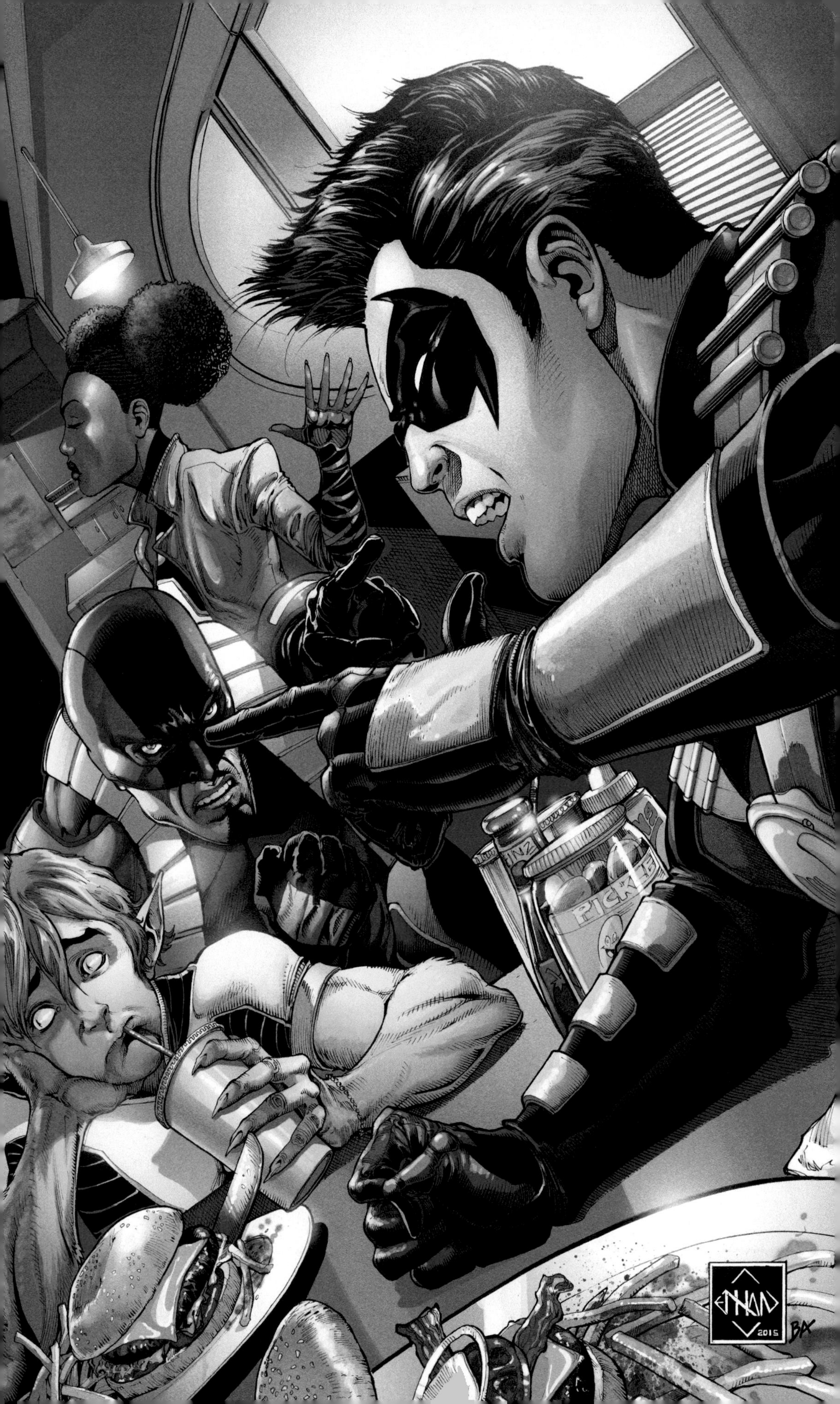

AFTERMATH

SCOTT LOBDELL WILL PFEIFER writers SCOTT McDANIEL breakdowns NOEL RODRIGUEZ penciller ART THIBERT finishes & inks TONY AVIÑA colorist COREY BREEN letterer
cover art by ETHAN VAN SCIVER & BRAD ANDERSON

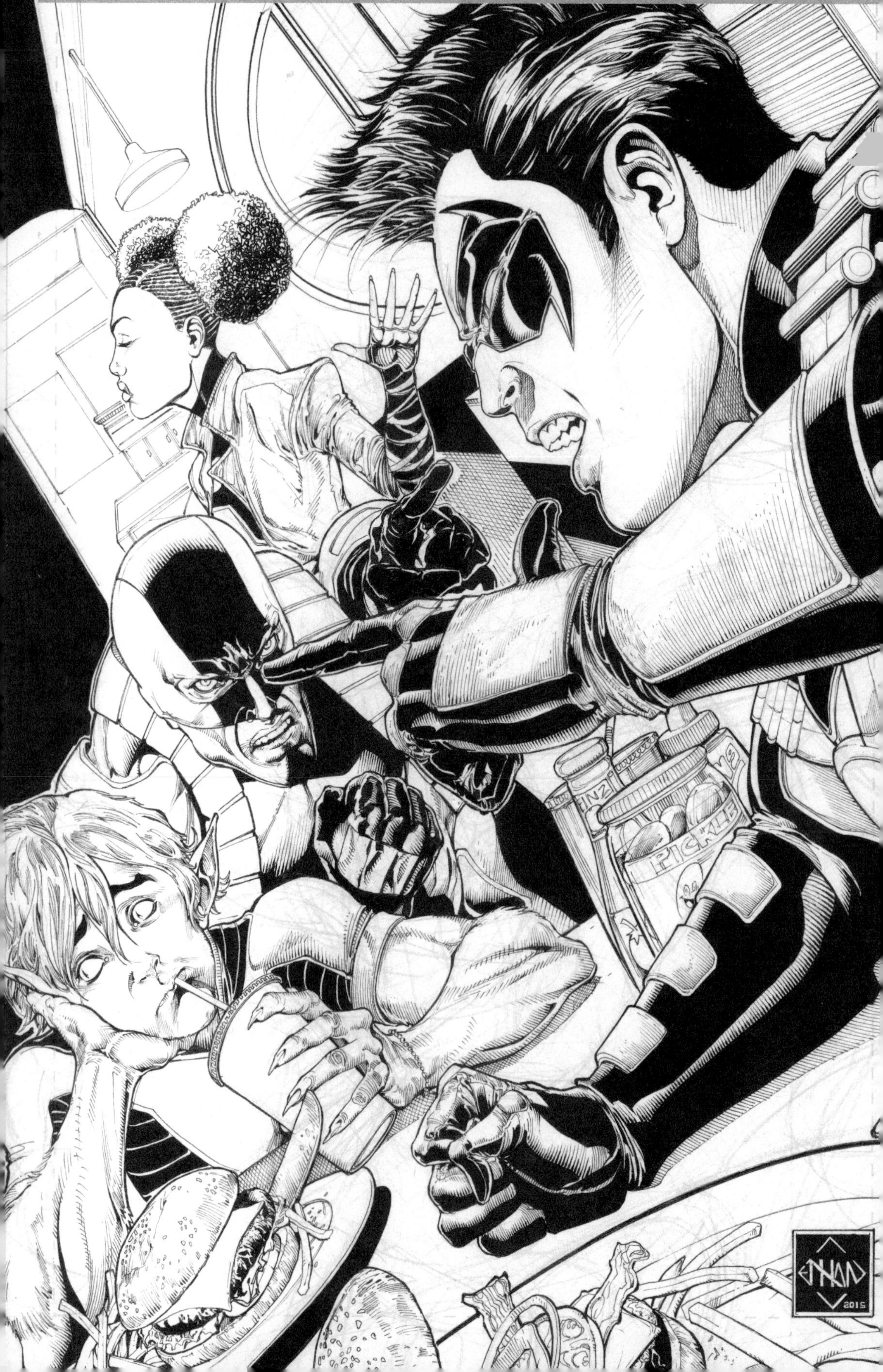
PICKLE
2015

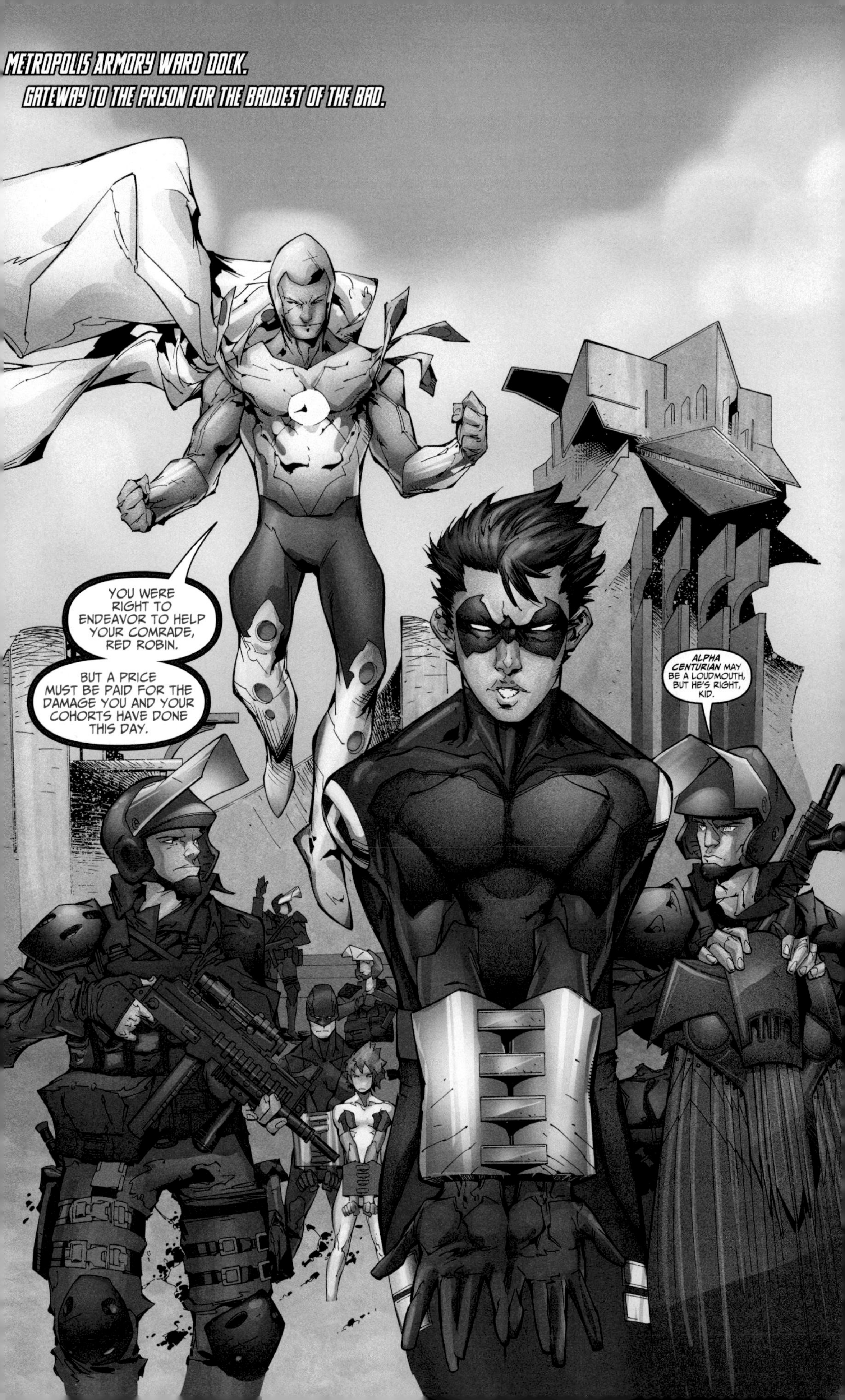
METROPOLIS ARMORY WARD DOCK.
GATEWAY TO THE PRISON FOR THE BADDEST OF THE BAD.
YOU WERE RIGHT TO ENDEAVOR TO HELP YOUR COMRADE, RED ROBIN.
BUT A PRICE MUST BE PAID FOR THE DAMAGE YOU AND YOUR COHORTS HAVE DONE THIS DAY.
ALPHA CENTURIAN MAY BE A LOUDMOUTH, BUT HE'S RIGHT, KID.

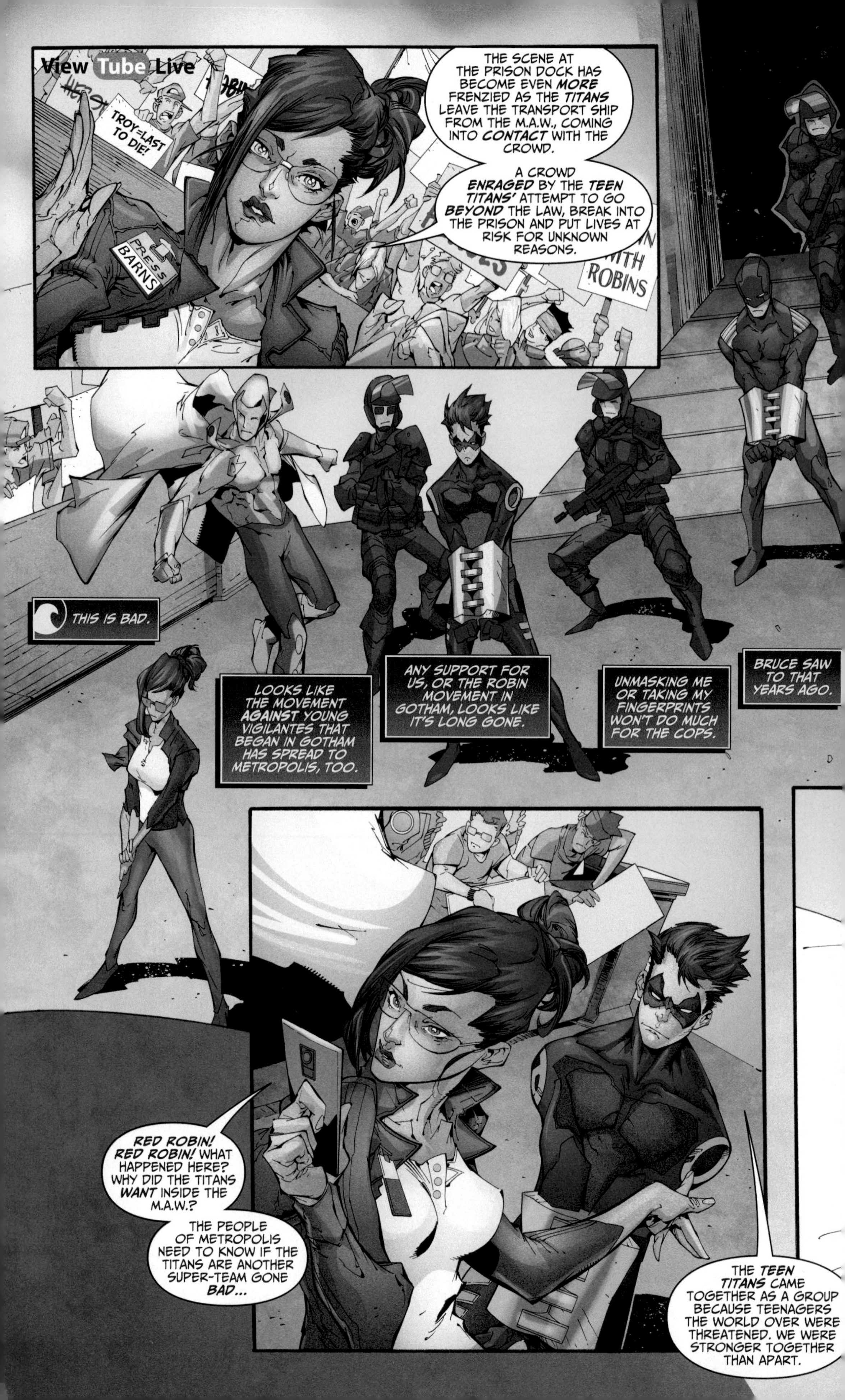

View Tube Live
TROY=LAST TO DIE!
PRESS BARNS
ROBINS
THE SCENE AT THE PRISON DOCK HAS BECOME EVEN MORE FRENZIED AS THE TITANS LEAVE THE TRANSPORT SHIP FROM THE M.A.W., COMING INTO CONTACT WITH THE CROWD.
A CROWD ENRAGED BY THE TEEN TITANS' ATTEMPT TO GO BEYOND THE LAW, BREAK INTO THE PRISON AND PUT LIVES AT RISK FOR UNKNOWN REASONS.
THIS IS BAD.
LOOKS LIKE THE MOVEMENT AGAINST YOUNG VIGILANTES THAT BEGAN IN GOTHAM HAS SPREAD TO METROPOLIS, TOO.
ANY SUPPORT FOR US, OR THE ROBIN MOVEMENT IN GOTHAM, LOOKS LIKE IT'S LONG GONE.
UNMASKING ME OR TAKING MY FINGERPRINTS WON'T DO MUCH FOR THE COPS.
BRUCE SAW TO THAT YEARS AGO.
RED ROBIN! RED ROBIN! WHAT HAPPENED HERE? WHY DID THE TITANS WANT INSIDE THE M.A.W.?
THE PEOPLE OF METROPOLIS NEED TO KNOW IF THE TITANS ARE ANOTHER SUPER-TEAM GONE BAD...
THE TEEN TITANS CAME TOGETHER AS A GROUP BECAUSE TEENAGERS THE WORLD OVER WERE THREATENED. WE WERE STRONGER TOGETHER THAN APART.

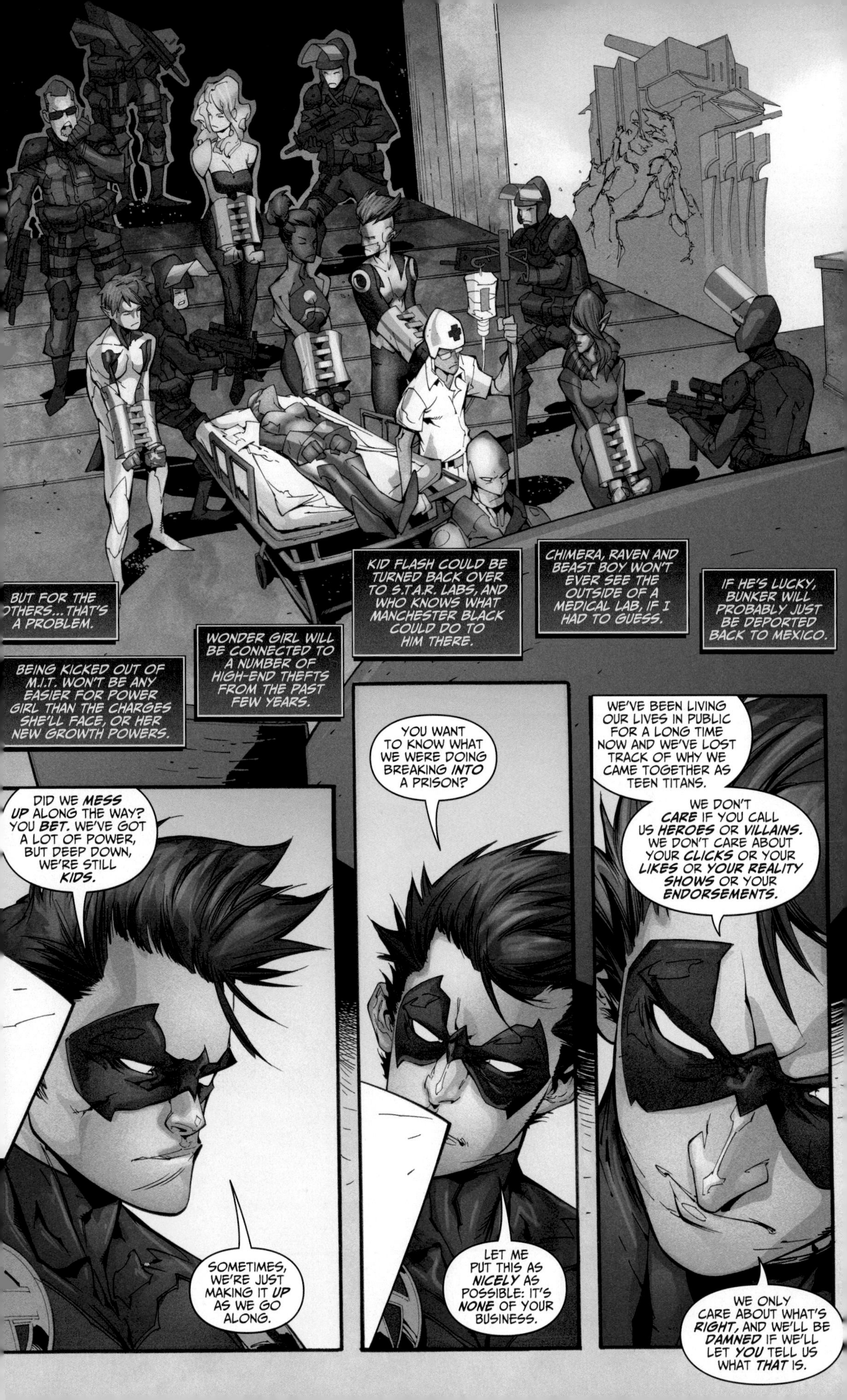
BUT FOR THE OTHERS... THAT'S A PROBLEM.
BEING KICKED OUT OF M.I.T. WON'T BE ANY EASIER FOR POWER GIRL THAN THE CHARGES SHE'LL FACE, OR HER NEW GROWTH POWERS.
WONDER GIRL WILL BE CONNECTED TO A NUMBER OF HIGH-END THEFTS FROM THE PAST FEW YEARS.
KID FLASH COULD BE TURNED BACK OVER TO S.T.A.R. LABS, AND WHO KNOWS WHAT MANCHESTER BLACK COULD DO TO HIM THERE.
CHIMERA, RAVEN AND BEAST BOY WON'T EVER SEE THE OUTSIDE OF A MEDICAL LAB, IF I HAD TO GUESS.
IF HE'S LUCKY, BUNKER WILL PROBABLY JUST BE DEPORTED BACK TO MEXICO.
DID WE MESS UP ALONG THE WAY? YOU BET. WE'VE GOT A LOT OF POWER, BUT DEEP DOWN, WE'RE STILL KIDS.
SOMETIMES, WE'RE JUST MAKING IT UP AS WE GO ALONG.
YOU WANT TO KNOW WHAT WE WERE DOING BREAKING INTO A PRISON?
LET ME PUT THIS AS NICELY AS POSSIBLE: IT'S NONE OF YOUR BUSINESS.
WE'VE BEEN LIVING OUR LIVES IN PUBLIC FOR A LONG TIME NOW AND WE'VE LOST TRACK OF WHY WE CAME TOGETHER AS TEEN TITANS.
WE DON'T CARE IF YOU CALL US HEROES OR VILLAINS. WE DON'T CARE ABOUT YOUR CLICKS OR YOUR LIKES OR YOUR REALITY SHOWS OR YOUR ENDORSEMENTS.
WE ONLY CARE ABOUT WHAT'S RIGHT, AND WE'LL BE DAMNED IF WE'LL LET YOU TELL US WHAT THAT IS.

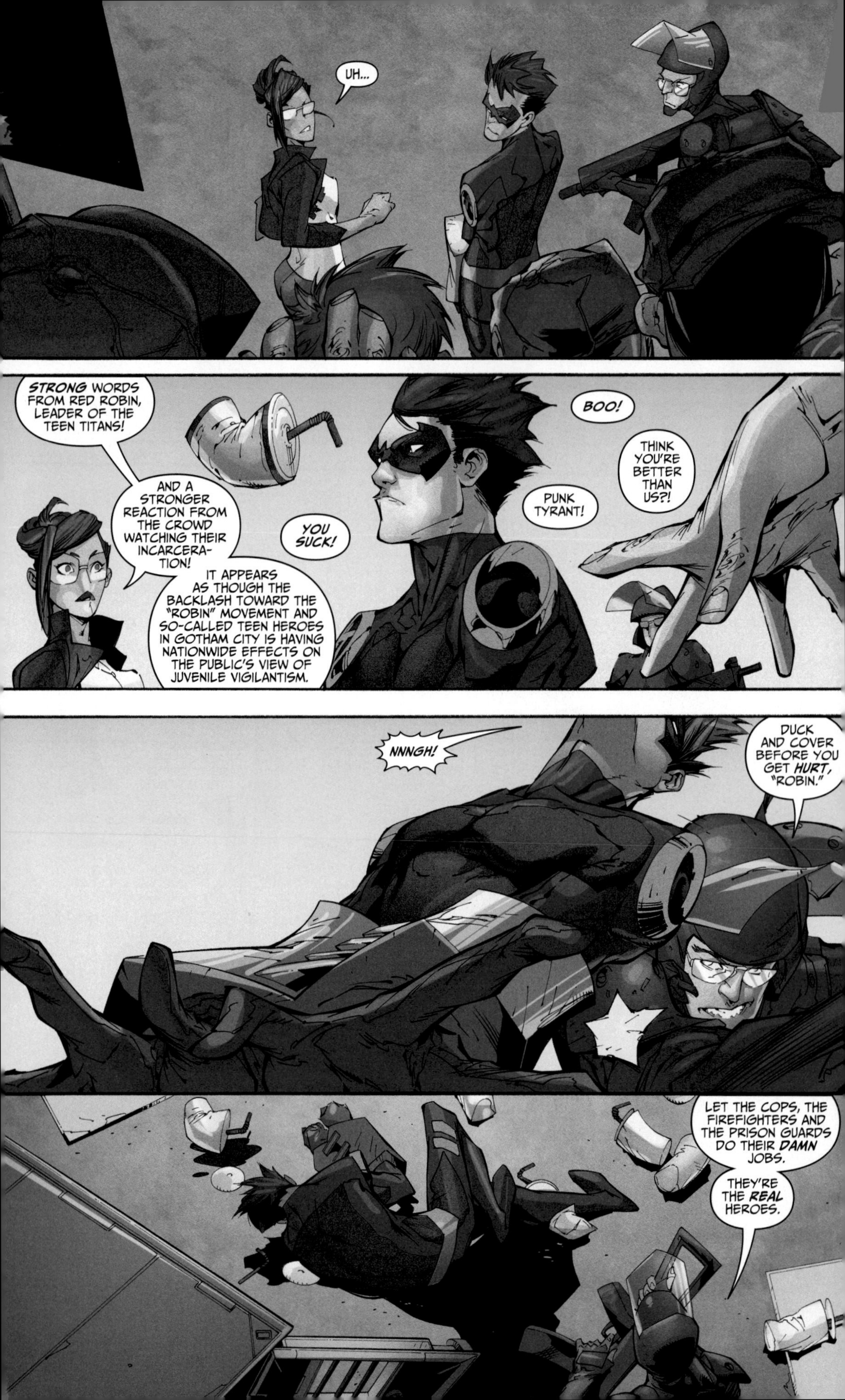
UH...
STRONG WORDS FROM RED ROBIN, LEADER OF THE TEEN TITANS!
AND A STRONGER REACTION FROM THE CROWD WATCHING THEIR INCARCERATION!
IT APPEARS AS THOUGH THE BACKLASH TOWARD THE "ROBIN" MOVEMENT AND SO-CALLED TEEN HEROES IN GOTHAM CITY IS HAVING NATIONWIDE EFFECTS ON THE PUBLIC'S VIEW OF JUVENILE VIGILANTISM.
YOU SUCK!
PUNK TYRANT!
BOO!
THINK YOU'RE BETTER THAN US?!
NNNGH!
DUCK AND COVER BEFORE YOU GET HURT, "ROBIN."
LET THE COPS, THE FIREFIGHTERS AND THE PRISON GUARDS DO THEIR DAMN JOBS.
THEY'RE THE REAL HEROES.

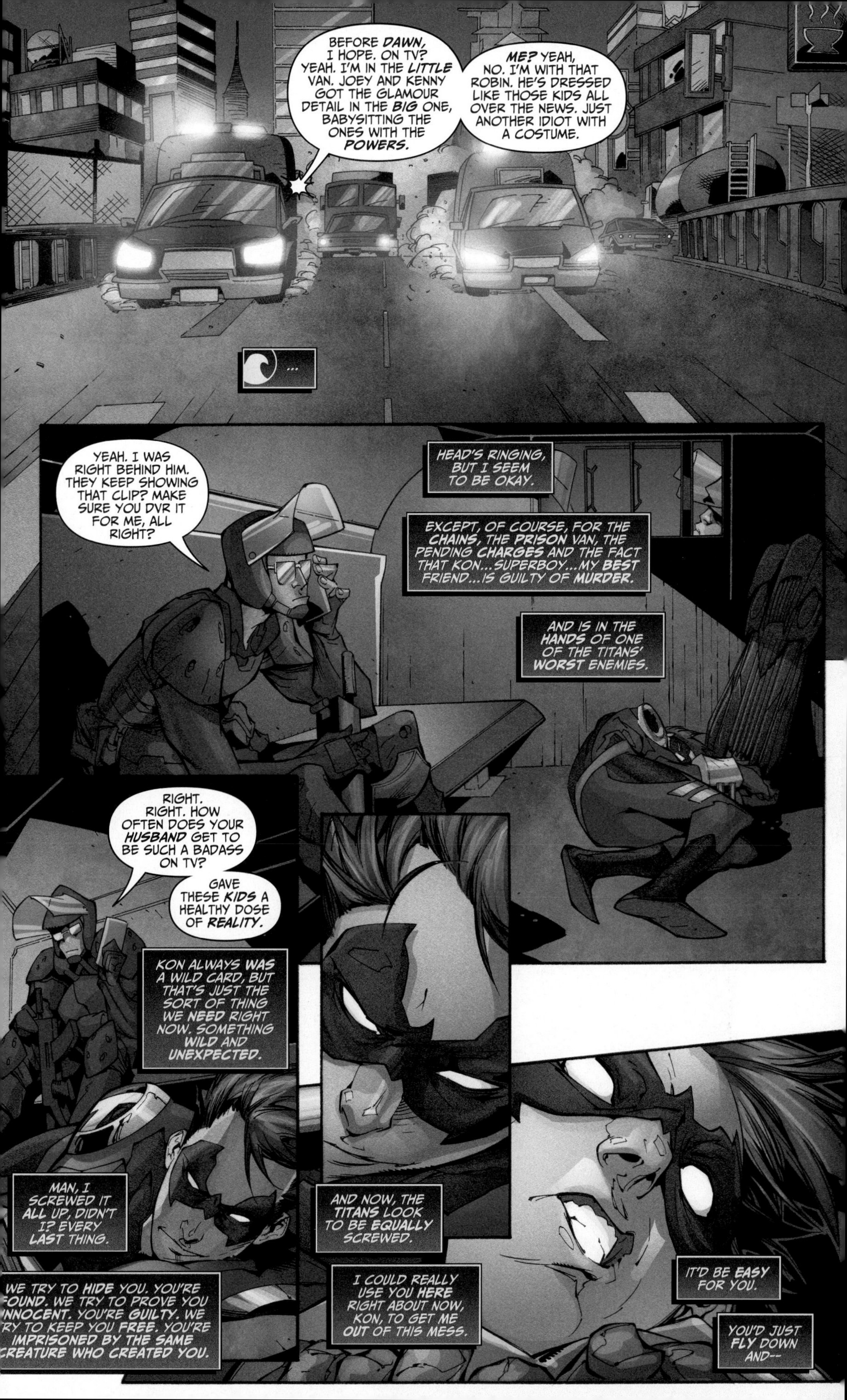
BEFORE DAWN, I HOPE. ON TV? YEAH. I'M IN THE LITTLE VAN. JOEY AND KENNY GOT THE GLAMOUR DETAIL IN THE BIG ONE, BABYSITTING THE ONES WITH THE POWERS.
ME? YEAH, NO. I'M WITH THAT ROBIN. HE'S DRESSED LIKE THOSE KIDS ALL OVER THE NEWS. JUST ANOTHER IDIOT WITH A COSTUME.
...
YEAH. I WAS RIGHT BEHIND HIM. THEY KEEP SHOWING THAT CLIP? MAKE SURE YOU DVR IT FOR ME, ALL RIGHT?
HEAD'S RINGING, BUT I SEEM TO BE OKAY.
EXCEPT, OF COURSE, FOR THE CHAINS, THE PRISON VAN, THE PENDING CHARGES AND THE FACT THAT KON...SUPERBOY...MY BEST FRIEND...IS GUILTY OF MURDER.
AND IS IN THE HANDS OF ONE OF THE TITANS' WORST ENEMIES.
RIGHT. RIGHT. HOW OFTEN DOES YOUR HUSBAND GET TO BE SUCH A BADASS ON TV?
GAVE THESE KIDS A HEALTHY DOSE OF REALITY.
KON ALWAYS WAS A WILD CARD, BUT THAT'S JUST THE SORT OF THING WE NEED RIGHT NOW. SOMETHING WILD AND UNEXPECTED.
MAN, I SCREWED IT ALL UP, DIDN'T I? EVERY LAST THING.
WE TRY TO HIDE YOU. YOU'RE FOUND. WE TRY TO PROVE YOU NNOCENT. YOU'RE GUILTY. WE RY TO KEEP YOU FREE. YOU'RE IMPRISONED BY THE SAME CREATURE WHO CREATED YOU.
AND NOW, THE TITANS LOOK TO BE EQUALLY SCREWED.
I COULD REALLY USE YOU HERE RIGHT ABOUT NOW, KON, TO GET ME OUT OF THIS MESS.
IT'D BE EASY FOR YOU.
YOU'D JUST FLY DOWN AND--

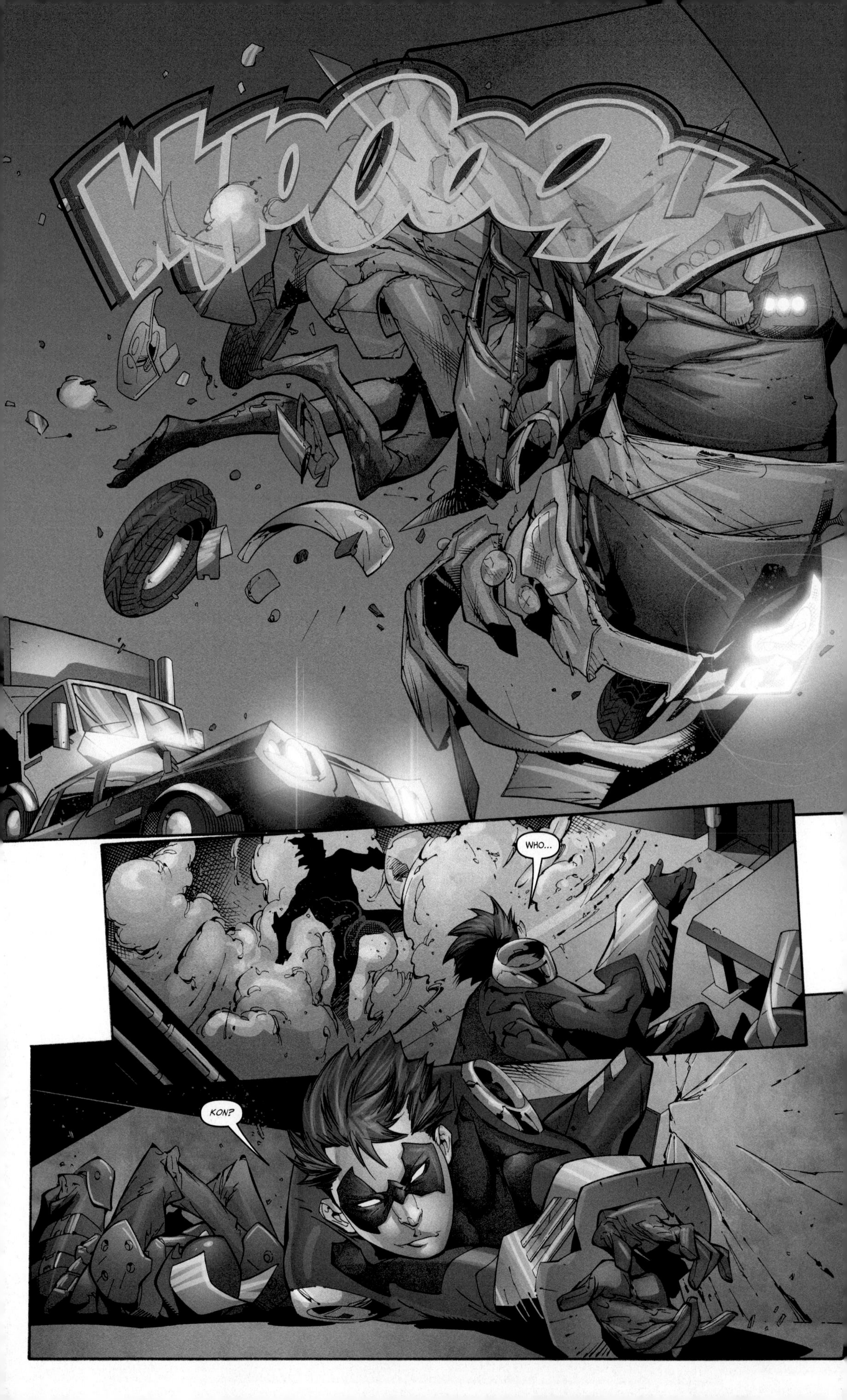
WHO...
KON?

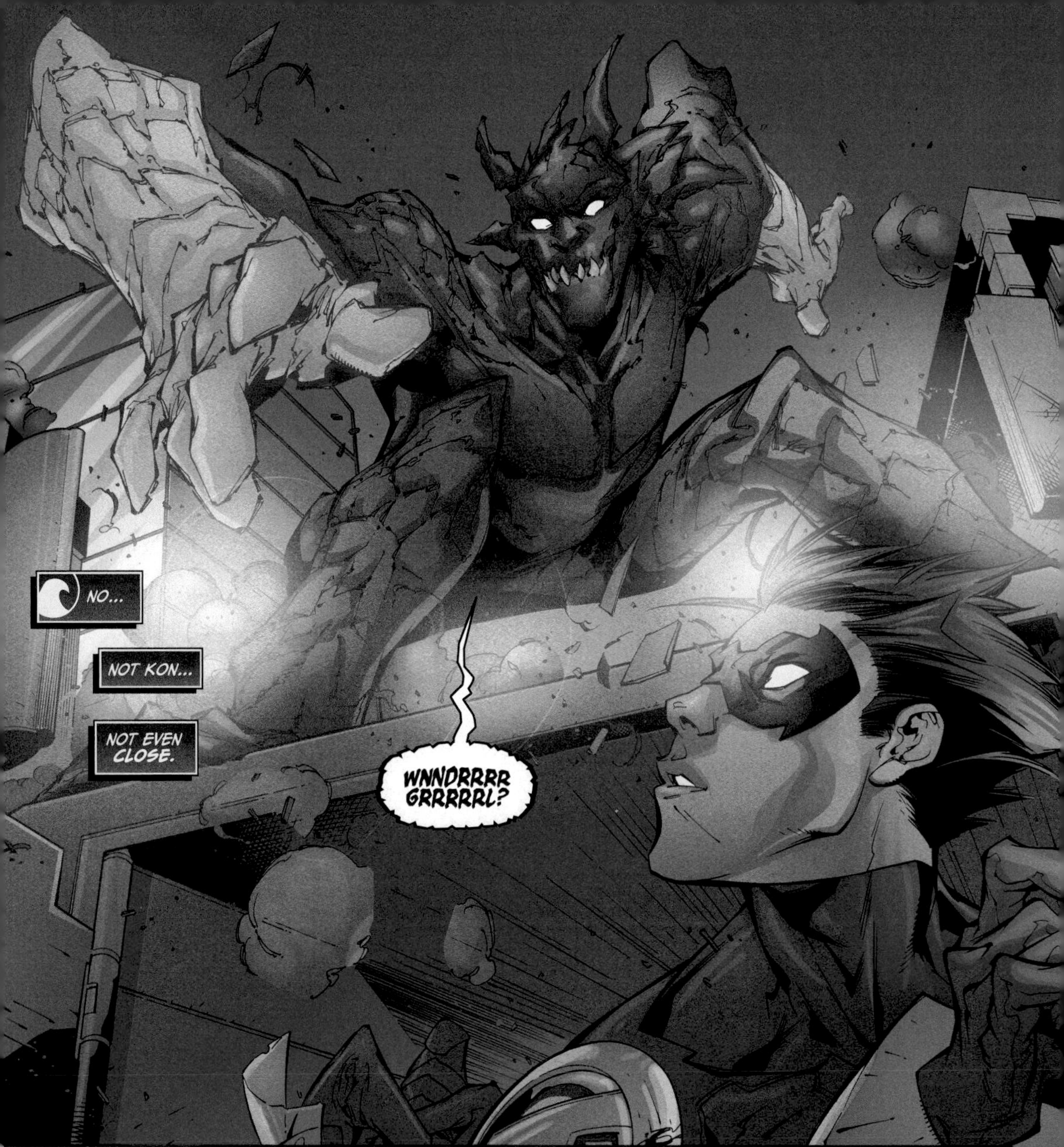
NO...
NOT KON...
NOT EVEN CLOSE.
WNNDRRRR GRRRRRL?

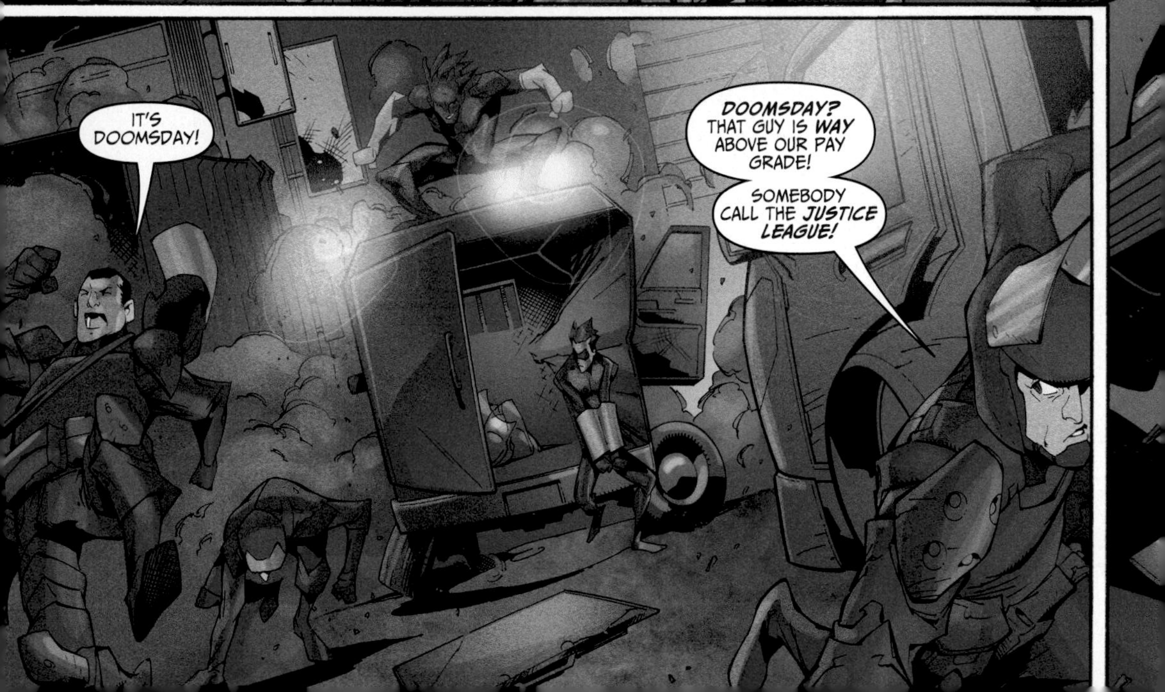
IT'S DOOMSDAY!
DOOMSDAY? THAT GUY IS WAY ABOVE OUR PAY GRADE!
SOMEBODY CALL THE JUSTICE LEAGUE!

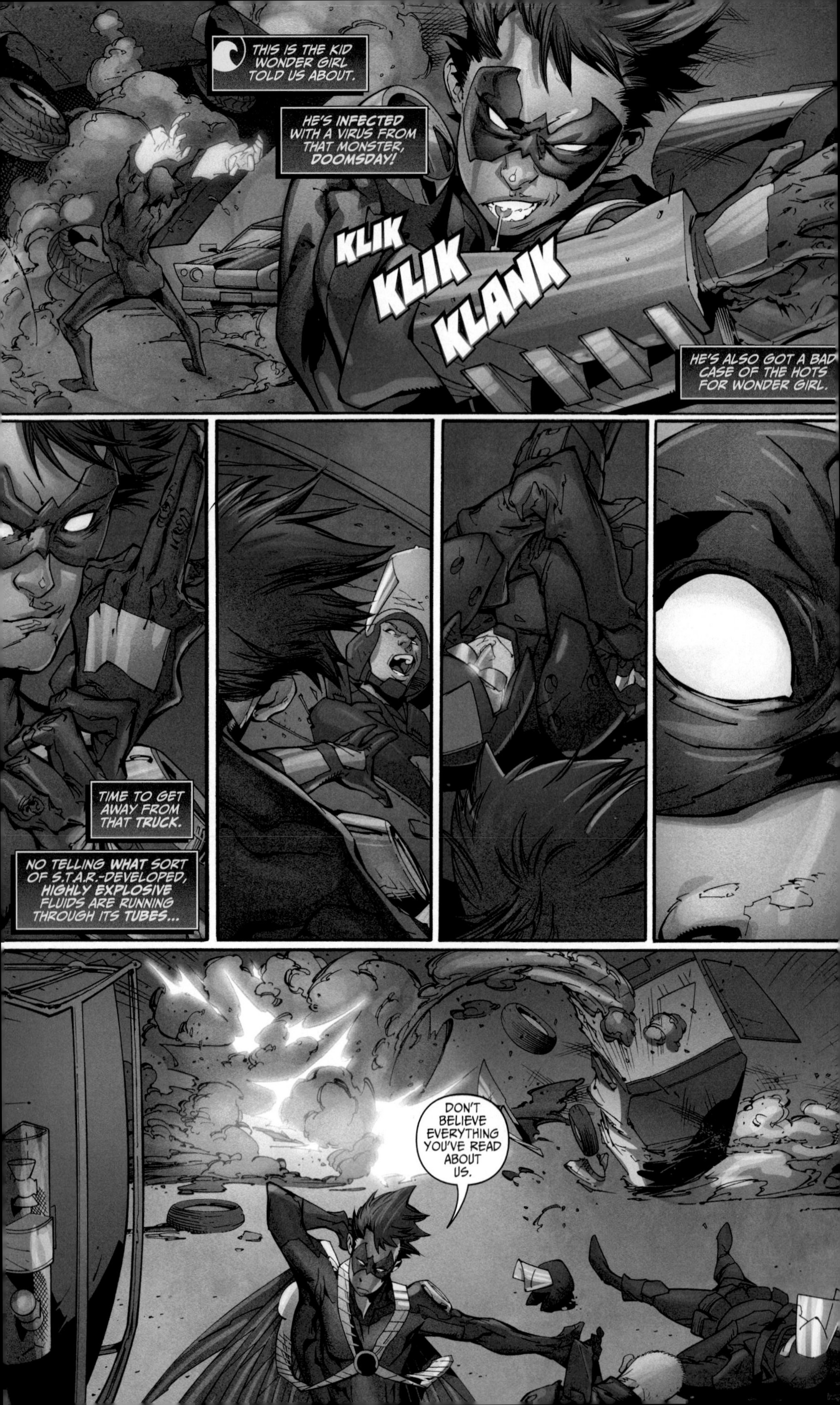

THIS IS THE KID WONDER GIRL TOLD US ABOUT.
HE'S INFECTED WITH A VIRUS FROM THAT MONSTER, DOOMSDAY!
KLIK
KLIK
KLANK
HE'S ALSO GOT A BAD CASE OF THE HOTS FOR WONDER GIRL.
TIME TO GET AWAY FROM THAT TRUCK.
NO TELLING WHAT SORT OF S.T.A.R.-DEVELOPED, HIGHLY EXPLOSIVE FLUIDS ARE RUNNING THROUGH ITS TUBES...
DON'T BELIEVE EVERYTHING YOU'VE READ ABOUT US.

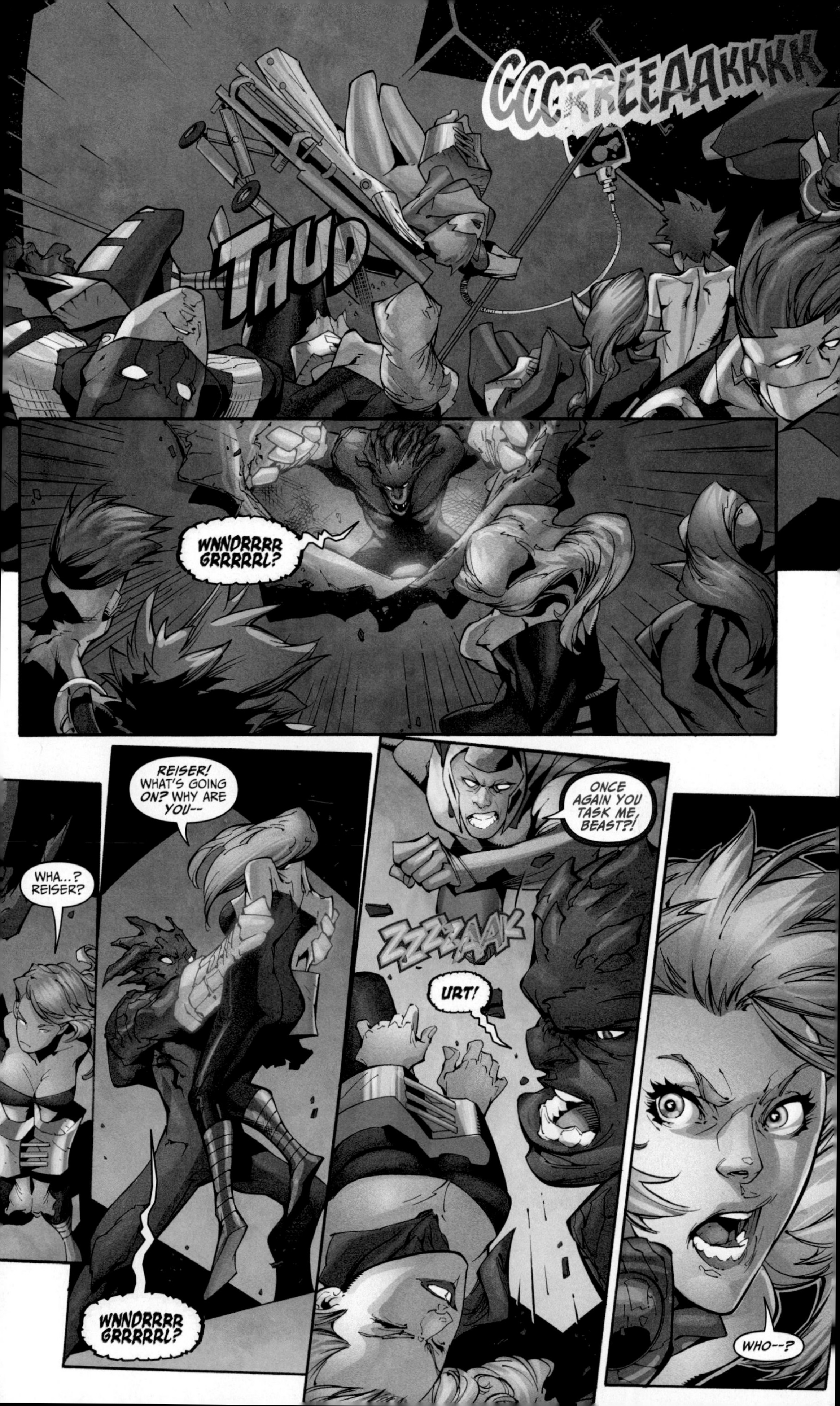
CCCRREEAAKKKK
THUD
WNNDRRRR GRRRRRL?
WHA...? REISER?
REISER! WHAT'S GOING ON? WHY ARE YOU--
WNNDRRRR GRRRRRL?
ONCE AGAIN YOU TASK ME, BEAST?!
ZZZZAAK
URT!
WHO--?

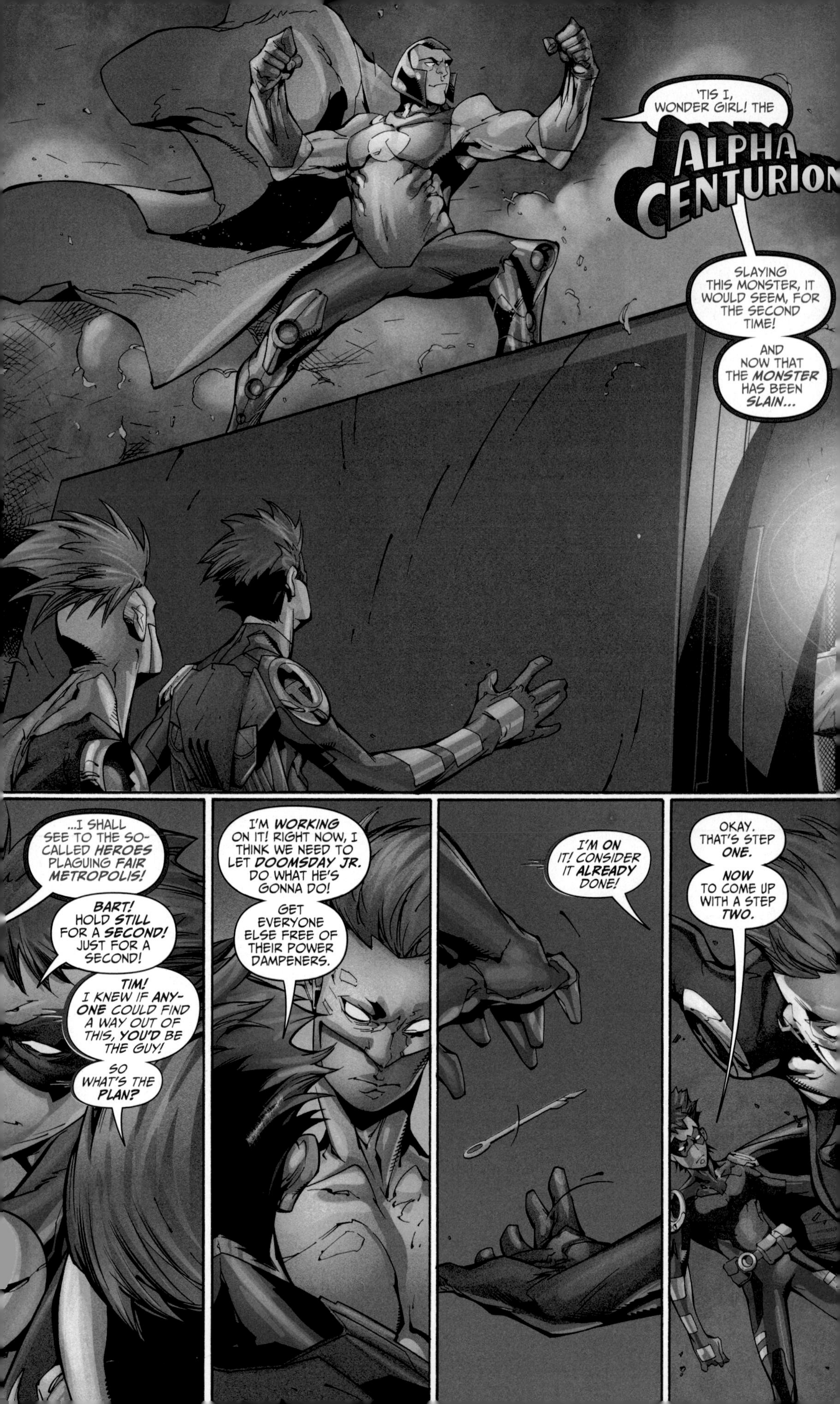

'TIS I, WONDER GIRL! THE
ALPHA CENTURION
SLAYING THIS MONSTER, IT WOULD SEEM, FOR THE SECOND TIME!
AND NOW THAT THE MONSTER HAS BEEN SLAIN...
...I SHALL SEE TO THE SO-CALLED HEROES PLAGUING FAIR METROPOLIS!
BART! HOLD STILL FOR A SECOND! JUST FOR A SECOND!
TIM! I KNEW IF ANY-ONE COULD FIND A WAY OUT OF THIS, YOU'D BE THE GUY!
SO WHAT'S THE PLAN?
I'M WORKING ON IT! RIGHT NOW, I THINK WE NEED TO LET DOOMSDAY JR. DO WHAT HE'S GONNA DO!
GET EVERYONE ELSE FREE OF THEIR POWER DAMPENERS.
I'M ON IT! CONSIDER IT ALREADY DONE!
OKAY. THAT'S STEP ONE.
NOW TO COME UP WITH A STEP TWO.

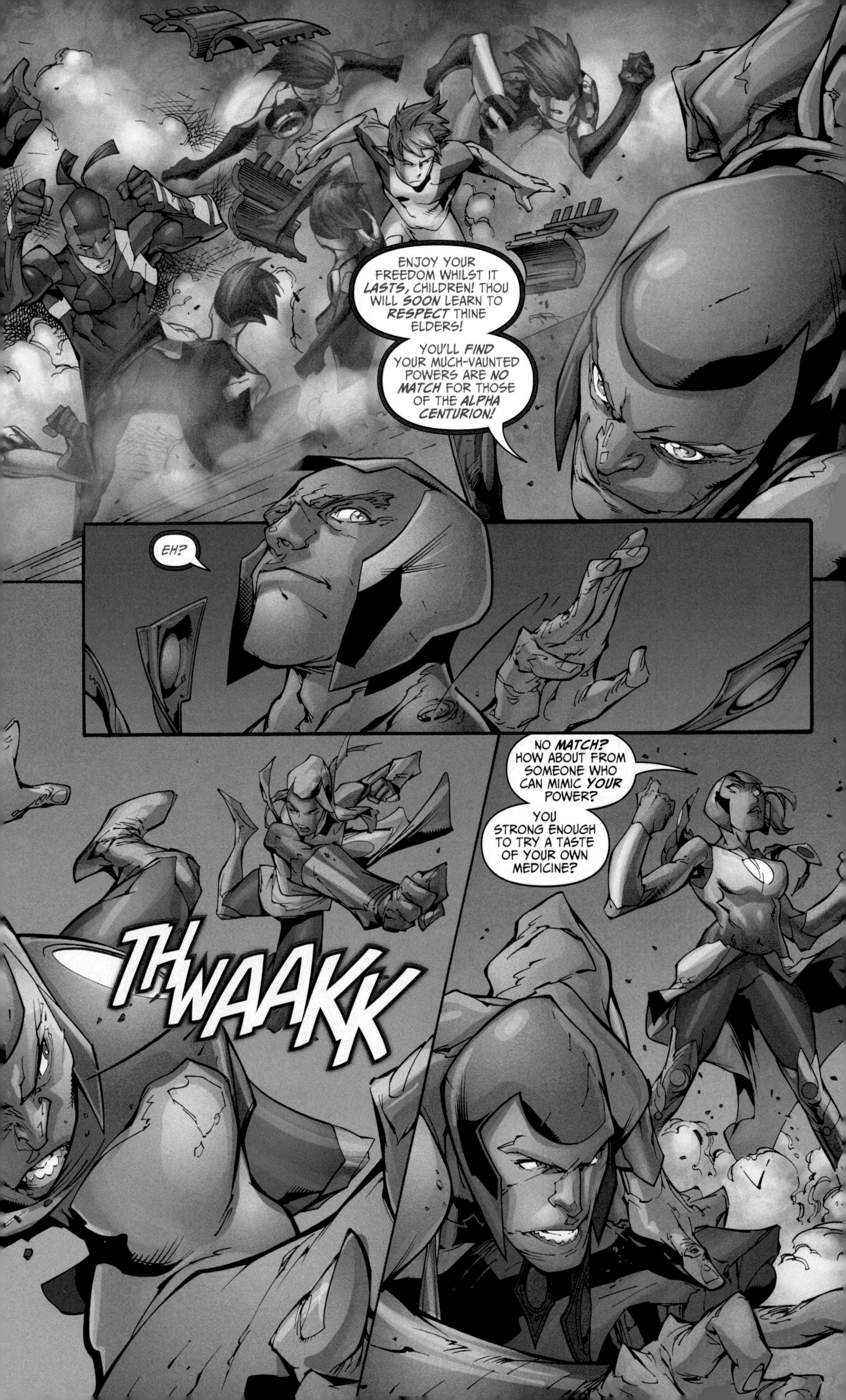
ENJOY YOUR FREEDOM WHILST IT LASTS, CHILDREN! THOU WILL SOON LEARN TO RESPECT THINE ELDERS!
YOU'LL FIND YOUR MUCH-VAUNTED POWERS ARE NO MATCH FOR THOSE OF THE ALPHA CENTURION!
EH?
NO MATCH? HOW ABOUT FROM SOMEONE WHO CAN MIMIC YOUR POWER?
YOU STRONG ENOUGH TO TRY A TASTE OF YOUR OWN MEDICINE?
THWAAKK

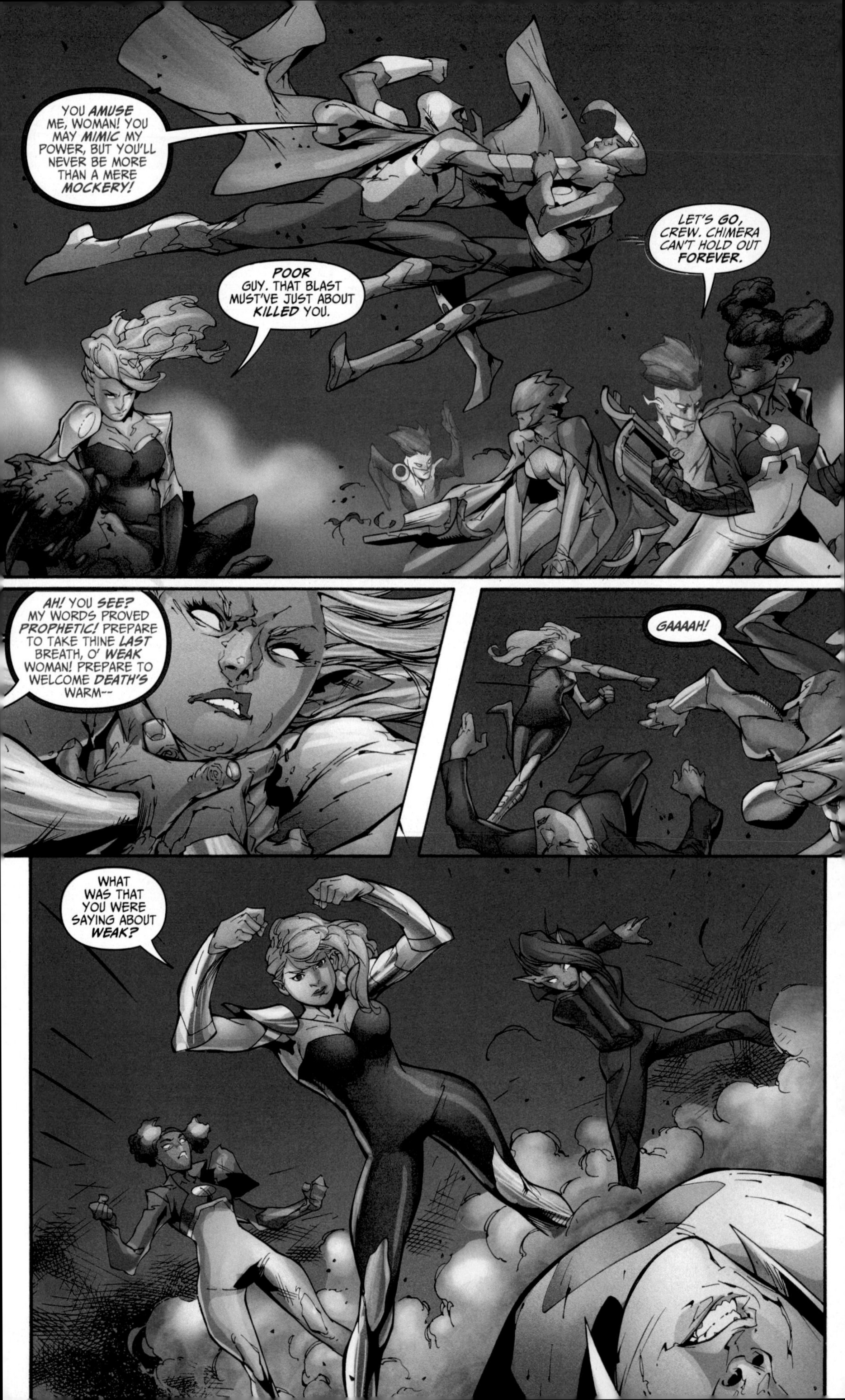
YOU AMUSE ME, WOMAN! YOU MAY MIMIC MY POWER, BUT YOU'LL NEVER BE MORE THAN A MERE MOCKERY!
POOR GUY. THAT BLAST MUST'VE JUST ABOUT KILLED YOU.
LET'S GO, CREW. CHIMERA CAN'T HOLD OUT FOREVER.
AH! YOU SEE? MY WORDS PROVED PROPHETIC! PREPARE TO TAKE THINE LAST BREATH, O' WEAK WOMAN! PREPARE TO WELCOME DEATH'S WARM--
GAAAAH!
WHAT WAS THAT YOU WERE SAYING ABOUT WEAK?

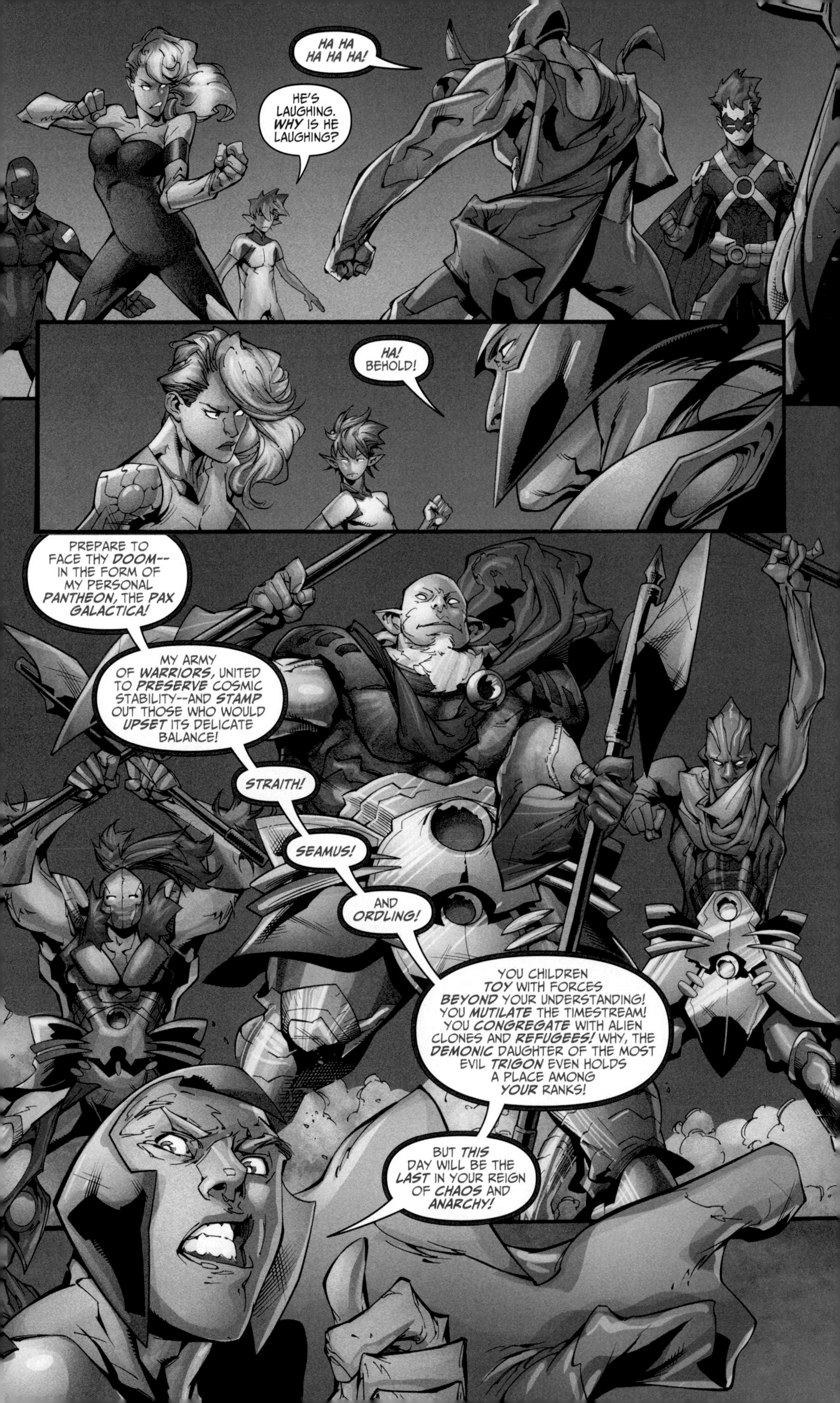
HA HA HA HA HA!
HE'S LAUGHING. WHY IS HE LAUGHING?
HA! BEHOLD!
PREPARE TO FACE THY DOOM-- IN THE FORM OF MY PERSONAL PANTHEON, THE PAX GALACTICA!
MY ARMY OF WARRIORS, UNITED TO PRESERVE COSMIC STABILITY--AND STAMP OUT THOSE WHO WOULD UPSET ITS DELICATE BALANCE!
STRAITH!
SEAMUS!
AND ORDLING!
YOU CHILDREN TOY WITH FORCES BEYOND YOUR UNDERSTANDING! YOU MUTILATE THE TIMESTREAM! YOU CONGREGATE WITH ALIEN CLONES AND REFUGEES! WHY, THE DEMONIC DAUGHTER OF THE MOST EVIL TRIGON EVEN HOLDS A PLACE AMONG YOUR RANKS!
BUT THIS DAY WILL BE THE LAST IN YOUR REIGN OF CHAOS AND ANARCHY!

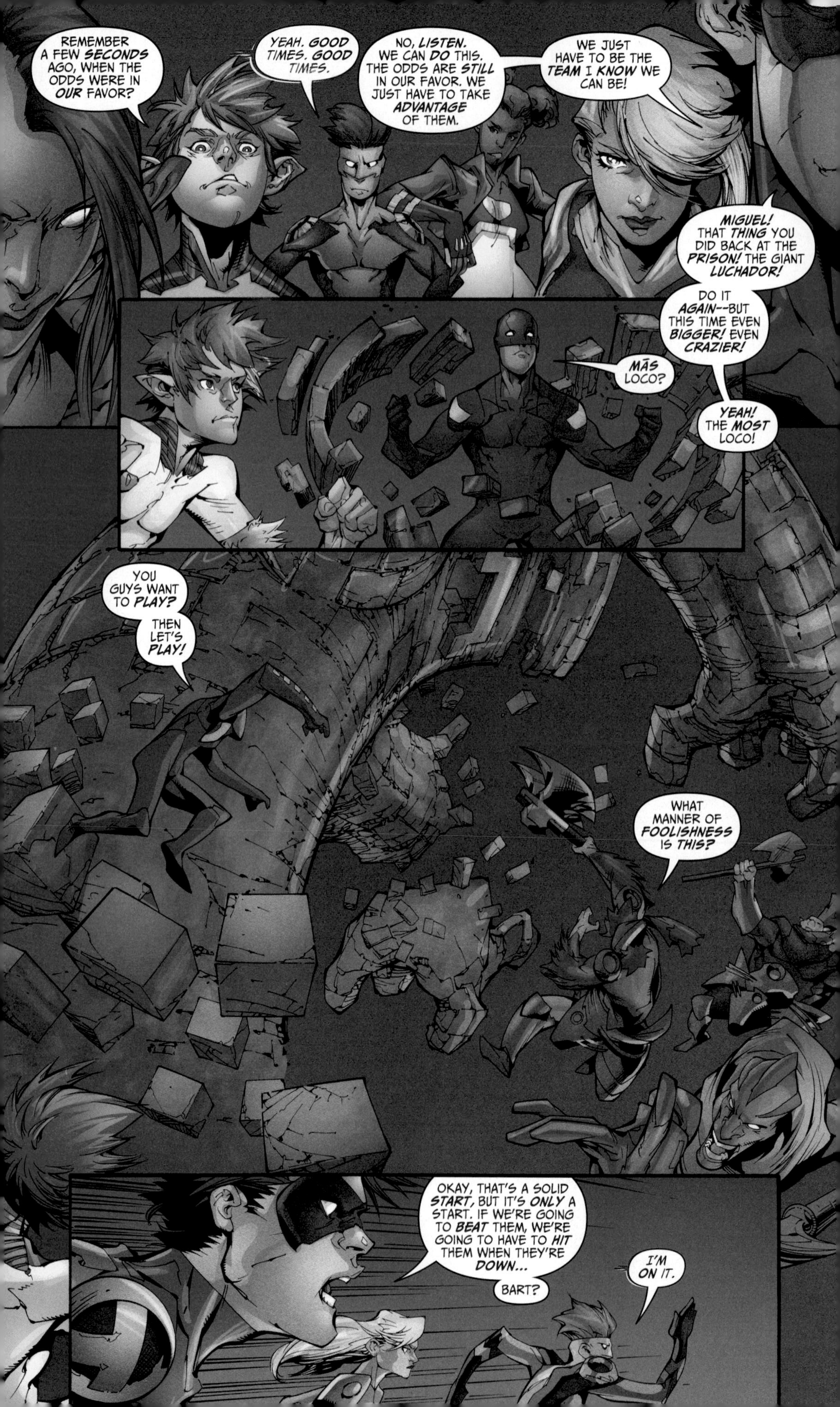
REMEMBER A FEW SECONDS AGO, WHEN THE ODDS WERE IN OUR FAVOR?
YEAH. GOOD TIMES. GOOD TIMES.
NO, LISTEN. WE CAN DO THIS. THE ODDS ARE STILL IN OUR FAVOR. WE JUST HAVE TO TAKE ADVANTAGE OF THEM.
WE JUST HAVE TO BE THE TEAM I KNOW WE CAN BE!
MIGUEL! THAT THING YOU DID BACK AT THE PRISON! THE GIANT LUCHADOR!
DO IT AGAIN--BUT THIS TIME EVEN BIGGER! EVEN CRAZIER!
MĀS LOCO?
YEAH! THE MOST LOCO!
YOU GUYS WANT TO PLAY?
THEN LET'S PLAY!
WHAT MANNER OF FOOLISHNESS IS THIS?
OKAY, THAT'S A SOLID START, BUT IT'S ONLY A START. IF WE'RE GOING TO BEAT THEM, WE'RE GOING TO HAVE TO HIT THEM WHEN THEY'RE DOWN...
BART?
I'M ON IT.

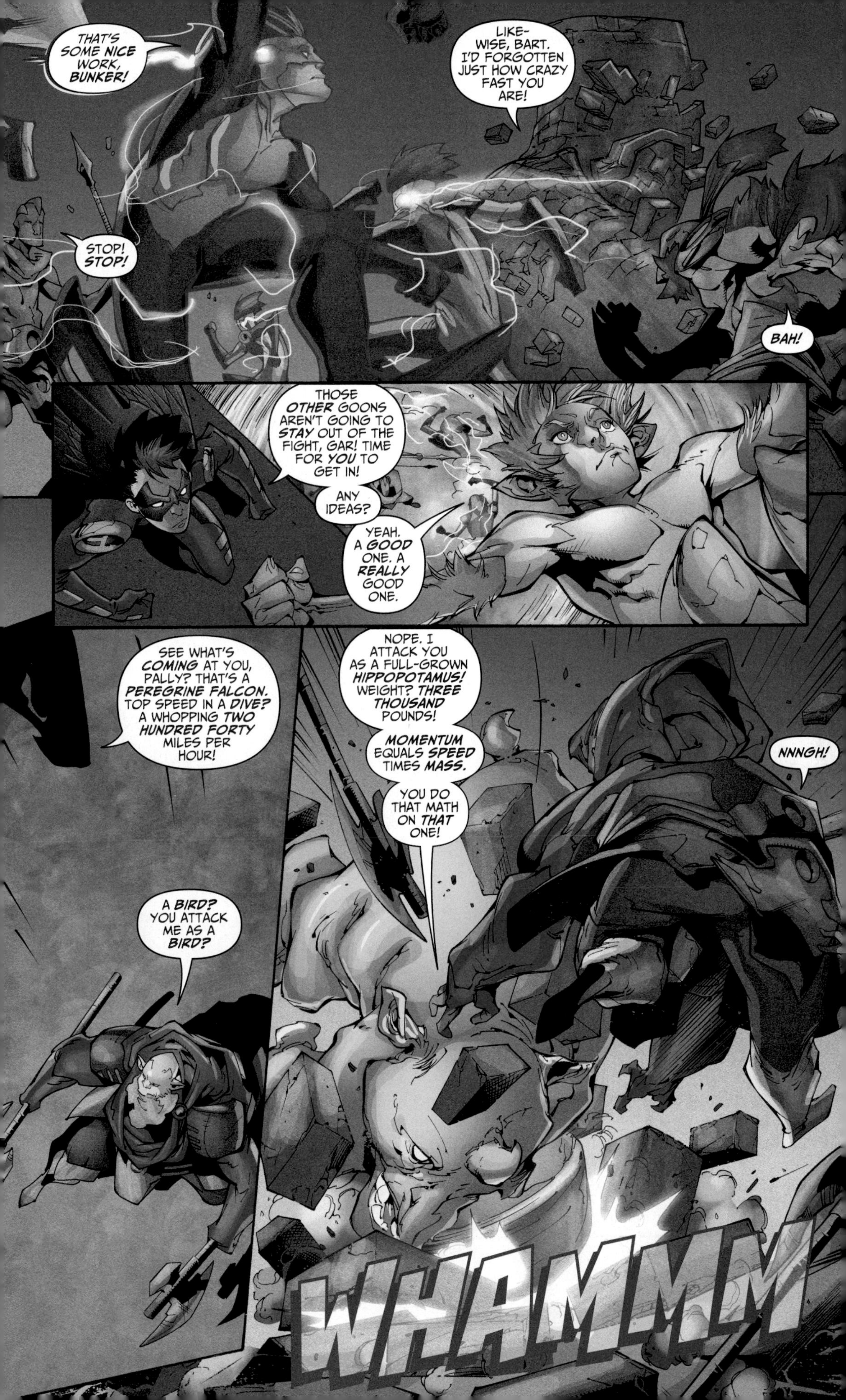
THAT'S SOME NICE WORK, BUNKER!
LIKE-WISE, BART. I'D FORGOTTEN JUST HOW CRAZY FAST YOU ARE!
STOP! STOP!
BAH!
THOSE OTHER GOONS AREN'T GOING TO STAY OUT OF THE FIGHT, GAR! TIME FOR YOU TO GET IN!
ANY IDEAS?
YEAH. A GOOD ONE. A REALLY GOOD ONE.
SEE WHAT'S COMING AT YOU, PALLY? THAT'S A PEREGRINE FALCON. TOP SPEED IN A DIVE? A WHOPPING TWO HUNDRED FORTY MILES PER HOUR!
A BIRD? YOU ATTACK ME AS A BIRD?
NOPE. I ATTACK YOU AS A FULL-GROWN HIPPOPOTAMUS! WEIGHT? THREE THOUSAND POUNDS!
MOMENTUM EQUALS SPEED TIMES MASS.
YOU DO THAT MATH ON THAT ONE!
NNNGH!
WHAMMM

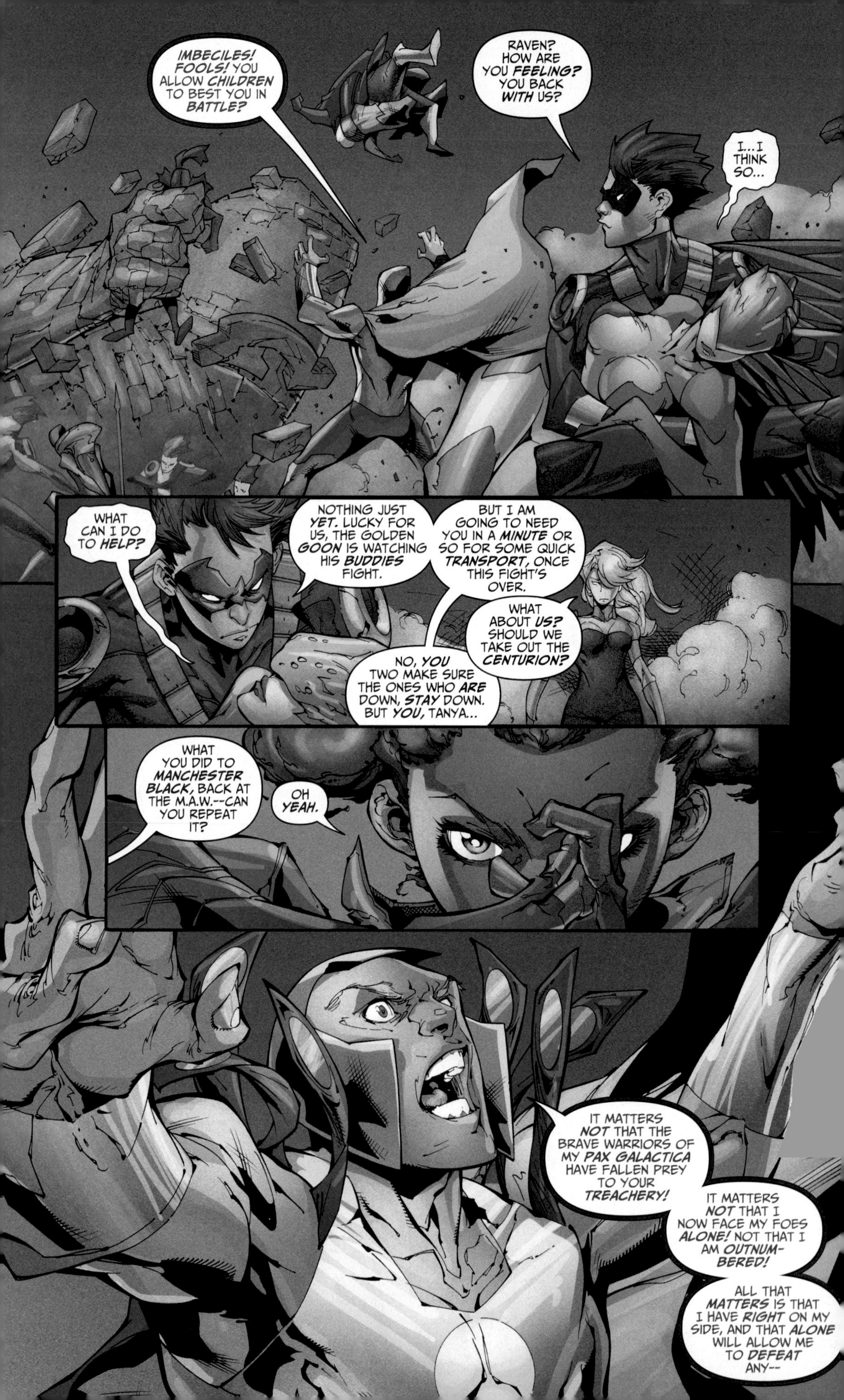

IMBECILES! FOOLS! YOU ALLOW CHILDREN TO BEST YOU IN BATTLE?
RAVEN? HOW ARE YOU FEELING? YOU BACK WITH US?
I...I THINK SO...
WHAT CAN I DO TO HELP?
NOTHING JUST YET. LUCKY FOR US, THE GOLDEN GOON IS WATCHING HIS BUDDIES FIGHT.
BUT I AM GOING TO NEED YOU IN A MINUTE OR SO FOR SOME QUICK TRANSPORT, ONCE THIS FIGHT'S OVER.
WHAT ABOUT US? SHOULD WE TAKE OUT THE CENTURION?
NO, YOU TWO MAKE SURE THE ONES WHO ARE DOWN, STAY DOWN. BUT YOU, TANYA...
WHAT YOU DID TO MANCHESTER BLACK, BACK AT THE M.A.W.--CAN YOU REPEAT IT?
OH YEAH.
IT MATTERS NOT THAT THE BRAVE WARRIORS OF MY PAX GALACTICA HAVE FALLEN PREY TO YOUR TREACHERY!
IT MATTERS NOT THAT I NOW FACE MY FOES ALONE! NOT THAT I AM OUTNUM-BERED!
ALL THAT MATTERS IS THAT I HAVE RIGHT ON MY SIDE, AND THAT ALONE WILL ALLOW ME TO DEFEAT ANY--

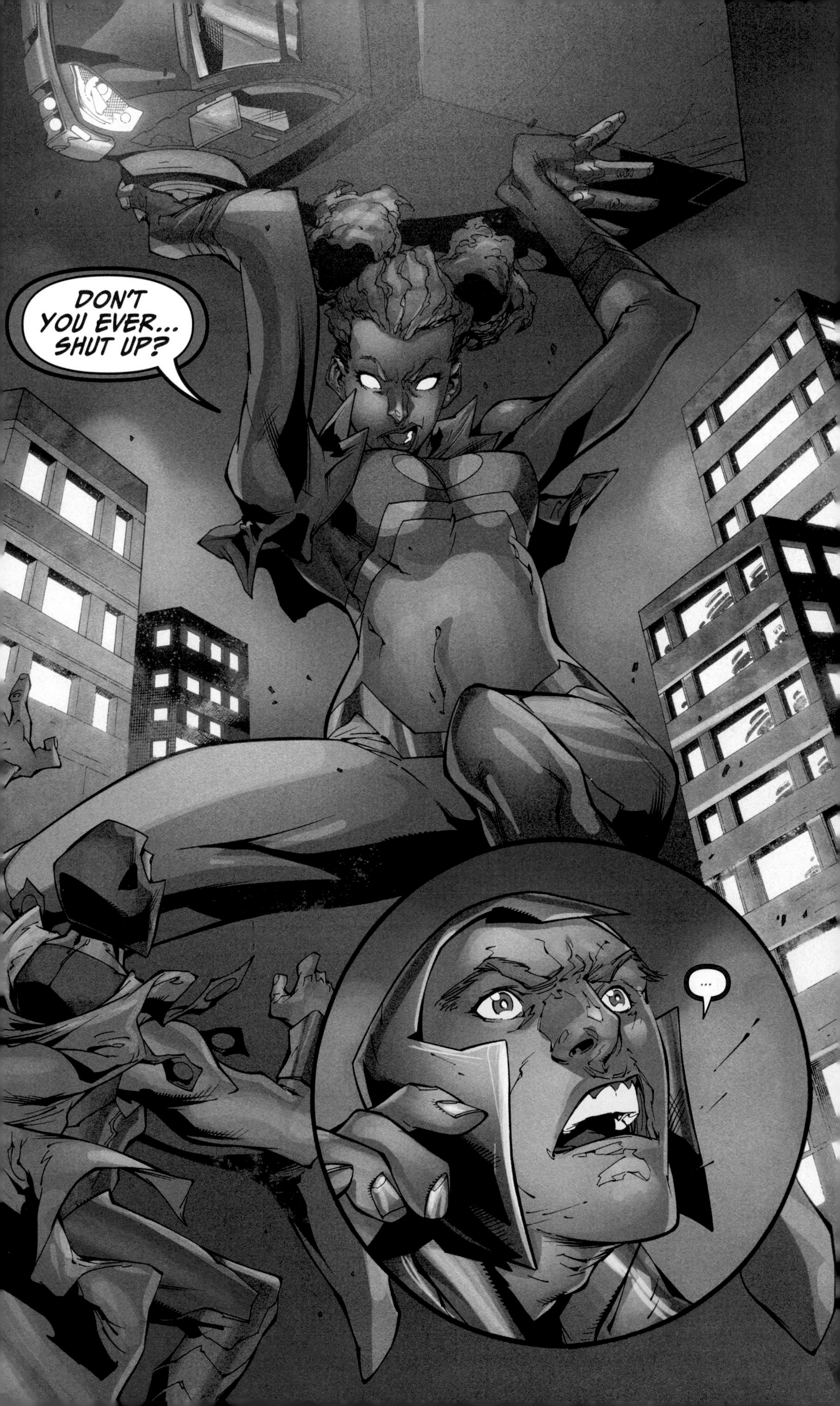
DON'T YOU EVER... SHUT UP?
...

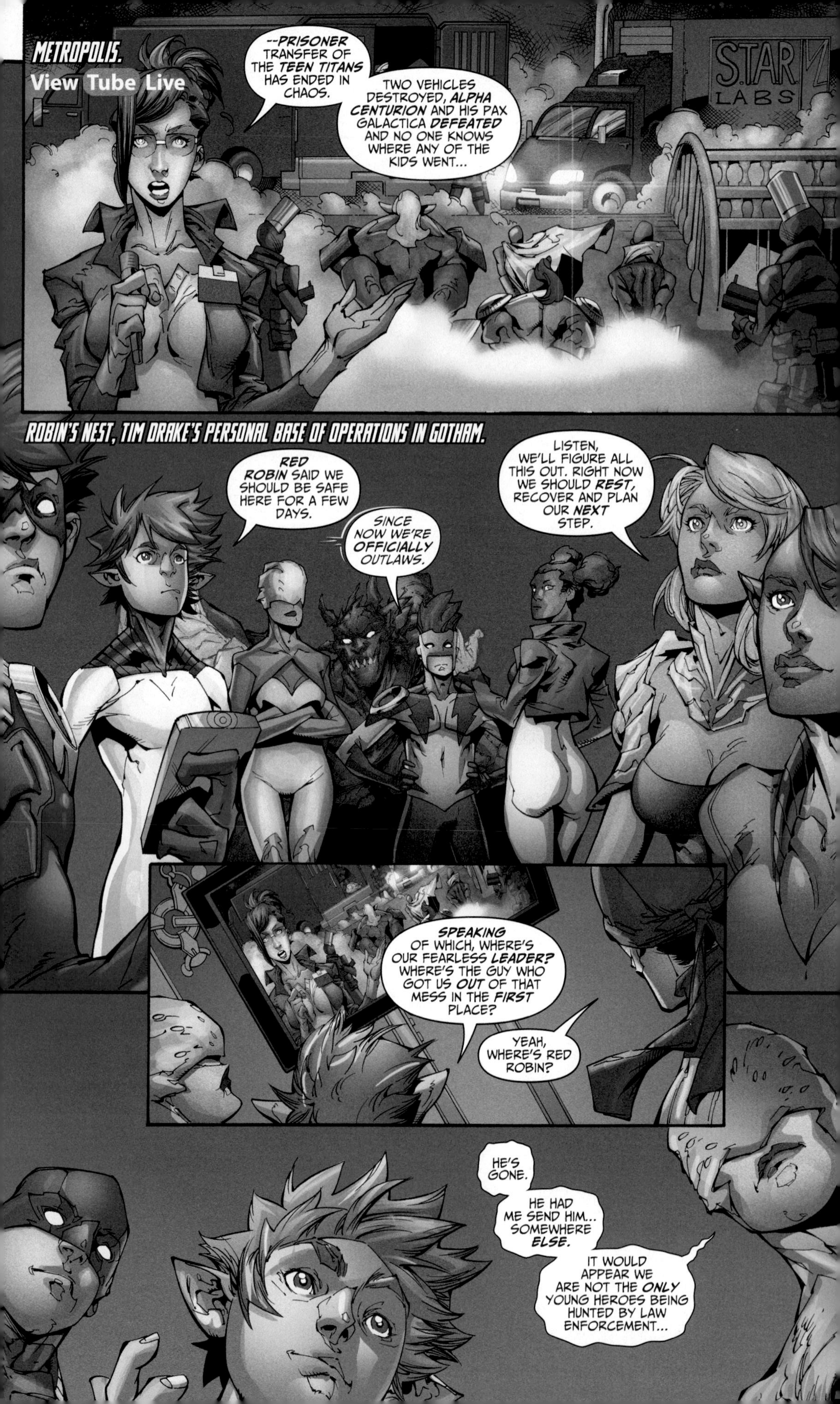
METROPOLIS.
View Tube Live
--PRISONER TRANSFER OF THE TEEN TITANS HAS ENDED IN CHAOS.
TWO VEHICLES DESTROYED, ALPHA CENTURION AND HIS PAX GALACTICA DEFEATED AND NO ONE KNOWS WHERE ANY OF THE KIDS WENT...
S.T.A.R. LABS
ROBIN'S NEST, TIM DRAKE'S PERSONAL BASE OF OPERATIONS IN GOTHAM.
RED ROBIN SAID WE SHOULD BE SAFE HERE FOR A FEW DAYS.
SINCE NOW WE'RE OFFICIALLY OUTLAWS.
LISTEN, WE'LL FIGURE ALL THIS OUT. RIGHT NOW WE SHOULD REST, RECOVER AND PLAN OUR NEXT STEP.
SPEAKING OF WHICH, WHERE'S OUR FEARLESS LEADER? WHERE'S THE GUY WHO GOT US OUT OF THAT MESS IN THE FIRST PLACE?
YEAH, WHERE'S RED ROBIN?
HE'S GONE.
HE HAD ME SEND HIM... SOMEWHERE ELSE.
IT WOULD APPEAR WE ARE NOT THE ONLY YOUNG HEROES BEING HUNTED BY LAW ENFORCEMENT...

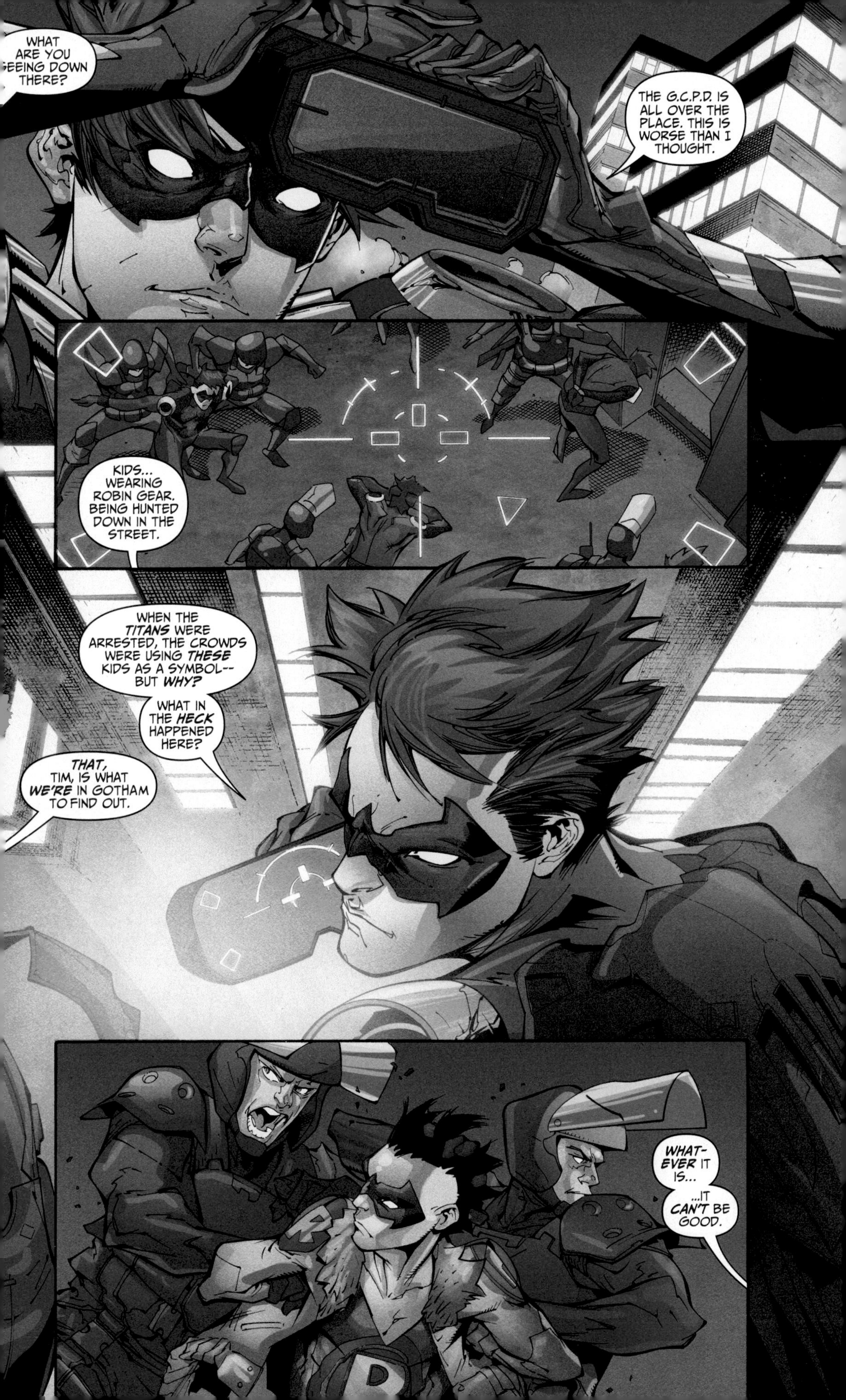

WHAT ARE YOU SEEING DOWN THERE?
THE G.C.P.D. IS ALL OVER THE PLACE. THIS IS WORSE THAN I THOUGHT.
KIDS... WEARING ROBIN GEAR. BEING HUNTED DOWN IN THE STREET.
WHEN THE *TITANS* WERE ARRESTED, THE CROWDS WERE USING *THESE* KIDS AS A SYMBOL-- BUT *WHY?*
WHAT IN THE *HECK* HAPPENED HERE?
THAT, TIM, IS WHAT *WE'RE* IN GOTHAM TO FIND OUT.
WHAT-EVER IT IS...
...IT *CAN'T* BE GOOD.

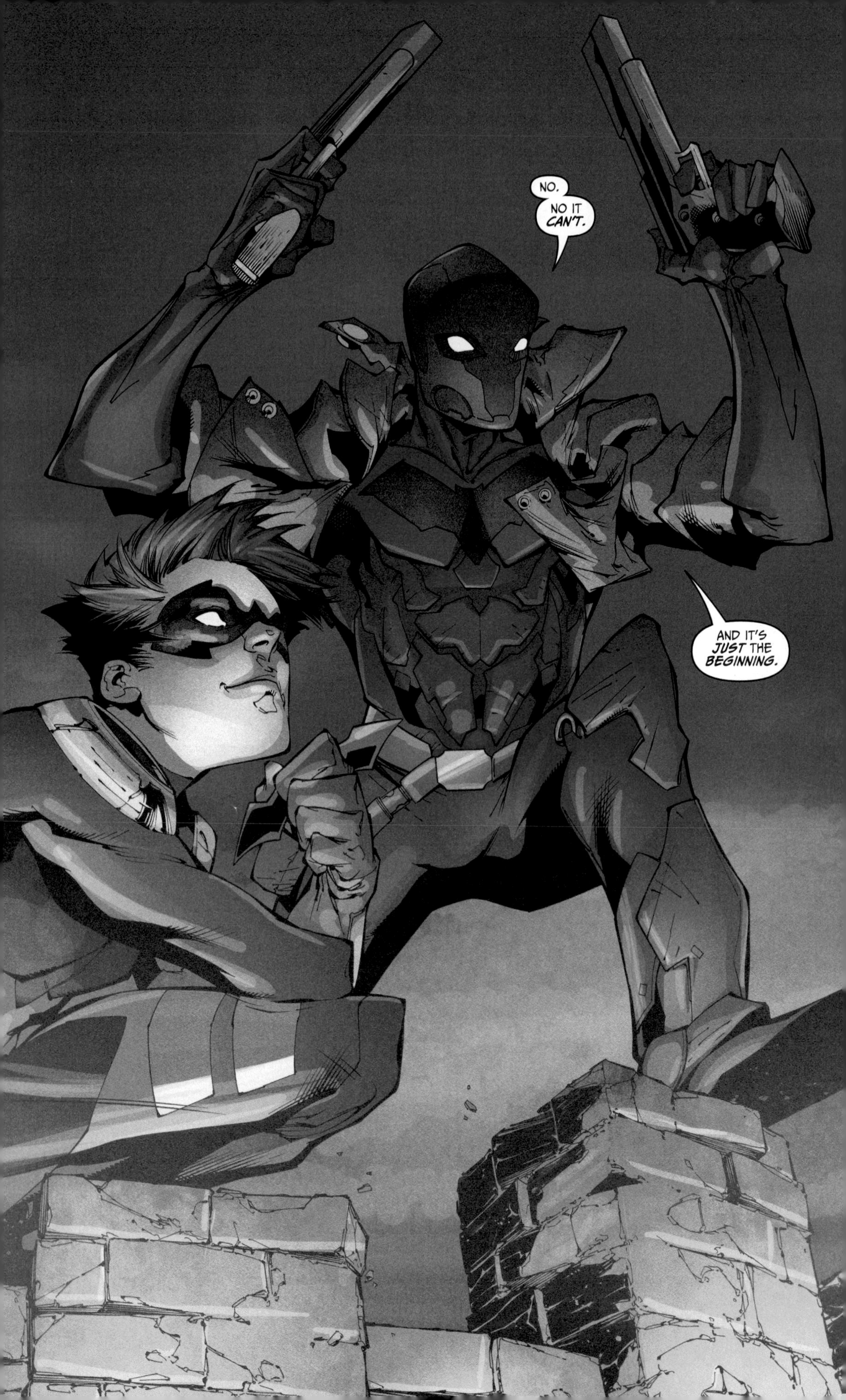
NO.
NO IT CAN'T.
AND IT'S JUST THE BEGINNING.

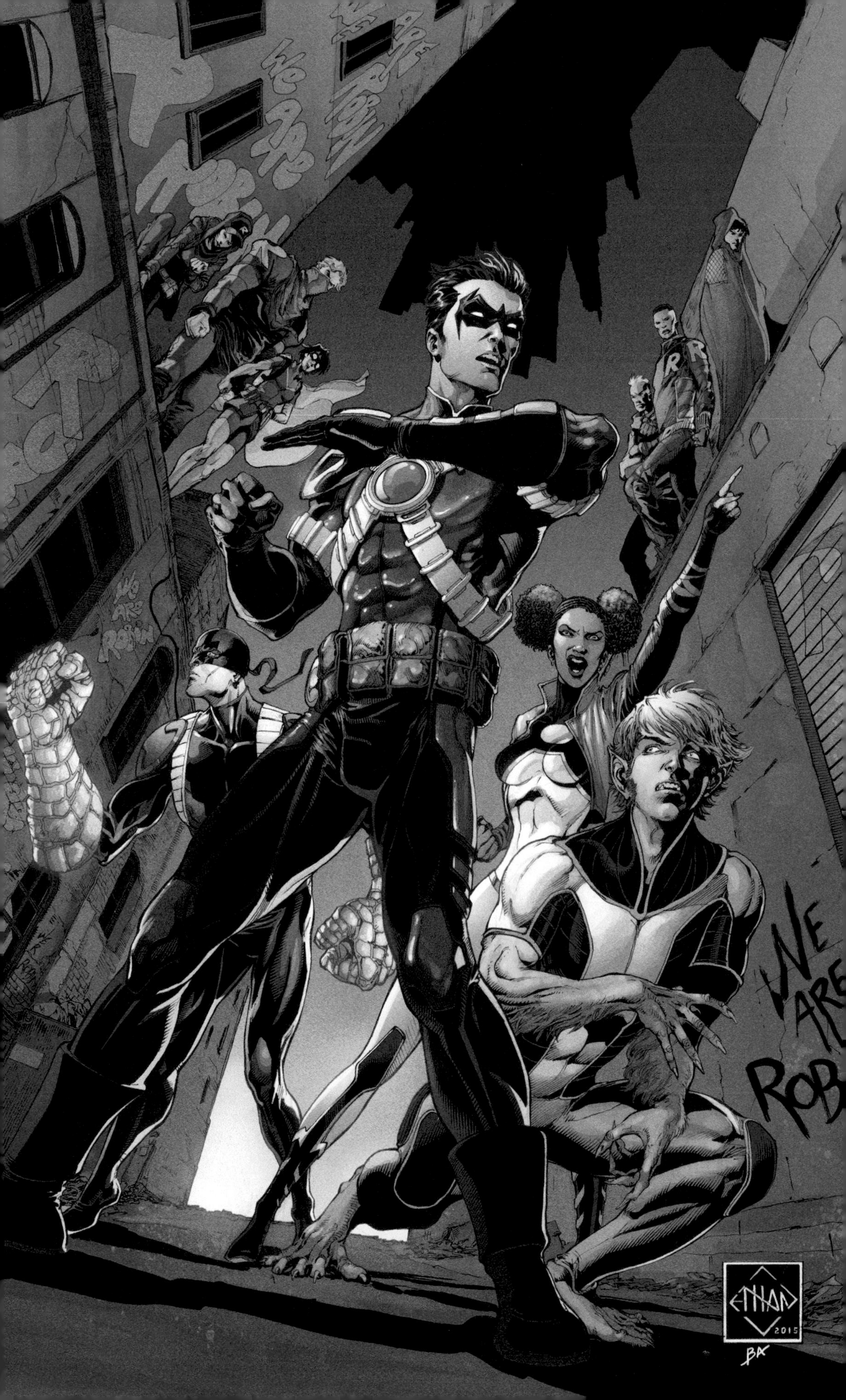

WE ARE ROBIN
WE ARE ROB
ETHAN 2015
BA

ON THE RUN

SCOTT LOBDELL WILL PFEIFER writers IAN CHURCHILL MIGUEL MENDONÇA pencillers NORM RAPMUND DEXTER VINES inkers TONY AVIÑA colorist COREY BREEN letterer
cover art by ETHAN VAN SCIVER & BRAD ANDERSON

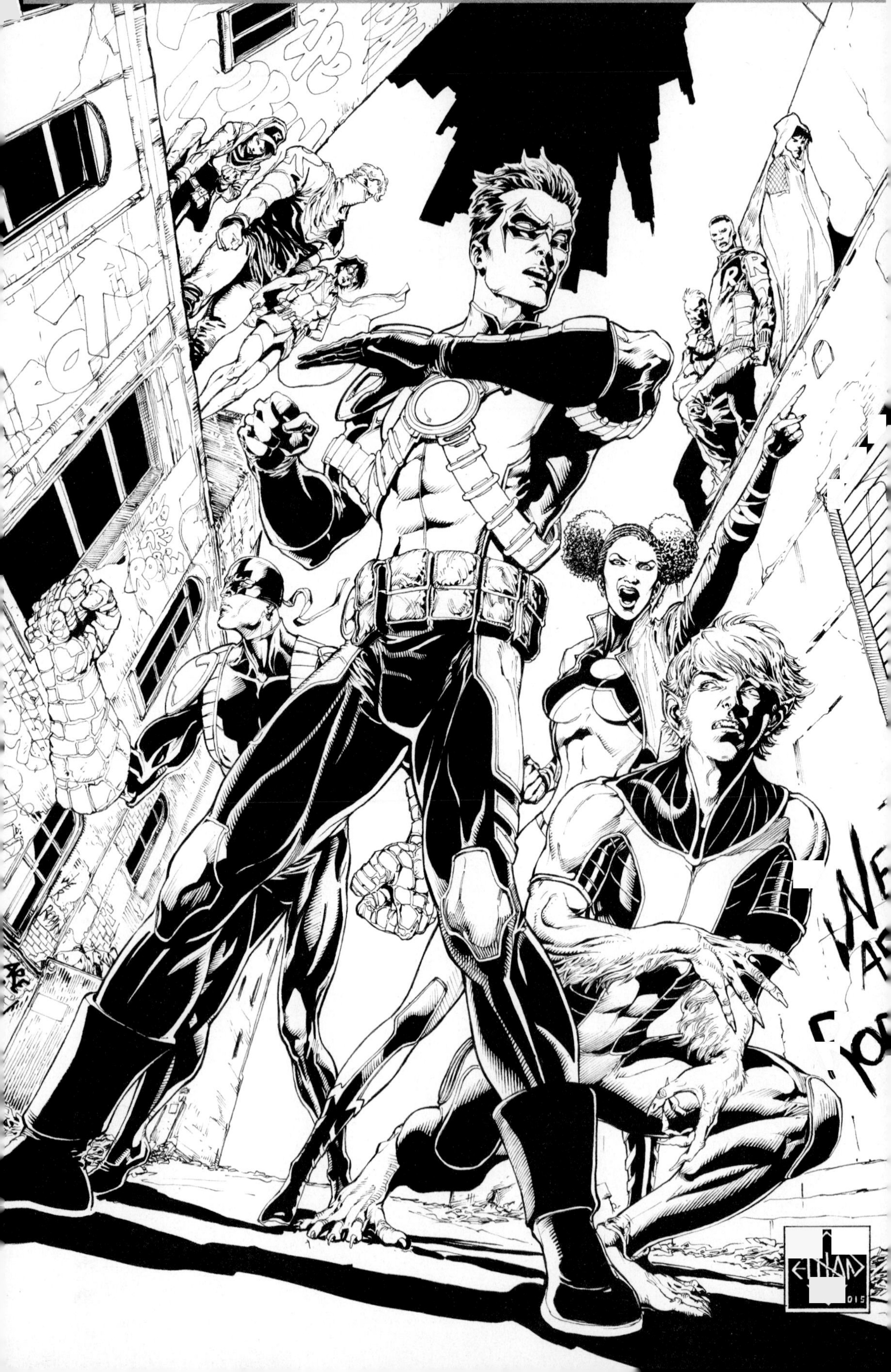
WE ARE ROBIN

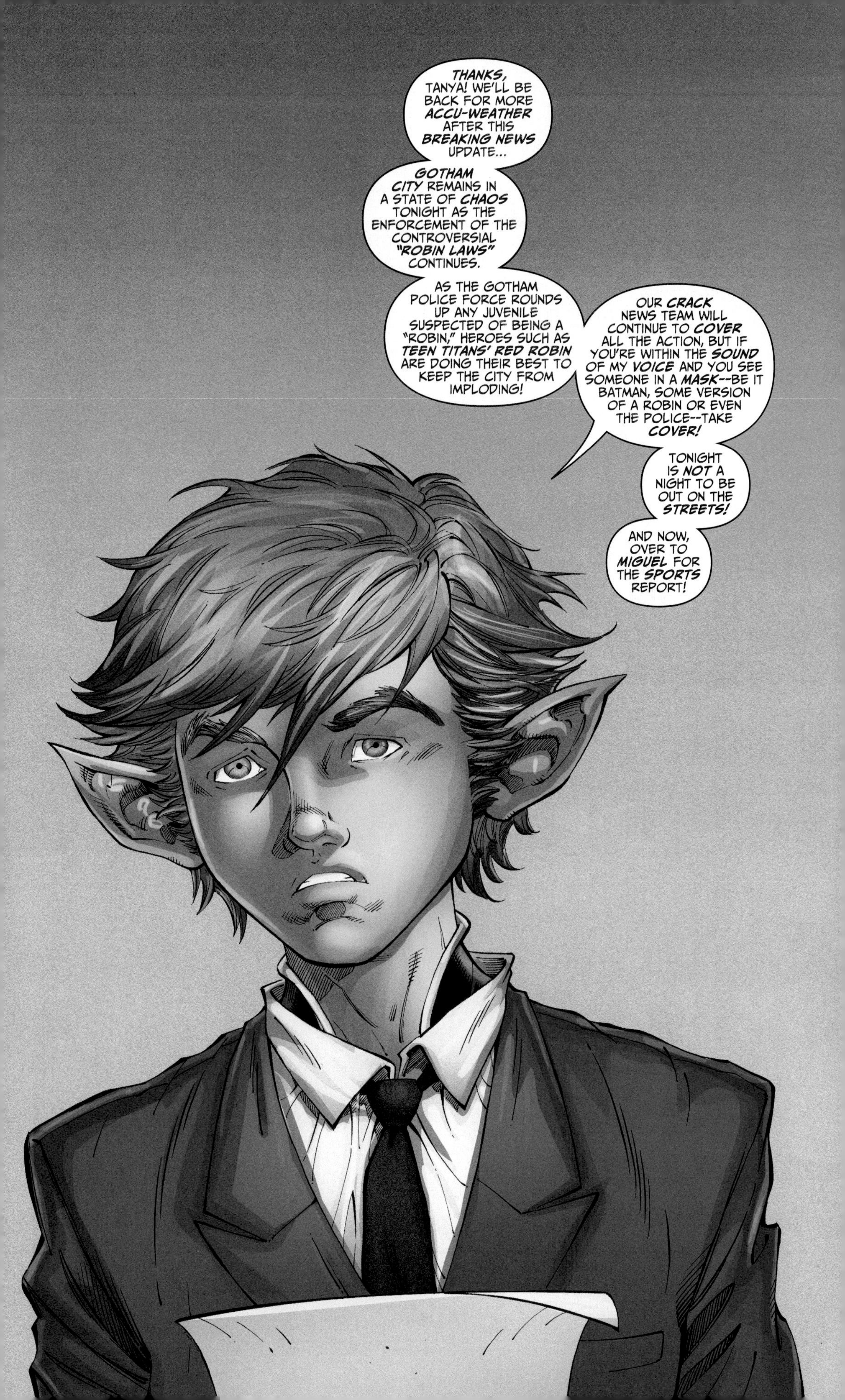
THANKS, TANYA! WE'LL BE BACK FOR MORE ACCU-WEATHER AFTER THIS BREAKING NEWS UPDATE...
GOTHAM CITY REMAINS IN A STATE OF CHAOS TONIGHT AS THE ENFORCEMENT OF THE CONTROVERSIAL "ROBIN LAWS" CONTINUES.
AS THE GOTHAM POLICE FORCE ROUNDS UP ANY JUVENILE SUSPECTED OF BEING A "ROBIN," HEROES SUCH AS TEEN TITANS' RED ROBIN ARE DOING THEIR BEST TO KEEP THE CITY FROM IMPLODING!
OUR CRACK NEWS TEAM WILL CONTINUE TO COVER ALL THE ACTION, BUT IF YOU'RE WITHIN THE SOUND OF MY VOICE AND YOU SEE SOMEONE IN A MASK--BE IT BATMAN, SOME VERSION OF A ROBIN OR EVEN THE POLICE--TAKE COVER!
TONIGHT IS NOT A NIGHT TO BE OUT ON THE STREETS!
AND NOW, OVER TO MIGUEL FOR THE SPORTS REPORT!

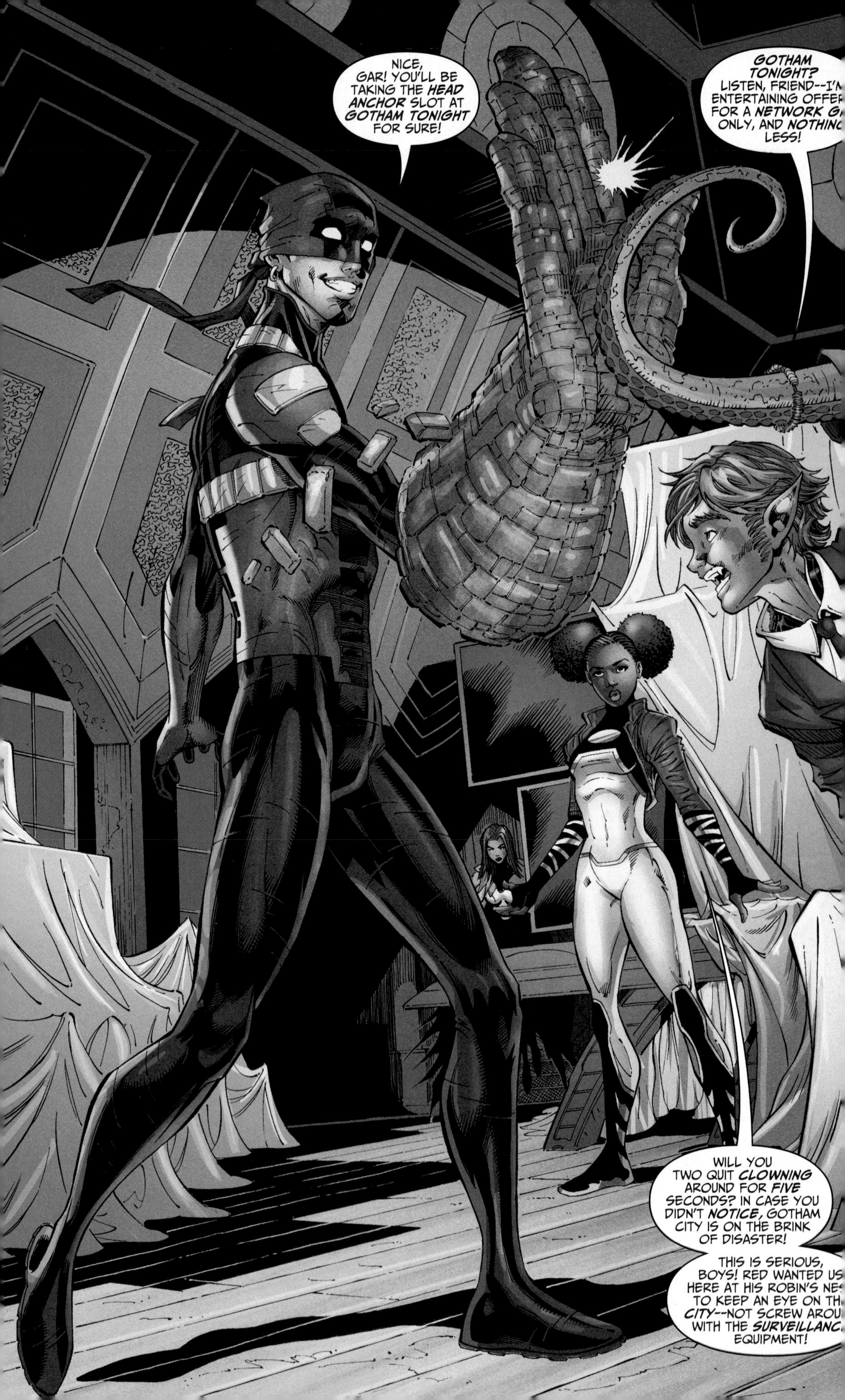
NICE, GAR! YOU'LL BE TAKING THE HEAD ANCHOR SLOT AT GOTHAM TONIGHT FOR SURE!
GOTHAM TONIGHT? LISTEN, FRIEND--I'M ENTERTAINING OFFER FOR A NETWORK G ONLY, AND NOTHIN LESS!
WILL YOU TWO QUIT CLOWNING AROUND FOR FIVE SECONDS? IN CASE YOU DIDN'T NOTICE, GOTHAM CITY IS ON THE BRINK OF DISASTER!
THIS IS SERIOUS, BOYS! RED WANTED US HERE AT HIS ROBIN'S NE TO KEEP AN EYE ON TH CITY--NOT SCREW ARO WITH THE SURVEILLANC EQUIPMENT!

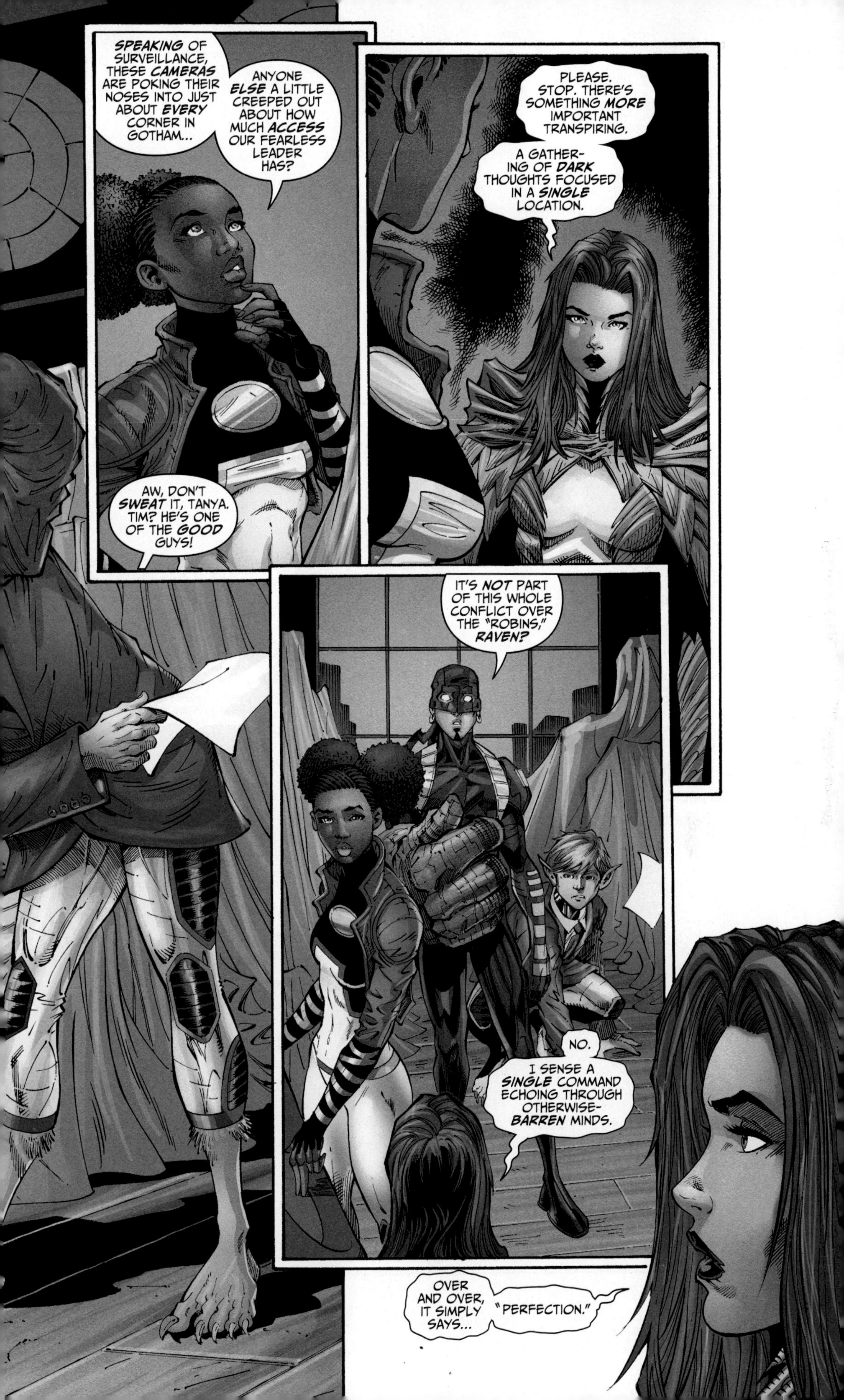

SPEAKING OF SURVEILLANCE, THESE CAMERAS ARE POKING THEIR NOSES INTO JUST ABOUT EVERY CORNER IN GOTHAM...
ANYONE ELSE A LITTLE CREEPED OUT ABOUT HOW MUCH ACCESS OUR FEARLESS LEADER HAS?
AW, DON'T SWEAT IT, TANYA. TIM? HE'S ONE OF THE GOOD GUYS!
PLEASE. STOP. THERE'S SOMETHING MORE IMPORTANT TRANSPIRING.
A GATHERING OF DARK THOUGHTS FOCUSED IN A SINGLE LOCATION.
IT'S NOT PART OF THIS WHOLE CONFLICT OVER THE "ROBINS," RAVEN?
NO.
I SENSE A SINGLE COMMAND ECHOING THROUGH OTHERWISE-BARREN MINDS.
OVER AND OVER, IT SIMPLY SAYS...
"PERFECTION."

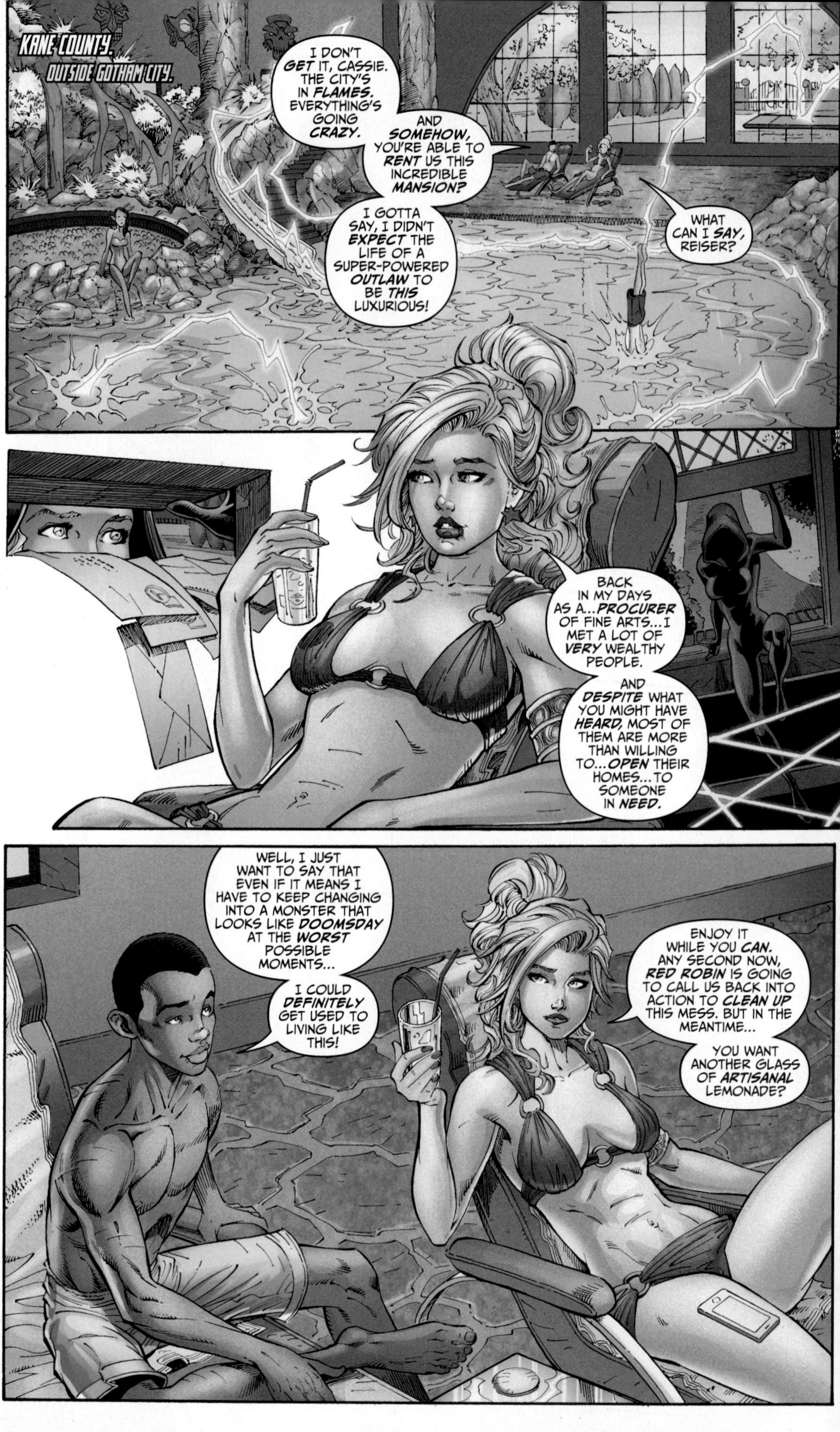
KANE COUNTY.
OUTSIDE GOTHAM CITY.
I DON'T GET IT, CASSIE. THE CITY'S IN FLAMES. EVERYTHING'S GOING CRAZY.
AND SOMEHOW, YOU'RE ABLE TO RENT US THIS INCREDIBLE MANSION?
I GOTTA SAY, I DIDN'T EXPECT THE LIFE OF A SUPER-POWERED OUTLAW TO BE THIS LUXURIOUS!
WHAT CAN I SAY, REISER?
BACK IN MY DAYS AS A...PROCURER OF FINE ARTS...I MET A LOT OF VERY WEALTHY PEOPLE.
AND DESPITE WHAT YOU MIGHT HAVE HEARD, MOST OF THEM ARE MORE THAN WILLING TO...OPEN THEIR HOMES...TO SOMEONE IN NEED.
WELL, I JUST WANT TO SAY THAT EVEN IF IT MEANS I HAVE TO KEEP CHANGING INTO A MONSTER THAT LOOKS LIKE DOOMSDAY AT THE WORST POSSIBLE MOMENTS...
I COULD DEFINITELY GET USED TO LIVING LIKE THIS!
ENJOY IT WHILE YOU CAN. ANY SECOND NOW, RED ROBIN IS GOING TO CALL US BACK INTO ACTION TO CLEAN UP THIS MESS. BUT IN THE MEANTIME...
YOU WANT ANOTHER GLASS OF ARTISANAL LEMONADE?

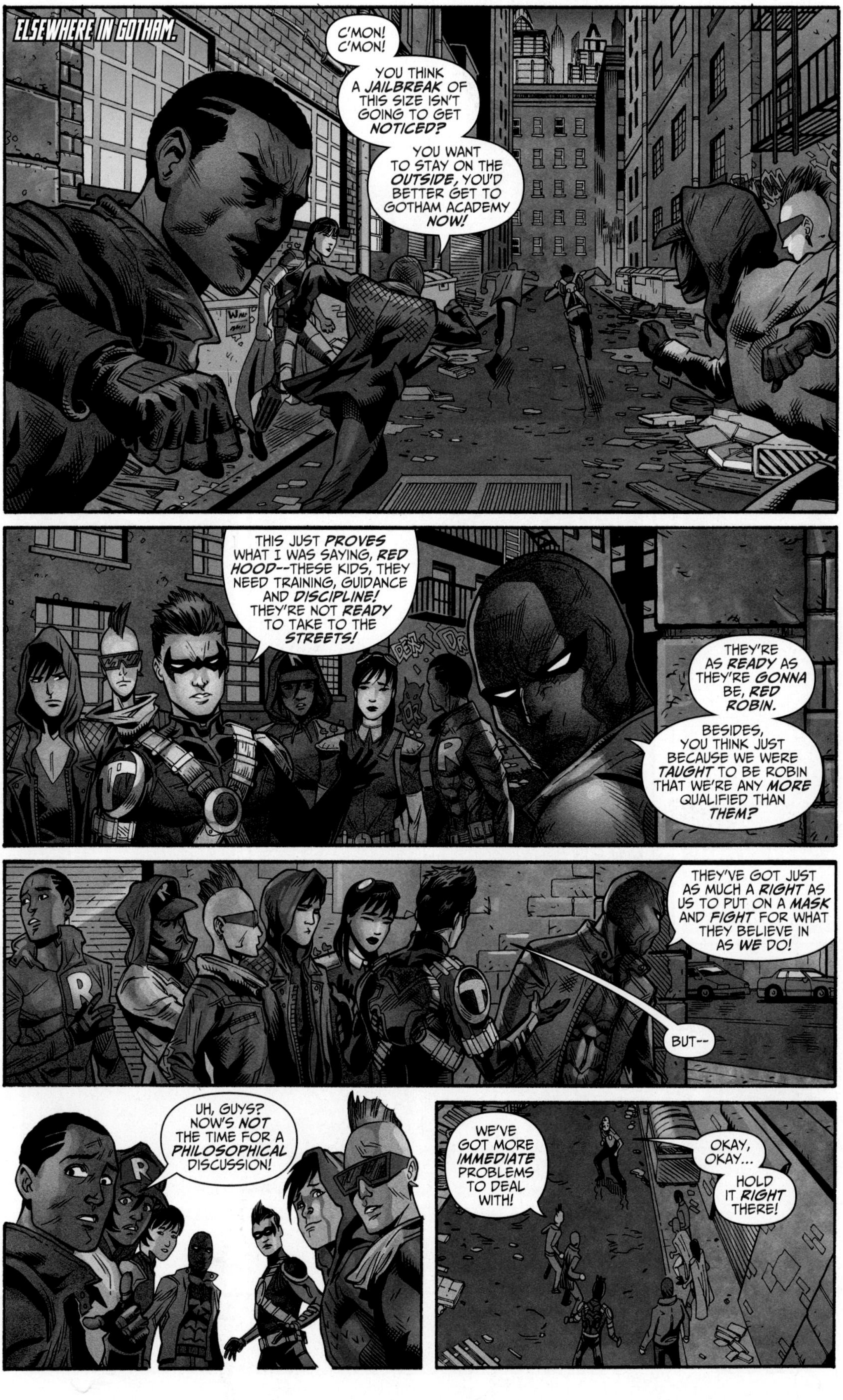
ELSEWHERE IN GOTHAM.
C'MON! C'MON!
YOU THINK A JAILBREAK OF THIS SIZE ISN'T GOING TO GET NOTICED?
YOU WANT TO STAY ON THE OUTSIDE, YOU'D BETTER GET TO GOTHAM ACADEMY NOW!
THIS JUST PROVES WHAT I WAS SAYING, RED HOOD--THESE KIDS, THEY NEED TRAINING, GUIDANCE AND DISCIPLINE! THEY'RE NOT READY TO TAKE TO THE STREETS!
THEY'RE AS READY AS THEY'RE GONNA BE, RED ROBIN.
BESIDES, YOU THINK JUST BECAUSE WE WERE TAUGHT TO BE ROBIN THAT WE'RE ANY MORE QUALIFIED THAN THEM?
THEY'VE GOT JUST AS MUCH A RIGHT AS US TO PUT ON A MASK AND FIGHT FOR WHAT THEY BELIEVE IN AS WE DO!
BUT--
UH, GUYS? NOW'S NOT THE TIME FOR A PHILOSOPHICAL DISCUSSION!
WE'VE GOT MORE IMMEDIATE PROBLEMS TO DEAL WITH!
OKAY, OKAY...
HOLD IT RIGHT THERE!

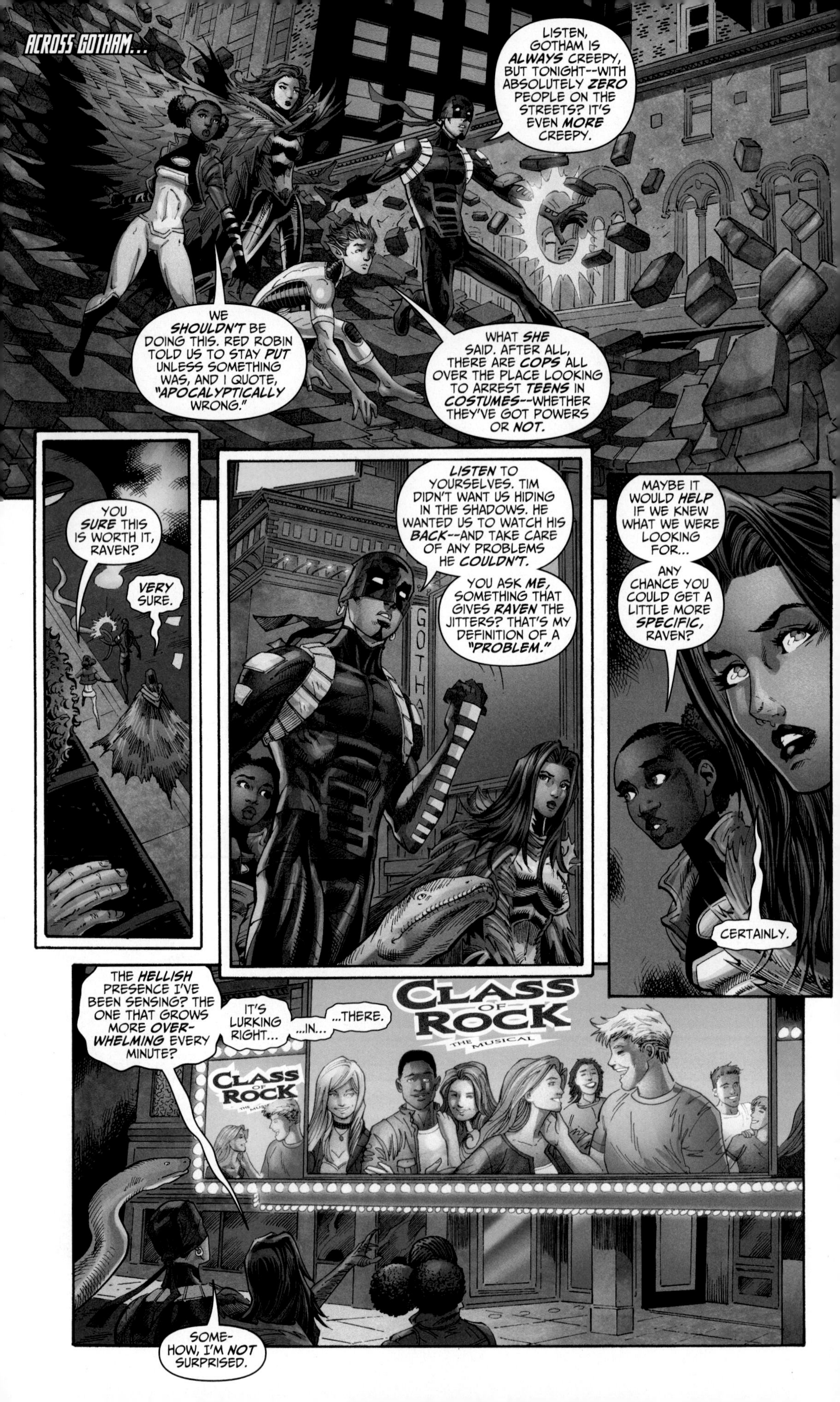
ACROSS GOTHAM...
LISTEN, GOTHAM IS ALWAYS CREEPY, BUT TONIGHT--WITH ABSOLUTELY ZERO PEOPLE ON THE STREETS? IT'S EVEN MORE CREEPY.
WE SHOULDN'T BE DOING THIS. RED ROBIN TOLD US TO STAY PUT UNLESS SOMETHING WAS, AND I QUOTE, "APOCALYPTICALLY WRONG."
WHAT SHE SAID. AFTER ALL, THERE ARE COPS ALL OVER THE PLACE LOOKING TO ARREST TEENS IN COSTUMES--WHETHER THEY'VE GOT POWERS OR NOT.
YOU SURE THIS IS WORTH IT, RAVEN?
VERY SURE.
LISTEN TO YOURSELVES. TIM DIDN'T WANT US HIDING IN THE SHADOWS. HE WANTED US TO WATCH HIS BACK--AND TAKE CARE OF ANY PROBLEMS HE COULDN'T.
YOU ASK ME, SOMETHING THAT GIVES RAVEN THE JITTERS? THAT'S MY DEFINITION OF A "PROBLEM."
MAYBE IT WOULD HELP IF WE KNEW WHAT WE WERE LOOKING FOR...
ANY CHANCE YOU COULD GET A LITTLE MORE SPECIFIC, RAVEN?
CERTAINLY.
THE HELLISH PRESENCE I'VE BEEN SENSING? THE ONE THAT GROWS MORE OVER-WHELMING EVERY MINUTE?
IT'S LURKING RIGHT...
...IN...
...THERE.
CLASS OF ROCK
THE MUSICAL
SOME-HOW, I'M NOT SURPRISED.

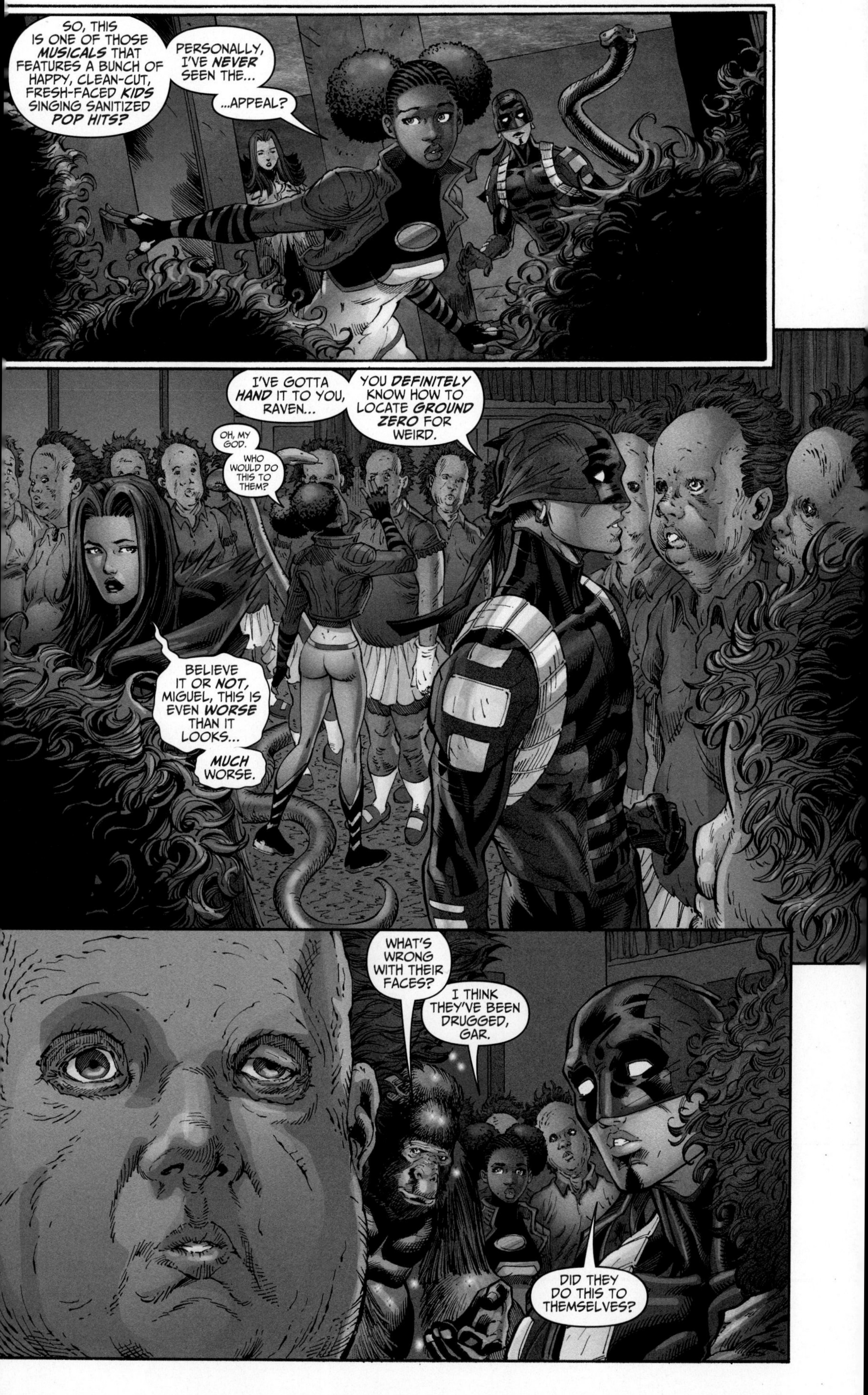
SO, THIS IS ONE OF THOSE MUSICALS THAT FEATURES A BUNCH OF HAPPY, CLEAN-CUT, FRESH-FACED KIDS SINGING SANITIZED POP HITS?
PERSONALLY, I'VE NEVER SEEN THE...
...APPEAL?
I'VE GOTTA HAND IT TO YOU, RAVEN...
YOU DEFINITELY KNOW HOW TO LOCATE GROUND ZERO FOR WEIRD.
OH, MY GOD.
WHO WOULD DO THIS TO THEM?
BELIEVE IT OR NOT, MIGUEL, THIS IS EVEN WORSE THAN IT LOOKS...
MUCH WORSE.
WHAT'S WRONG WITH THEIR FACES?
I THINK THEY'VE BEEN DRUGGED, GAR.
DID THEY DO THIS TO THEMSELVES?

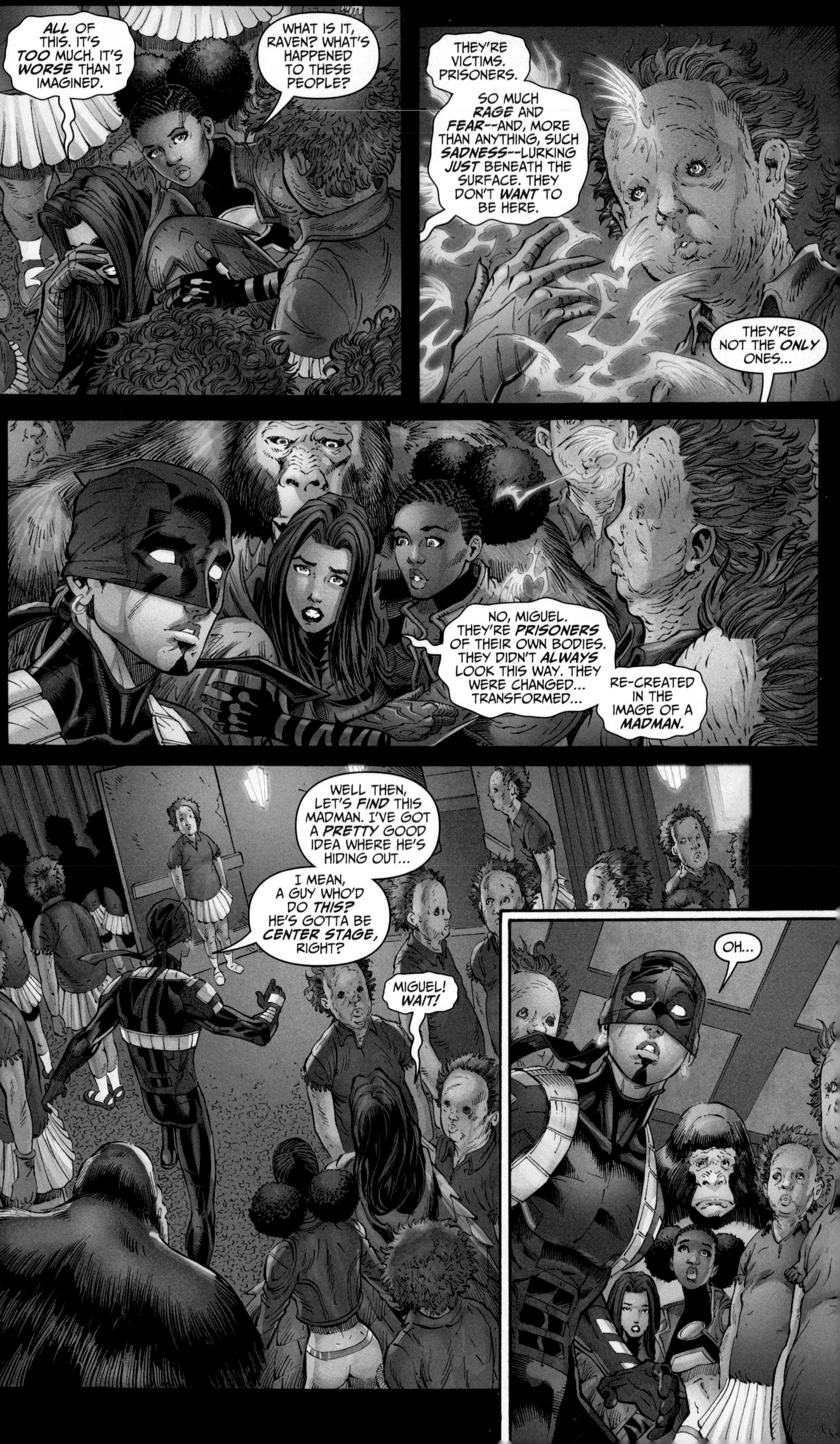

ALL OF THIS. IT'S TOO MUCH. IT'S WORSE THAN I IMAGINED.
WHAT IS IT, RAVEN? WHAT'S HAPPENED TO THESE PEOPLE?
THEY'RE VICTIMS. PRISONERS.
SO MUCH RAGE AND FEAR--AND, MORE THAN ANYTHING, SUCH SADNESS--LURKING JUST BENEATH THE SURFACE. THEY DON'T WANT TO BE HERE.
THEY'RE NOT THE ONLY ONES...
NO, MIGUEL. THEY'RE PRISONERS OF THEIR OWN BODIES. THEY DIDN'T ALWAYS LOOK THIS WAY. THEY WERE CHANGED... TRANSFORMED...
RE-CREATED IN THE IMAGE OF A MADMAN.
WELL THEN, LET'S FIND THIS MADMAN. I'VE GOT A PRETTY GOOD IDEA WHERE HE'S HIDING OUT...
I MEAN, A GUY WHO'D DO THIS? HE'S GOTTA BE CENTER STAGE, RIGHT?
MIGUEL! WAIT!
OH...

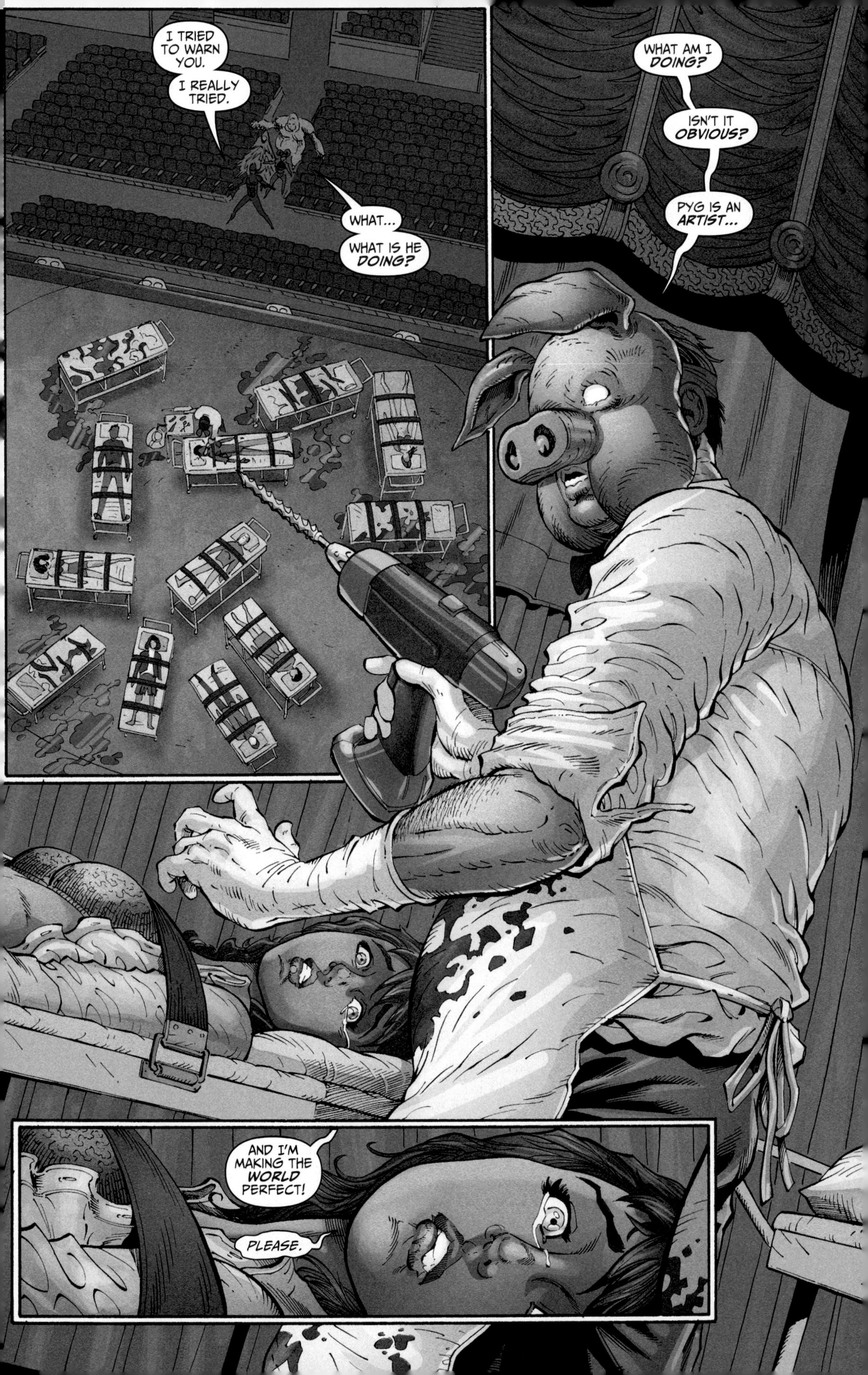
I TRIED TO WARN YOU.
I REALLY TRIED.
WHAT...
WHAT IS HE DOING?
WHAT AM I DOING?
ISN'T IT OBVIOUS?
PYG IS AN ARTIST...
AND I'M MAKING THE WORLD PERFECT!
PLEASE.

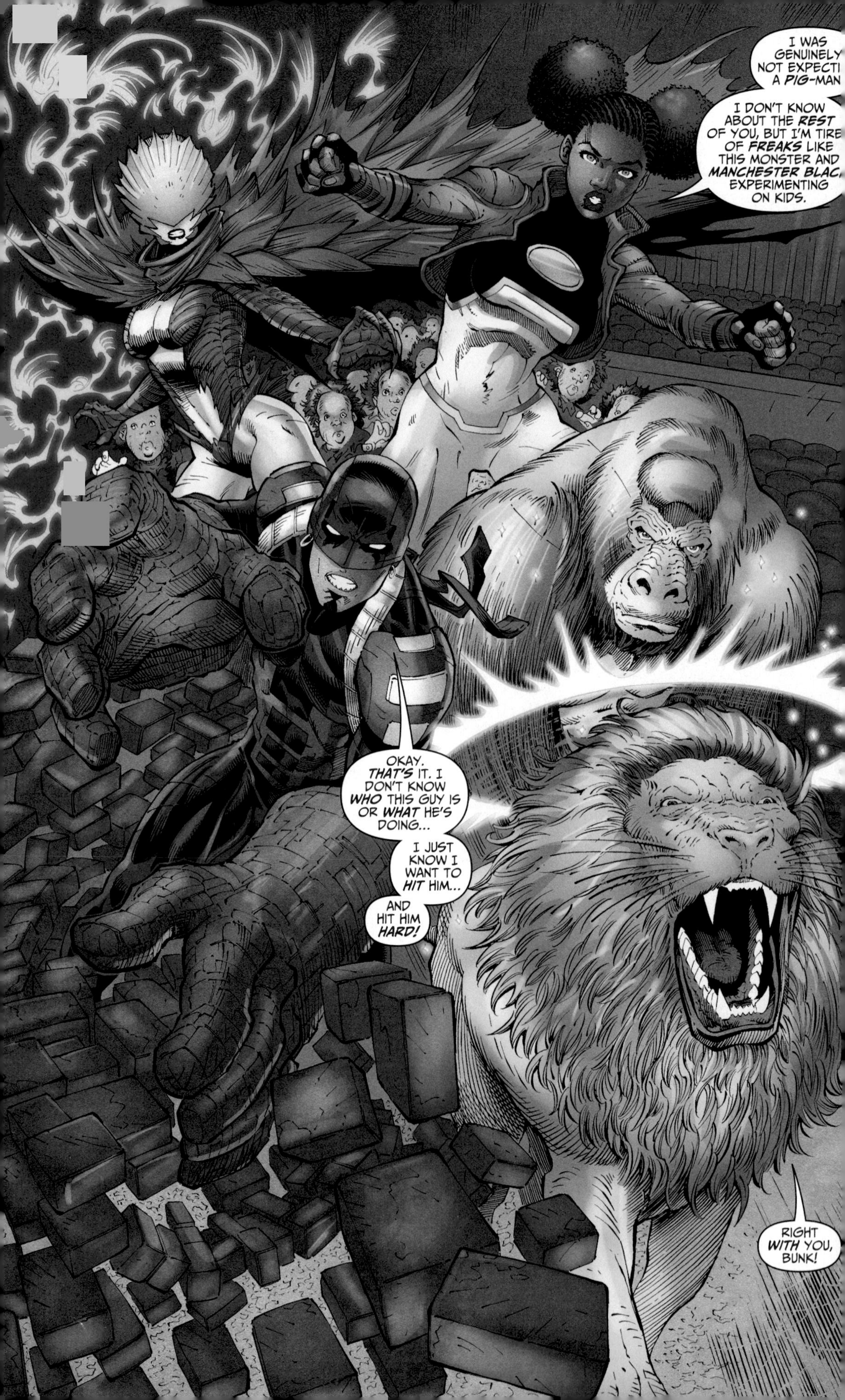

I WAS GENUINELY NOT EXPECTI A PIG-MAN
I DON'T KNOW ABOUT THE REST OF YOU, BUT I'M TIRE OF FREAKS LIKE THIS MONSTER AND MANCHESTER BLAC EXPERIMENTING ON KIDS.
OKAY. THAT'S IT. I DON'T KNOW WHO THIS GUY IS OR WHAT HE'S DOING...
I JUST KNOW I WANT TO HIT HIM...
AND HIT HIM HARD!
RIGHT WITH YOU, BUNK!

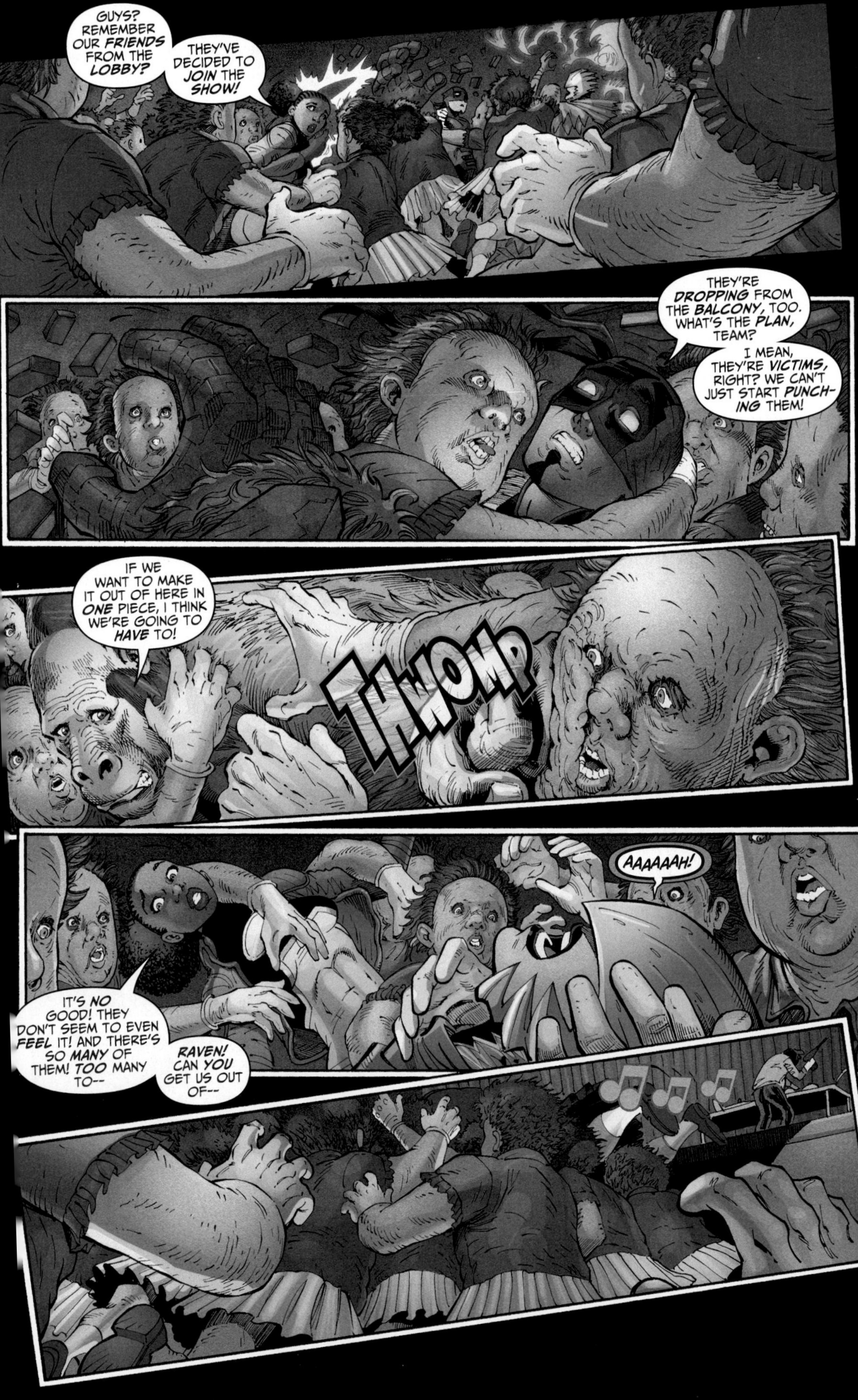
GUYS? REMEMBER OUR FRIENDS FROM THE LOBBY?
THEY'VE DECIDED TO JOIN THE SHOW!
THEY'RE DROPPING FROM THE BALCONY, TOO. WHAT'S THE PLAN, TEAM?
I MEAN, THEY'RE VICTIMS, RIGHT? WE CAN'T JUST START PUNCHING THEM!
IF WE WANT TO MAKE IT OUT OF HERE IN ONE PIECE, I THINK WE'RE GOING TO HAVE TO!
THWOMP
AAAAAAH!
IT'S NO GOOD! THEY DON'T SEEM TO EVEN FEEL IT! AND THERE'S SO MANY OF THEM! TOO MANY TO--
RAVEN! CAN YOU GET US OUT OF--

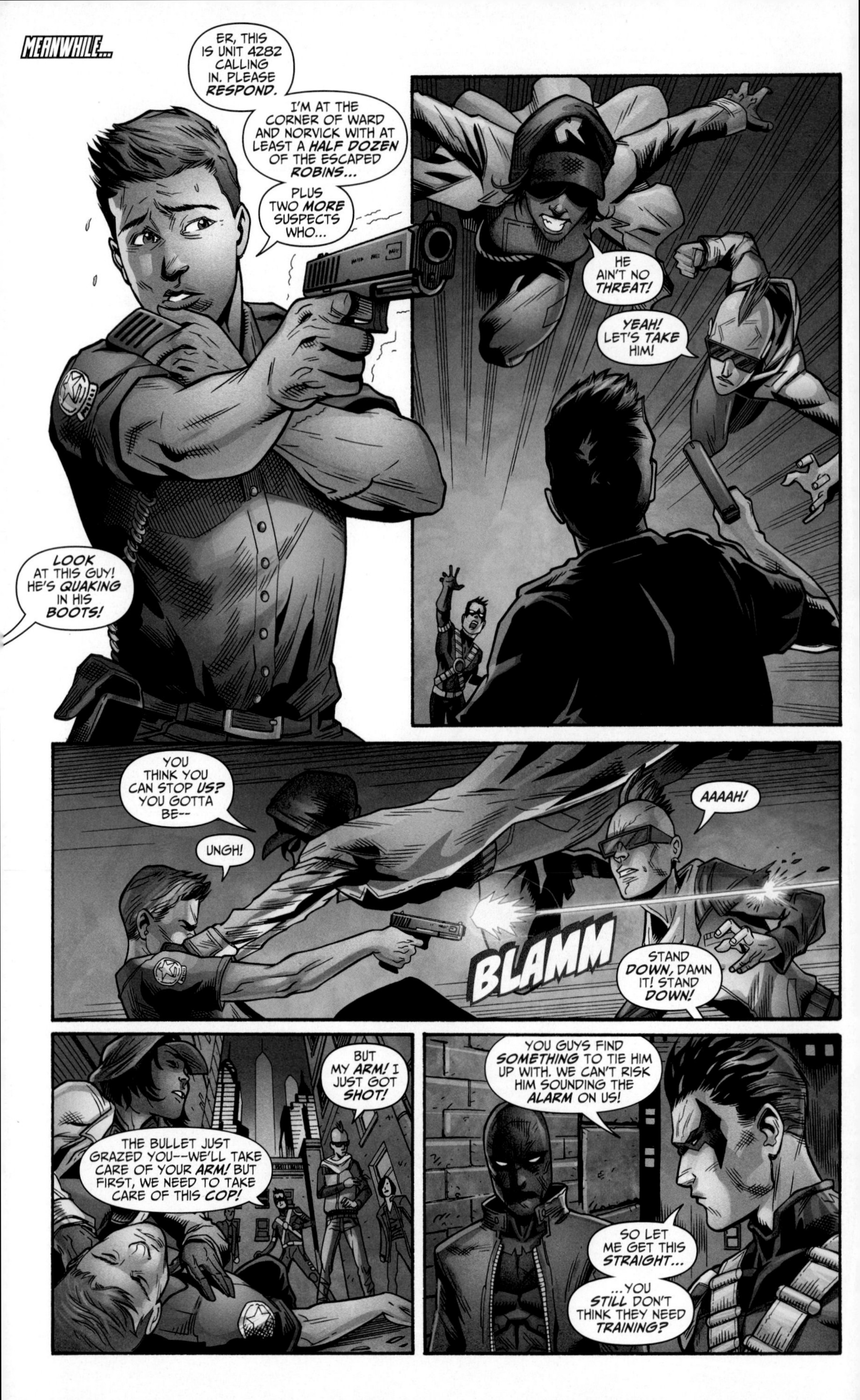
MEANWHILE...
ER, THIS IS UNIT 4282 CALLING IN. PLEASE RESPOND.
I'M AT THE CORNER OF WARD AND NORVICK WITH AT LEAST A HALF DOZEN OF THE ESCAPED ROBINS...
PLUS TWO MORE SUSPECTS WHO...
HE AIN'T NO THREAT!
YEAH! LET'S TAKE HIM!
LOOK AT THIS GUY! HE'S QUAKING IN HIS BOOTS!
YOU THINK YOU CAN STOP US? YOU GOTTA BE--
UNGH!
AAAAH!
BLAMM
STAND DOWN, DAMN IT! STAND DOWN!
BUT MY ARM! I JUST GOT SHOT!
THE BULLET JUST GRAZED YOU--WE'LL TAKE CARE OF YOUR ARM! BUT FIRST, WE NEED TO TAKE CARE OF THIS COP!
YOU GUYS FIND SOMETHING TO TIE HIM UP WITH. WE CAN'T RISK HIM SOUNDING THE ALARM ON US!
SO LET ME GET THIS STRAIGHT...
...YOU STILL DON'T THINK THEY NEED TRAINING?

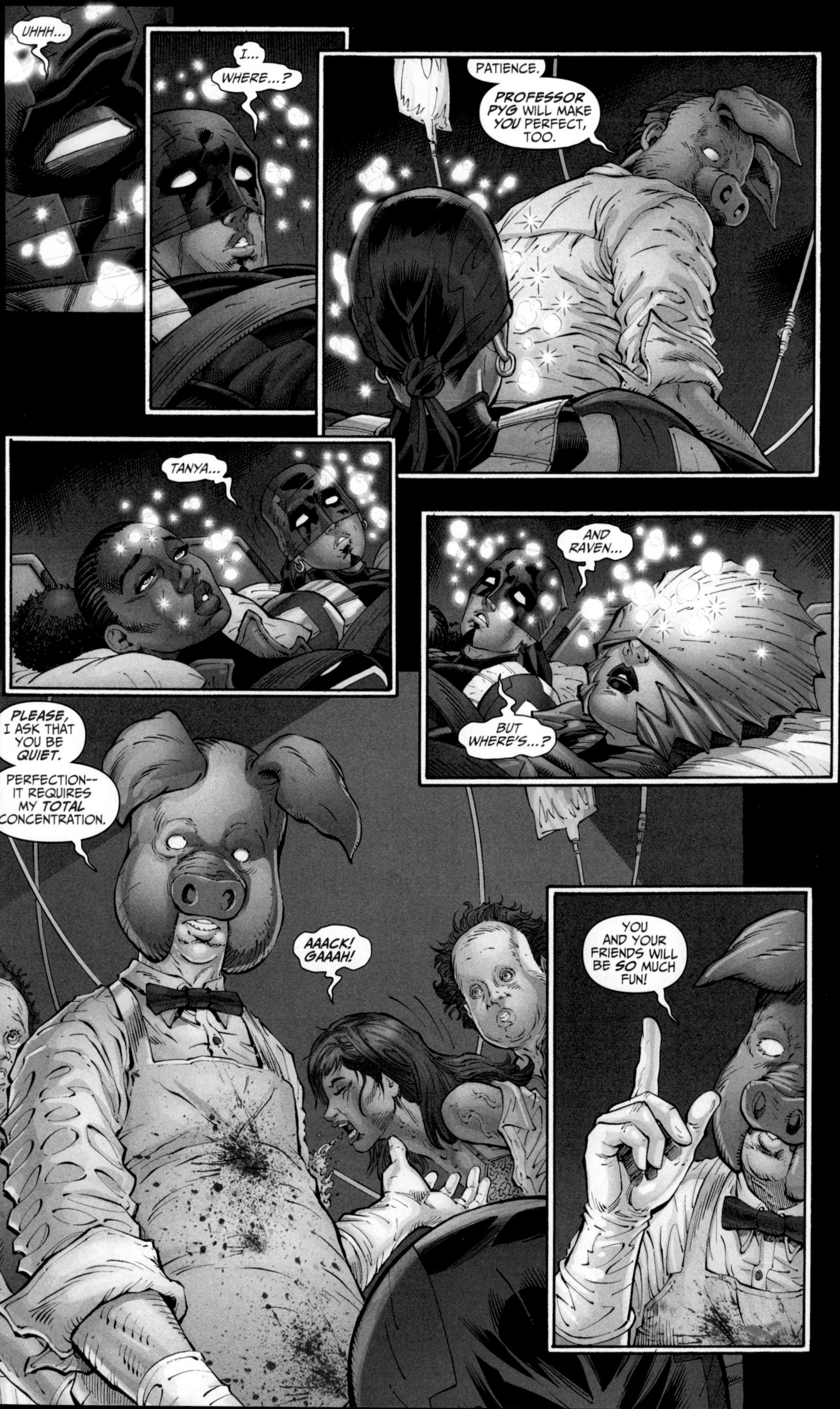
UHHH...
I... WHERE...?
PATIENCE.
PROFESSOR PYG WILL MAKE YOU PERFECT, TOO.
TANYA...
AND RAVEN...
BUT WHERE'S...?
PLEASE, I ASK THAT YOU BE QUIET.
PERFECTION-- IT REQUIRES MY TOTAL CONCENTRATION.
AAACK! GAAAH!
YOU AND YOUR FRIENDS WILL BE SO MUCH FUN!

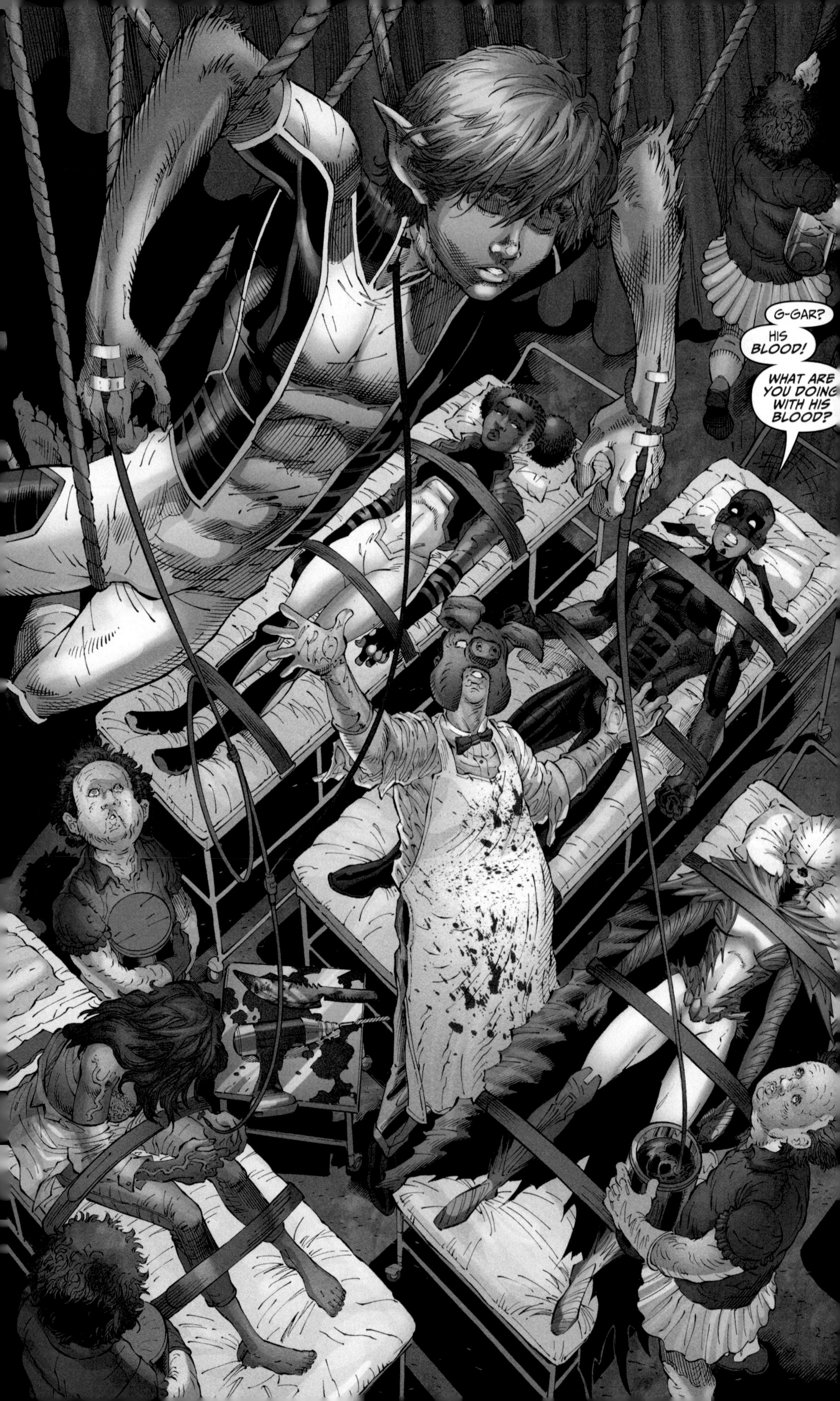
G-GAR?
HIS BLOOD!
WHAT ARE YOU DOING WITH HIS BLOOD?

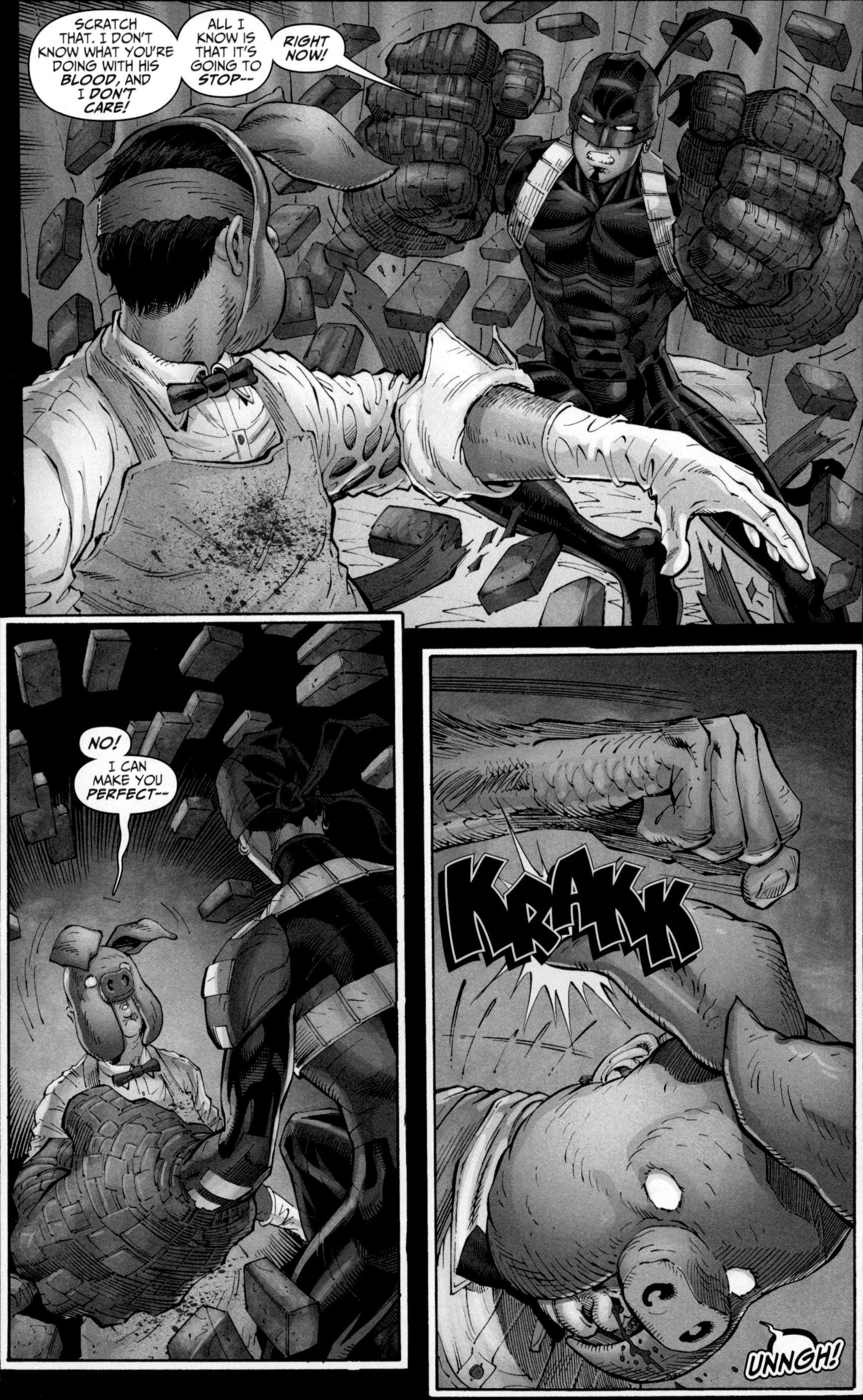
SCRATCH THAT. I DON'T KNOW WHAT YOU'RE DOING WITH HIS BLOOD, AND I DON'T CARE!
ALL I KNOW IS THAT IT'S GOING TO STOP--
RIGHT NOW!
NO! I CAN MAKE YOU PERFECT--
KRAKK
UNNGH!

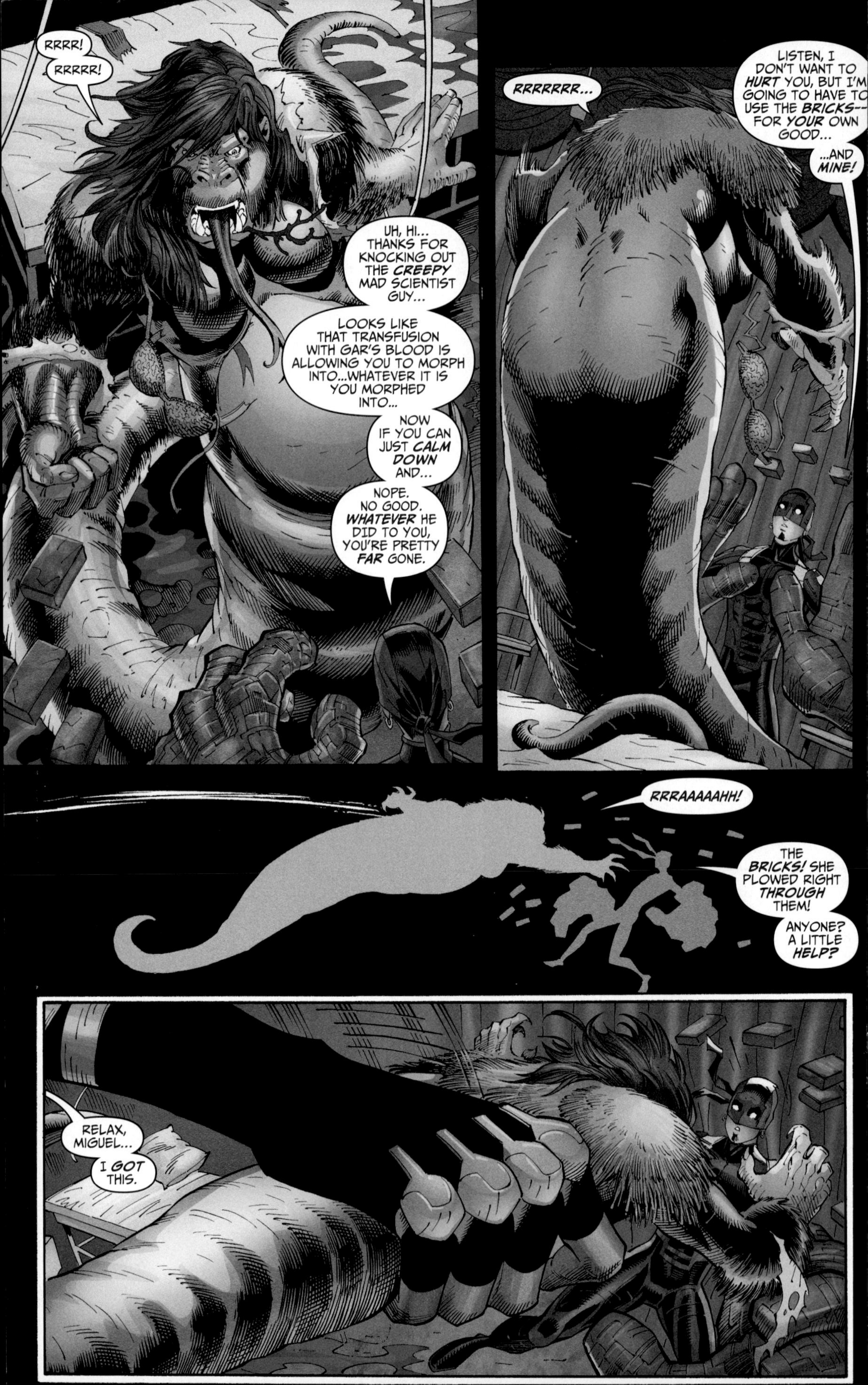
RRRR!
RRRRR!
UH, HI... THANKS FOR KNOCKING OUT THE CREEPY MAD SCIENTIST GUY...
LOOKS LIKE THAT TRANSFUSION WITH GAR'S BLOOD IS ALLOWING YOU TO MORPH INTO...WHATEVER IT IS YOU MORPHED INTO...
NOW IF YOU CAN JUST CALM DOWN AND...
NOPE. NO GOOD. WHATEVER HE DID TO YOU, YOU'RE PRETTY FAR GONE.
RRRRRRR...
LISTEN, I DON'T WANT TO HURT YOU, BUT I'M GOING TO HAVE TO USE THE BRICKS-- FOR YOUR OWN GOOD...
...AND MINE!
RRRAAAAAHH!
THE BRICKS! SHE PLOWED RIGHT THROUGH THEM!
ANYONE? A LITTLE HELP?
RELAX, MIGUEL...
I GOT THIS.

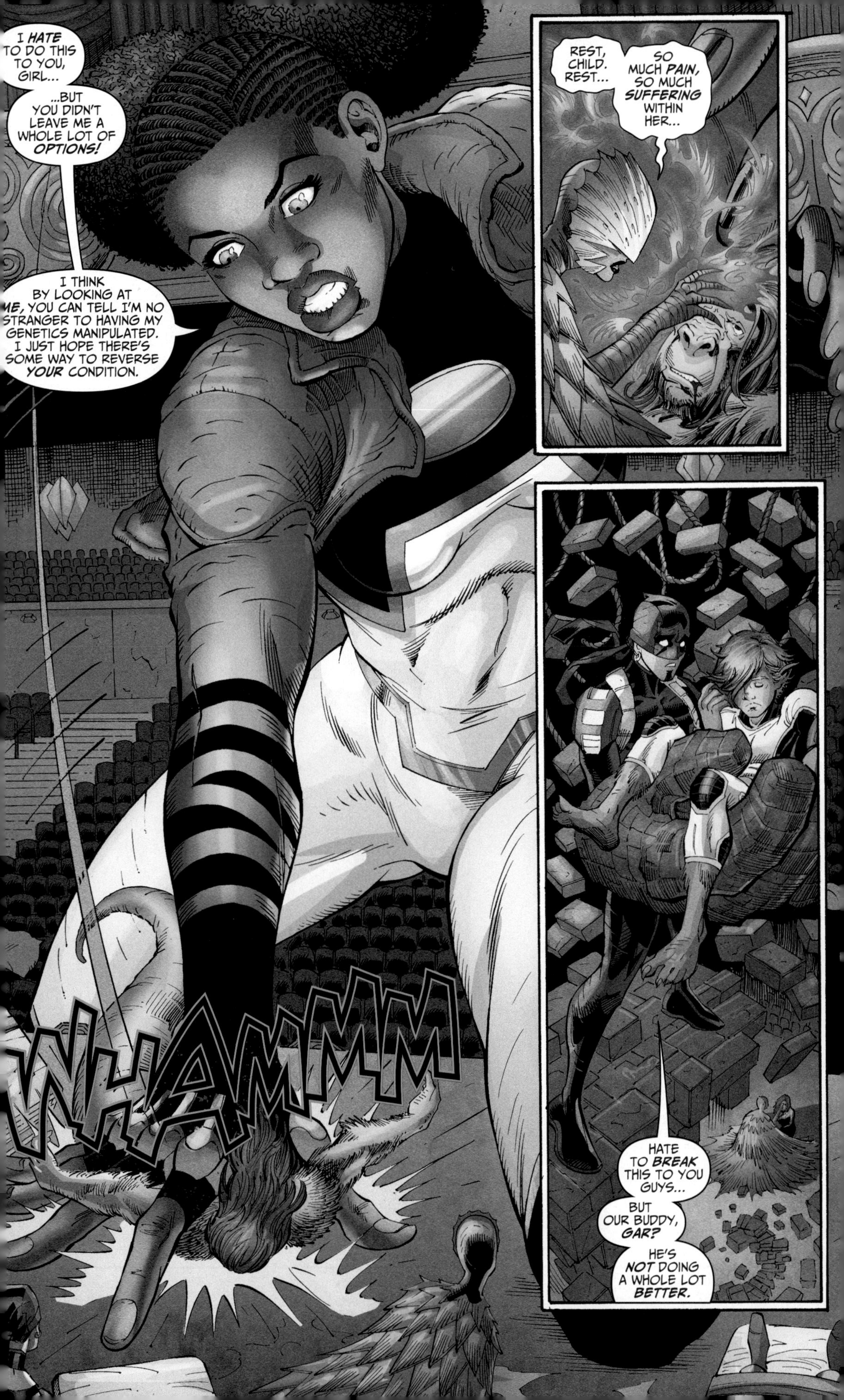
I HATE TO DO THIS TO YOU, GIRL...
...BUT YOU DIDN'T LEAVE ME A WHOLE LOT OF OPTIONS!
I THINK BY LOOKING AT ME, YOU CAN TELL I'M NO STRANGER TO HAVING MY GENETICS MANIPULATED. I JUST HOPE THERE'S SOME WAY TO REVERSE YOUR CONDITION.
WHAMMM
REST, CHILD. REST...
SO MUCH PAIN, SO MUCH SUFFERING WITHIN HER...
HATE TO BREAK THIS TO YOU GUYS...
BUT OUR BUDDY, GAR?
HE'S NOT DOING A WHOLE LOT BETTER.

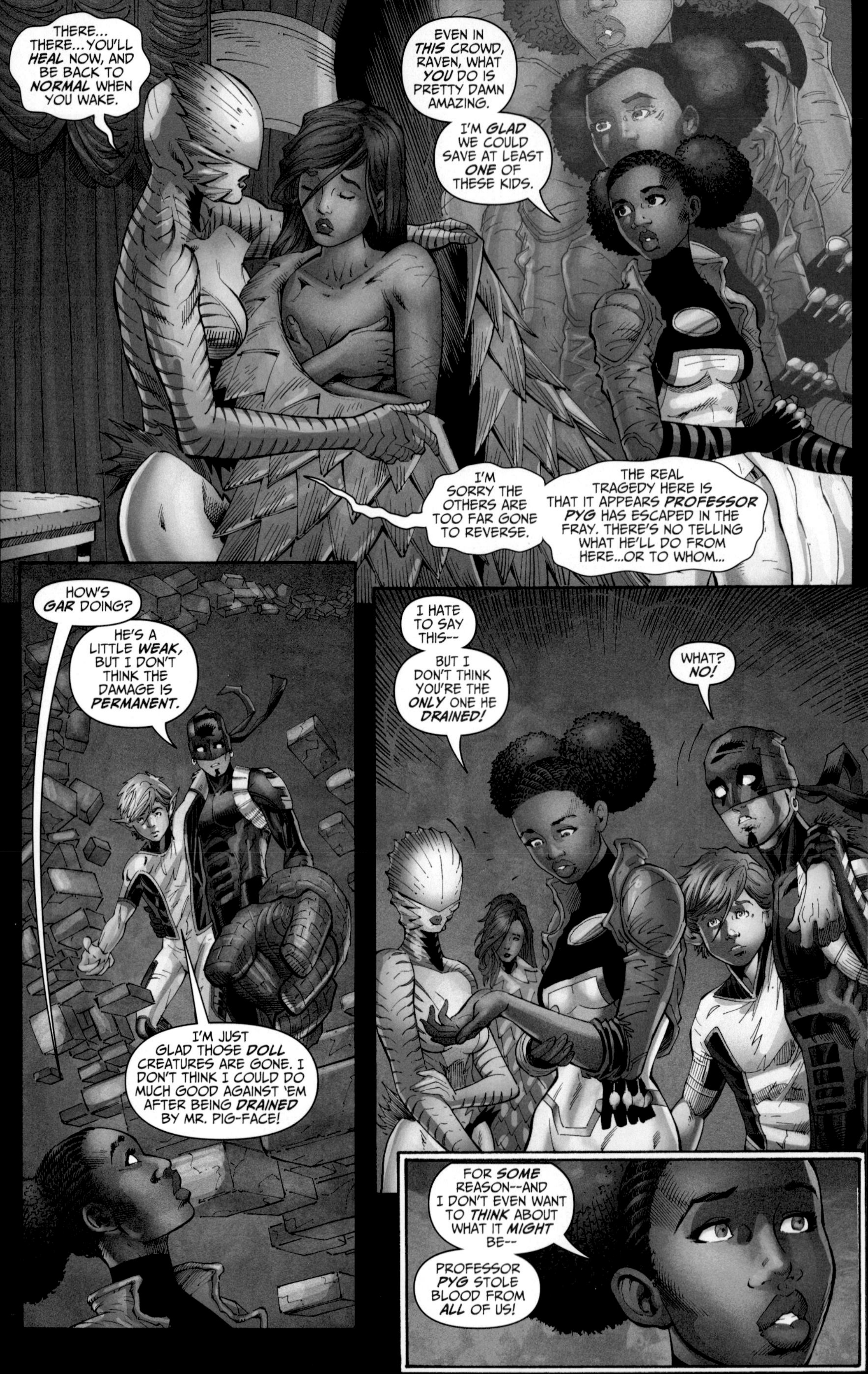
THERE... THERE...YOU'LL HEAL NOW, AND BE BACK TO NORMAL WHEN YOU WAKE.
EVEN IN THIS CROWD, RAVEN, WHAT YOU DO IS PRETTY DAMN AMAZING.
I'M GLAD WE COULD SAVE AT LEAST ONE OF THESE KIDS.
I'M SORRY THE OTHERS ARE TOO FAR GONE TO REVERSE.
THE REAL TRAGEDY HERE IS THAT IT APPEARS PROFESSOR PYG HAS ESCAPED IN THE FRAY. THERE'S NO TELLING WHAT HE'LL DO FROM HERE...OR TO WHOM...
HOW'S GAR DOING?
HE'S A LITTLE WEAK, BUT I DON'T THINK THE DAMAGE IS PERMANENT.
I'M JUST GLAD THOSE DOLL CREATURES ARE GONE. I DON'T THINK I COULD DO MUCH GOOD AGAINST 'EM AFTER BEING DRAINED BY MR. PIG-FACE!
I HATE TO SAY THIS--
BUT I DON'T THINK YOU'RE THE ONLY ONE HE DRAINED!
WHAT? NO!
FOR SOME REASON--AND I DON'T EVEN WANT TO THINK ABOUT WHAT IT MIGHT BE--
PROFESSOR PYG STOLE BLOOD FROM ALL OF US!

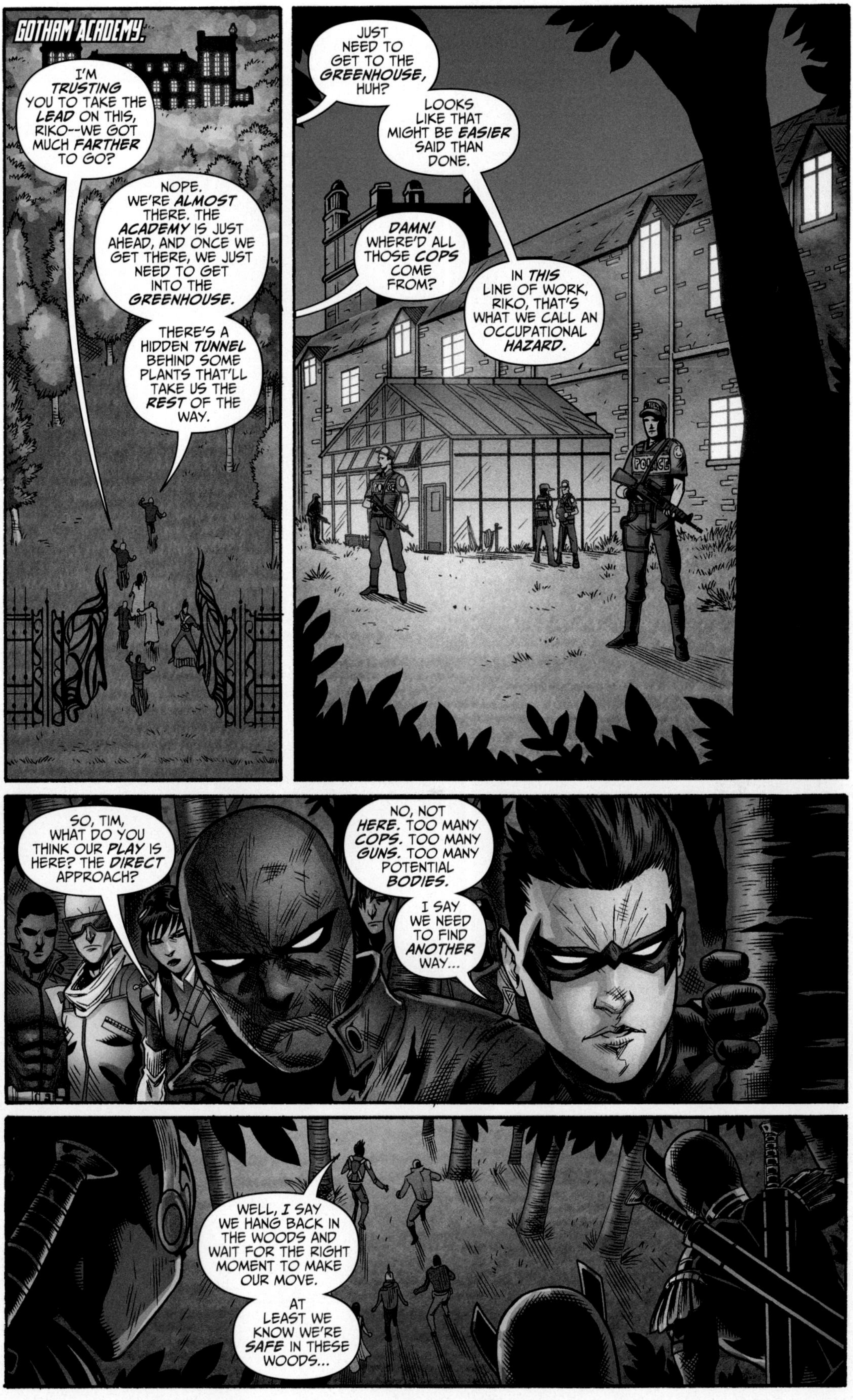
GOTHAM ACADEMY.
I'M TRUSTING YOU TO TAKE THE LEAD ON THIS, RIKO--WE GOT MUCH FARTHER TO GO?
NOPE. WE'RE ALMOST THERE. THE ACADEMY IS JUST AHEAD, AND ONCE WE GET THERE, WE JUST NEED TO GET INTO THE GREENHOUSE.
THERE'S A HIDDEN TUNNEL BEHIND SOME PLANTS THAT'LL TAKE US THE REST OF THE WAY.
JUST NEED TO GET TO THE GREENHOUSE, HUH?
LOOKS LIKE THAT MIGHT BE EASIER SAID THAN DONE.
DAMN! WHERE'D ALL THOSE COPS COME FROM?
IN THIS LINE OF WORK, RIKO, THAT'S WHAT WE CALL AN OCCUPATIONAL HAZARD.
POLICE
SO, TIM, WHAT DO YOU THINK OUR PLAY IS HERE? THE DIRECT APPROACH?
NO, NOT HERE. TOO MANY COPS. TOO MANY GUNS. TOO MANY POTENTIAL BODIES.
I SAY WE NEED TO FIND ANOTHER WAY...
WELL, I SAY WE HANG BACK IN THE WOODS AND WAIT FOR THE RIGHT MOMENT TO MAKE OUR MOVE.
AT LEAST WE KNOW WE'RE SAFE IN THESE WOODS...

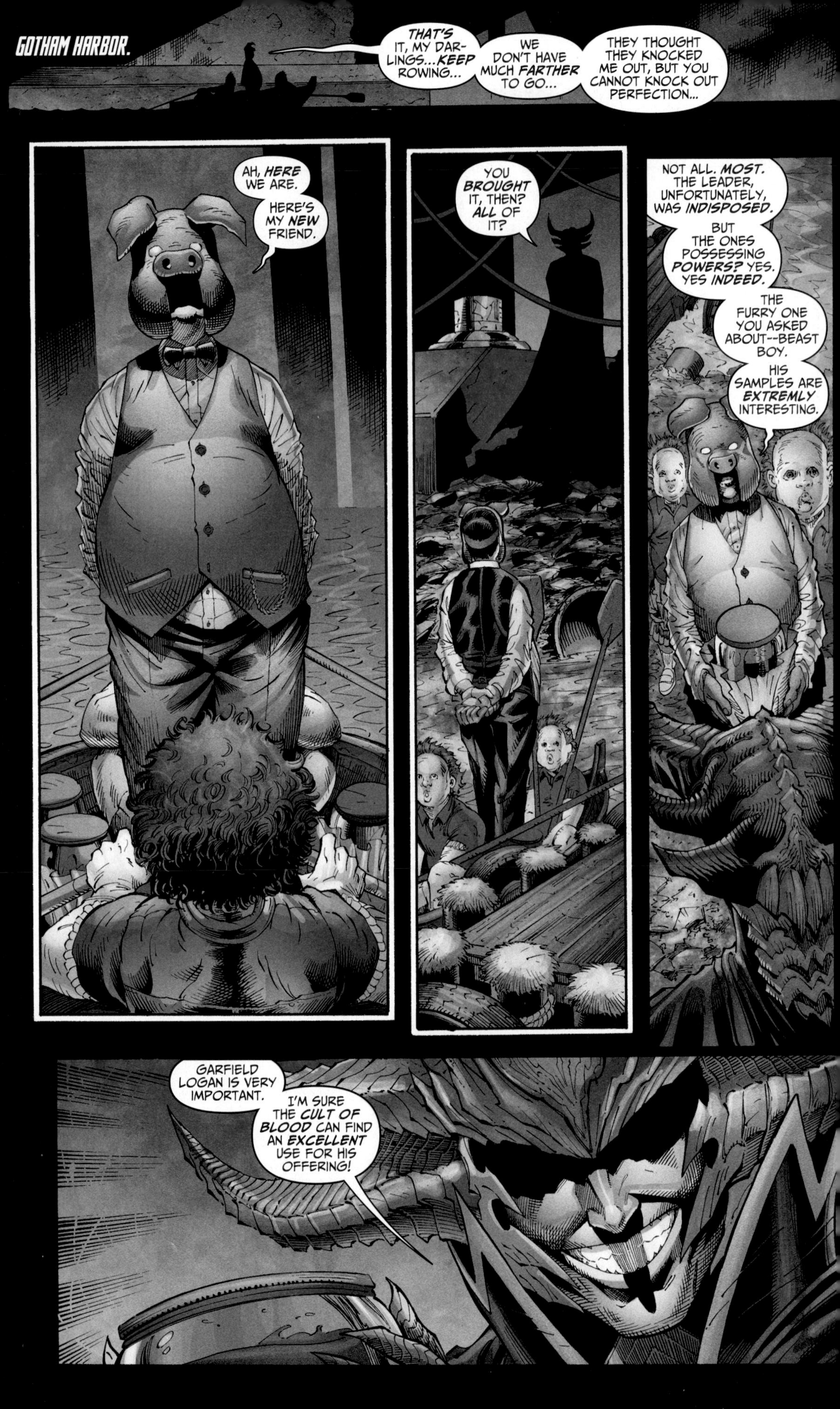
GOTHAM HARBOR.
THAT'S IT, MY DARLINGS... KEEP ROWING...
WE DON'T HAVE MUCH FARTHER TO GO...
THEY THOUGHT THEY KNOCKED ME OUT, BUT YOU CANNOT KNOCK OUT PERFECTION...
AH, HERE WE ARE.
HERE'S MY NEW FRIEND.
YOU BROUGHT IT, THEN? ALL OF IT?
NOT ALL. MOST. THE LEADER, UNFORTUNATELY, WAS INDISPOSED.
BUT THE ONES POSSESSING POWERS? YES. YES INDEED.
THE FURRY ONE YOU ASKED ABOUT--BEAST BOY.
HIS SAMPLES ARE EXTREMLY INTERESTING.
GARFIELD LOGAN IS VERY IMPORTANT.
I'M SURE THE CULT OF BLOOD CAN FIND AN EXCELLENT USE FOR HIS OFFERING!

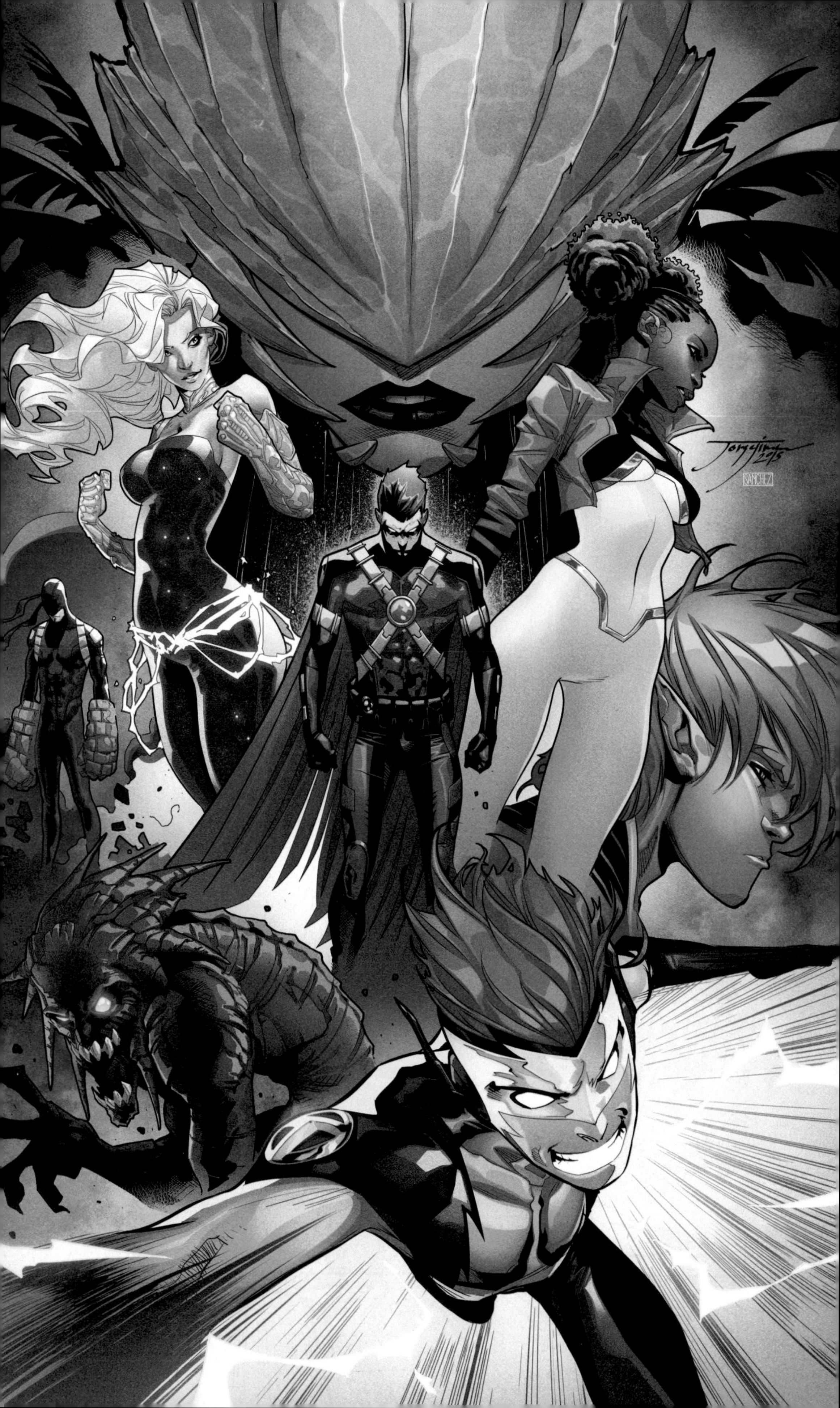
SANCHEZ

THE SUM OF ITS PARTS

WILL PFEIFER writer MIGUEL MENDONÇA penciller DEXTER VINES inker TONY AVIÑA colorist COREY BREEN letterer cover art by JORGE JIMÉNEZ & ALEJANDRO SANCHEZ

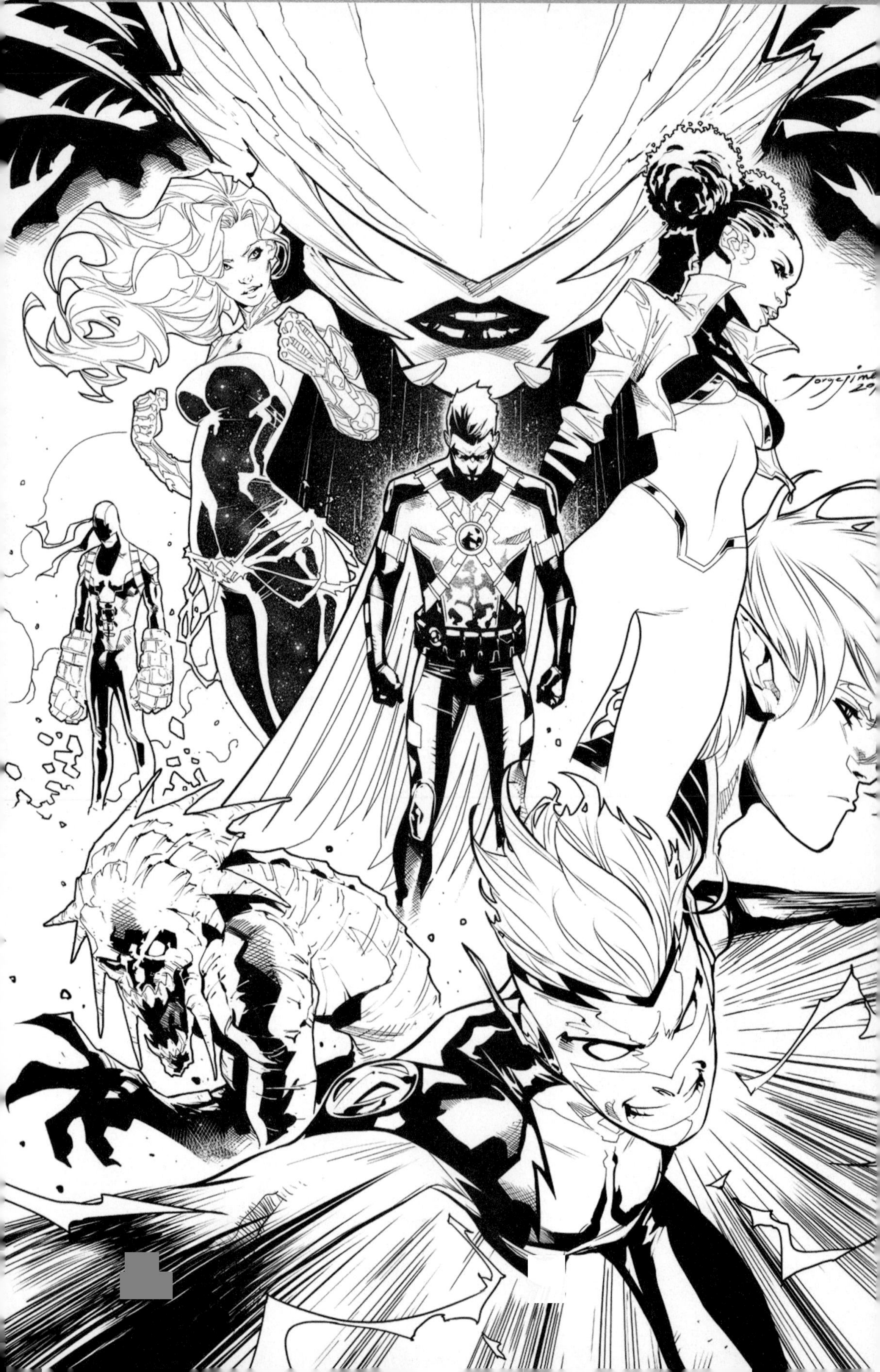

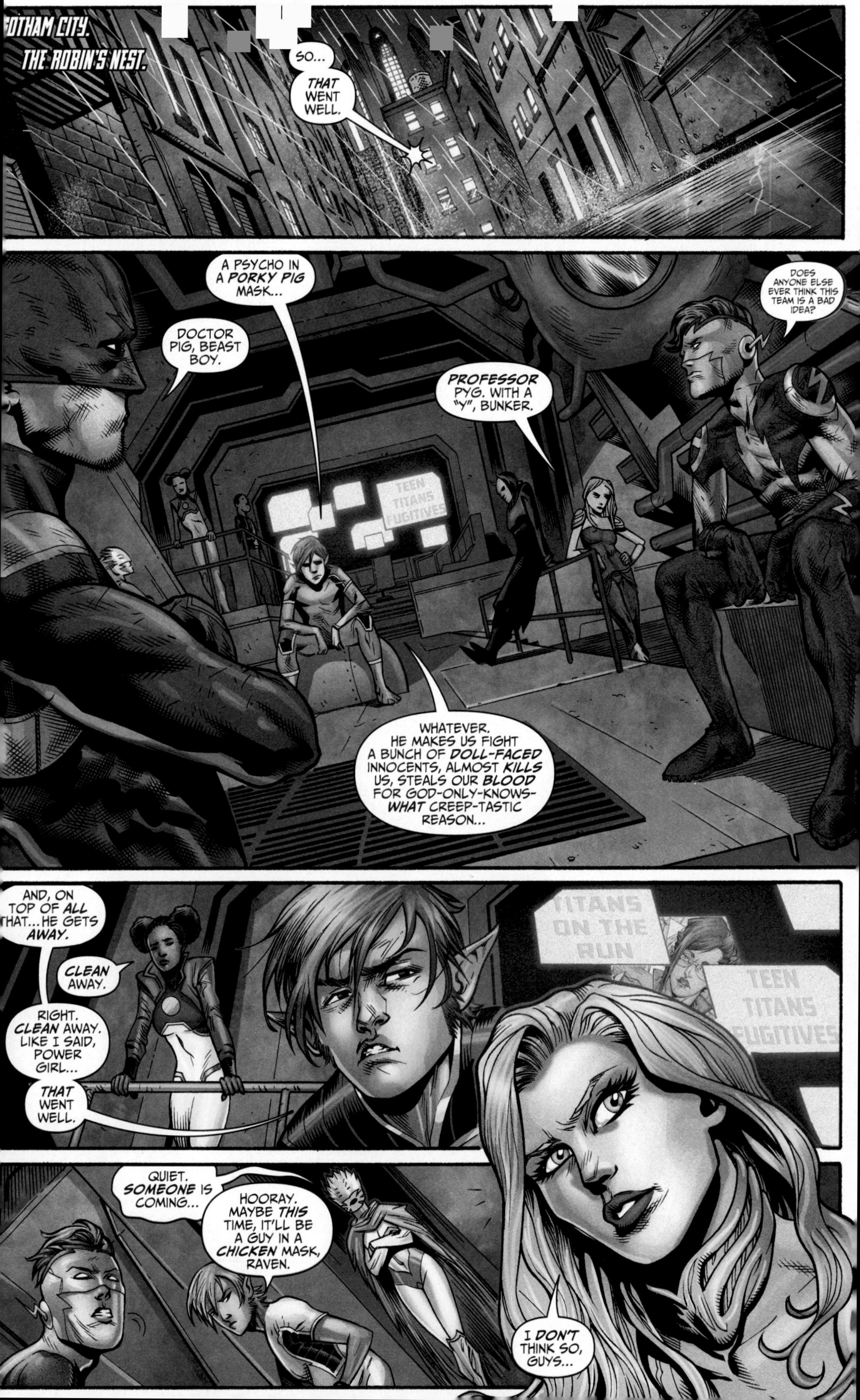

OTHAM CITY.
THE ROBIN'S NEST.
SO... THAT WENT WELL.
A PSYCHO IN A PORKY PIG MASK...
DOCTOR PIG, BEAST BOY.
PROFESSOR PYG. WITH A "Y", BUNKER.
DOES ANYONE ELSE EVER THINK THIS TEAM IS A BAD IDEA?
TEEN TITANS FUGITIVES
WHATEVER. HE MAKES US FIGHT A BUNCH OF DOLL-FACED INNOCENTS, ALMOST KILLS US, STEALS OUR BLOOD FOR GOD-ONLY-KNOWS-WHAT CREEP-TASTIC REASON...
AND, ON TOP OF ALL THAT... HE GETS AWAY.
CLEAN AWAY.
RIGHT. CLEAN AWAY. LIKE I SAID, POWER GIRL...
THAT WENT WELL.
TITANS ON THE RUN
TEEN TITANS FUGITIVES
QUIET. SOMEONE IS COMING...
HOORAY. MAYBE THIS TIME, IT'LL BE A GUY IN A CHICKEN MASK, RAVEN.
I DON'T THINK SO, GUYS...

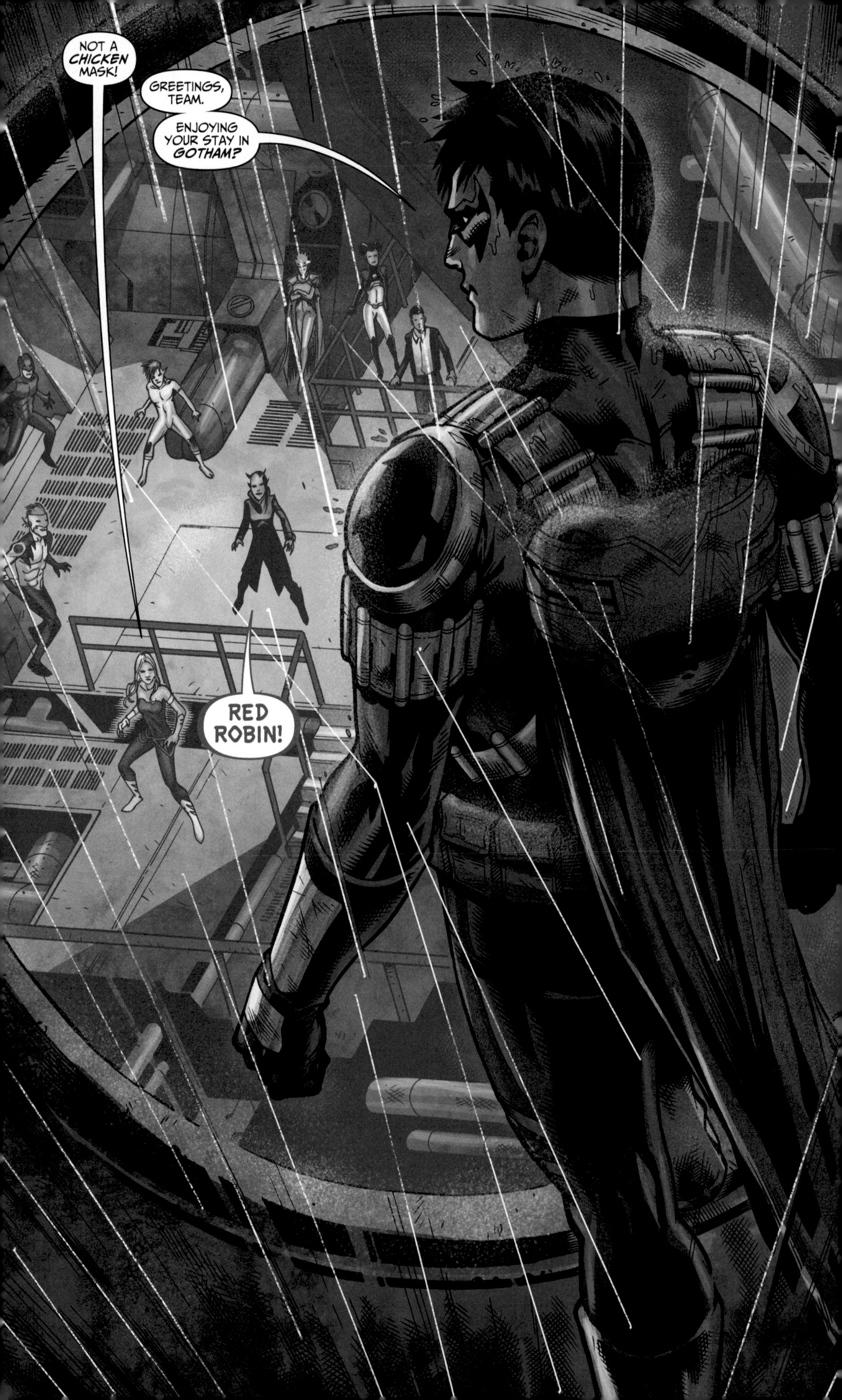
NOT A CHICKEN MASK!
GREETINGS, TEAM.
ENJOYING YOUR STAY IN GOTHAM?
RED ROBIN!

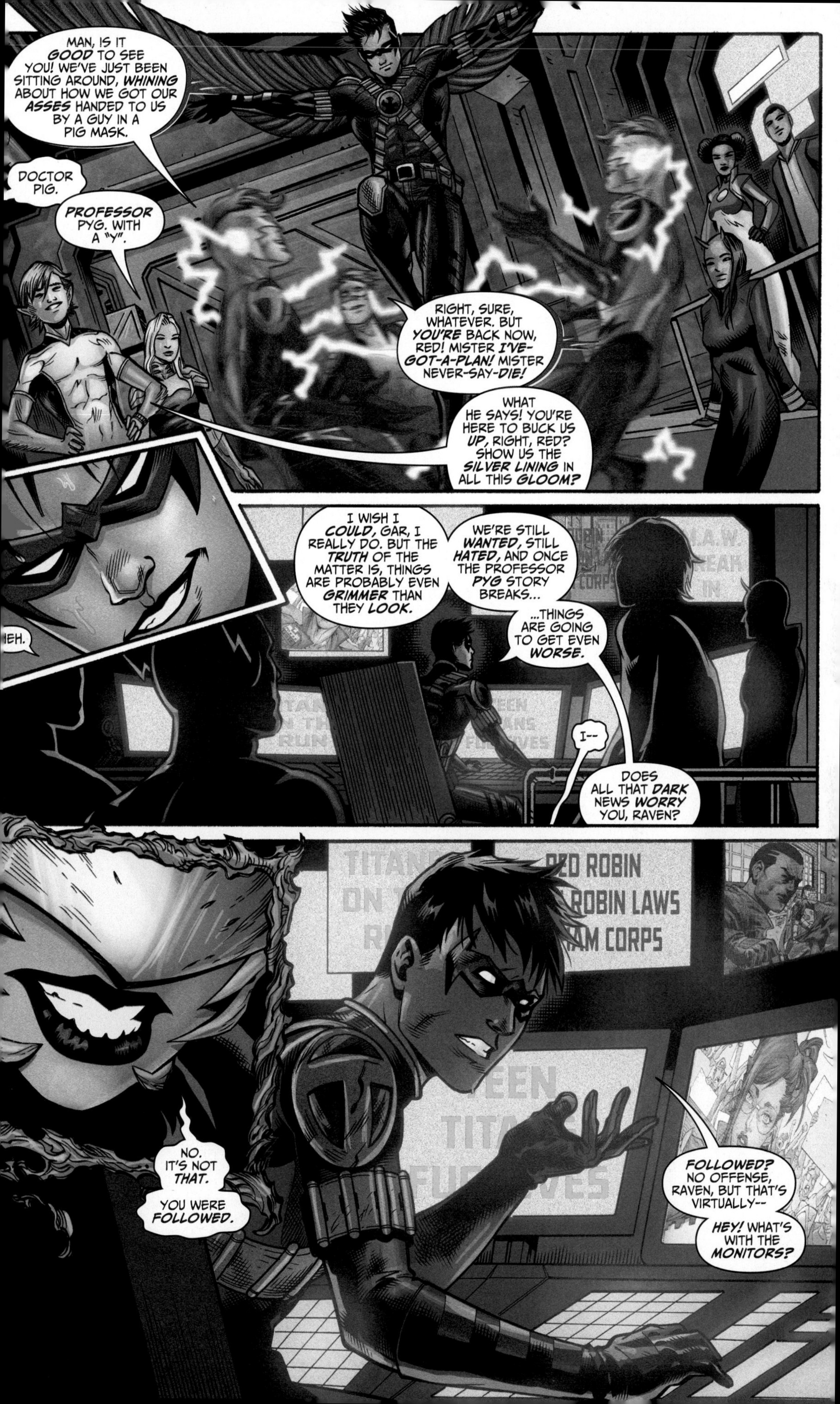

MAN, IS IT GOOD TO SEE YOU! WE'VE JUST BEEN SITTING AROUND, WHINING ABOUT HOW WE GOT OUR ASSES HANDED TO US BY A GUY IN A PIG MASK.
DOCTOR PIG.
PROFESSOR PYG. WITH A "Y".
RIGHT, SURE, WHATEVER. BUT YOU'RE BACK NOW, RED! MISTER I'VE-GOT-A-PLAN! MISTER NEVER-SAY-DIE!
WHAT HE SAYS! YOU'RE HERE TO BUCK US UP, RIGHT, RED? SHOW US THE SILVER LINING IN ALL THIS GLOOM?
I WISH I COULD, GAR, I REALLY DO. BUT THE TRUTH OF THE MATTER IS, THINGS ARE PROBABLY EVEN GRIMMER THAN THEY LOOK.
WE'RE STILL WANTED, STILL HATED, AND ONCE THE PROFESSOR PYG STORY BREAKS...
...THINGS ARE GOING TO GET EVEN WORSE.
I--
DOES ALL THAT DARK NEWS WORRY YOU, RAVEN?
NO. IT'S NOT THAT.
YOU WERE FOLLOWED.
FOLLOWED? NO OFFENSE, RAVEN, BUT THAT'S VIRTUALLY--
HEY! WHAT'S WITH THE MONITORS?

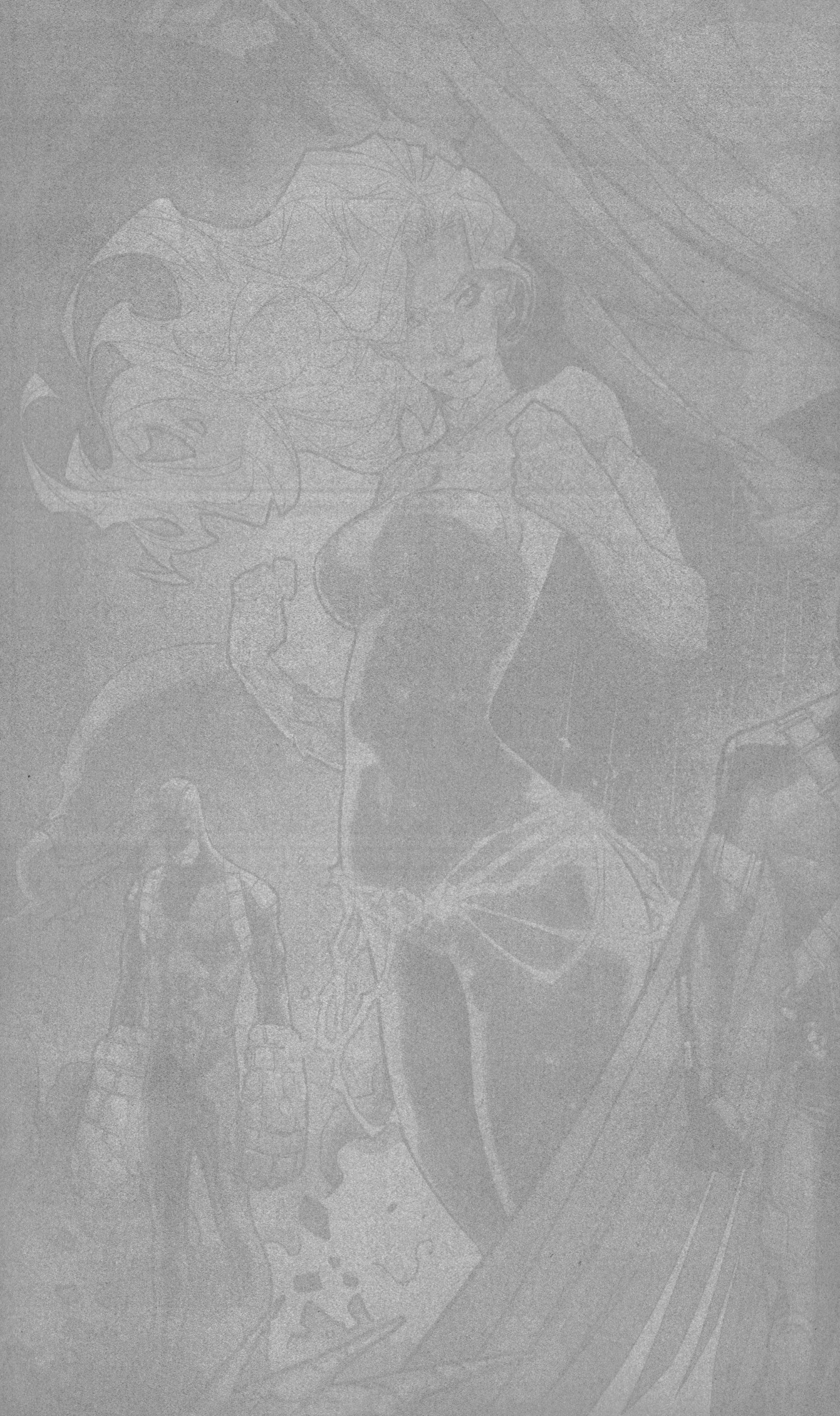

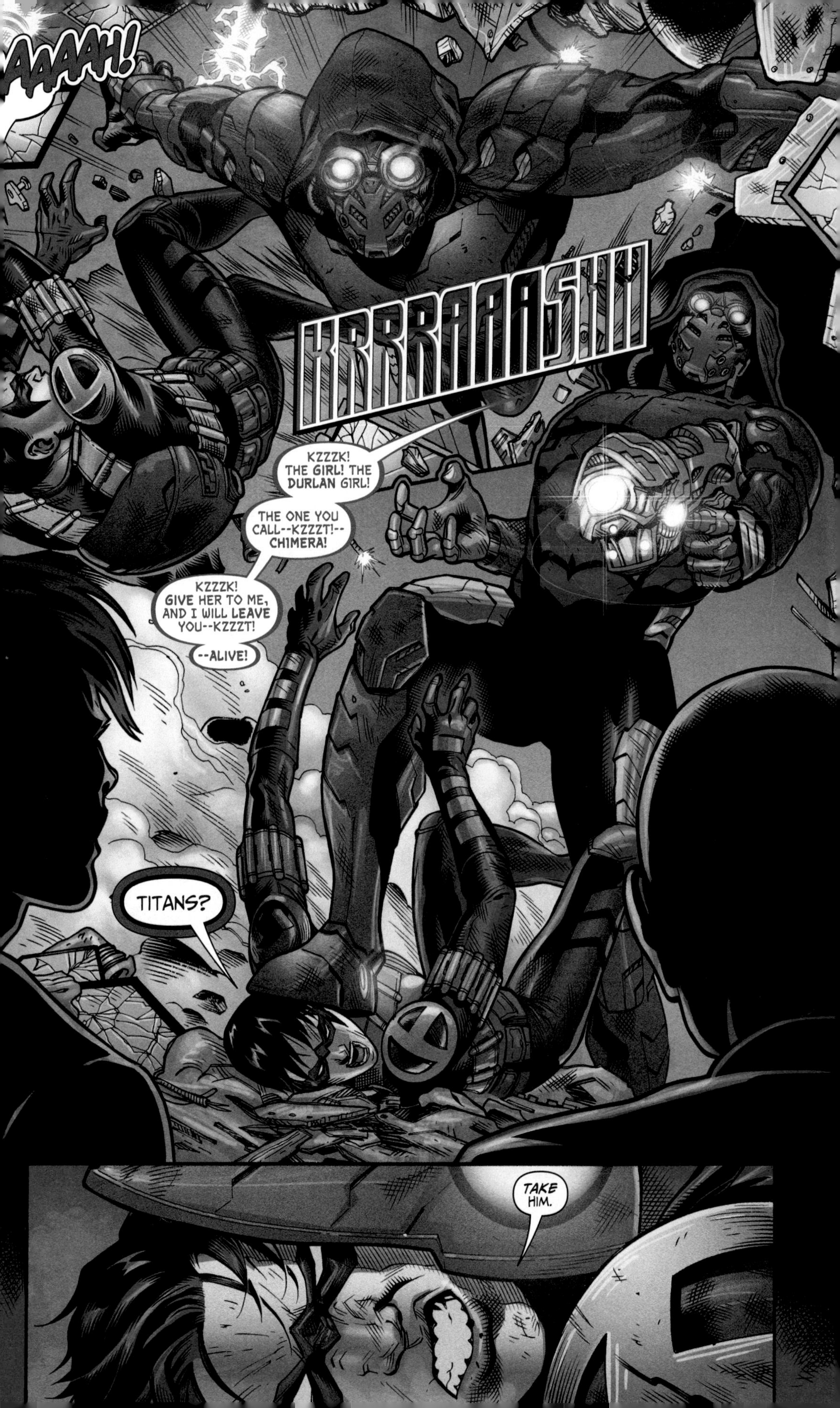
AAAAH!
KRRRAAASHH
KZZZK! THE GIRL! THE DURLAN GIRL!
THE ONE YOU CALL--KZZZT!--CHIMERA!
KZZZK! GIVE HER TO ME, AND I WILL LEAVE YOU--KZZZT!
--ALIVE!
TITANS?
TAKE HIM.

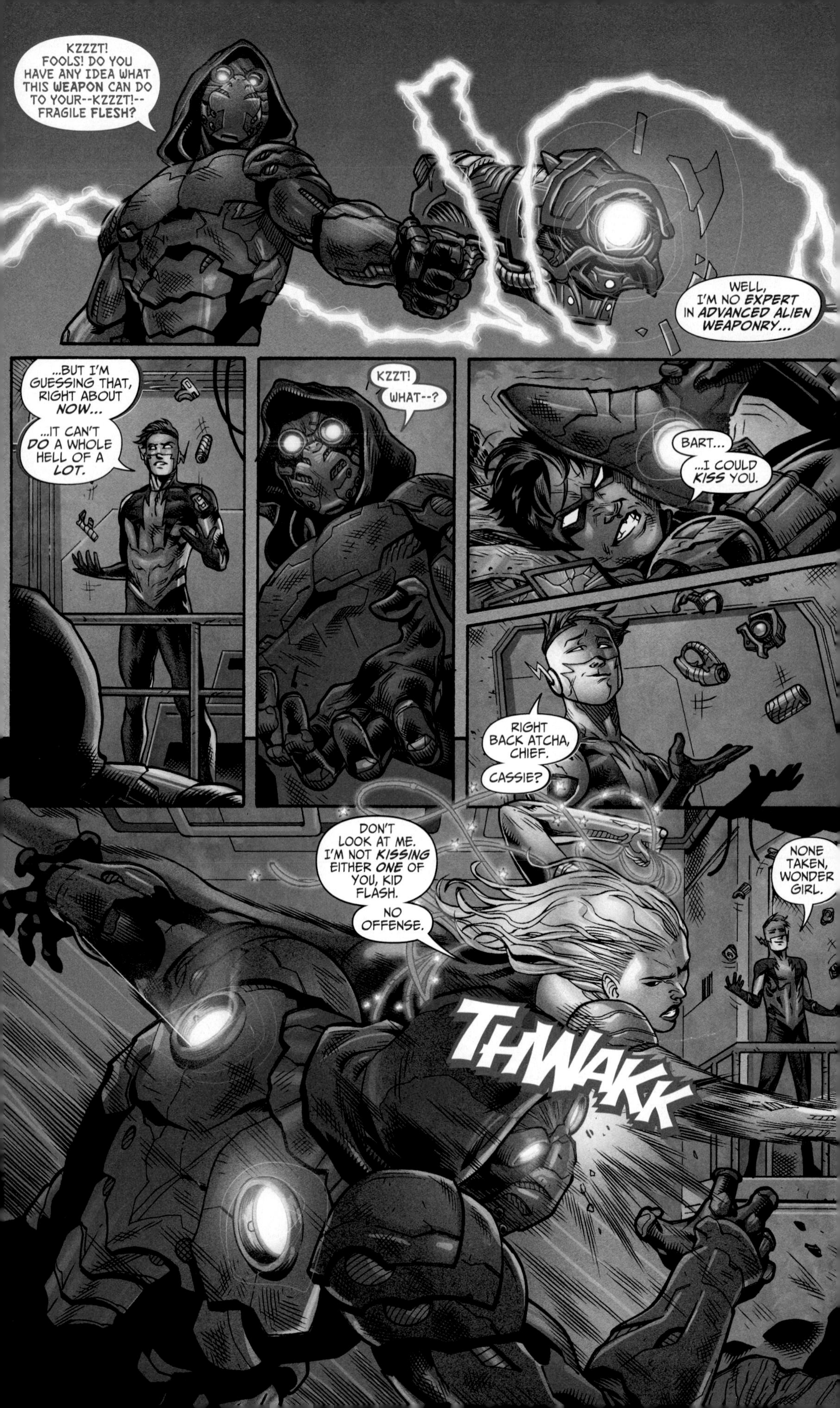
KZZZT! FOOLS! DO YOU HAVE ANY IDEA WHAT THIS WEAPON CAN DO TO YOUR--KZZZT!--FRAGILE FLESH?
WELL, I'M NO EXPERT IN ADVANCED ALIEN WEAPONRY...
...BUT I'M GUESSING THAT, RIGHT ABOUT NOW...
...IT CAN'T DO A WHOLE HELL OF A LOT.
KZZT!
WHAT--?
BART...
...I COULD KISS YOU.
RIGHT BACK ATCHA, CHIEF.
CASSIE?
DON'T LOOK AT ME. I'M NOT KISSING EITHER ONE OF YOU, KID FLASH.
NO OFFENSE.
NONE TAKEN, WONDER GIRL.
THWAKK

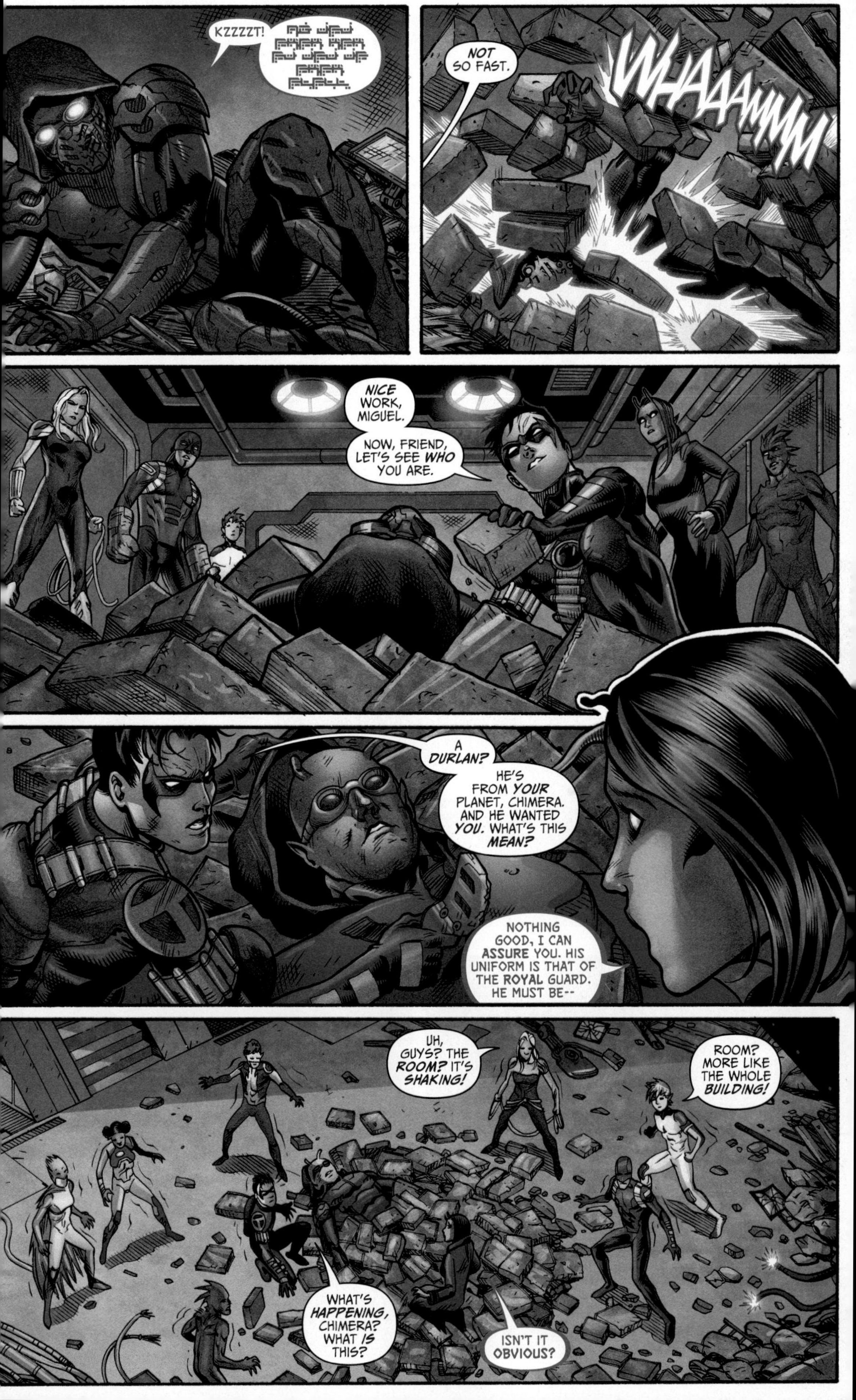
KZZZZT!
NOT SO FAST.
WHAAAMMM
NICE WORK, MIGUEL.
NOW, FRIEND, LET'S SEE WHO YOU ARE.
A DURLAN?
HE'S FROM YOUR PLANET, CHIMERA. AND HE WANTED YOU. WHAT'S THIS MEAN?
NOTHING GOOD, I CAN ASSURE YOU. HIS UNIFORM IS THAT OF THE ROYAL GUARD. HE MUST BE--
UH, GUYS? THE ROOM? IT'S SHAKING!
ROOM? MORE LIKE THE WHOLE BUILDING!
WHAT'S HAPPENING, CHIMERA? WHAT IS THIS?
ISN'T IT OBVIOUS?

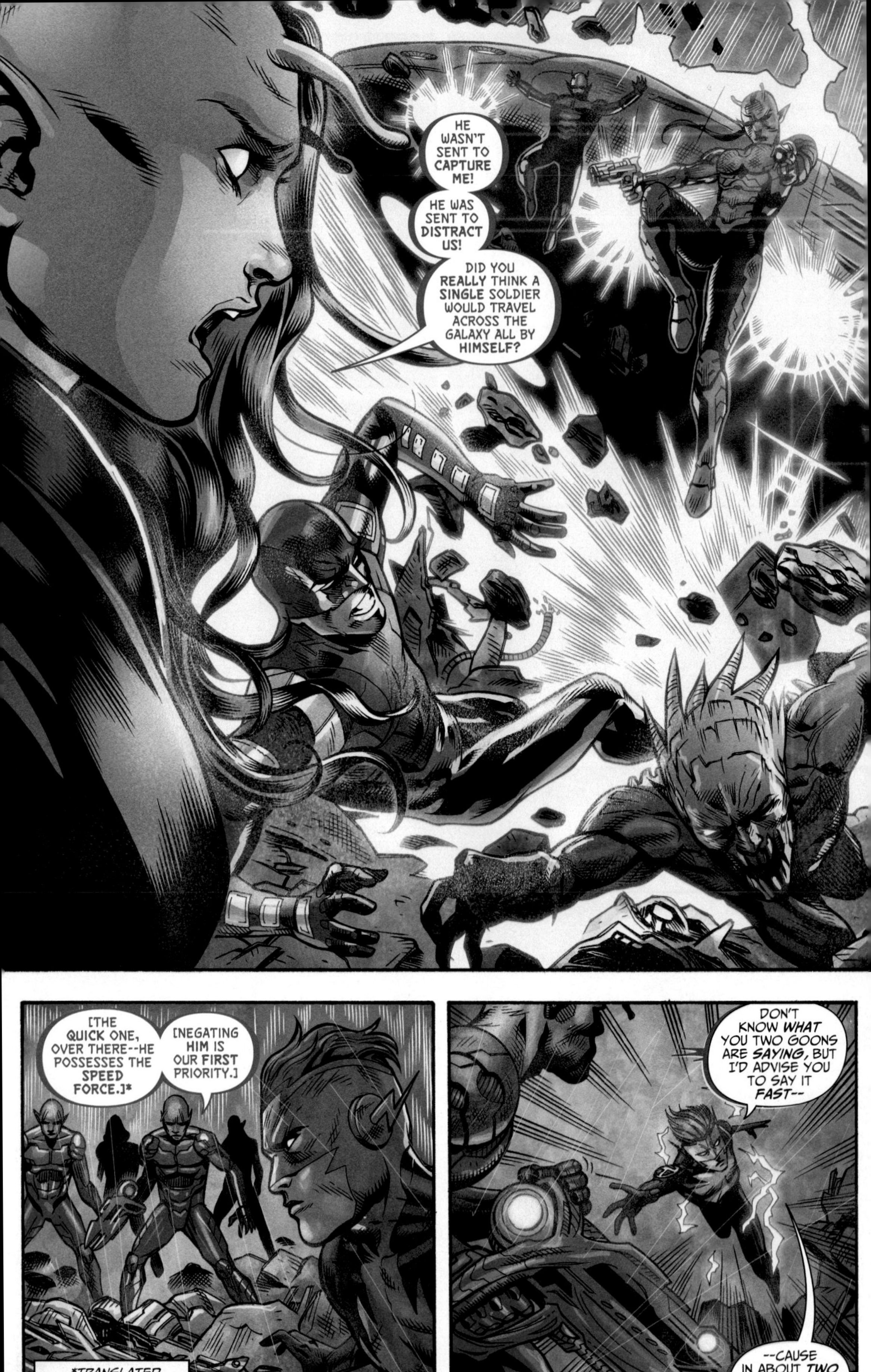
HE WASN'T SENT TO CAPTURE ME!
HE WAS SENT TO DISTRACT US!
DID YOU REALLY THINK A SINGLE SOLDIER WOULD TRAVEL ACROSS THE GALAXY ALL BY HIMSELF?
[THE QUICK ONE, OVER THERE--HE POSSESSES THE SPEED FORCE.]*
[NEGATING HIM IS OUR FIRST PRIORITY.]
*TRANSLATED FROM DURLAN - MIKE
DON'T KNOW WHAT YOU TWO GOONS ARE SAYING, BUT I'D ADVISE YOU TO SAY IT FAST--
--CAUSE IN ABOUT TWO SECONDS, I'M GOING TO--

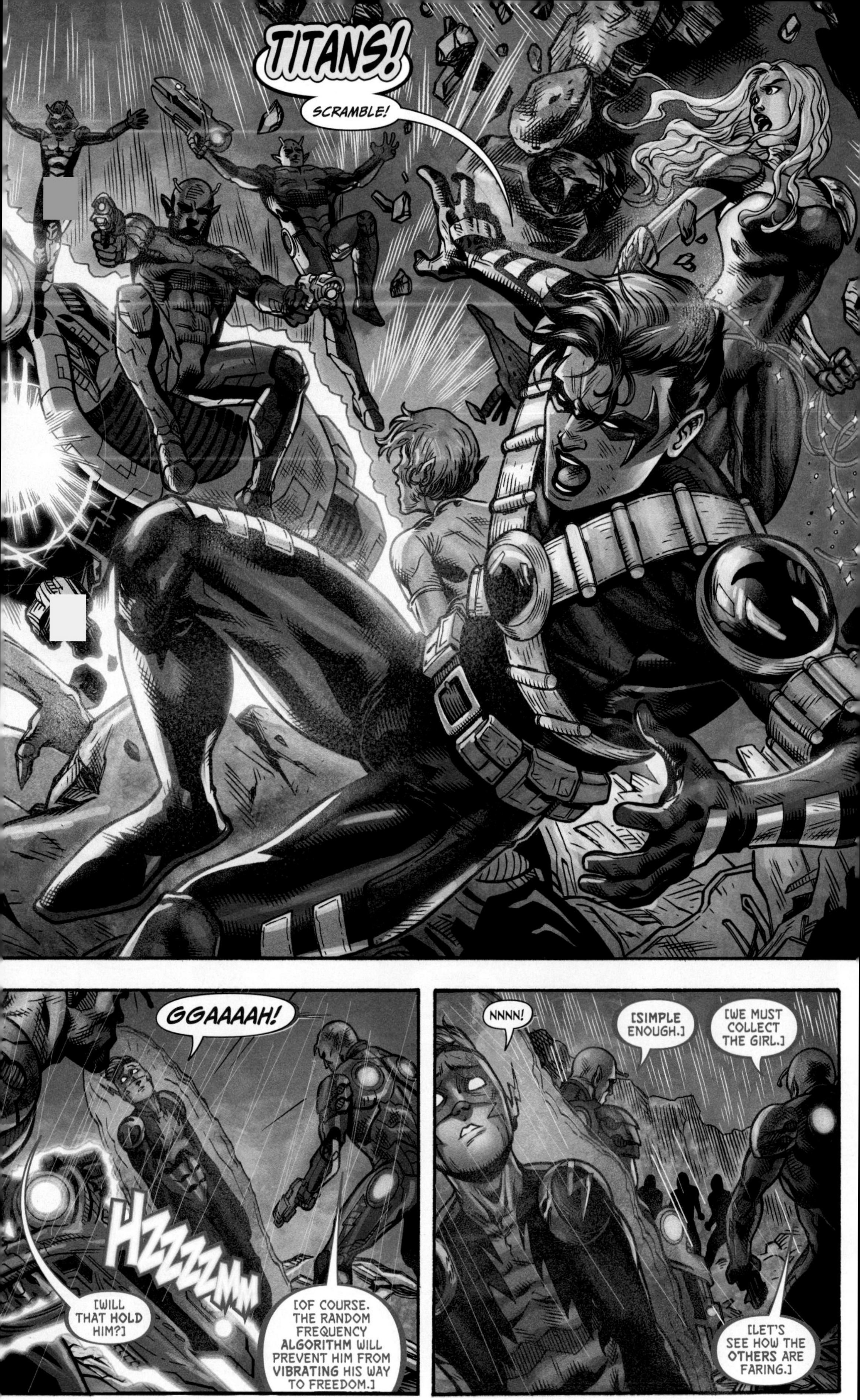
TITANS!
SCRAMBLE!
GGAAAAH!
[WILL THAT HOLD HIM?]
HZZZZMM
[OF COURSE. THE RANDOM FREQUENCY ALGORITHM WILL PREVENT HIM FROM VIBRATING HIS WAY TO FREEDOM.]
NNNN!
[SIMPLE ENOUGH.]
[WE MUST COLLECT THE GIRL.]
[LET'S SEE HOW THE OTHERS ARE FARING.]

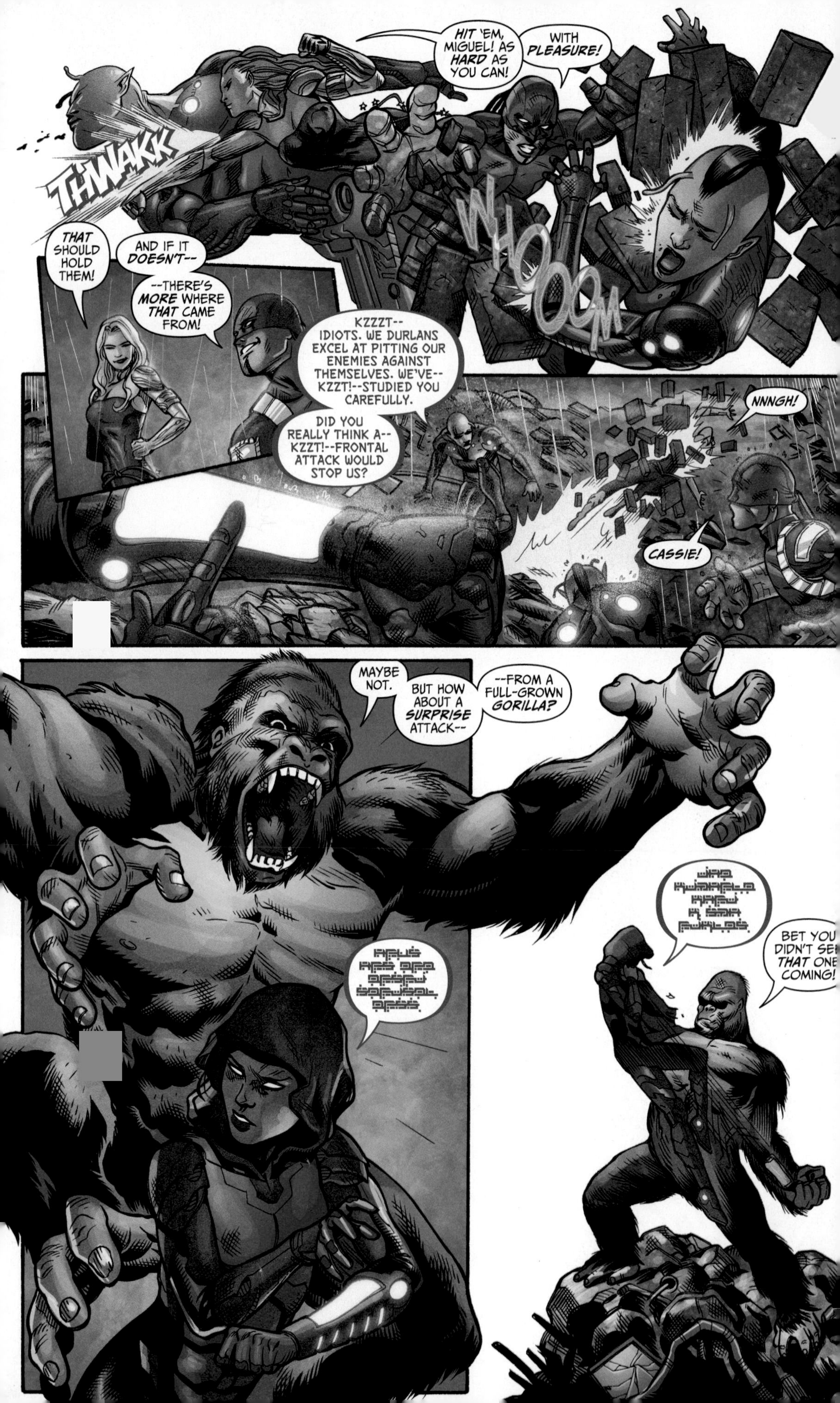
HIT 'EM, MIGUEL! AS HARD AS YOU CAN!
WITH PLEASURE!
THWAKK
WHOOOM
THAT SHOULD HOLD THEM!
AND IF IT DOESN'T--
--THERE'S MORE WHERE THAT CAME FROM!
KZZZT-- IDIOTS. WE DURLANS EXCEL AT PITTING OUR ENEMIES AGAINST THEMSELVES. WE'VE-- KZZT!--STUDIED YOU CAREFULLY.
DID YOU REALLY THINK A-- KZZT!--FRONTAL ATTACK WOULD STOP US?
NNNGH!
CASSIE!
MAYBE NOT.
BUT HOW ABOUT A SURPRISE ATTACK--
--FROM A FULL-GROWN GORILLA?
BET YOU DIDN'T SE THAT ONE COMING!

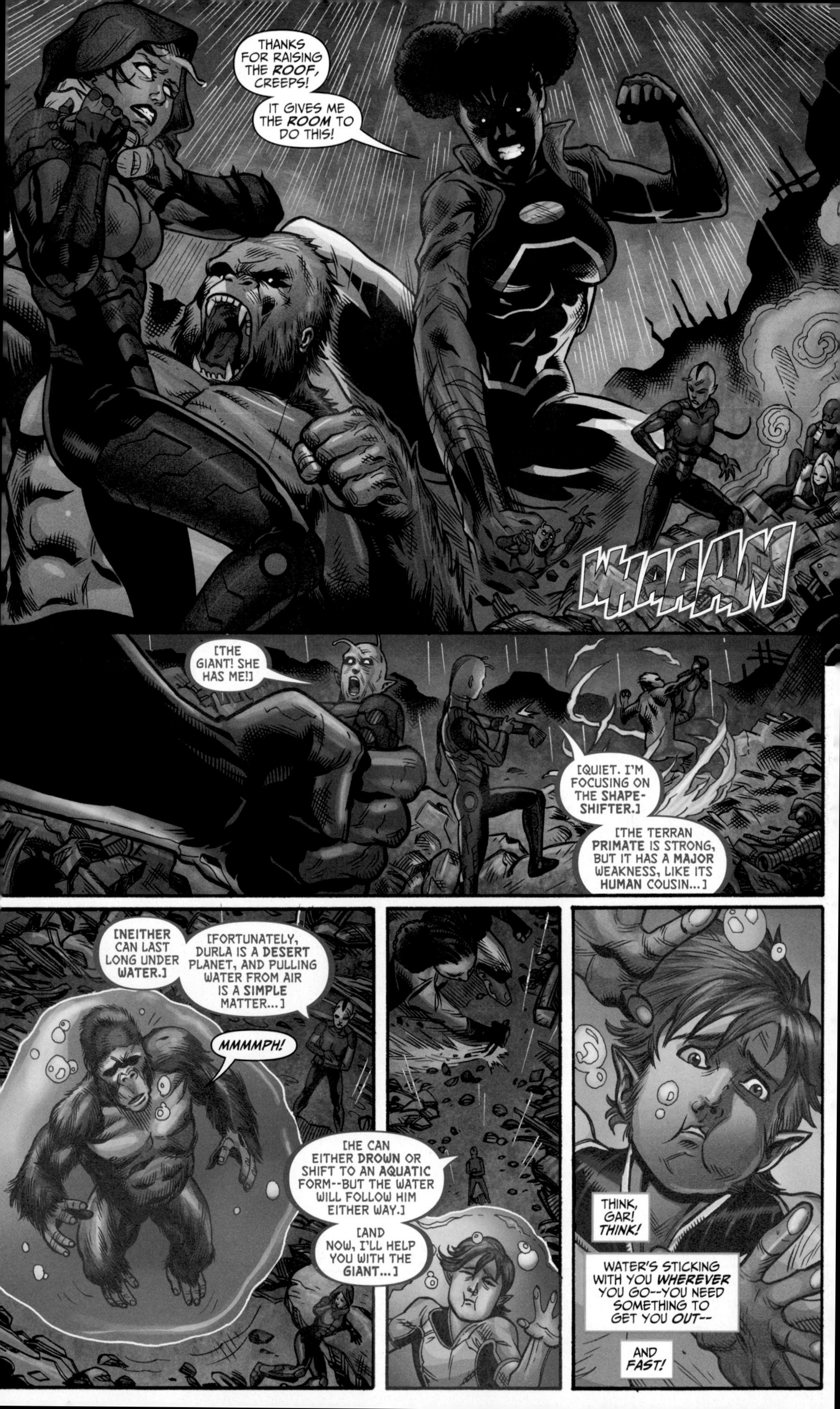
THANKS FOR RAISING THE ROOF, CREEPS!
IT GIVES ME THE ROOM TO DO THIS!
WHAAAM
[THE GIANT! SHE HAS ME!]
[QUIET. I'M FOCUSING ON THE SHAPE-SHIFTER.]
[THE TERRAN PRIMATE IS STRONG, BUT IT HAS A MAJOR WEAKNESS, LIKE ITS HUMAN COUSIN...]
[NEITHER CAN LAST LONG UNDER WATER.]
[FORTUNATELY, DURLA IS A DESERT PLANET, AND PULLING WATER FROM AIR IS A SIMPLE MATTER...]
MMMMPH!
[HE CAN EITHER DROWN OR SHIFT TO AN AQUATIC FORM--BUT THE WATER WILL FOLLOW HIM EITHER WAY.]
[AND NOW, I'LL HELP YOU WITH THE GIANT...]
THINK, GAR! THINK!
WATER'S STICKING WITH YOU WHEREVER YOU GO--YOU NEED SOMETHING TO GET YOU OUT--
AND FAST!

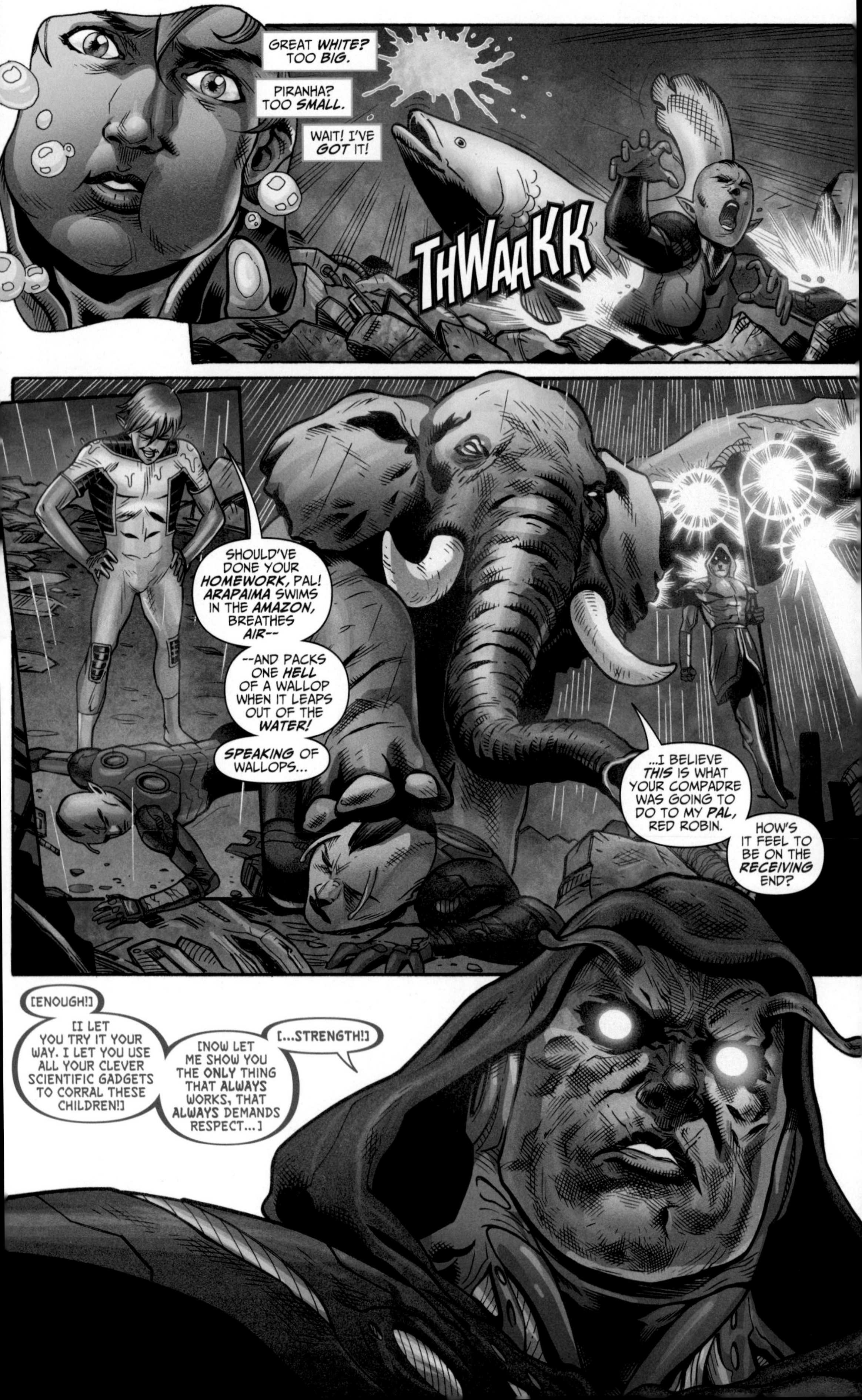
GREAT WHITE? TOO BIG.
PIRANHA? TOO SMALL.
WAIT! I'VE GOT IT!
THWAAKK
SHOULD'VE DONE YOUR HOMEWORK, PAL! ARAPAIMA SWIMS IN THE AMAZON, BREATHES AIR--
--AND PACKS ONE HELL OF A WALLOP WHEN IT LEAPS OUT OF THE WATER!
SPEAKING OF WALLOPS...
...I BELIEVE THIS IS WHAT YOUR COMPADRE WAS GOING TO DO TO MY PAL, RED ROBIN.
HOW'S IT FEEL TO BE ON THE RECEIVING END?
[ENOUGH!]
[I LET YOU TRY IT YOUR WAY. I LET YOU USE ALL YOUR CLEVER SCIENTIFIC GADGETS TO CORRAL THESE CHILDREN!]
[NOW LET ME SHOW YOU THE ONLY THING THAT ALWAYS WORKS, THAT ALWAYS DEMANDS RESPECT...]
[...STRENGTH!]

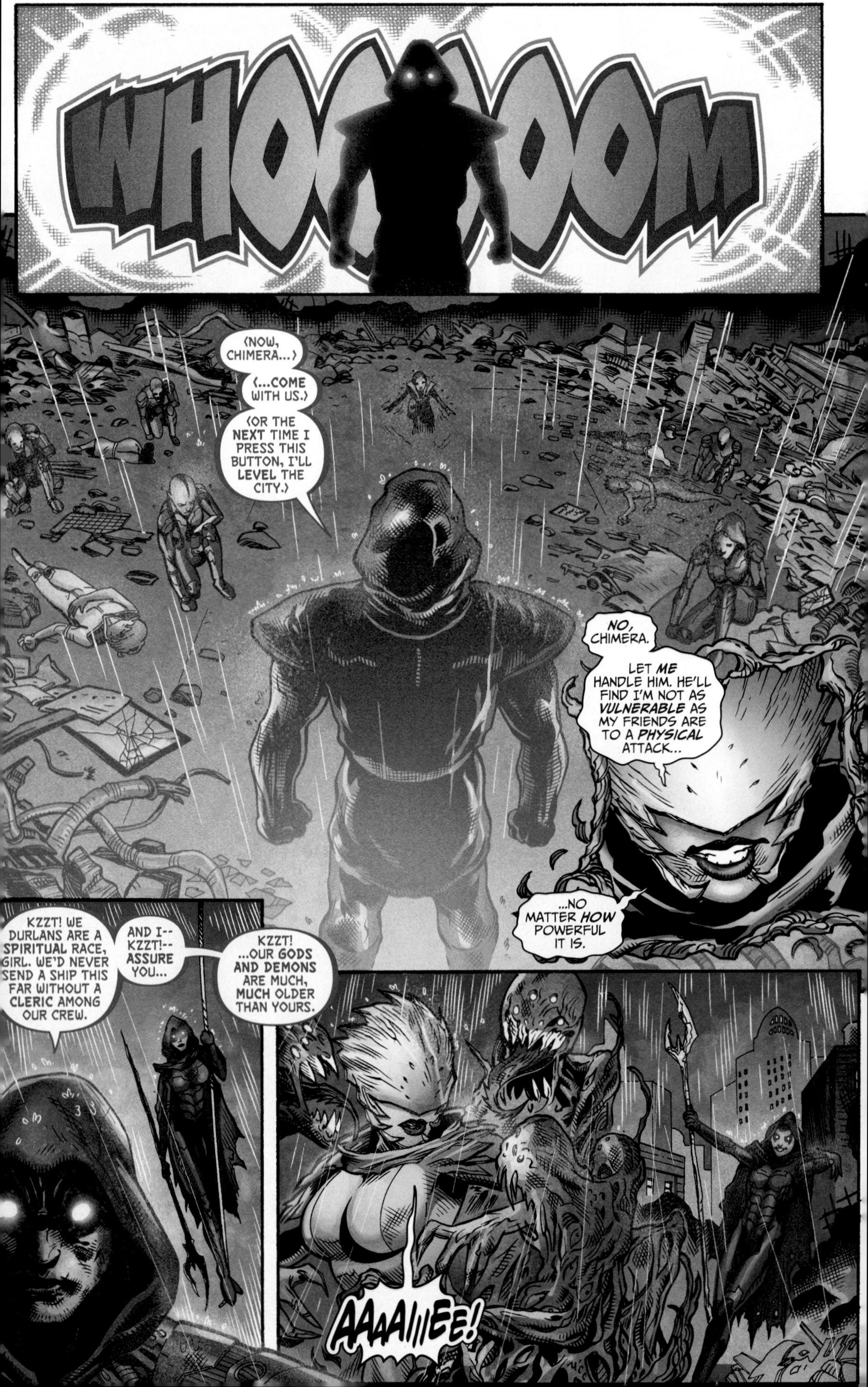
WHOOOOOM
‹NOW, CHIMERA...›
‹...COME WITH US.›
‹OR THE NEXT TIME I PRESS THIS BUTTON, I'LL LEVEL THE CITY.›
NO, CHIMERA.
LET ME HANDLE HIM. HE'LL FIND I'M NOT AS VULNERABLE AS MY FRIENDS ARE TO A PHYSICAL ATTACK...
...NO MATTER HOW POWERFUL IT IS.
KZZT! WE DURLANS ARE A SPIRITUAL RACE, GIRL. WE'D NEVER SEND A SHIP THIS FAR WITHOUT A CLERIC AMONG OUR CREW.
AND I--KZZT!--ASSURE YOU...
KZZT! ...OUR GODS AND DEMONS ARE MUCH, MUCH OLDER THAN YOURS.
AAAAIIIIEEE!

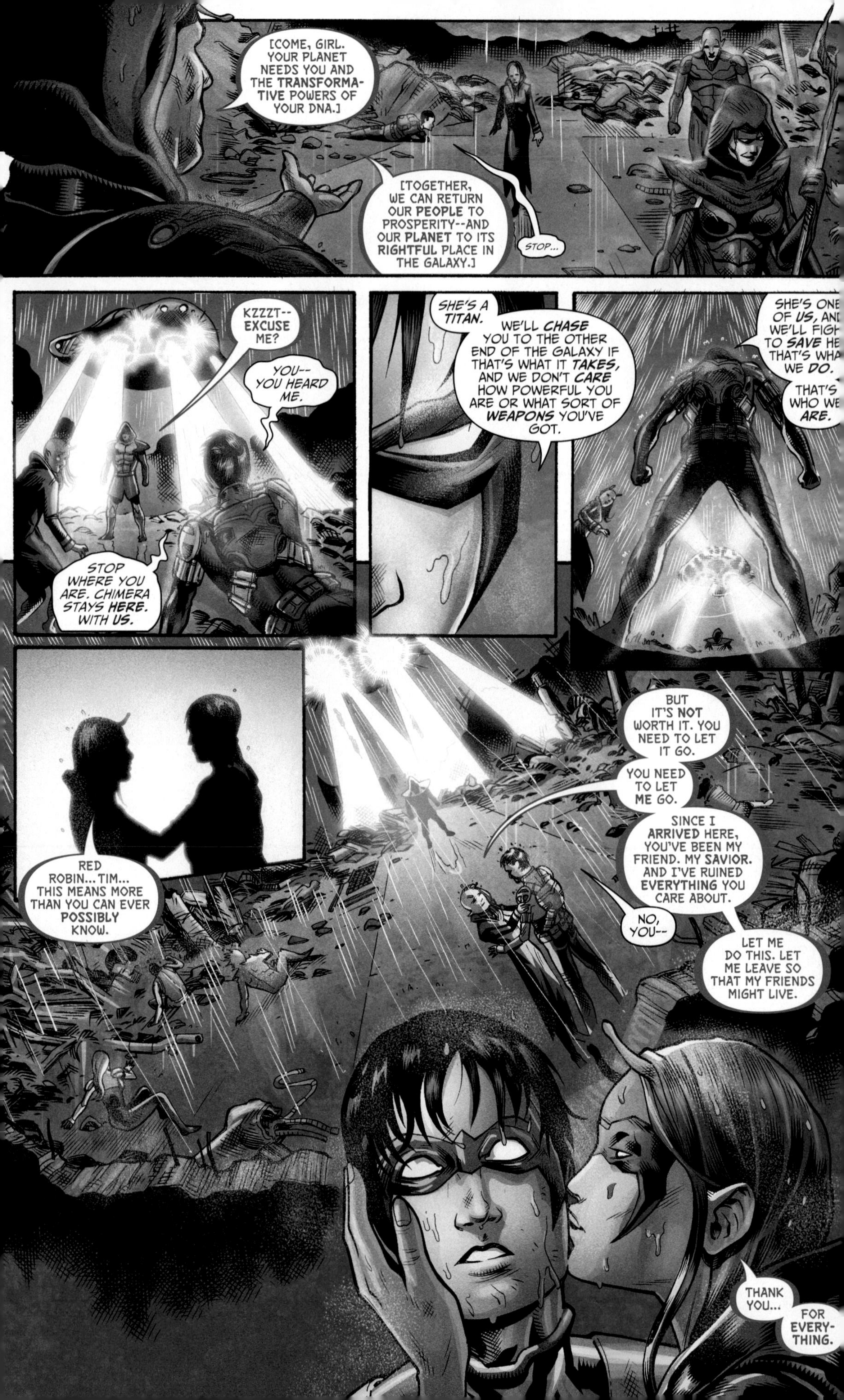
[COME, GIRL. YOUR PLANET NEEDS YOU AND THE TRANSFORMATIVE POWERS OF YOUR DNA.]
[TOGETHER, WE CAN RETURN OUR PEOPLE TO PROSPERITY--AND OUR PLANET TO ITS RIGHTFUL PLACE IN THE GALAXY.]
STOP...
KZZZT--EXCUSE ME?
YOU--YOU HEARD ME.
STOP WHERE YOU ARE. CHIMERA STAYS HERE. WITH US.
SHE'S A TITAN.
WE'LL CHASE YOU TO THE OTHER END OF THE GALAXY IF THAT'S WHAT IT TAKES, AND WE DON'T CARE HOW POWERFUL YOU ARE OR WHAT SORT OF WEAPONS YOU'VE GOT.
SHE'S ONE OF US, AND WE'LL FIGHT TO SAVE HER. THAT'S WHAT WE DO.
THAT'S WHO WE ARE.
BUT IT'S NOT WORTH IT. YOU NEED TO LET IT GO.
YOU NEED TO LET ME GO.
SINCE I ARRIVED HERE, YOU'VE BEEN MY FRIEND. MY SAVIOR. AND I'VE RUINED EVERYTHING YOU CARE ABOUT.
NO, YOU--
LET ME DO THIS. LET ME LEAVE SO THAT MY FRIENDS MIGHT LIVE.
RED ROBIN...TIM... THIS MEANS MORE THAN YOU CAN EVER POSSIBLY KNOW.
THANK YOU...
FOR EVERYTHING.

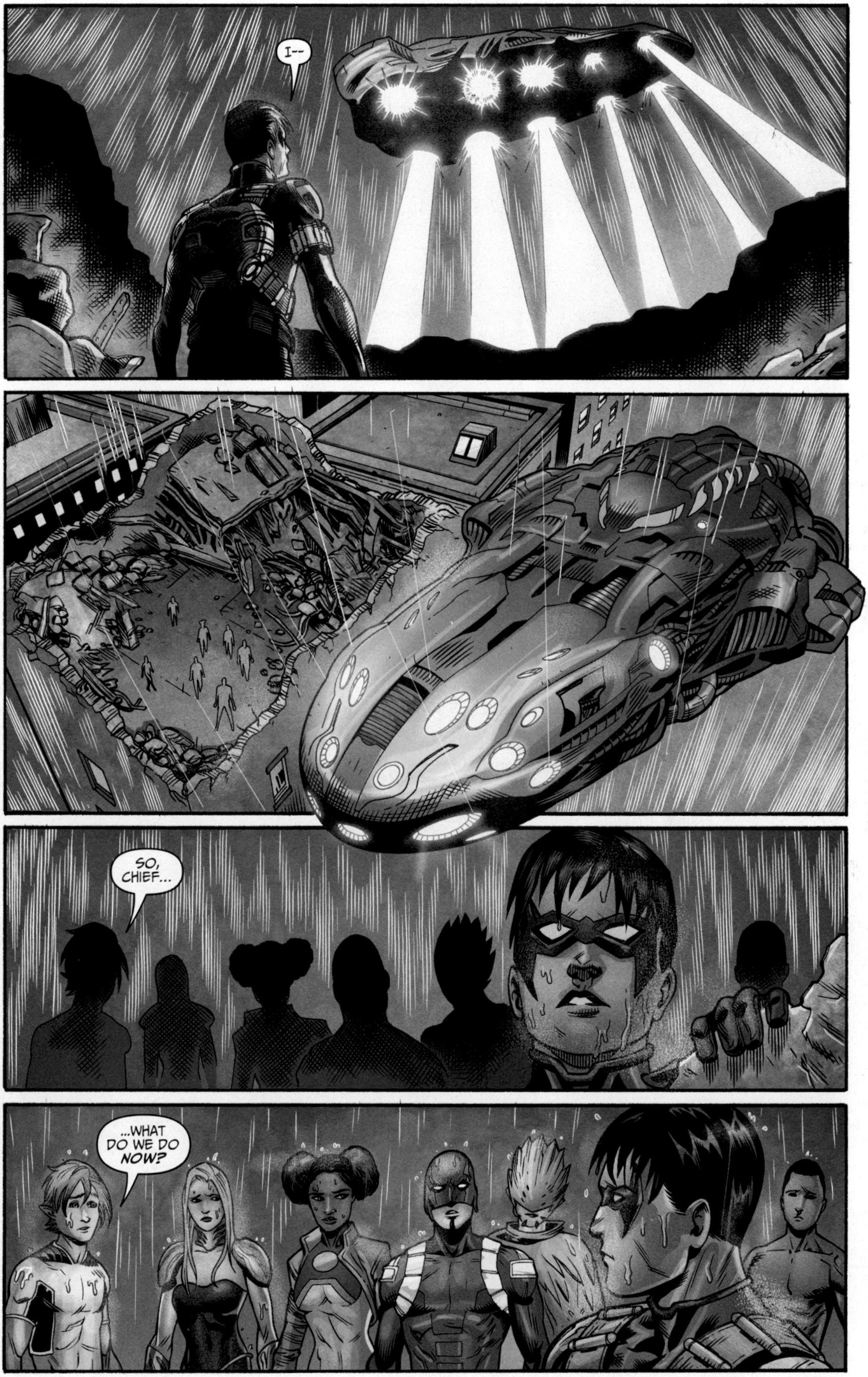

I--
SO, CHIEF...
...WHAT DO WE DO NOW?

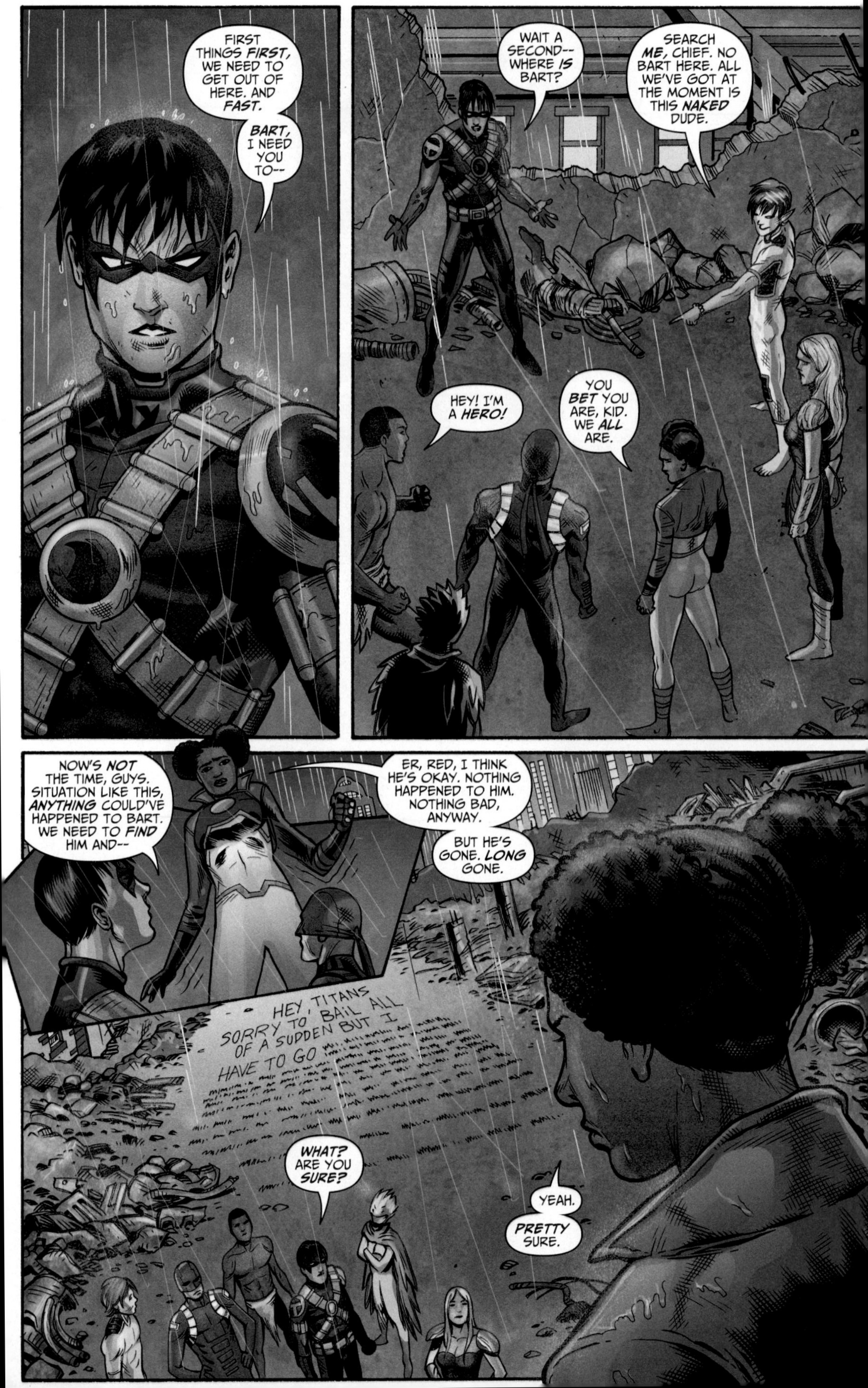

FIRST THINGS *FIRST,* WE NEED TO GET OUT OF HERE. AND *FAST.*
BART, I NEED YOU TO--
WAIT A SECOND-- WHERE *IS* BART?
SEARCH *ME,* CHIEF. NO BART HERE. ALL WE'VE GOT AT THE MOMENT IS THIS *NAKED* DUDE.
HEY! I'M A *HERO!*
YOU *BET* YOU ARE, KID. WE *ALL* ARE.
NOW'S *NOT* THE TIME, GUYS. SITUATION LIKE THIS, *ANYTHING* COULD'VE HAPPENED TO BART. WE NEED TO *FIND* HIM AND--
ER, RED, I THINK HE'S OKAY. NOTHING HAPPENED TO HIM. NOTHING BAD, ANYWAY.
BUT HE'S GONE. *LONG* GONE.
HEY, TITANS
SORRY TO BAIL ALL OF A SUDDEN BUT I HAVE TO GO
WHAT? ARE YOU *SURE?*
YEAH.
PRETTY SURE.

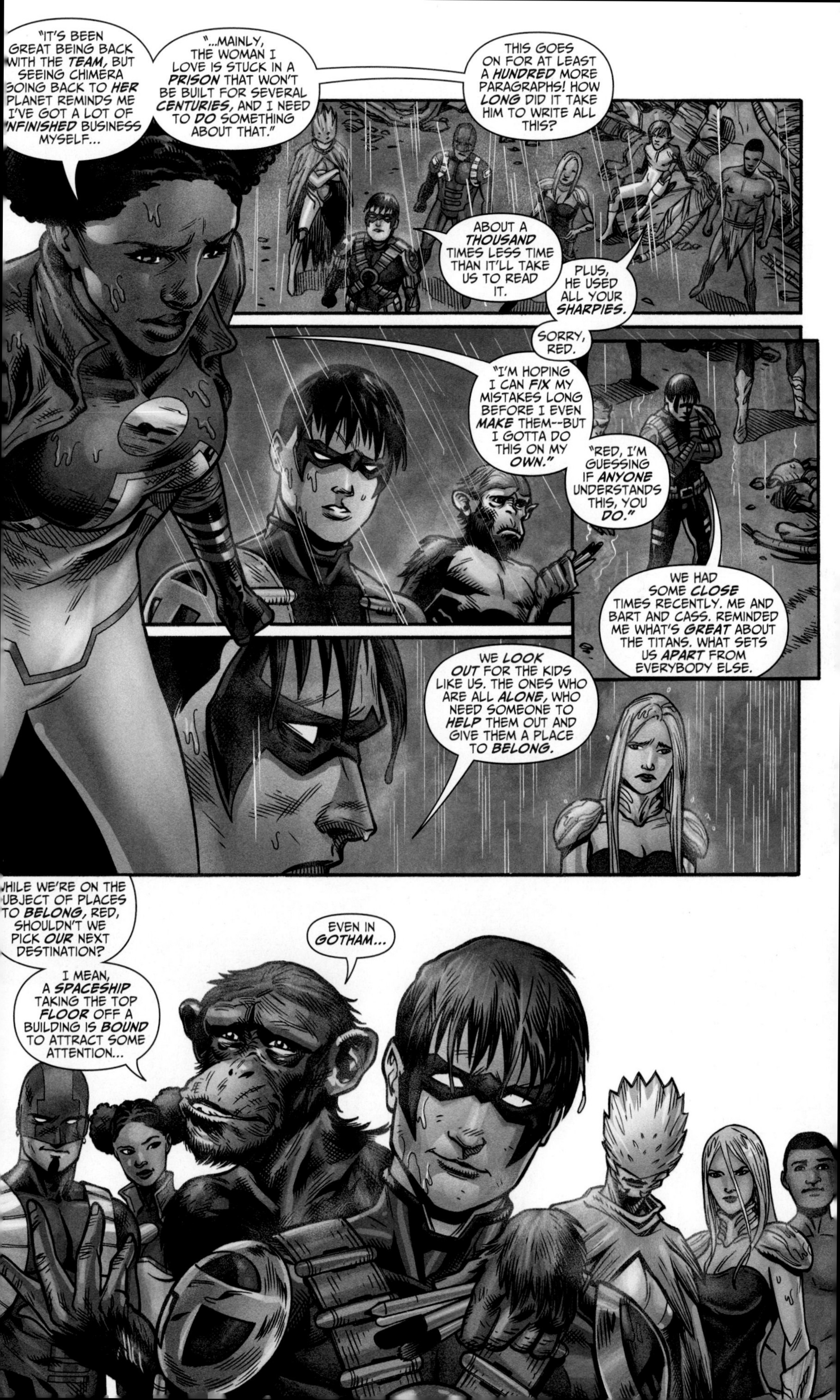
"IT'S BEEN GREAT BEING BACK WITH THE TEAM, BUT SEEING CHIMERA GOING BACK TO HER PLANET REMINDS ME I'VE GOT A LOT OF UNFINISHED BUSINESS MYSELF...
"...MAINLY, THE WOMAN I LOVE IS STUCK IN A PRISON THAT WON'T BE BUILT FOR SEVERAL CENTURIES, AND I NEED TO DO SOMETHING ABOUT THAT."
THIS GOES ON FOR AT LEAST A HUNDRED MORE PARAGRAPHS! HOW LONG DID IT TAKE HIM TO WRITE ALL THIS?
ABOUT A THOUSAND TIMES LESS TIME THAN IT'LL TAKE US TO READ IT.
PLUS, HE USED ALL YOUR SHARPIES.
SORRY, RED.
"I'M HOPING I CAN FIX MY MISTAKES LONG BEFORE I EVEN MAKE THEM--BUT I GOTTA DO THIS ON MY OWN."
"RED, I'M GUESSING IF ANYONE UNDERSTANDS THIS, YOU DO."
WE HAD SOME CLOSE TIMES RECENTLY. ME AND BART AND CASS. REMINDED ME WHAT'S GREAT ABOUT THE TITANS. WHAT SETS US APART FROM EVERYBODY ELSE.
WE LOOK OUT FOR THE KIDS LIKE US. THE ONES WHO ARE ALL ALONE, WHO NEED SOMEONE TO HELP THEM OUT AND GIVE THEM A PLACE TO BELONG.
WHILE WE'RE ON THE SUBJECT OF PLACES TO BELONG, RED, SHOULDN'T WE PICK OUR NEXT DESTINATION?
I MEAN, A SPACESHIP TAKING THE TOP FLOOR OFF A BUILDING IS BOUND TO ATTRACT SOME ATTENTION...
EVEN IN GOTHAM...

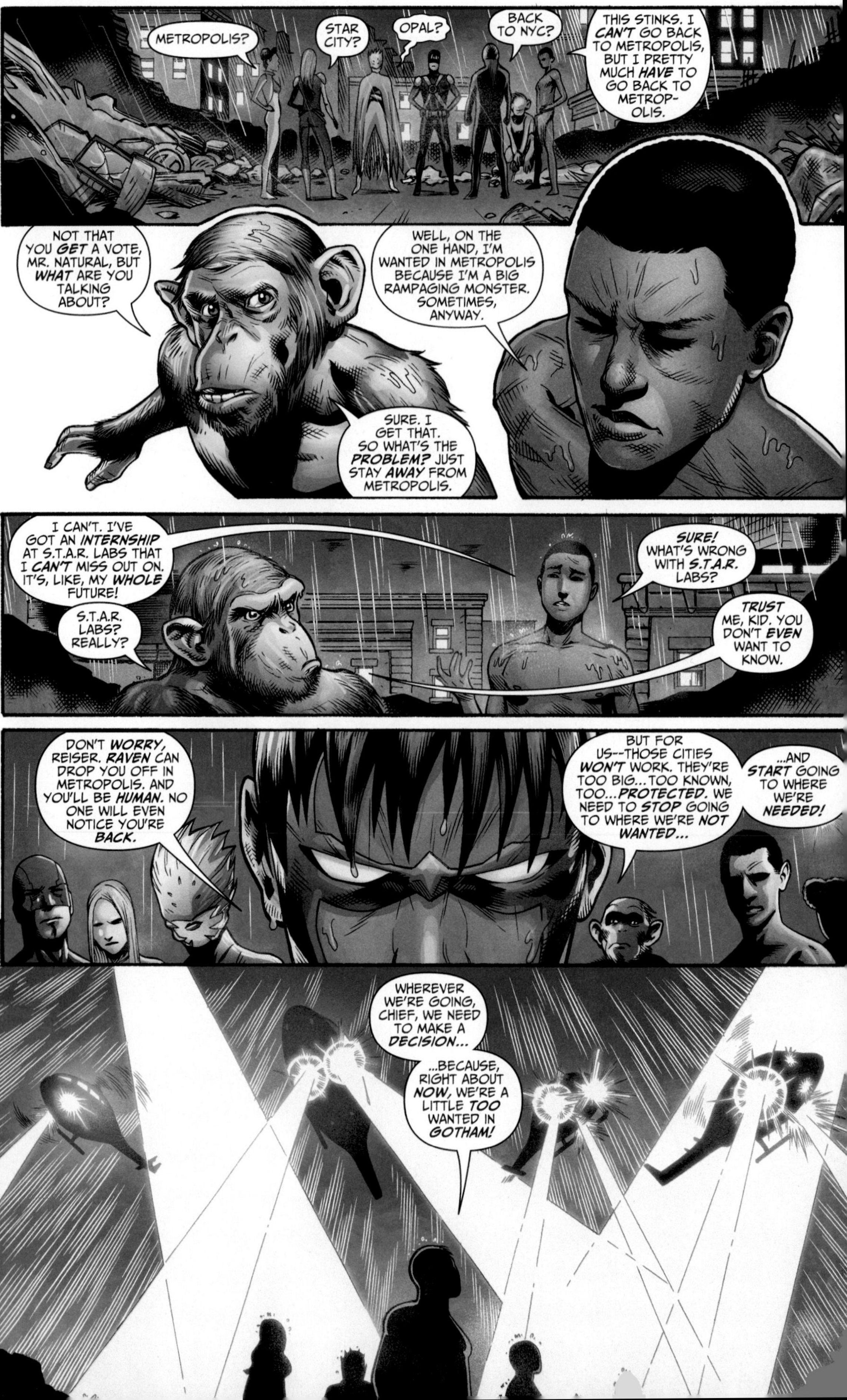
METROPOLIS?
STAR CITY?
OPAL?
BACK TO NYC?
THIS STINKS. I CAN'T GO BACK TO METROPOLIS, BUT I PRETTY MUCH HAVE TO GO BACK TO METROPOLIS.
NOT THAT YOU GET A VOTE, MR. NATURAL, BUT WHAT ARE YOU TALKING ABOUT?
WELL, ON THE ONE HAND, I'M WANTED IN METROPOLIS BECAUSE I'M A BIG RAMPAGING MONSTER. SOMETIMES, ANYWAY.
SURE. I GET THAT. SO WHAT'S THE PROBLEM? JUST STAY AWAY FROM METROPOLIS.
I CAN'T. I'VE GOT AN INTERNSHIP AT S.T.A.R. LABS THAT I CAN'T MISS OUT ON. IT'S, LIKE, MY WHOLE FUTURE!
S.T.A.R. LABS? REALLY?
SURE! WHAT'S WRONG WITH S.T.A.R. LABS?
TRUST ME, KID. YOU DON'T EVEN WANT TO KNOW.
DON'T WORRY, REISER. RAVEN CAN DROP YOU OFF IN METROPOLIS. AND YOU'LL BE HUMAN. NO ONE WILL EVEN NOTICE YOU'RE BACK.
BUT FOR US--THOSE CITIES WON'T WORK. THEY'RE TOO BIG...TOO KNOWN, TOO...PROTECTED. WE NEED TO STOP GOING TO WHERE WE'RE NOT WANTED...
...AND START GOING TO WHERE WE'RE NEEDED!
WHEREVER WE'RE GOING, CHIEF, WE NEED TO MAKE A DECISION...
...BECAUSE, RIGHT ABOUT NOW, WE'RE A LITTLE TOO WANTED IN GOTHAM!

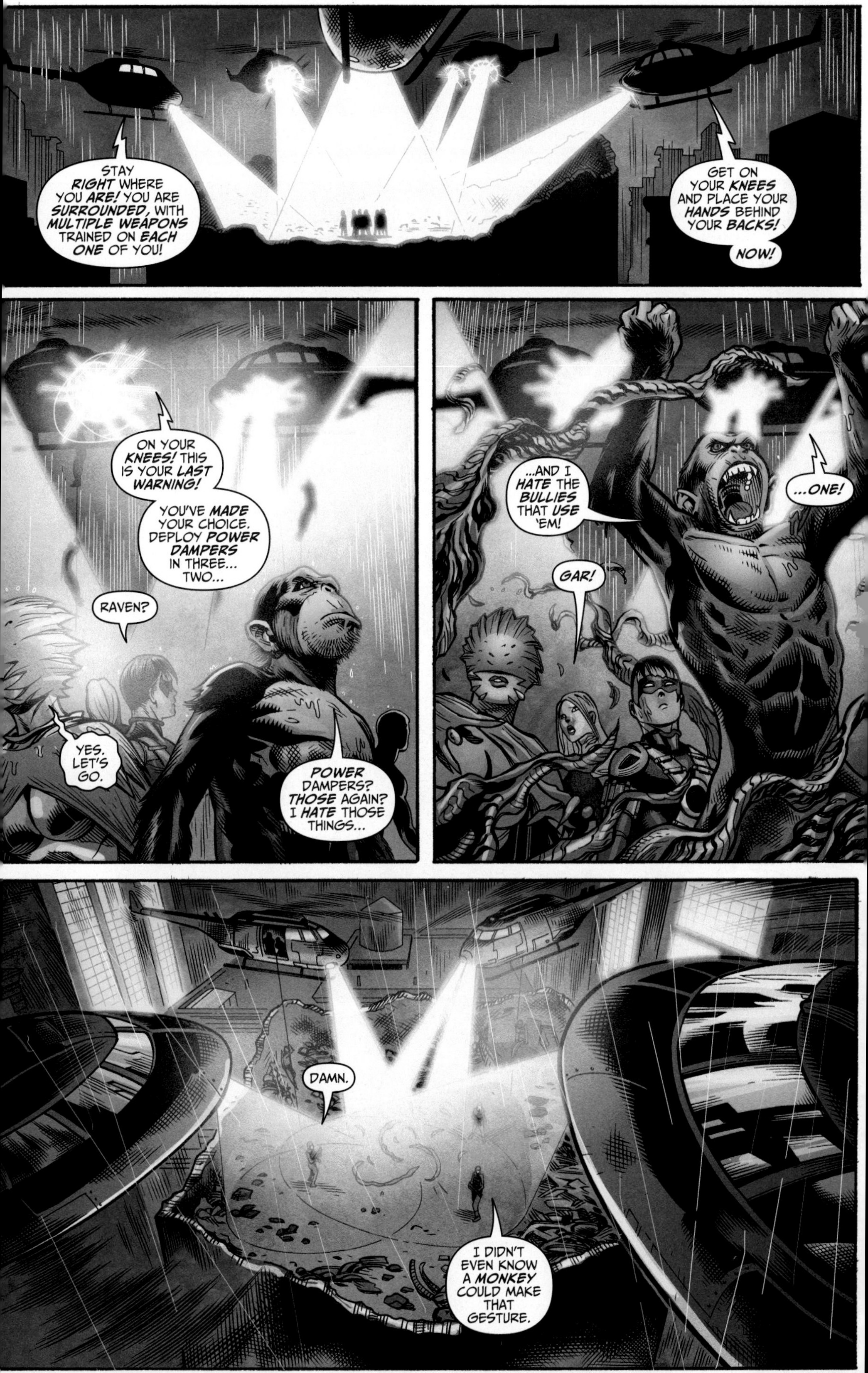
STAY RIGHT WHERE YOU ARE! YOU ARE SURROUNDED, WITH MULTIPLE WEAPONS TRAINED ON EACH ONE OF YOU!
GET ON YOUR KNEES AND PLACE YOUR HANDS BEHIND YOUR BACKS!
NOW!
ON YOUR KNEES! THIS IS YOUR LAST WARNING!
YOU'VE MADE YOUR CHOICE. DEPLOY POWER DAMPERS IN THREE... TWO...
RAVEN?
YES. LET'S GO.
POWER DAMPERS? THOSE AGAIN? I HATE THOSE THINGS...
...AND I HATE THE BULLIES THAT USE 'EM!
...ONE!
GAR!
DAMN.
I DIDN'T EVEN KNOW A MONKEY COULD MAKE THAT GESTURE.

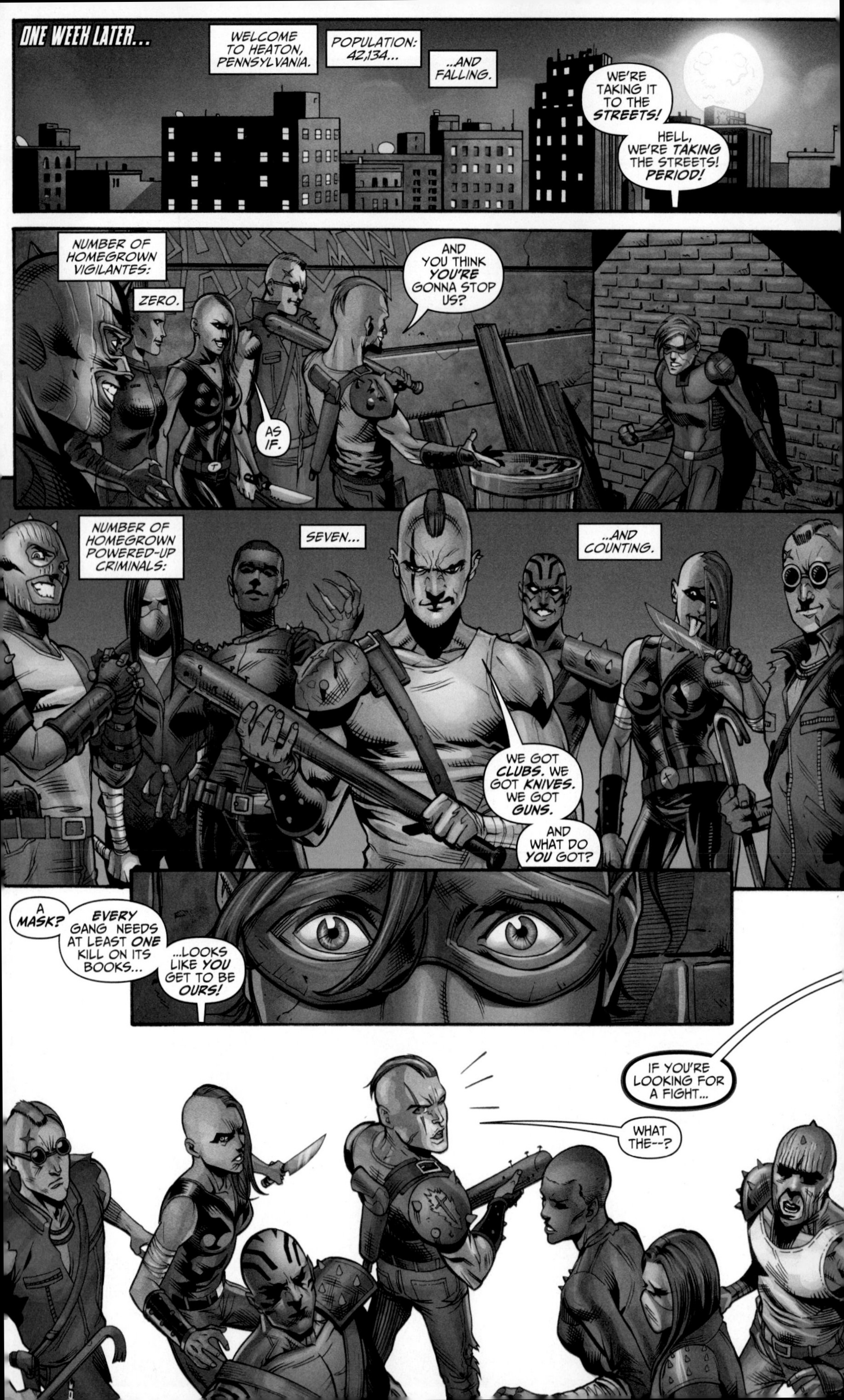
ONE WEEK LATER...
WELCOME TO HEATON, PENNSYLVANIA.
POPULATION: 42,134...
...AND FALLING.
WE'RE TAKING IT TO THE STREETS!
HELL, WE'RE TAKING THE STREETS! PERIOD!
NUMBER OF HOMEGROWN VIGILANTES:
ZERO.
AND YOU THINK YOU'RE GONNA STOP US?
AS IF.
NUMBER OF HOMEGROWN POWERED-UP CRIMINALS:
SEVEN...
...AND COUNTING.
WE GOT CLUBS. WE GOT KNIVES. WE GOT GUNS.
AND WHAT DO YOU GOT?
A MASK?
EVERY GANG NEEDS AT LEAST ONE KILL ON ITS BOOKS...
...LOOKS LIKE YOU GET TO BE OURS!
IF YOU'RE LOOKING FOR A FIGHT...
WHAT THE--?

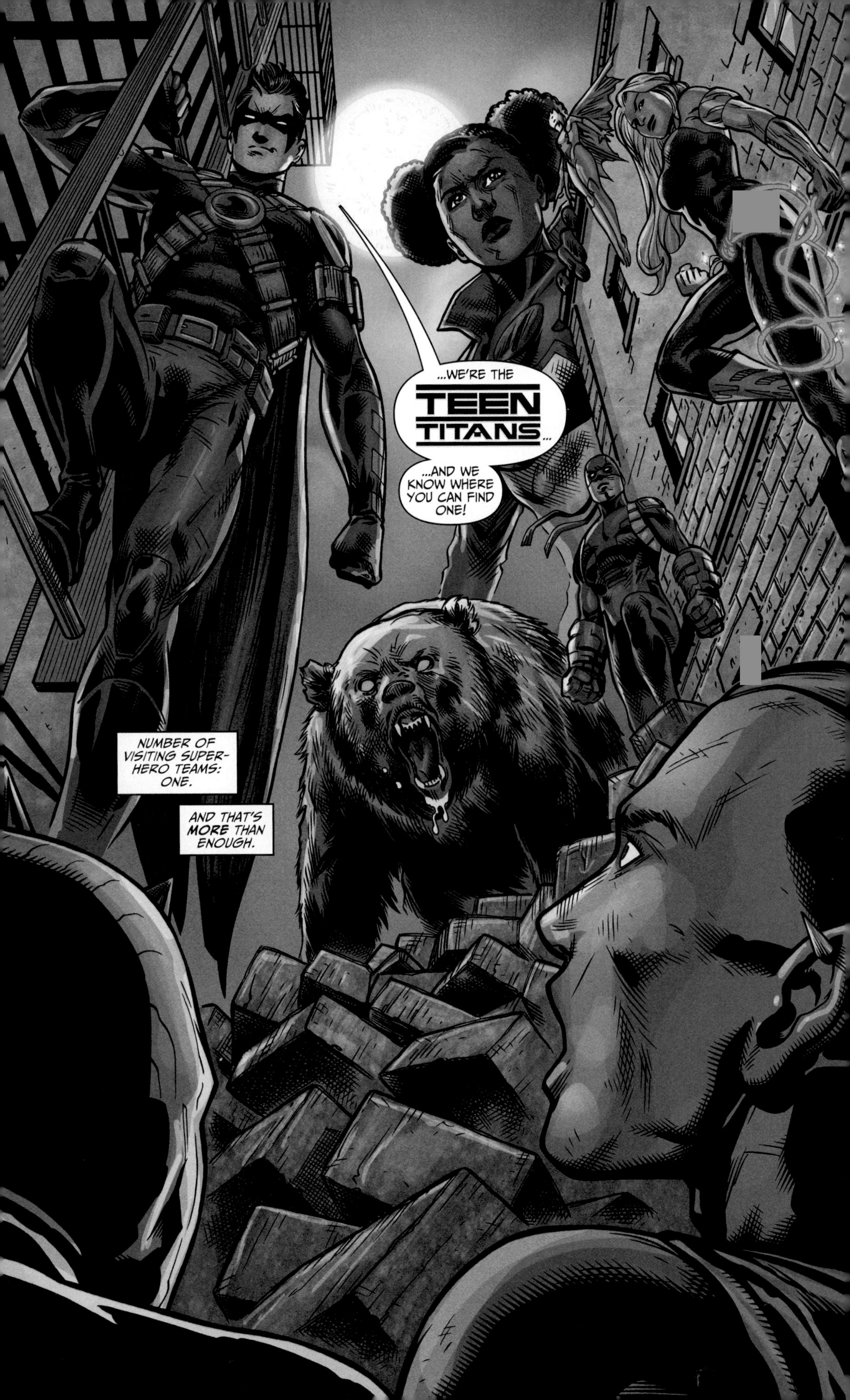
...WE'RE THE
TEEN TITANS...
...AND WE KNOW WHERE YOU CAN FIND ONE!
NUMBER OF VISITING SUPER-HERO TEAMS: ONE.
AND THAT'S MORE THAN ENOUGH.

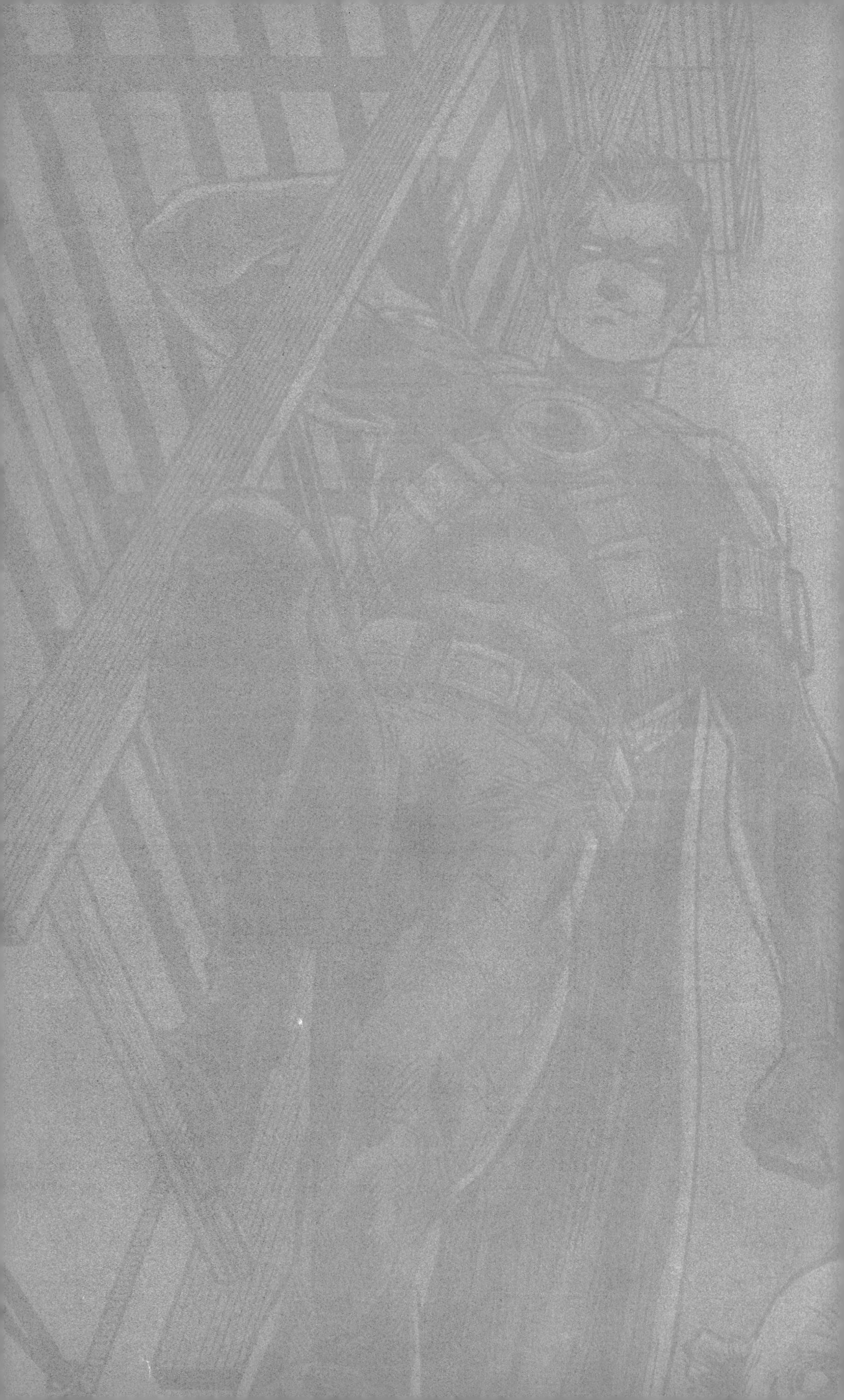

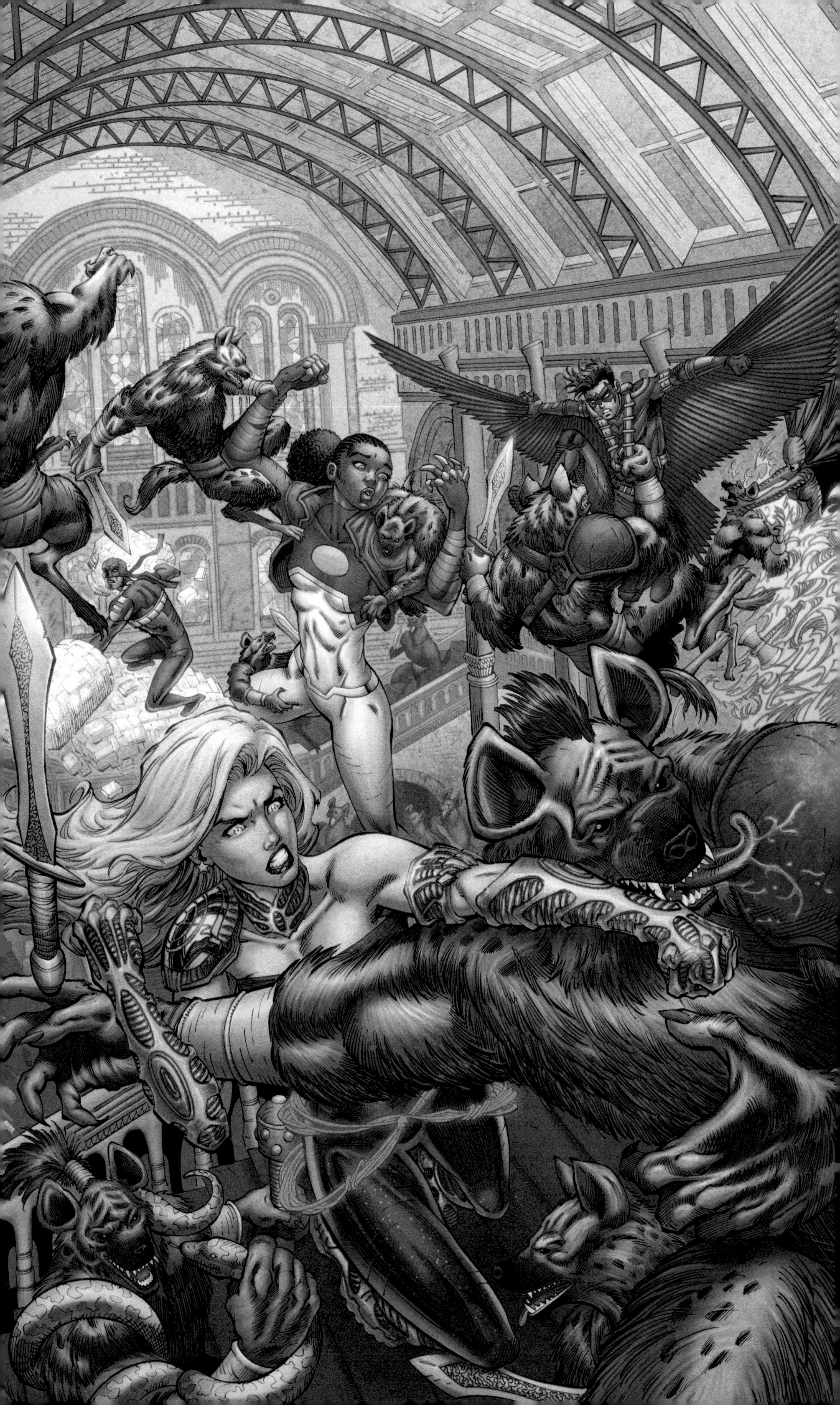

WHO IS WONDER GIRL?

GREG PAK writer IAN CHURCHILL penciller NORM RAPMUND inker TONY AVIÑA colorist COREY BREEN letterer
cover art by IAN CHURCHILL, NORM RAPMUND & ANDREW DALHOUSE

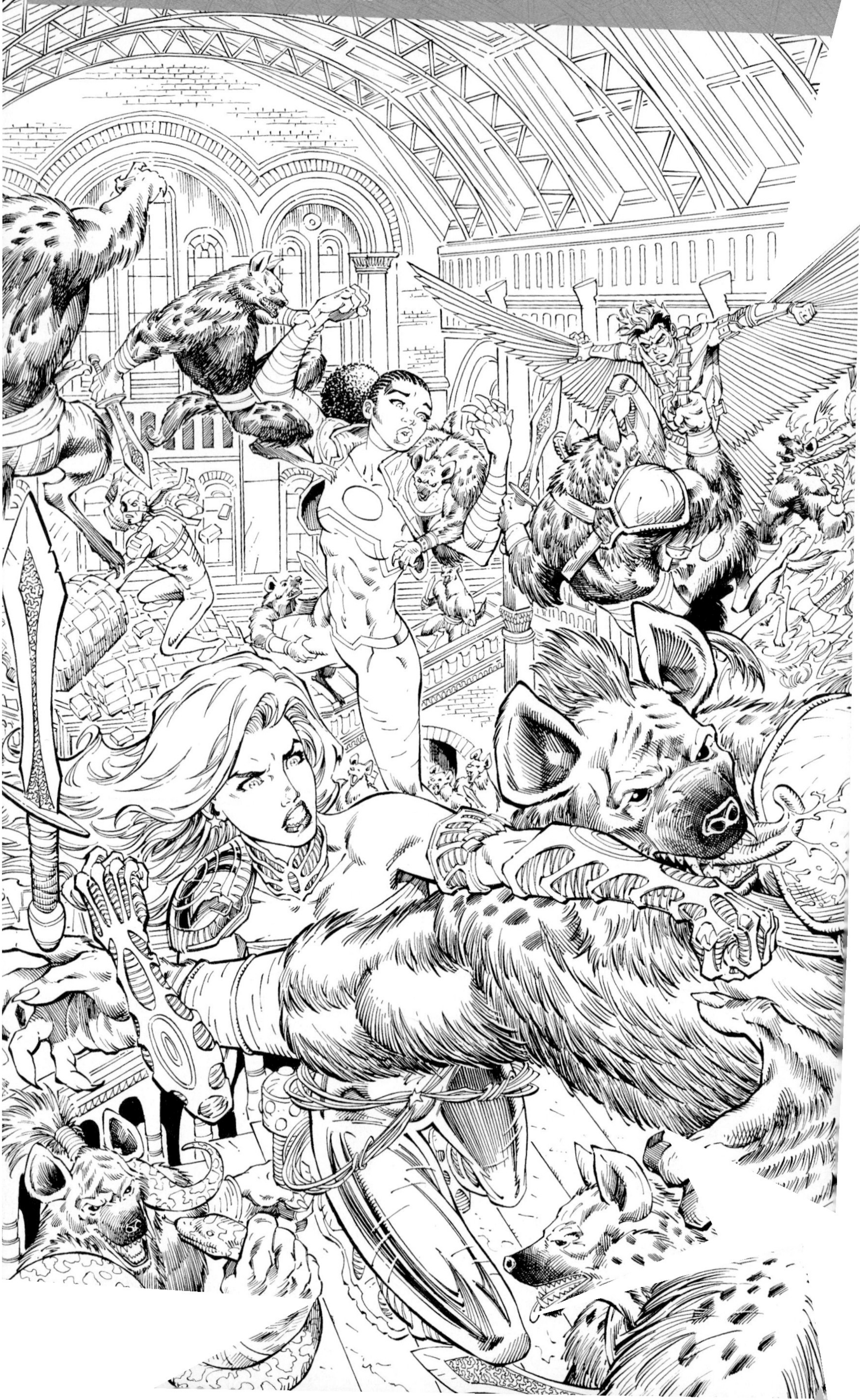

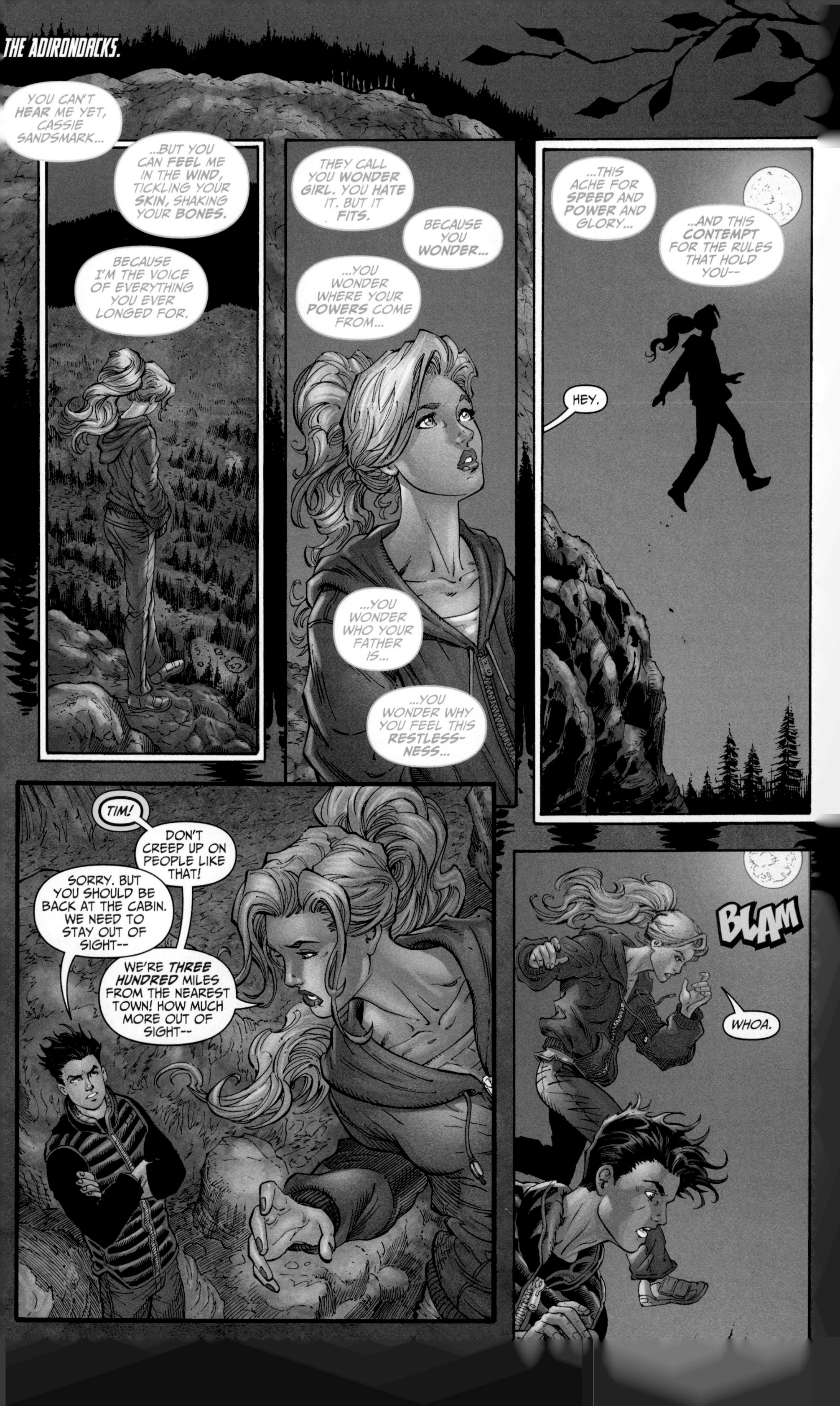
THE ADIRONDACKS.
YOU CAN'T HEAR ME YET, CASSIE SANDSMARK...
...BUT YOU CAN FEEL ME IN THE WIND, TICKLING YOUR SKIN, SHAKING YOUR BONES.
BECAUSE I'M THE VOICE OF EVERYTHING YOU EVER LONGED FOR.
THEY CALL YOU WONDER GIRL. YOU HATE IT. BUT IT FITS.
BECAUSE YOU WONDER...
...YOU WONDER WHERE YOUR POWERS COME FROM...
...YOU WONDER WHO YOUR FATHER IS...
...YOU WONDER WHY YOU FEEL THIS RESTLESS-NESS...
...THIS ACHE FOR SPEED AND POWER AND GLORY...
..AND THIS CONTEMPT FOR THE RULES THAT HOLD YOU--
HEY.
TIM!
DON'T CREEP UP ON PEOPLE LIKE THAT!
SORRY. BUT YOU SHOULD BE BACK AT THE CABIN. WE NEED TO STAY OUT OF SIGHT--
WE'RE THREE HUNDRED MILES FROM THE NEAREST TOWN! HOW MUCH MORE OUT OF SIGHT--
BLAM
WHOA.

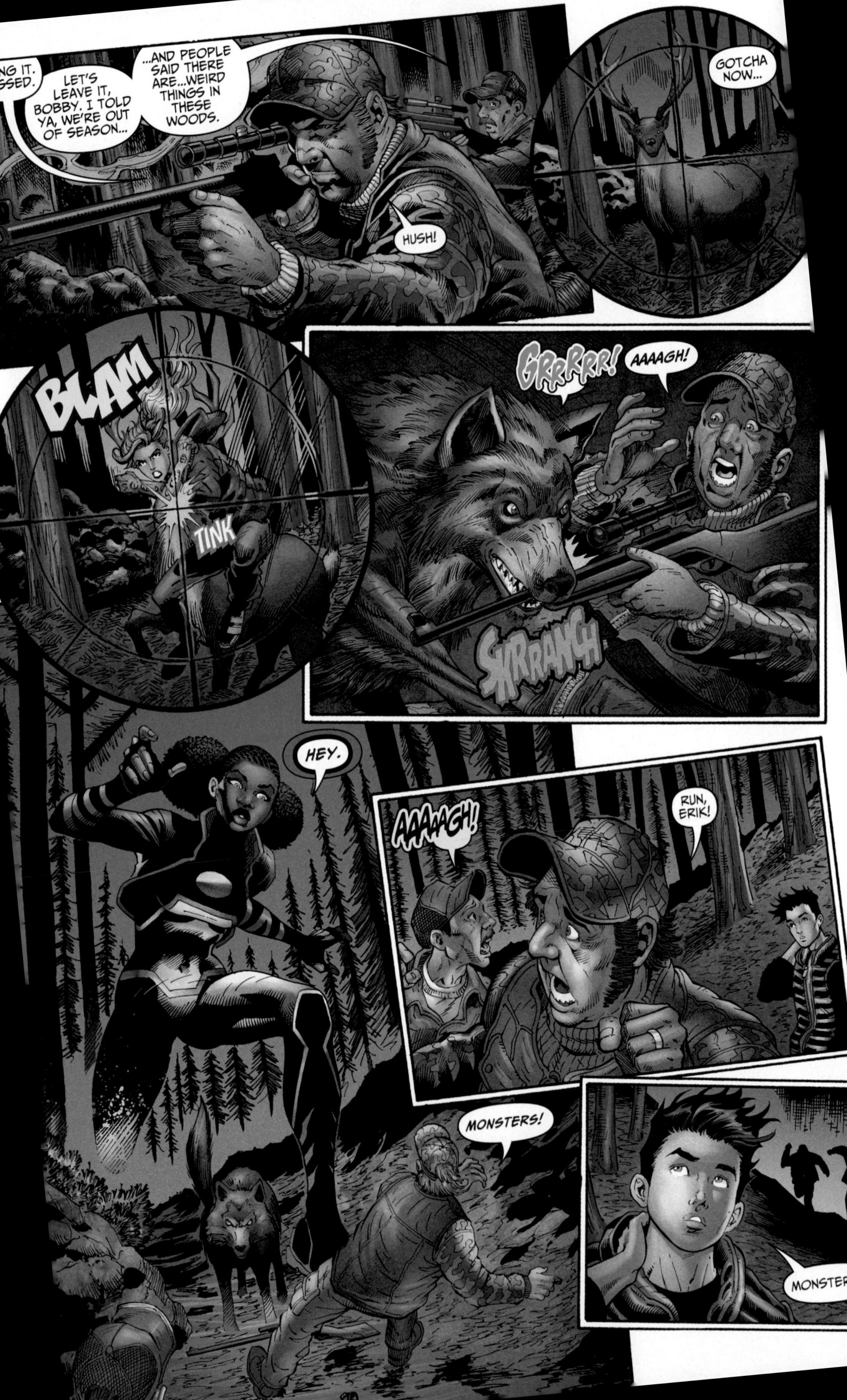
NG IT.
SSED.
LET'S LEAVE IT, BOBBY. I TOLD YA, WE'RE OUT OF SEASON...
...AND PEOPLE SAID THERE ARE...WEIRD THINGS IN THESE WOODS.
HUSH!
GOTCHA NOW...
BLAM
TINK
GRRRRR!
AAAAGH!
SKRRANCH
HEY.
AAAAAGH!
RUN, ERIK!
MONSTERS!
MONSTER

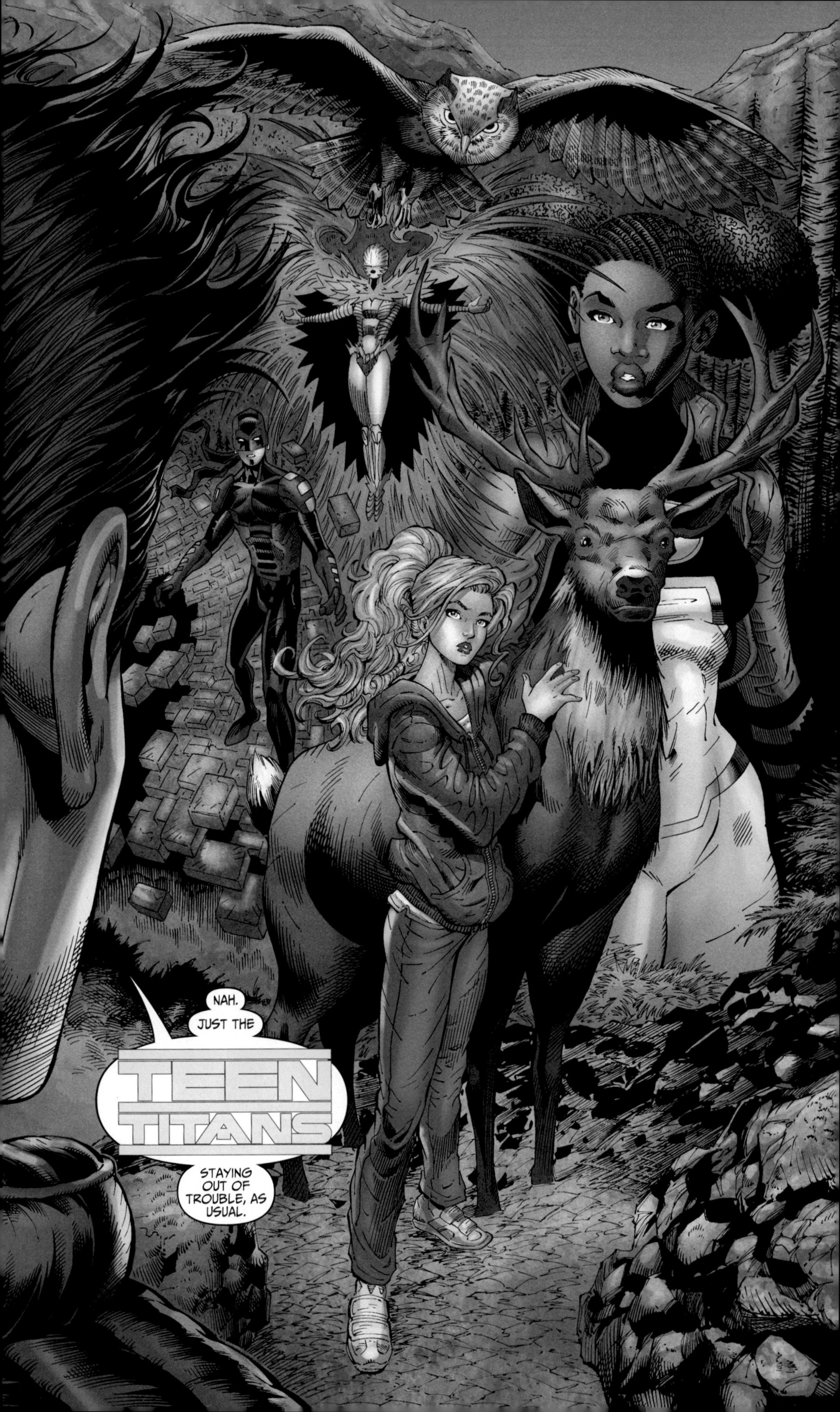
NAH. JUST THE
TEEN TITANS
STAYING OUT OF TROUBLE, AS USUAL.

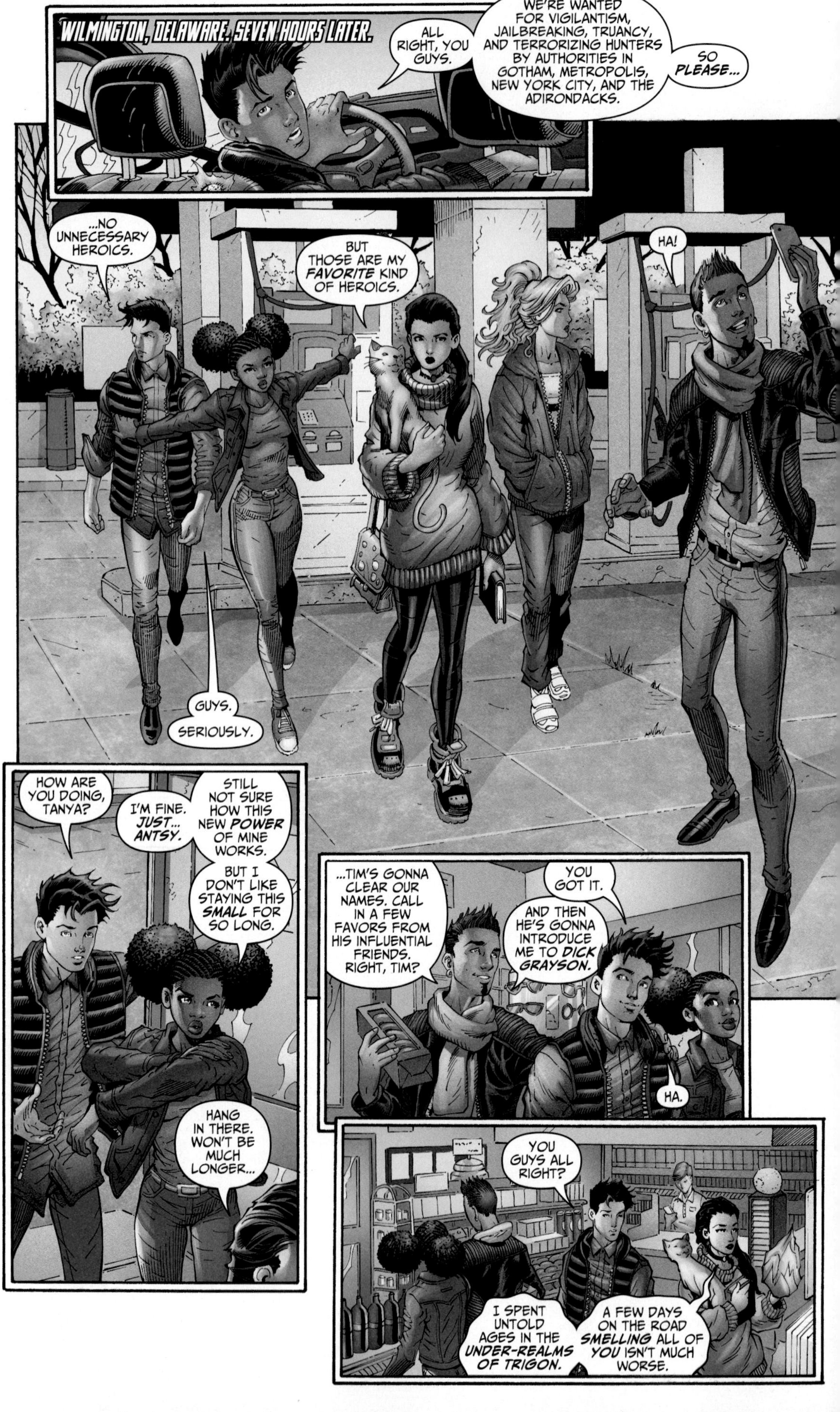
WILMINGTON, DELAWARE. SEVEN HOURS LATER.
ALL RIGHT, YOU GUYS.
WE'RE WANTED FOR VIGILANTISM, JAILBREAKING, TRUANCY, AND TERRORIZING HUNTERS BY AUTHORITIES IN GOTHAM, METROPOLIS, NEW YORK CITY, AND THE ADIRONDACKS.
SO PLEASE...
...NO UNNECESSARY HEROICS.
BUT THOSE ARE MY FAVORITE KIND OF HEROICS.
HA!
GUYS.
SERIOUSLY.
HOW ARE YOU DOING, TANYA?
I'M FINE. JUST... ANTSY.
STILL NOT SURE HOW THIS NEW POWER OF MINE WORKS.
BUT I DON'T LIKE STAYING THIS SMALL FOR SO LONG.
HANG IN THERE. WON'T BE MUCH LONGER...
...TIM'S GONNA CLEAR OUR NAMES. CALL IN A FEW FAVORS FROM HIS INFLUENTIAL FRIENDS. RIGHT, TIM?
YOU GOT IT.
AND THEN HE'S GONNA INTRODUCE ME TO DICK GRAYSON.
HA.
YOU GUYS ALL RIGHT?
I SPENT UNTOLD AGES IN THE UNDER-REALMS OF TRIGON.
A FEW DAYS ON THE ROAD SMELLING ALL OF YOU ISN'T MUCH WORSE.

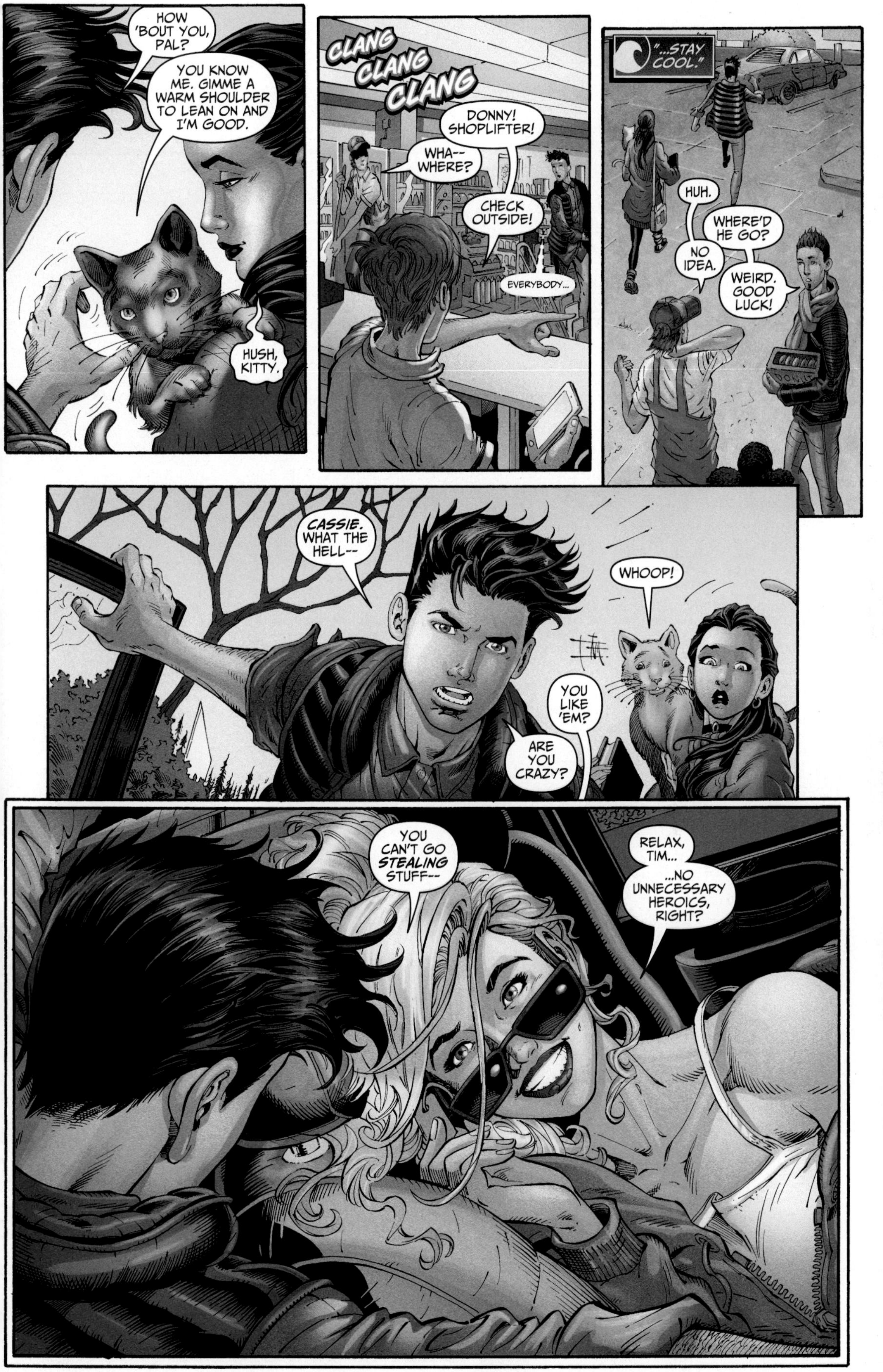
HOW 'BOUT YOU, PAL?
YOU KNOW ME. GIMME A WARM SHOULDER TO LEAN ON AND I'M GOOD.
HUSH, KITTY.
CLANG CLANG CLANG
DONNY! SHOPLIFTER!
WHA-- WHERE?
CHECK OUTSIDE!
EVERYBODY...
"...STAY COOL."
HUH.
WHERE'D HE GO?
NO IDEA.
WEIRD. GOOD LUCK!
CASSIE. WHAT THE HELL--
WHOOP!
YOU LIKE 'EM?
ARE YOU CRAZY?
YOU CAN'T GO STEALING STUFF--
RELAX, TIM...
...NO UNNECESSARY HEROICS, RIGHT?

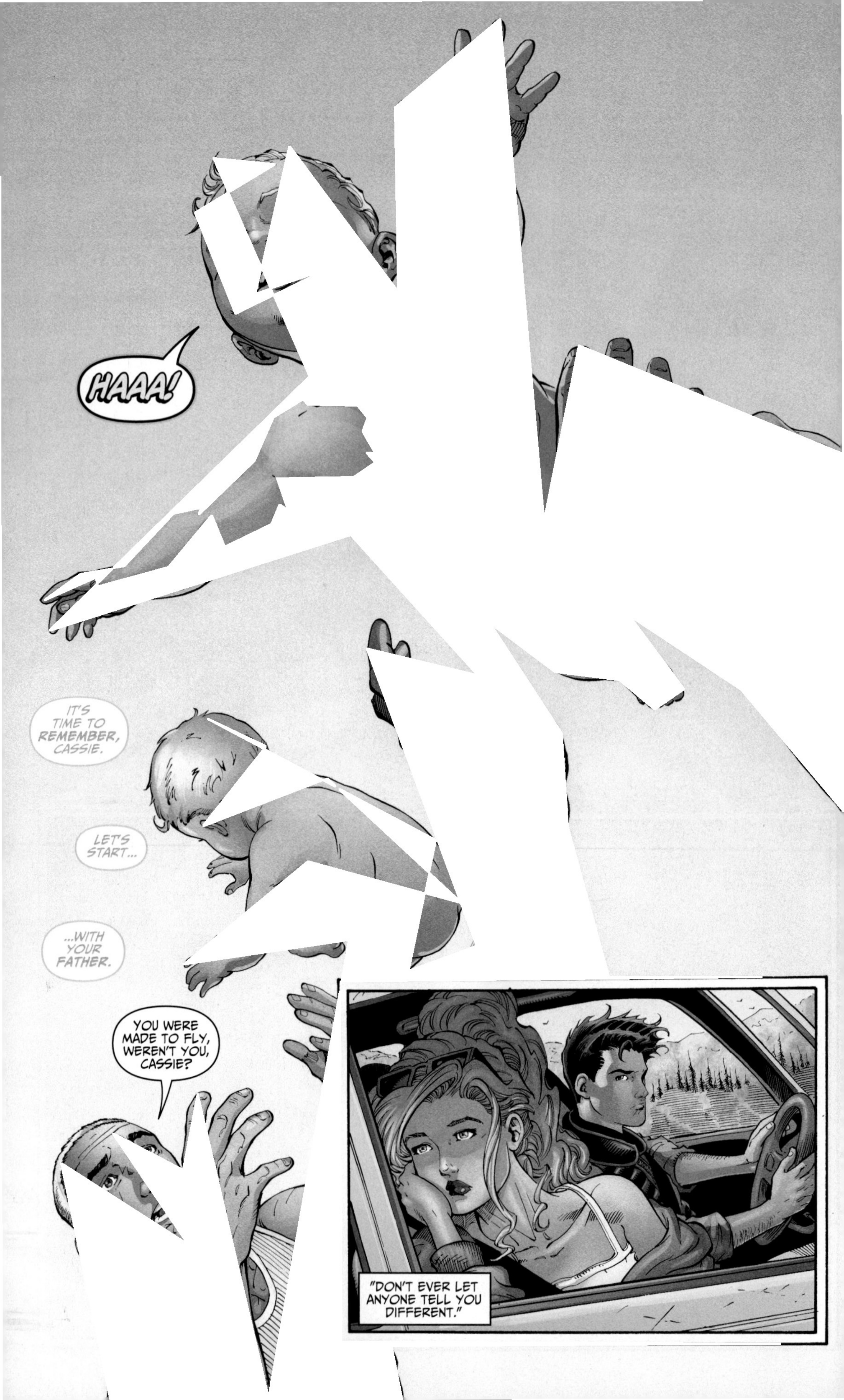
HAAA!
IT'S TIME TO REMEMBER, CASSIE.
LET'S START...
...WITH YOUR FATHER.
YOU WERE MADE TO FLY, WEREN'T YOU, CASSIE?
"DON'T EVER LET ANYONE TELL YOU DIFFERENT."

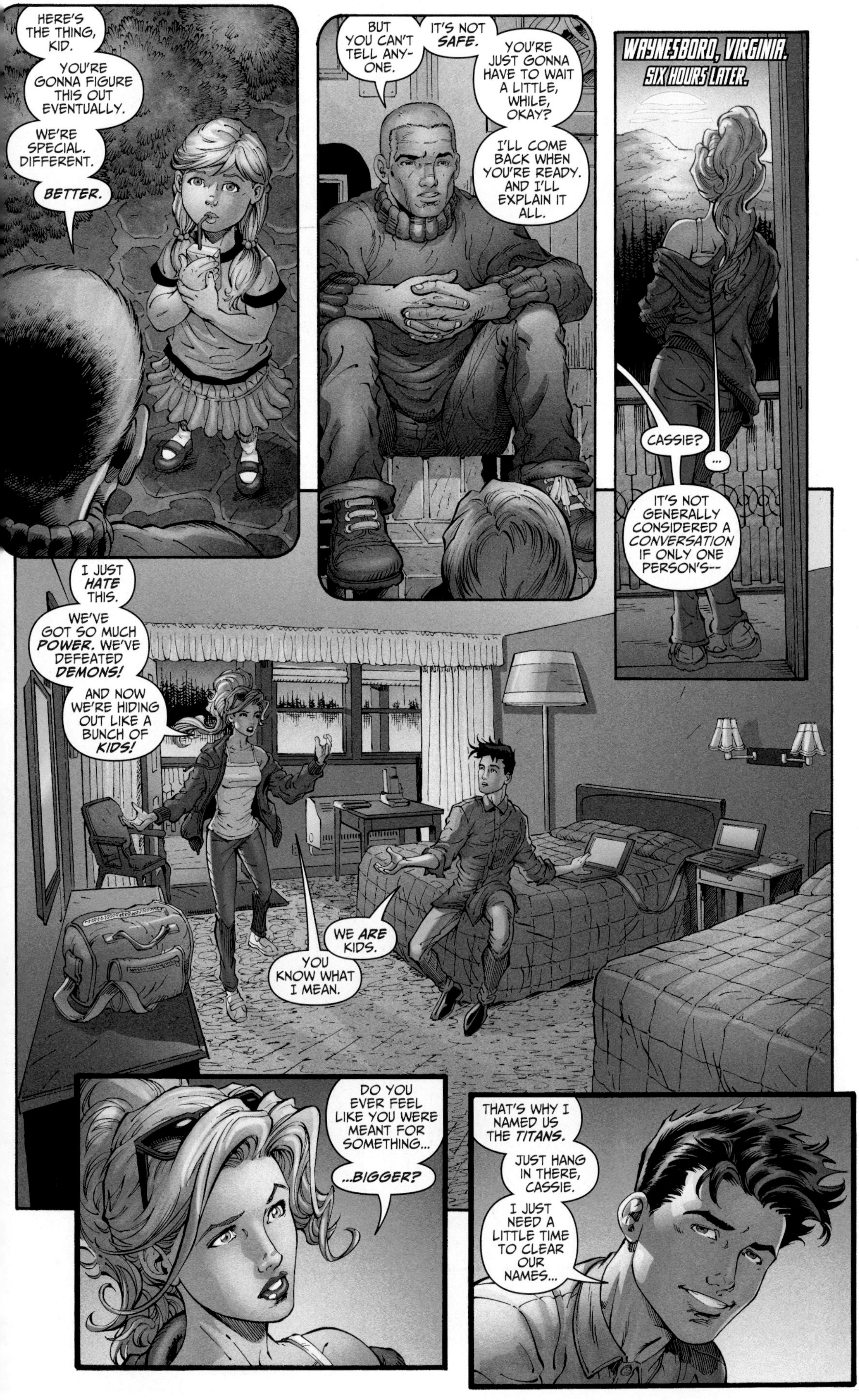

HERE'S THE THING, KID.
YOU'RE GONNA FIGURE THIS OUT EVENTUALLY.
WE'RE SPECIAL. DIFFERENT.
BETTER.
BUT YOU CAN'T TELL ANY-ONE.
IT'S NOT SAFE.
YOU'RE JUST GONNA HAVE TO WAIT A LITTLE, WHILE, OKAY?
I'LL COME BACK WHEN YOU'RE READY. AND I'LL EXPLAIN IT ALL.
WAYNESBORO, VIRGINIA.
SIX HOURS LATER.
CASSIE?
...
IT'S NOT GENERALLY CONSIDERED A CONVERSATION IF ONLY ONE PERSON'S--
I JUST HATE THIS.
WE'VE GOT SO MUCH POWER. WE'VE DEFEATED DEMONS!
AND NOW WE'RE HIDING OUT LIKE A BUNCH OF KIDS!
WE ARE KIDS.
YOU KNOW WHAT I MEAN.
DO YOU EVER FEEL LIKE YOU WERE MEANT FOR SOMETHING...
...BIGGER?
THAT'S WHY I NAMED US THE TITANS.
JUST HANG IN THERE, CASSIE.
I JUST NEED A LITTLE TIME TO CLEAR OUR NAMES...

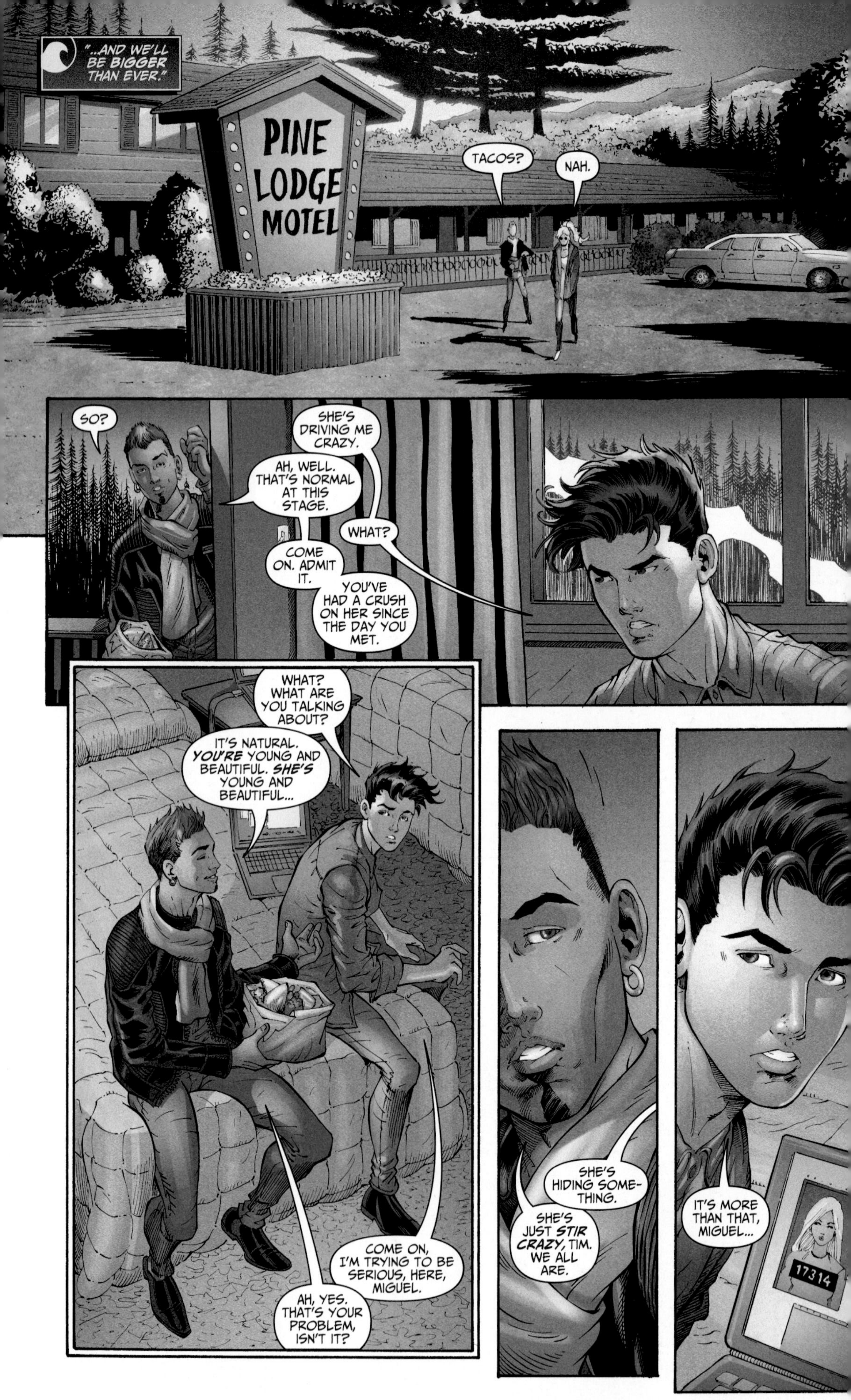
"...AND WE'LL BE BIGGER THAN EVER."
PINE LODGE MOTEL
TACOS?
NAH.
SO?
SHE'S DRIVING ME CRAZY.
AH, WELL. THAT'S NORMAL AT THIS STAGE.
WHAT?
COME ON. ADMIT IT.
YOU'VE HAD A CRUSH ON HER SINCE THE DAY YOU MET.
WHAT? WHAT ARE YOU TALKING ABOUT?
IT'S NATURAL. ***YOU'RE*** YOUNG AND BEAUTIFUL. ***SHE'S*** YOUNG AND BEAUTIFUL...
COME ON, I'M TRYING TO BE SERIOUS, HERE, MIGUEL.
AH, YES. THAT'S YOUR PROBLEM, ISN'T IT?
SHE'S HIDING SOME-THING.
SHE'S JUST ***STIR CRAZY***, TIM. WE ALL ARE.
IT'S MORE THAN THAT, MIGUEL...
17314

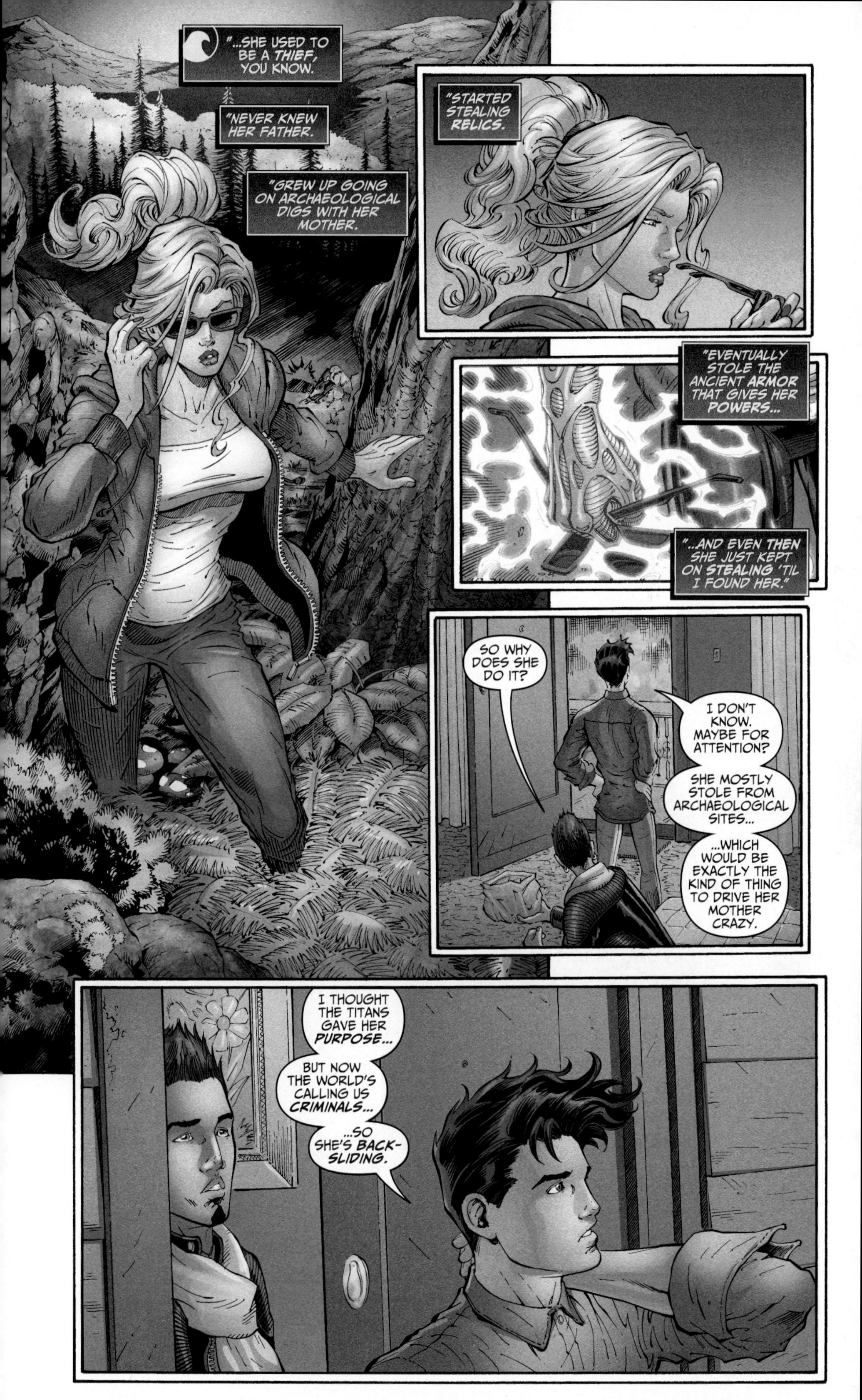
"...SHE USED TO BE A THIEF, YOU KNOW.
"NEVER KNEW HER FATHER.
"GREW UP GOING ON ARCHAEOLOGICAL DIGS WITH HER MOTHER.
"STARTED STEALING RELICS.
"EVENTUALLY STOLE THE ANCIENT ARMOR THAT GIVES HER POWERS...
"...AND EVEN THEN SHE JUST KEPT ON STEALING 'TIL I FOUND HER."
SO WHY DOES SHE DO IT?
I DON'T KNOW. MAYBE FOR ATTENTION?
SHE MOSTLY STOLE FROM ARCHAEOLOGICAL SITES...
...WHICH WOULD BE EXACTLY THE KIND OF THING TO DRIVE HER MOTHER CRAZY.
I THOUGHT THE TITANS GAVE HER PURPOSE...
BUT NOW THE WORLD'S CALLING US CRIMINALS...
...SO SHE'S BACK-SLIDING.

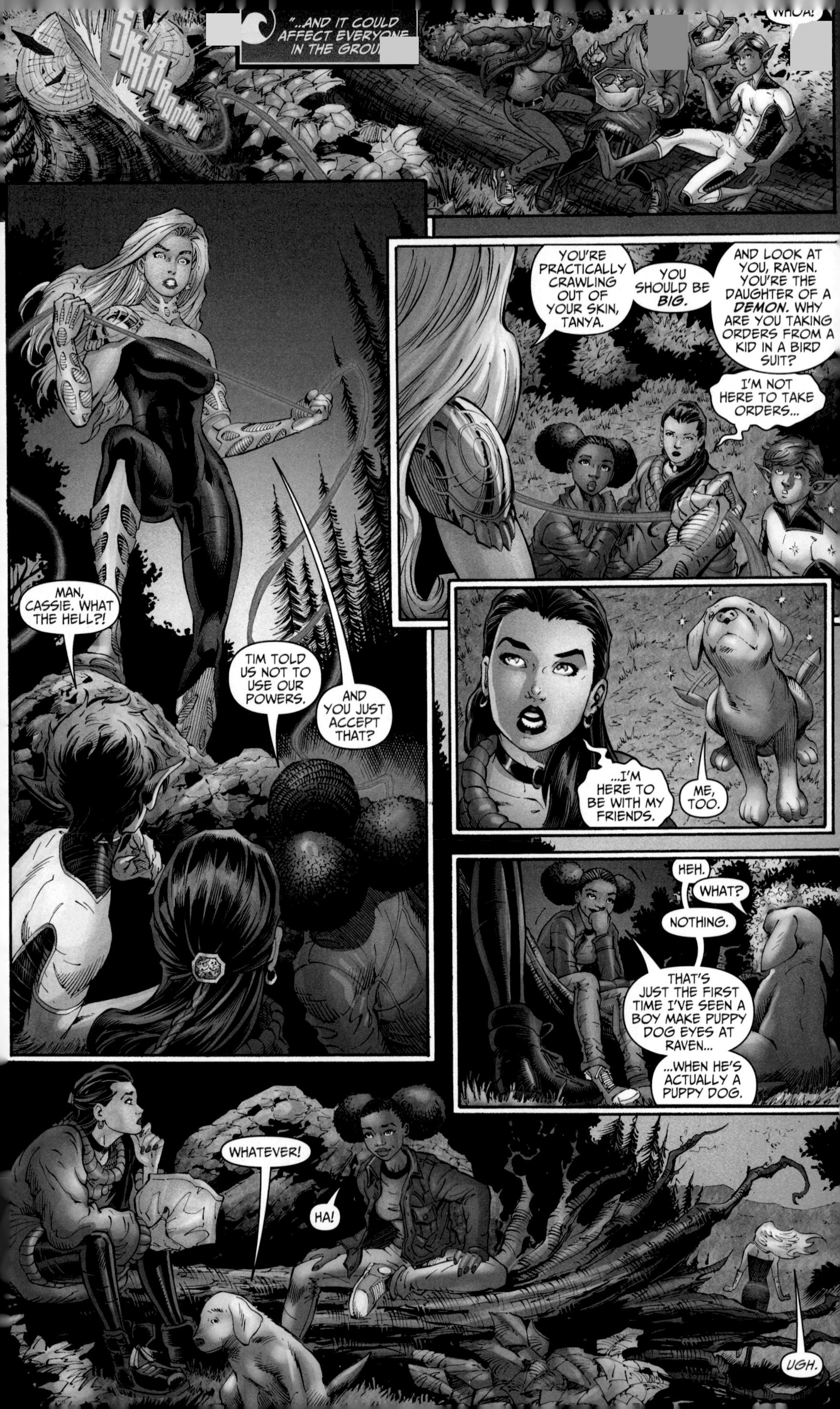
SKRRRoooKKK
"...AND IT COULD AFFECT EVERYONE IN THE GROU
WHOA!
MAN, CASSIE. WHAT THE HELL?!
TIM TOLD US NOT TO USE OUR POWERS.
AND YOU JUST ACCEPT THAT?
YOU'RE PRACTICALLY CRAWLING OUT OF YOUR SKIN, TANYA.
YOU SHOULD BE BIG.
AND LOOK AT YOU, RAVEN. YOU'RE THE DAUGHTER OF A DEMON. WHY ARE YOU TAKING ORDERS FROM A KID IN A BIRD SUIT?
I'M NOT HERE TO TAKE ORDERS...
...I'M HERE TO BE WITH MY FRIENDS.
ME, TOO.
HEH.
WHAT?
NOTHING.
THAT'S JUST THE FIRST TIME I'VE SEEN A BOY MAKE PUPPY DOG EYES AT RAVEN...
...WHEN HE'S ACTUALLY A PUPPY DOG.
WHATEVER!
HA!
UGH.

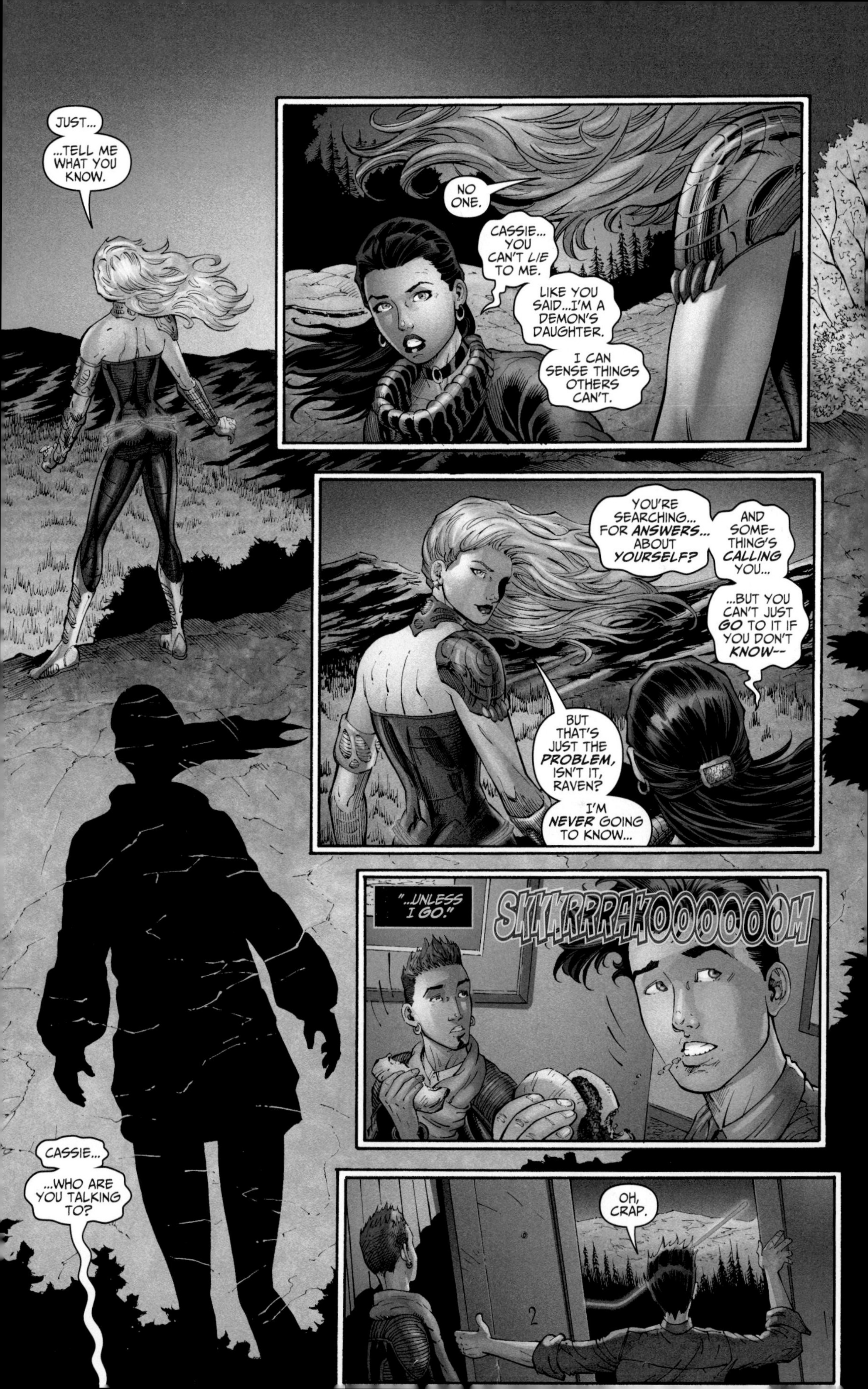

JUST...
...TELL ME WHAT YOU KNOW.
NO ONE.
CASSIE... YOU CAN'T LIE TO ME.
LIKE YOU SAID...I'M A DEMON'S DAUGHTER.
I CAN SENSE THINGS OTHERS CAN'T.
YOU'RE SEARCHING... FOR ANSWERS... ABOUT YOURSELF?
AND SOME-THING'S CALLING YOU...
...BUT YOU CAN'T JUST GO TO IT IF YOU DON'T KNOW--
BUT THAT'S JUST THE PROBLEM, ISN'T IT, RAVEN?
I'M NEVER GOING TO KNOW...
"...UNLESS I GO."
SKKKRRRAKOOOOOOOM
CASSIE...
...WHO ARE YOU TALKING TO?
OH, CRAP.
2

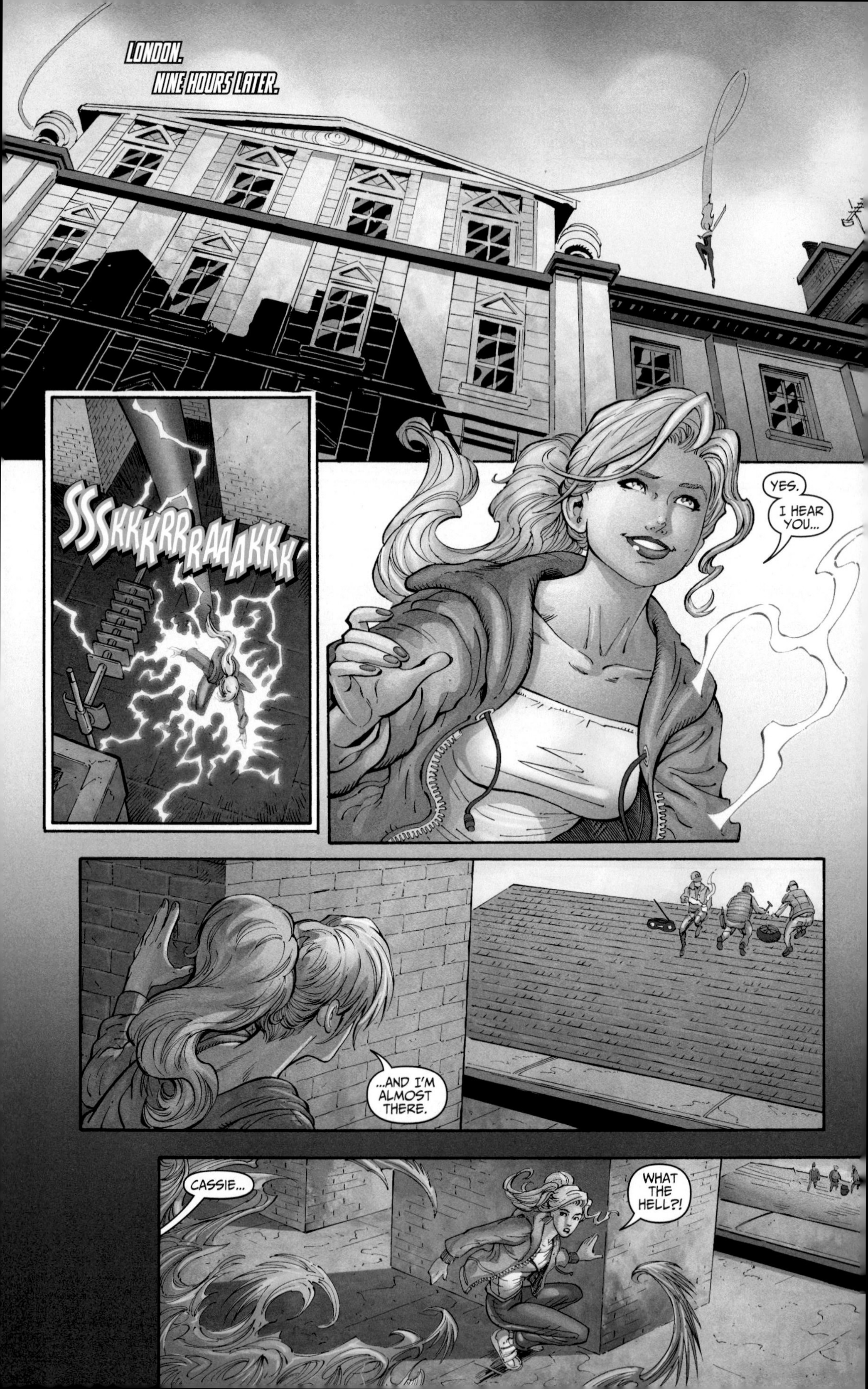
LONDON.
NINE HOURS LATER.
SSSKKKRRRAAAKKK
YES. I HEAR YOU...
...AND I'M ALMOST THERE.
CASSIE...
WHAT THE HELL?!

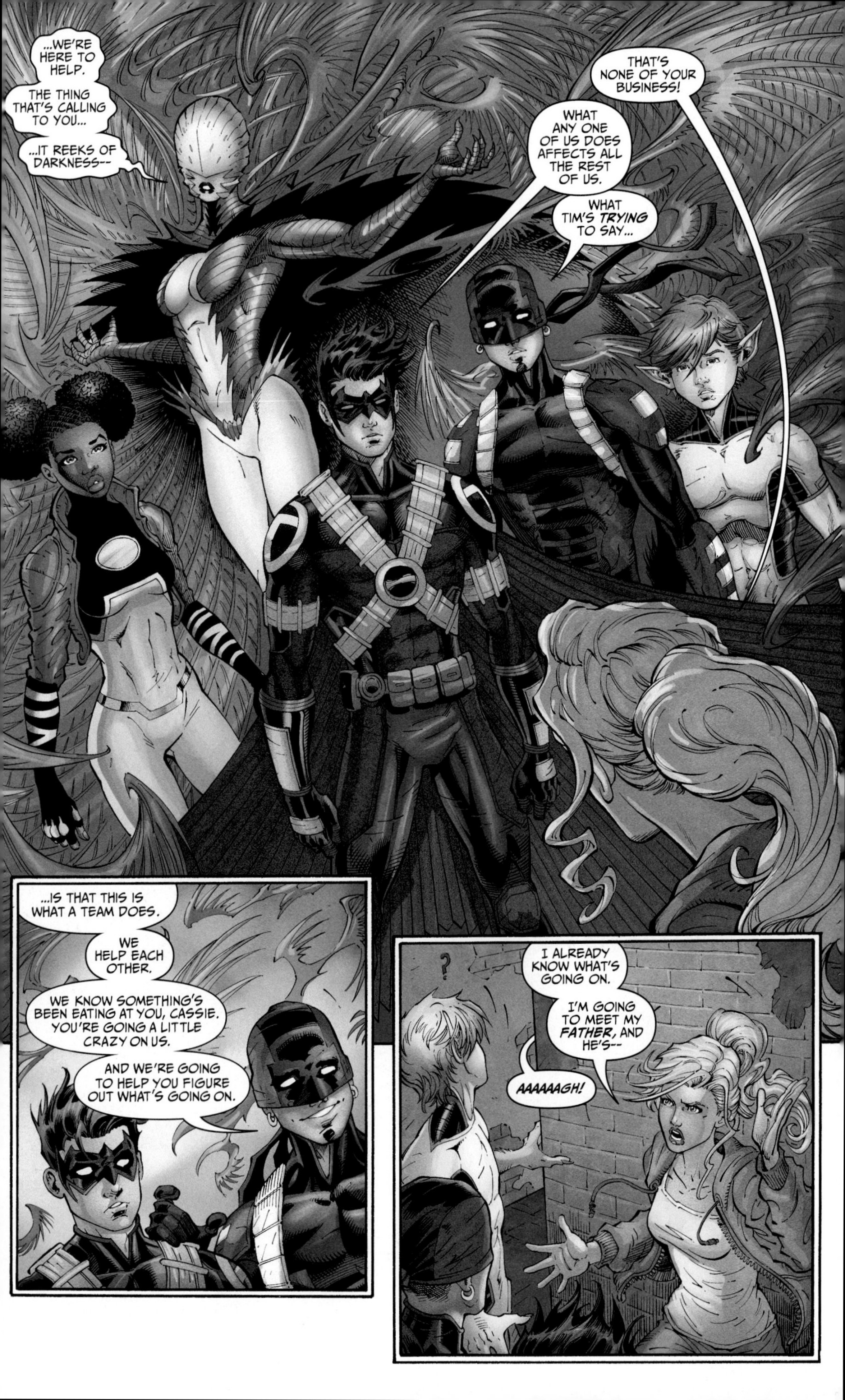
...WE'RE HERE TO HELP.
THE THING THAT'S CALLING TO YOU...
...IT REEKS OF DARKNESS--
THAT'S NONE OF YOUR BUSINESS!
WHAT ANY ONE OF US DOES AFFECTS ALL THE REST OF US.
WHAT TIM'S *TRYING* TO SAY...
...IS THAT THIS IS WHAT A TEAM DOES.
WE HELP EACH OTHER.
WE KNOW SOMETHING'S BEEN EATING AT YOU, CASSIE. YOU'RE GOING A LITTLE CRAZY ON US.
AND WE'RE GOING TO HELP YOU FIGURE OUT WHAT'S GOING ON.
?
I ALREADY KNOW WHAT'S GOING ON.
I'M GOING TO MEET MY *FATHER*, AND HE'S--
AAAAAAGH!

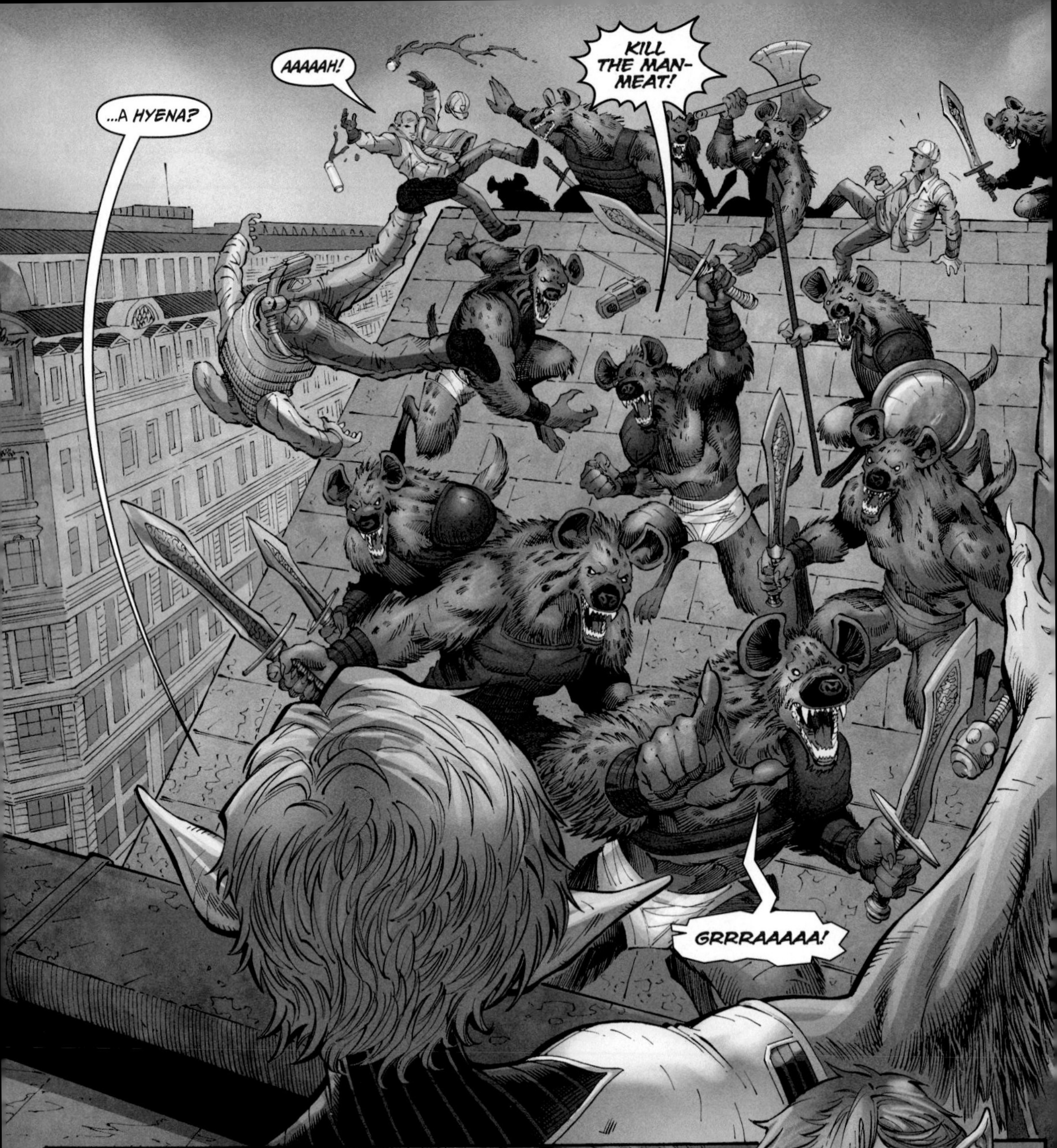
...A HYENA?
AAAAAH!
KILL THE MAN-MEAT!
GRRRAAAAA!

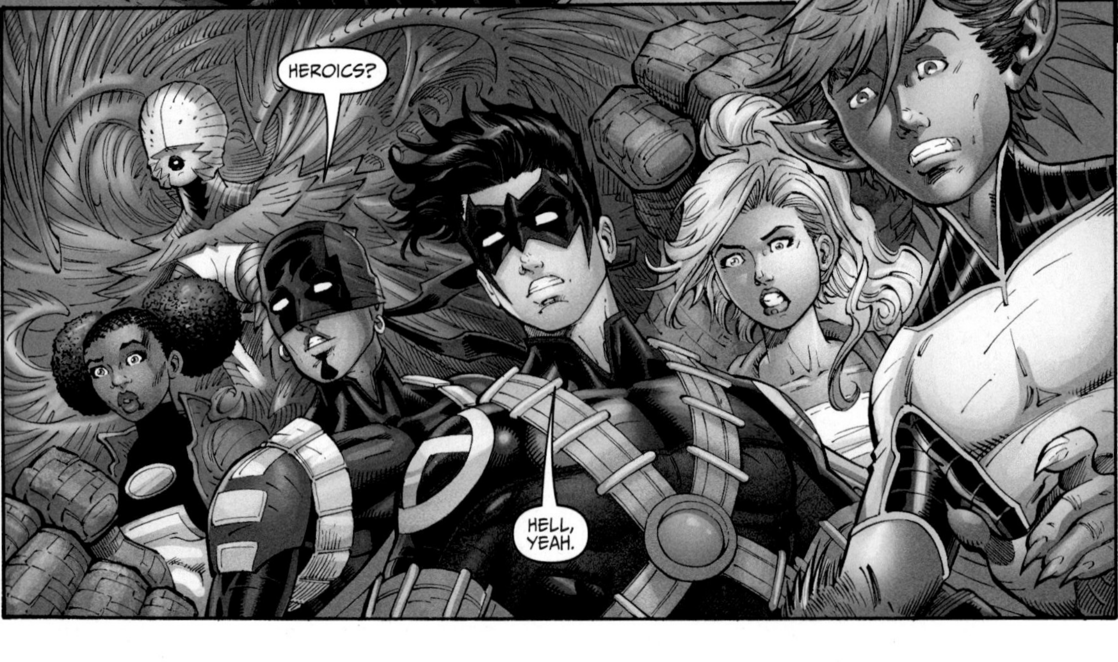
HEROICS?
HELL, YEAH.

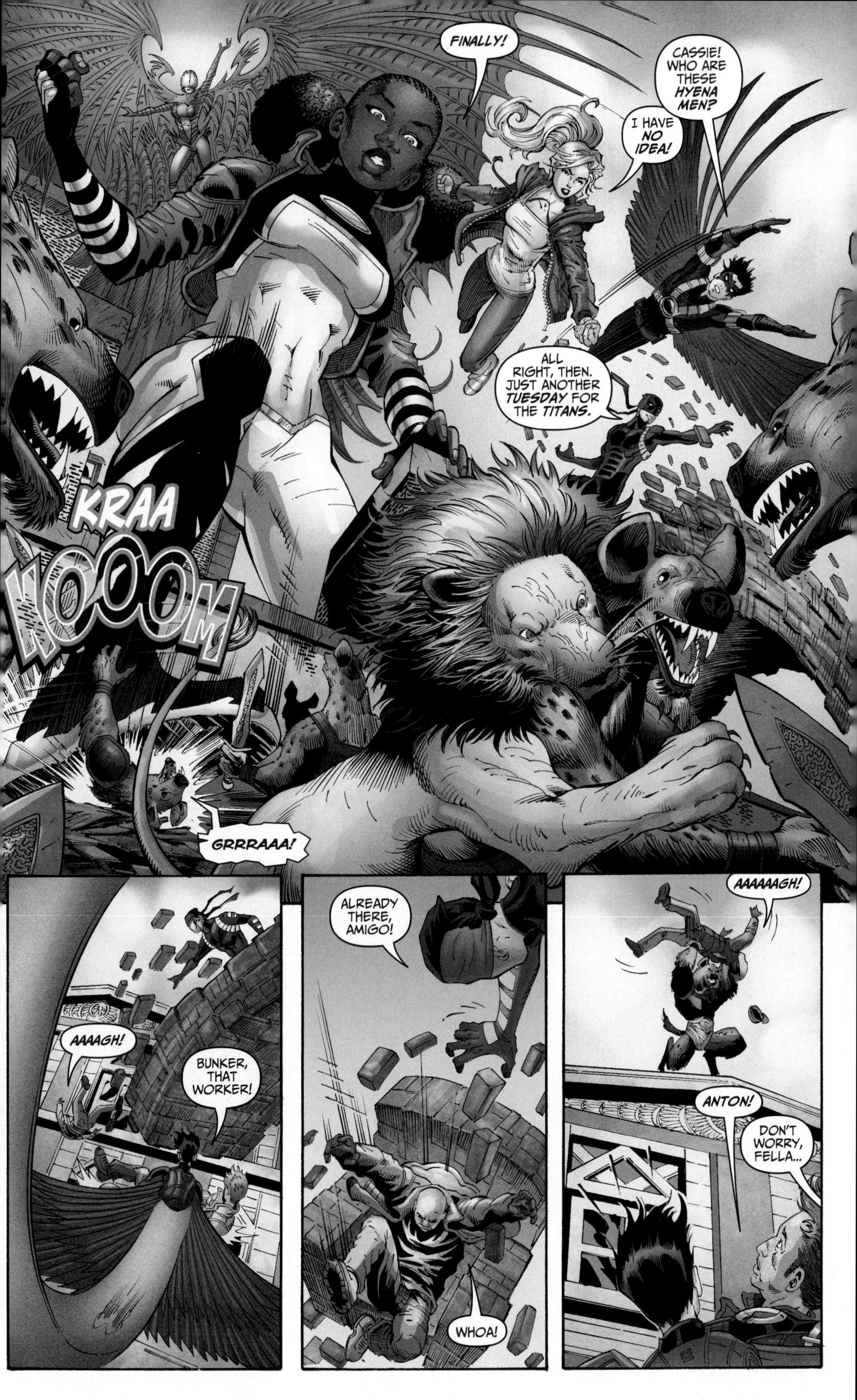
FINALLY!
CASSIE! WHO ARE THESE HYENA MEN?
I HAVE NO IDEA!
ALL RIGHT, THEN. JUST ANOTHER TUESDAY FOR THE TITANS.
KRAA
KOOOM
GRRRAAA!
AAAAGH!
BUNKER, THAT WORKER!
ALREADY THERE, AMIGO!
WHOA!
AAAAAAGH!
ANTON!
DON'T WORRY, FELLA...

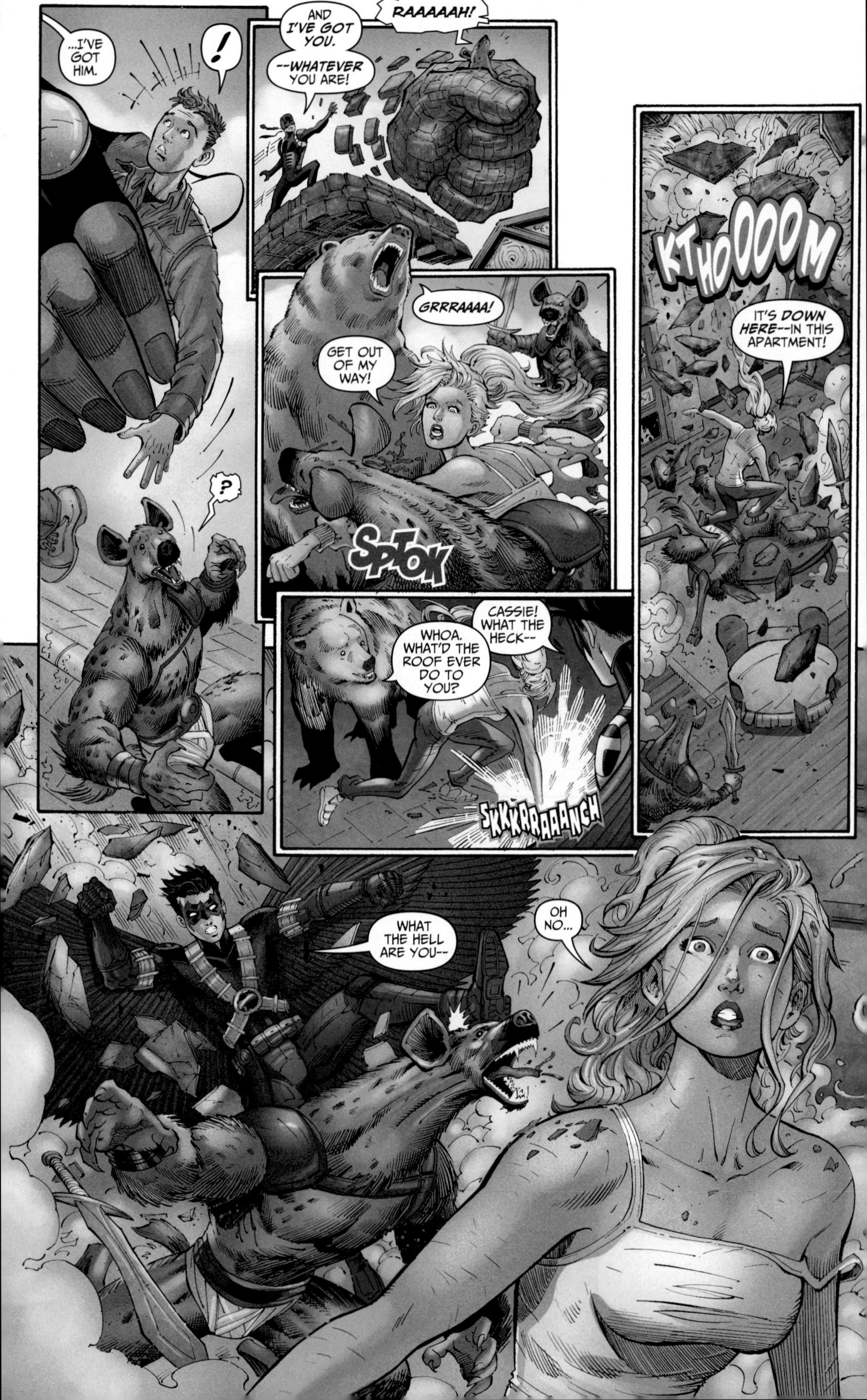
...I'VE GOT HIM.
!
AND I'VE GOT YOU.
--WHATEVER YOU ARE!
RAAAAAH!
GRRRAAAA!
GET OUT OF MY WAY!
SPTOK
?
CASSIE! WHAT THE HECK--
WHOA. WHAT'D THE ROOF EVER DO TO YOU?
SKKKRRAAANCH
KTHOOOOM
IT'S DOWN HERE--IN THIS APARTMENT!
WHAT THE HELL ARE YOU--
OH NO...

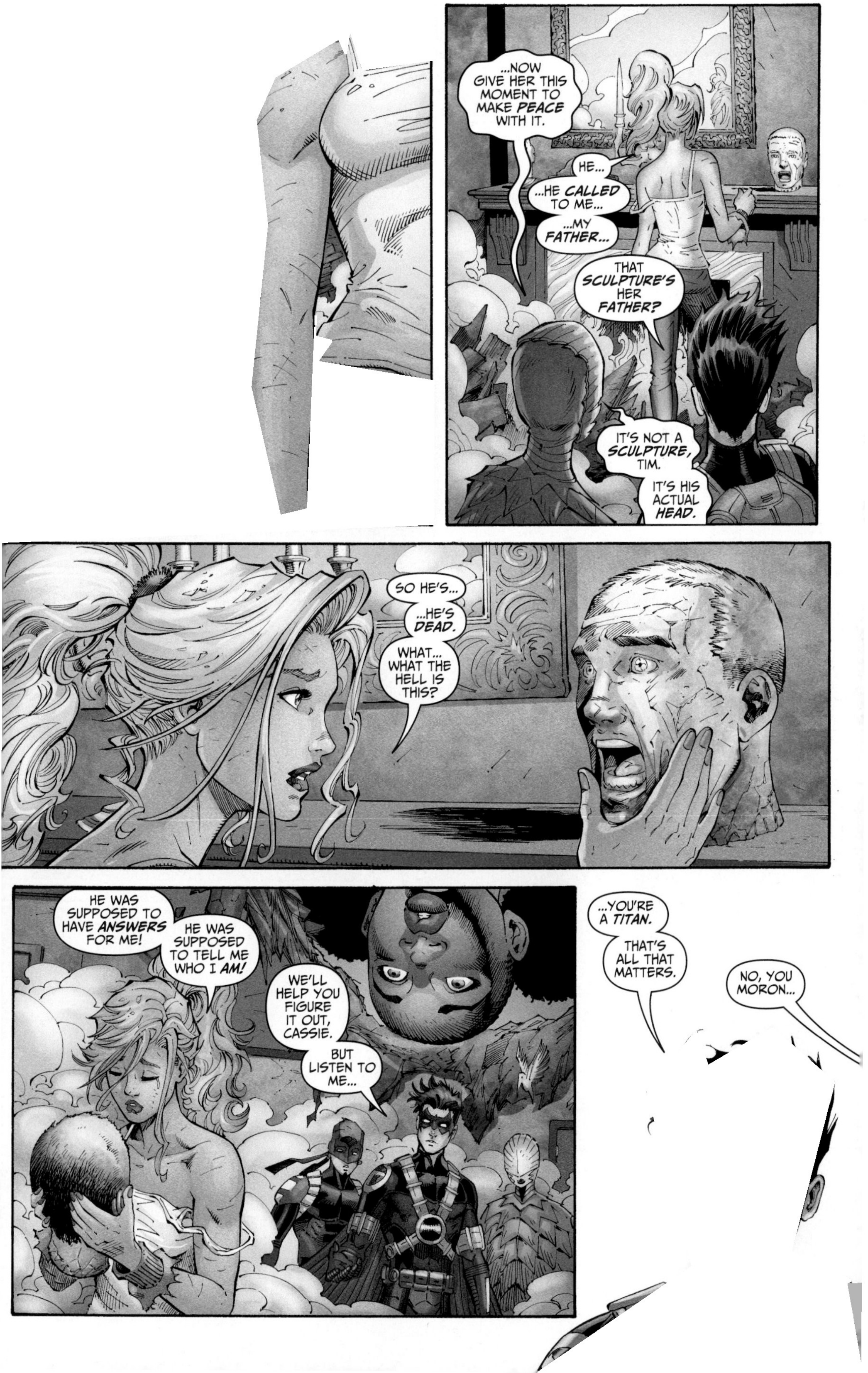
...NOW GIVE HER THIS MOMENT TO MAKE PEACE WITH IT.
HE...
...HE CALLED TO ME...
...MY FATHER...
THAT SCULPTURE'S HER FATHER?
IT'S NOT A SCULPTURE, TIM.
IT'S HIS ACTUAL HEAD.
SO HE'S...
...HE'S DEAD.
WHAT... WHAT THE HELL IS THIS?
HE WAS SUPPOSED TO HAVE ANSWERS FOR ME!
HE WAS SUPPOSED TO TELL ME WHO I AM!
WE'LL HELP YOU FIGURE IT OUT, CASSIE.
BUT LISTEN TO ME...
...YOU'RE A TITAN.
THAT'S ALL THAT MATTERS.
NO, YOU MORON...

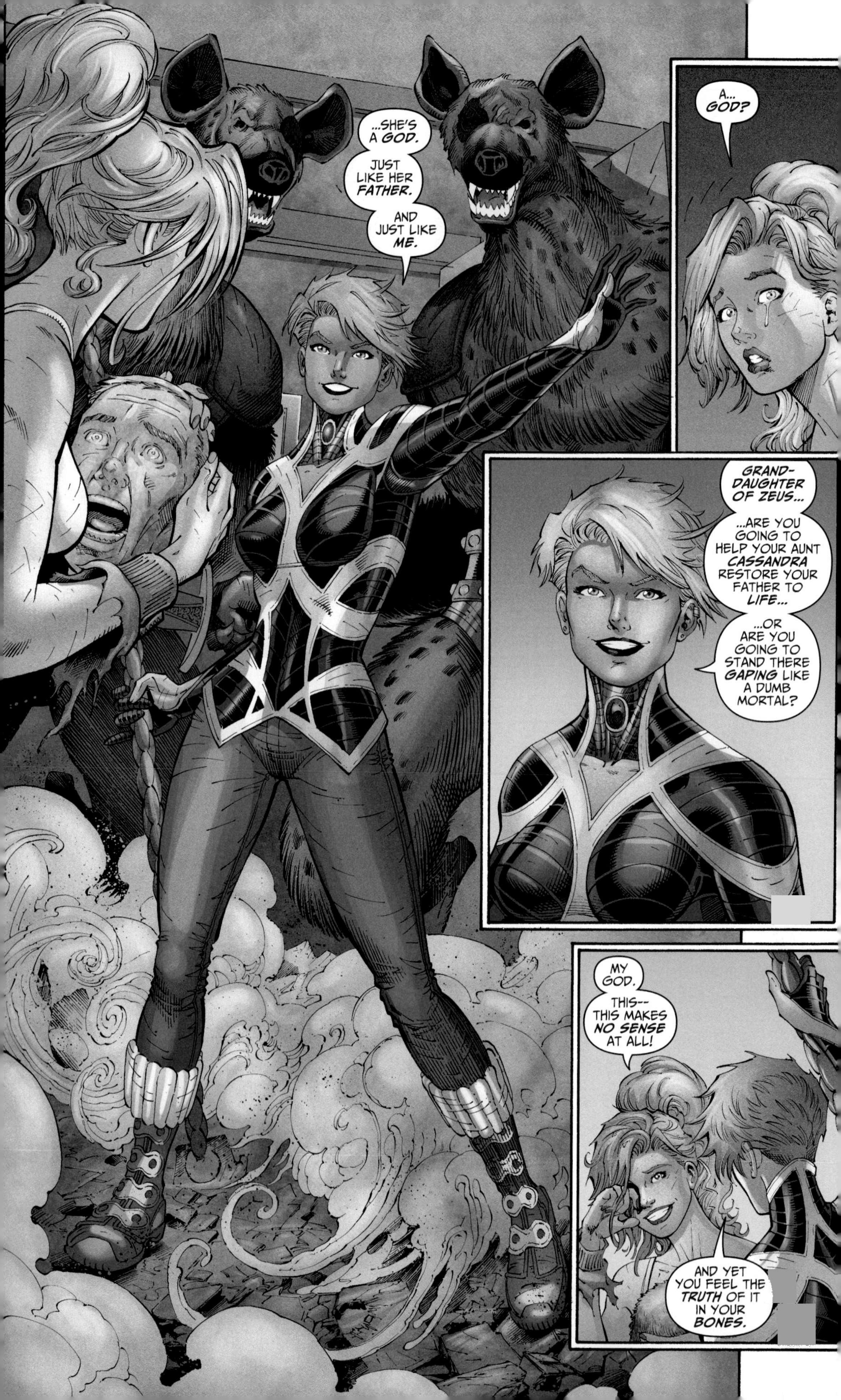
...SHE'S A GOD.
JUST LIKE HER FATHER.
AND JUST LIKE ME.
A... GOD?
GRAND-DAUGHTER OF ZEUS...
...ARE YOU GOING TO HELP YOUR AUNT CASSANDRA RESTORE YOUR FATHER TO LIFE...
...OR ARE YOU GOING TO STAND THERE GAPING LIKE A DUMB MORTAL?
MY GOD. THIS-- THIS MAKES NO SENSE AT ALL!
AND YET YOU FEEL THE TRUTH OF IT IN YOUR BONES.

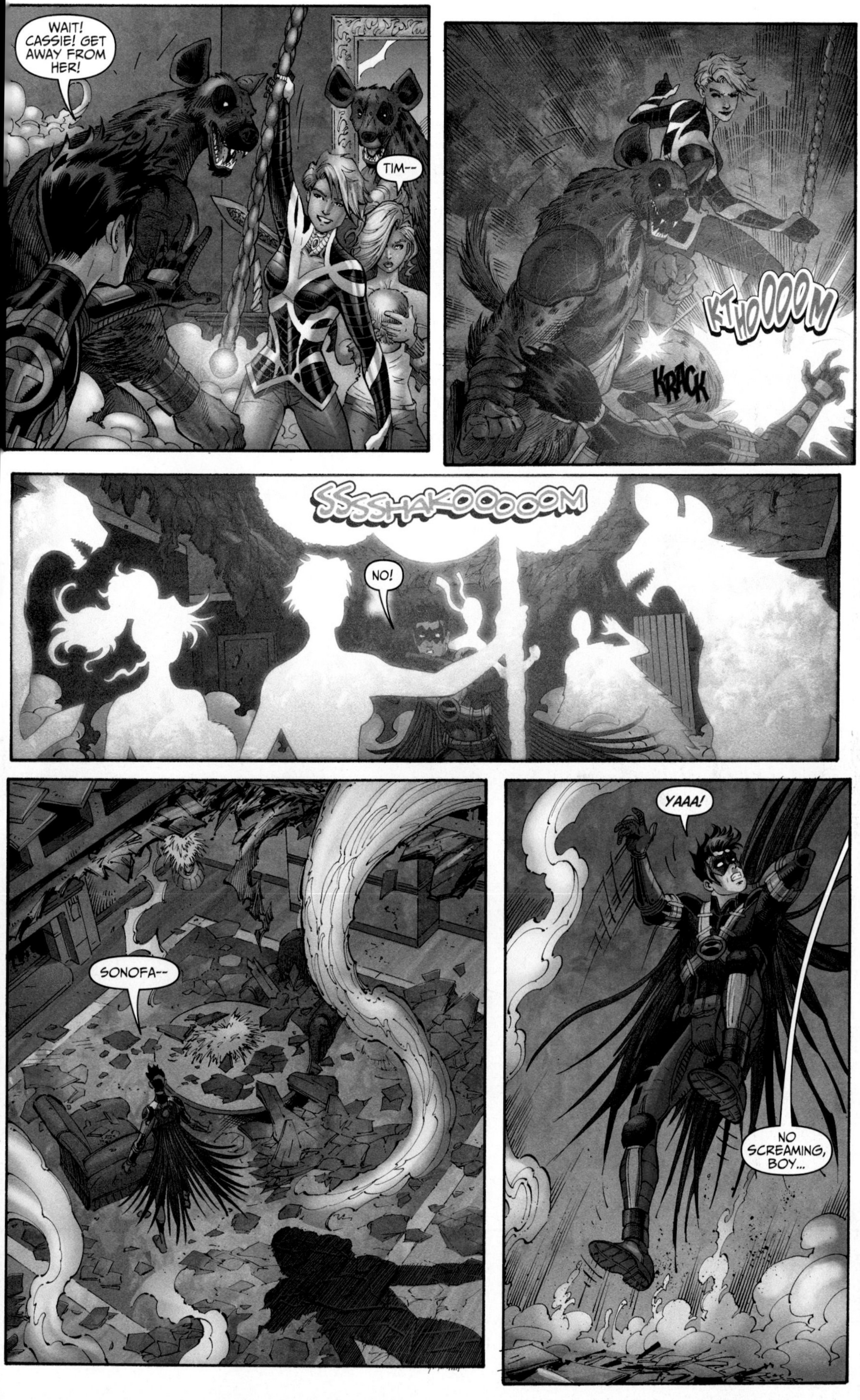
WAIT! CASSIE! GET AWAY FROM HER!
TIM--
KTHOOOOM
KRACK
SSSSHAKOOOOOOM
NO!
SONOFA--
YAAA!
NO SCREAMING, BOY...

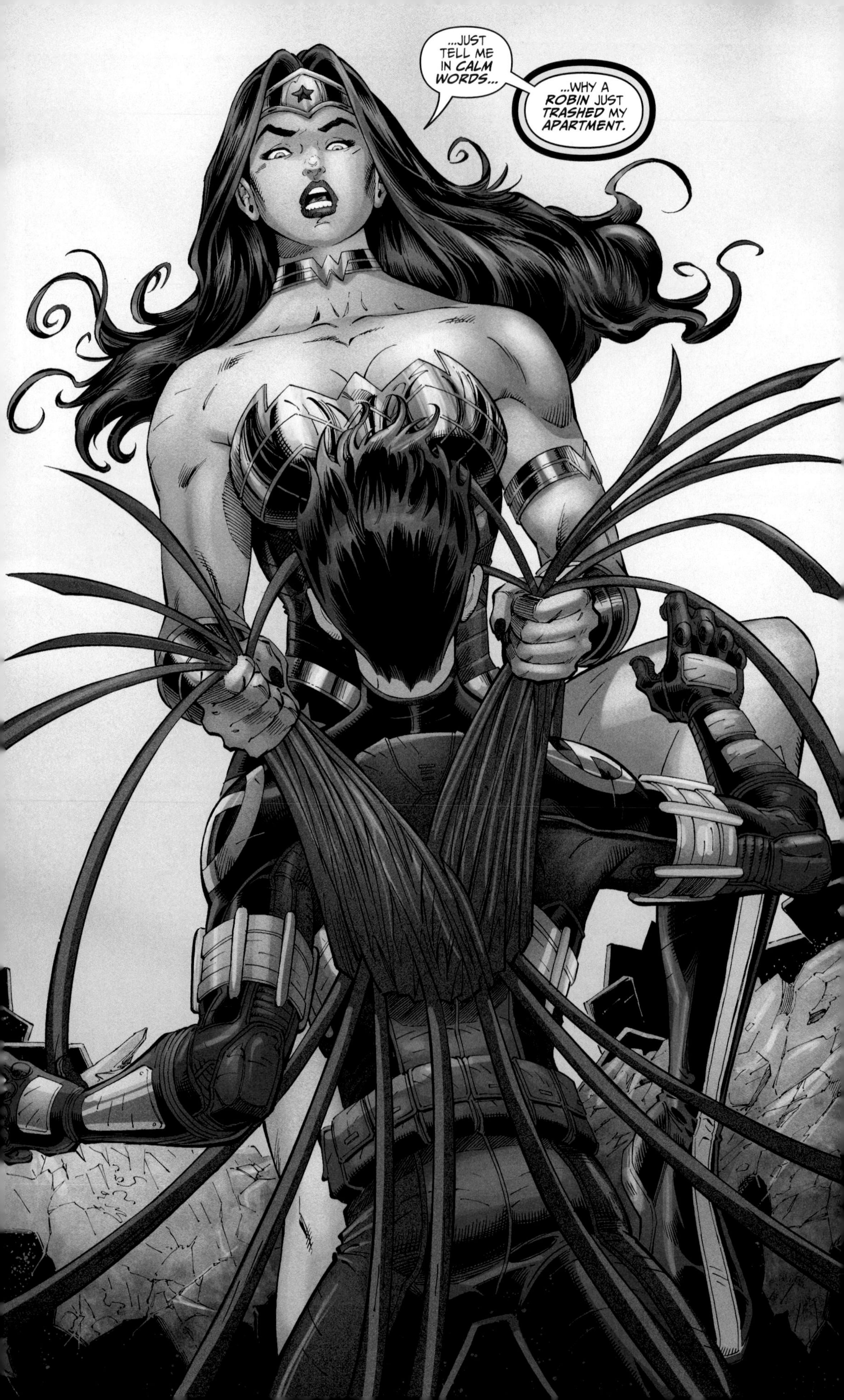
...JUST TELL ME IN CALM WORDS...
...WHY A ROBIN JUST TRASHED MY APARTMENT.

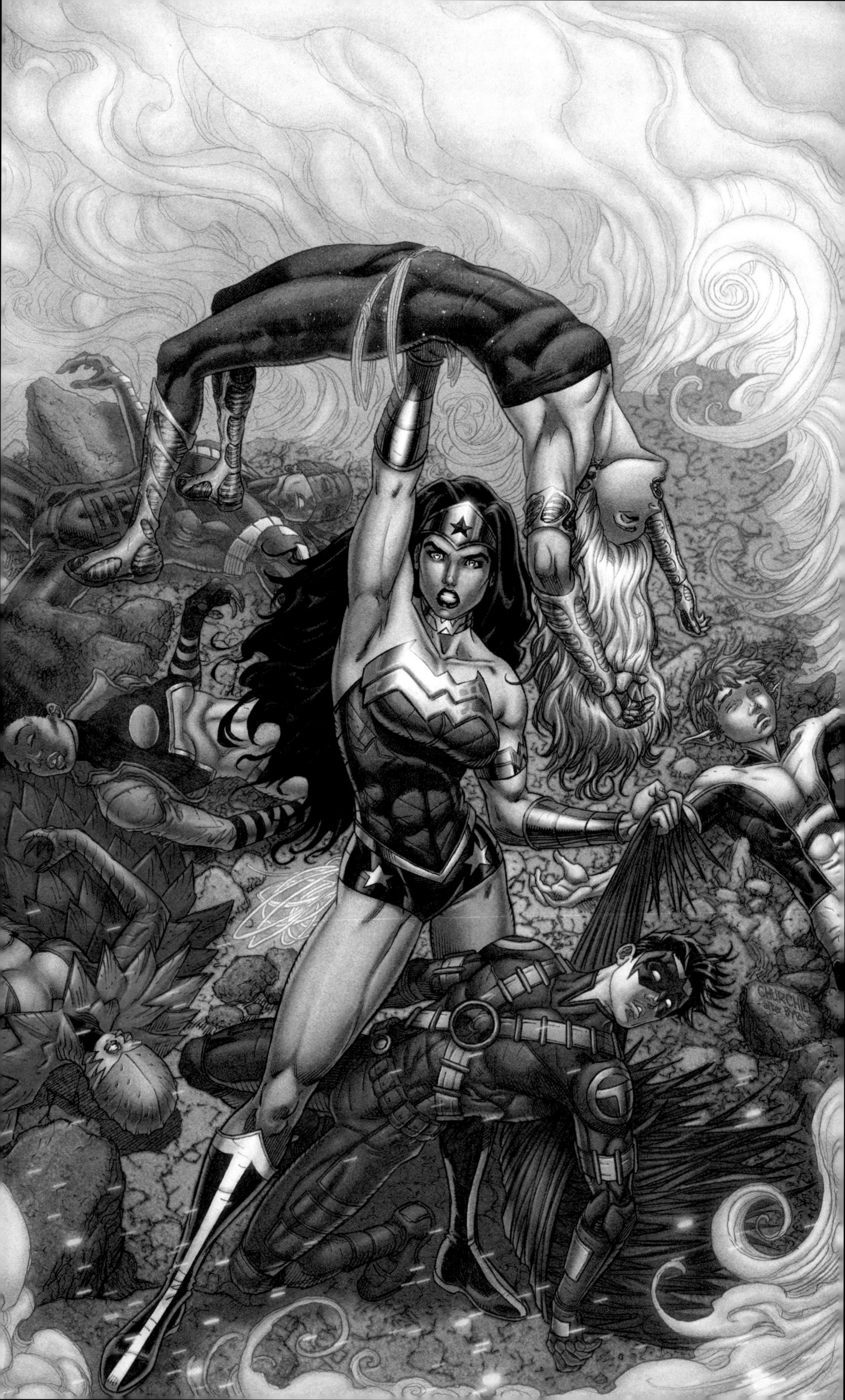
CHURCHILL

WHO IS WONDER GIRL? PART TWO

GREG PAK writer IAN CHURCHILL TOM DERENICK pencillers NORM RAPMUND ART THIBERT inkers TONY AVIÑA colorist COREY BREEN letterer
cover art by IAN CHURCHILL & ANDREW DALHOUSE

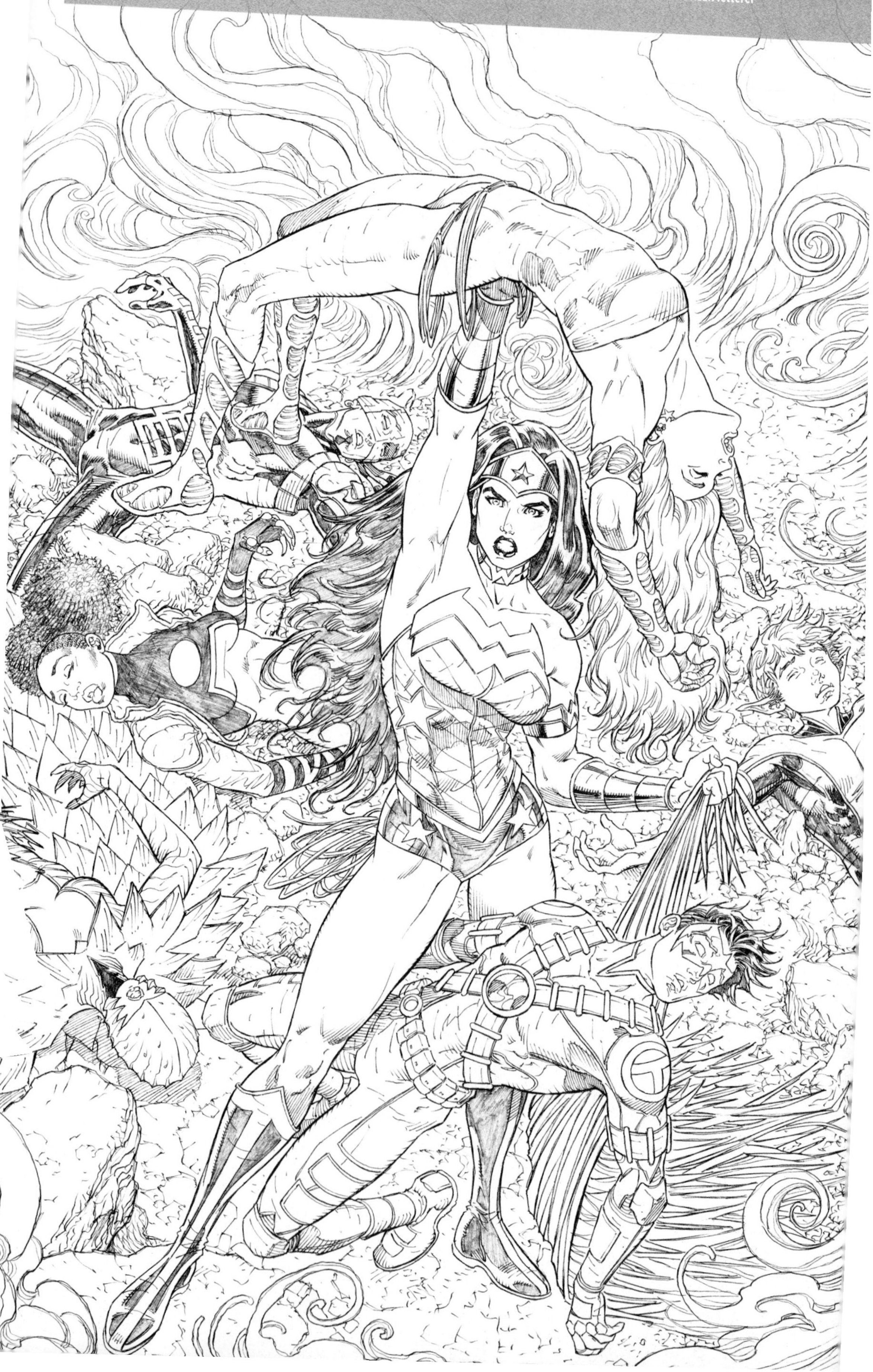

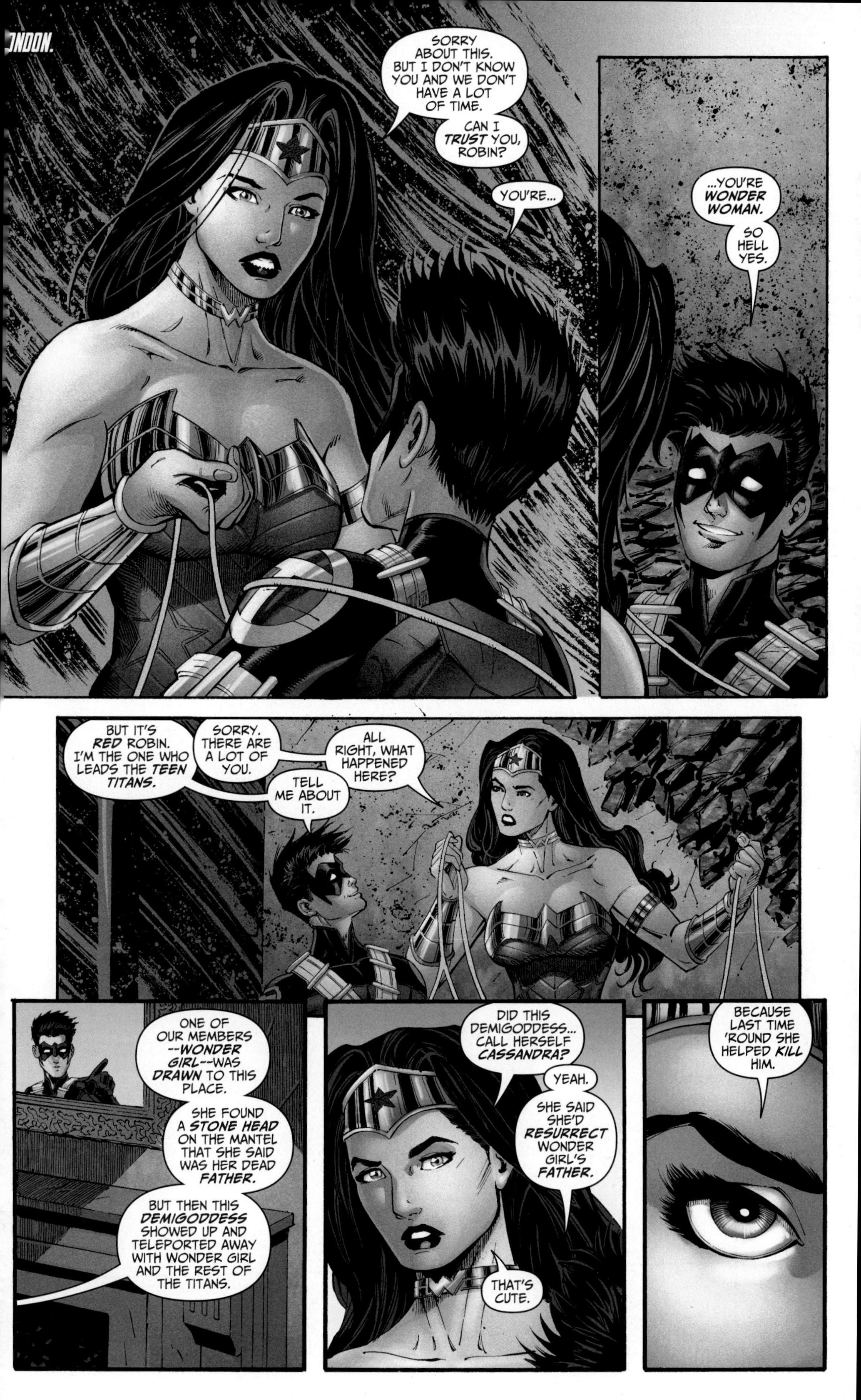

NDON.
SORRY ABOUT THIS. BUT I DON'T KNOW YOU AND WE DON'T HAVE A LOT OF TIME.
CAN I TRUST YOU, ROBIN?
YOU'RE...
...YOU'RE WONDER WOMAN.
SO HELL YES.
BUT IT'S RED ROBIN. I'M THE ONE WHO LEADS THE TEEN TITANS.
SORRY. THERE ARE A LOT OF YOU.
TELL ME ABOUT IT.
ALL RIGHT, WHAT HAPPENED HERE?
ONE OF OUR MEMBERS --WONDER GIRL--WAS DRAWN TO THIS PLACE.
SHE FOUND A STONE HEAD ON THE MANTEL THAT SHE SAID WAS HER DEAD FATHER.
BUT THEN THIS DEMIGODDESS SHOWED UP AND TELEPORTED AWAY WITH WONDER GIRL AND THE REST OF THE TITANS.
DID THIS DEMIGODDESS... CALL HERSELF CASSANDRA?
YEAH.
SHE SAID SHE'D RESURRECT WONDER GIRL'S FATHER.
THAT'S CUTE.
BECAUSE LAST TIME 'ROUND SHE HELPED KILL HIM.

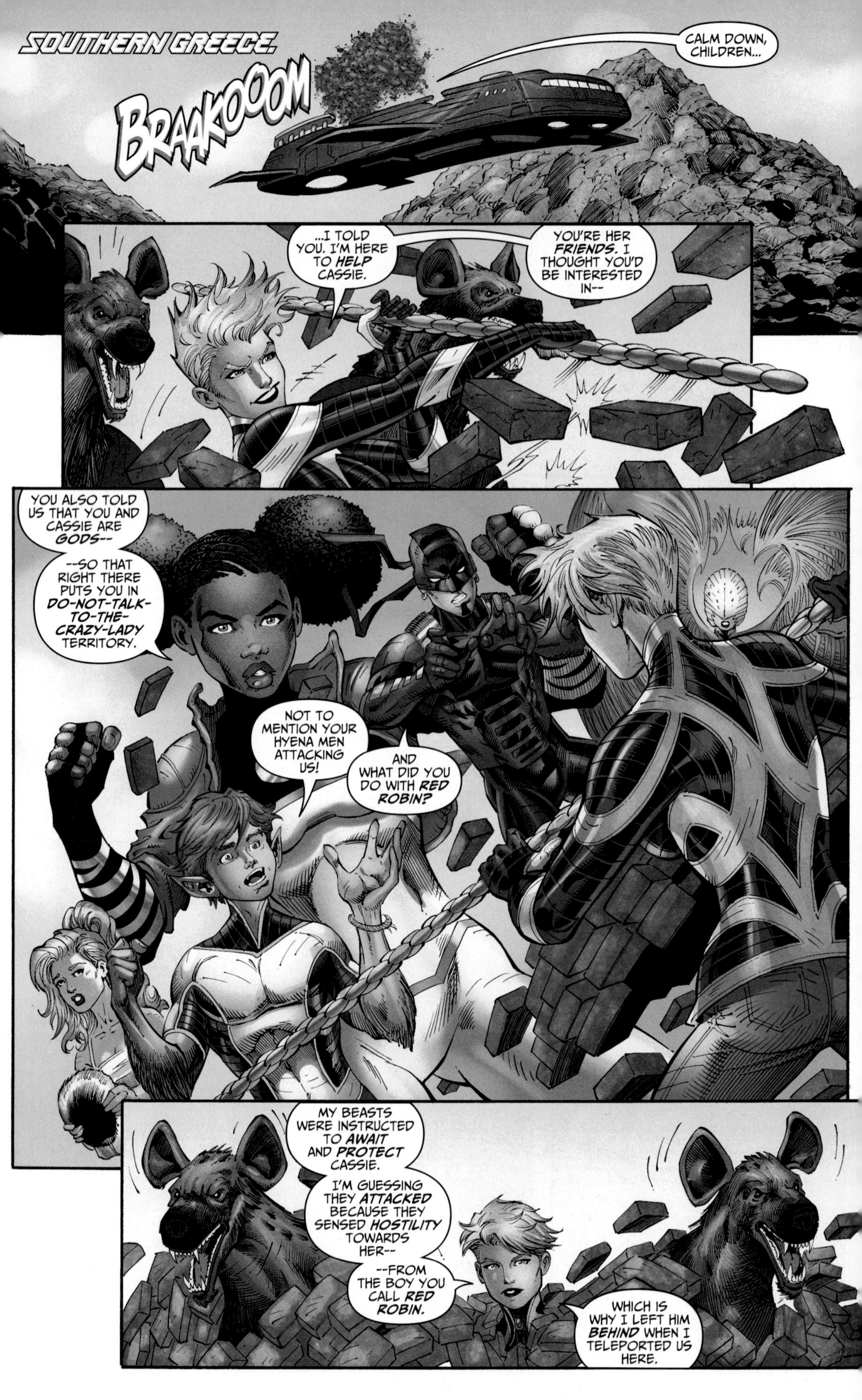
SOUTHERN GREECE.
CALM DOWN, CHILDREN...
BRAAKOOOM
...I TOLD YOU. I'M HERE TO HELP CASSIE.
YOU'RE HER FRIENDS. I THOUGHT YOU'D BE INTERESTED IN--
YOU ALSO TOLD US THAT YOU AND CASSIE ARE GODS--
--SO THAT RIGHT THERE PUTS YOU IN DO-NOT-TALK-TO-THE-CRAZY-LADY TERRITORY.
NOT TO MENTION YOUR HYENA MEN ATTACKING US!
AND WHAT DID YOU DO WITH RED ROBIN?
MY BEASTS WERE INSTRUCTED TO AWAIT AND PROTECT CASSIE.
I'M GUESSING THEY ATTACKED BECAUSE THEY SENSED HOSTILITY TOWARDS HER--
--FROM THE BOY YOU CALL RED ROBIN.
WHICH IS WHY I LEFT HIM BEHIND WHEN I TELEPORTED US HERE.

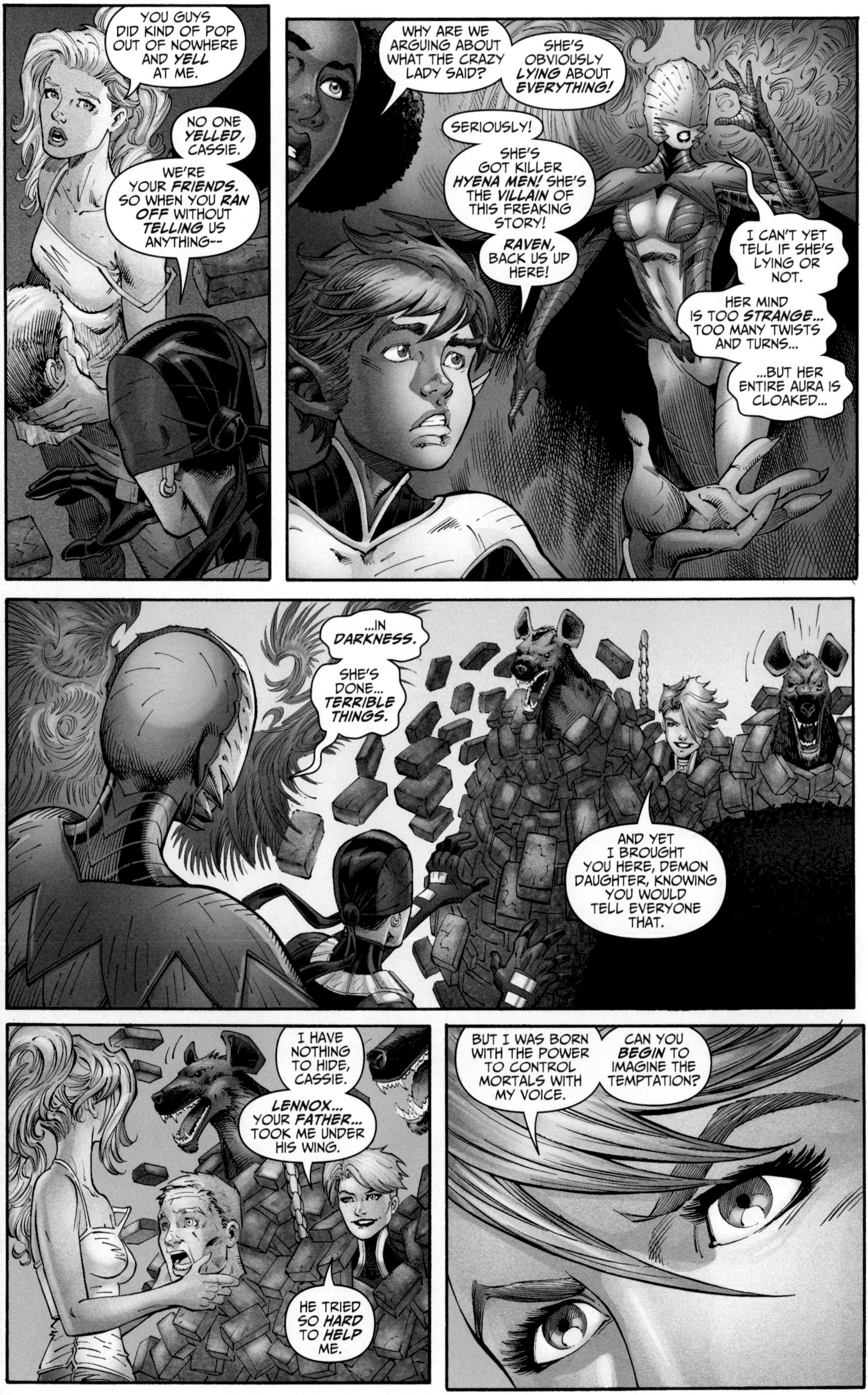

YOU GUYS DID KIND OF POP OUT OF NOWHERE AND YELL AT ME.
NO ONE YELLED, CASSIE.
WE'RE YOUR FRIENDS. SO WHEN YOU RAN OFF WITHOUT TELLING US ANYTHING--
WHY ARE WE ARGUING ABOUT WHAT THE CRAZY LADY SAID?
SHE'S OBVIOUSLY LYING ABOUT EVERYTHING!
SERIOUSLY!
SHE'S GOT KILLER HYENA MEN! SHE'S THE VILLAIN OF THIS FREAKING STORY!
RAVEN, BACK US UP HERE!
I CAN'T YET TELL IF SHE'S LYING OR NOT.
HER MIND IS TOO STRANGE... TOO MANY TWISTS AND TURNS...
...BUT HER ENTIRE AURA IS CLOAKED...
...IN DARKNESS.
SHE'S DONE... TERRIBLE THINGS.
AND YET I BROUGHT YOU HERE, DEMON DAUGHTER, KNOWING YOU WOULD TELL EVERYONE THAT.
I HAVE NOTHING TO HIDE, CASSIE.
LENNOX... YOUR FATHER... TOOK ME UNDER HIS WING.
HE TRIED SO HARD TO HELP ME.
BUT I WAS BORN WITH THE POWER TO CONTROL MORTALS WITH MY VOICE.
CAN YOU BEGIN TO IMAGINE THE TEMPTATION?

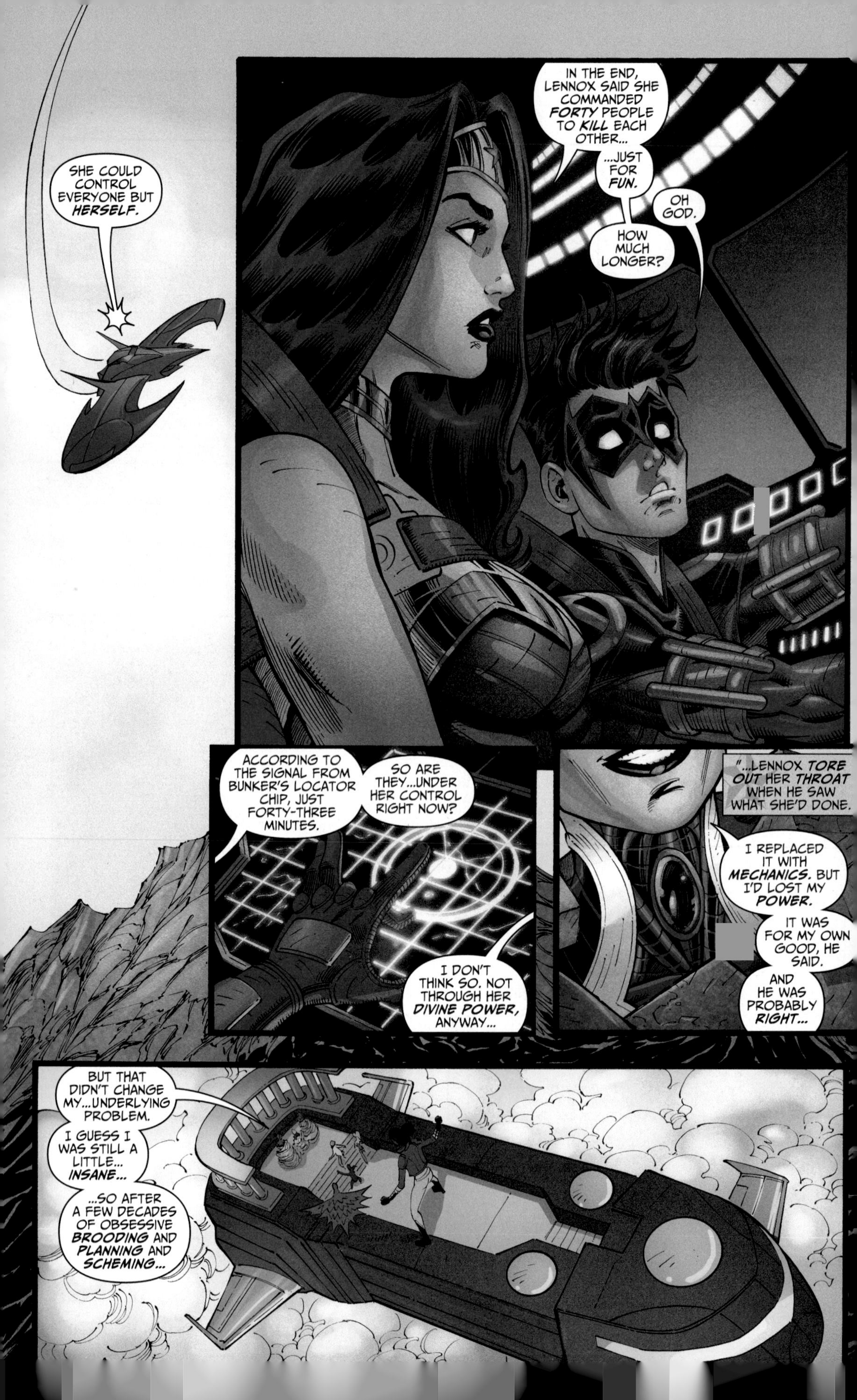
SHE COULD CONTROL EVERYONE BUT HERSELF.
IN THE END, LENNOX SAID SHE COMMANDED FORTY PEOPLE TO KILL EACH OTHER...
...JUST FOR FUN.
OH GOD.
HOW MUCH LONGER?
ACCORDING TO THE SIGNAL FROM BUNKER'S LOCATOR CHIP, JUST FORTY-THREE MINUTES.
SO ARE THEY...UNDER HER CONTROL RIGHT NOW?
I DON'T THINK SO. NOT THROUGH HER DIVINE POWER, ANYWAY...
"...LENNOX TORE OUT HER THROAT WHEN HE SAW WHAT SHE'D DONE.
I REPLACED IT WITH MECHANICS. BUT I'D LOST MY POWER.
IT WAS FOR MY OWN GOOD, HE SAID.
AND HE WAS PROBABLY RIGHT...
BUT THAT DIDN'T CHANGE MY...UNDERLYING PROBLEM.
I GUESS I WAS STILL A LITTLE... INSANE...
...SO AFTER A FEW DECADES OF OBSESSIVE BROODING AND PLANNING AND SCHEMING...

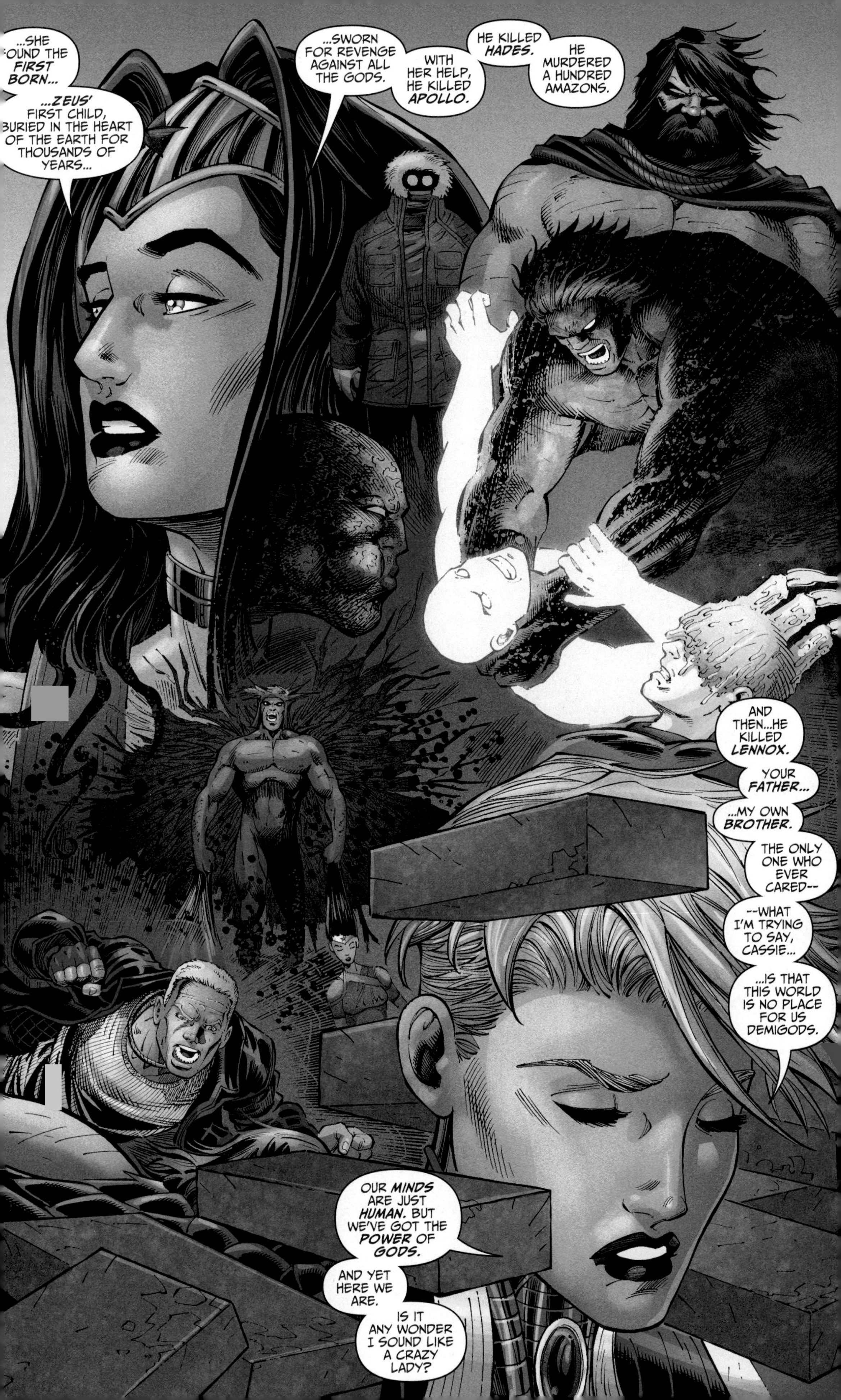
...SHE FOUND THE FIRST BORN...
...ZEUS' FIRST CHILD, BURIED IN THE HEART OF THE EARTH FOR THOUSANDS OF YEARS...
...SWORN FOR REVENGE AGAINST ALL THE GODS.
WITH HER HELP, HE KILLED APOLLO.
HE KILLED HADES.
HE MURDERED A HUNDRED AMAZONS.
AND THEN...HE KILLED LENNOX.
YOUR FATHER...
...MY OWN BROTHER.
THE ONLY ONE WHO EVER CARED--
--WHAT I'M TRYING TO SAY, CASSIE...
...IS THAT THIS WORLD IS NO PLACE FOR US DEMIGODS.
OUR MINDS ARE JUST HUMAN. BUT WE'VE GOT THE POWER OF GODS.
AND YET HERE WE ARE.
IS IT ANY WONDER I SOUND LIKE A CRAZY LADY?

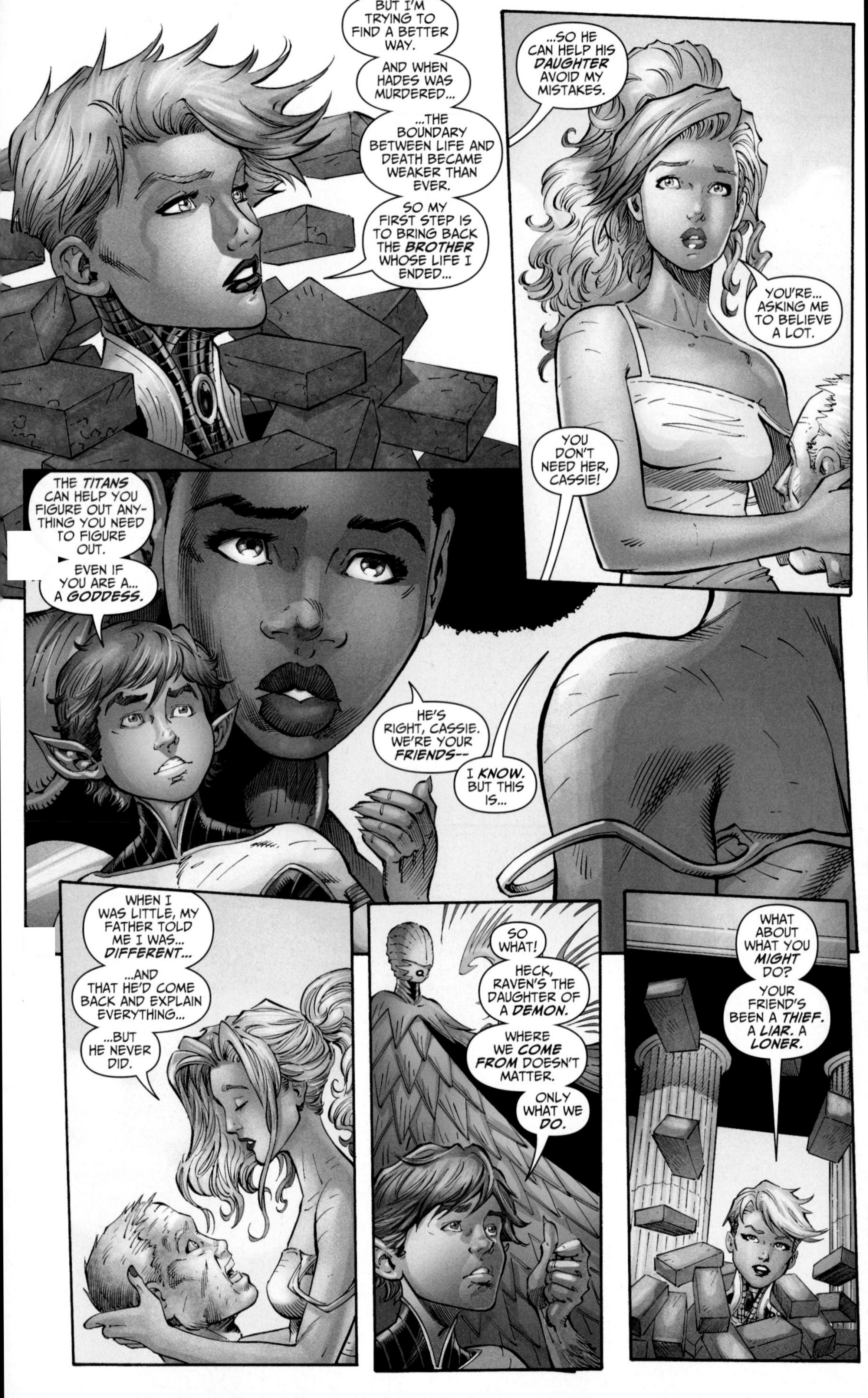

BUT I'M TRYING TO FIND A BETTER WAY.
AND WHEN HADES WAS MURDERED...
...THE BOUNDARY BETWEEN LIFE AND DEATH BECAME WEAKER THAN EVER.
SO MY FIRST STEP IS TO BRING BACK THE BROTHER WHOSE LIFE I ENDED...
...SO HE CAN HELP HIS DAUGHTER AVOID MY MISTAKES.
YOU'RE... ASKING ME TO BELIEVE A LOT.
YOU DON'T NEED HER, CASSIE!
THE TITANS CAN HELP YOU FIGURE OUT ANYTHING YOU NEED TO FIGURE OUT.
EVEN IF YOU ARE A... A GODDESS.
HE'S RIGHT, CASSIE. WE'RE YOUR FRIENDS--
I KNOW. BUT THIS IS...
WHEN I WAS LITTLE, MY FATHER TOLD ME I WAS... DIFFERENT...
...AND THAT HE'D COME BACK AND EXPLAIN EVERYTHING...
...BUT HE NEVER DID.
SO WHAT!
HECK, RAVEN'S THE DAUGHTER OF A DEMON.
WHERE WE COME FROM DOESN'T MATTER.
ONLY WHAT WE DO.
WHAT ABOUT WHAT YOU MIGHT DO?
YOUR FRIEND'S BEEN A THIEF. A LIAR. A LONER.

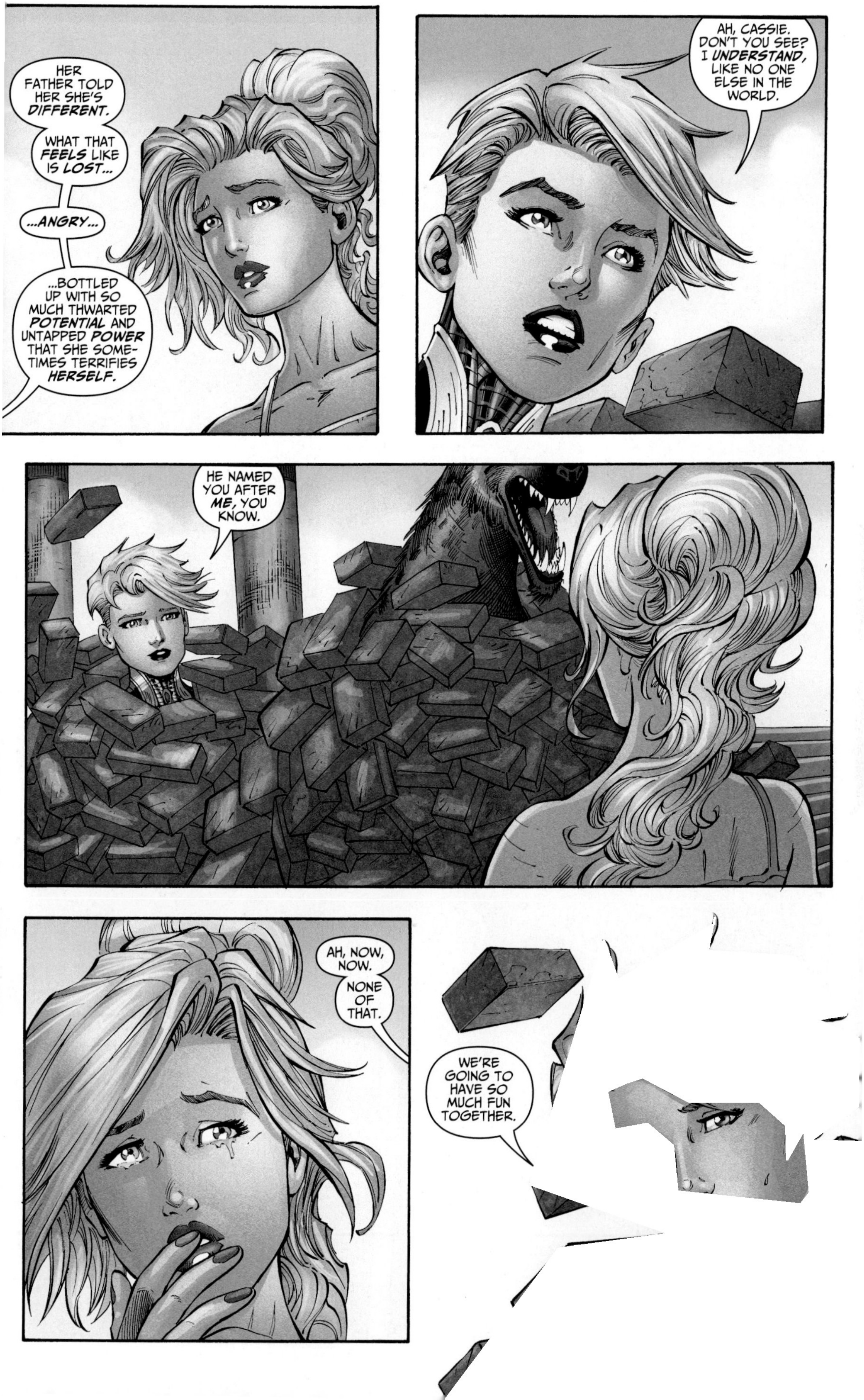

HER FATHER TOLD HER SHE'S DIFFERENT.
WHAT THAT FEELS LIKE IS LOST...
...ANGRY...
...BOTTLED UP WITH SO MUCH THWARTED POTENTIAL AND UNTAPPED POWER THAT SHE SOMETIMES TERRIFIES HERSELF.
AH, CASSIE. DON'T YOU SEE? I UNDERSTAND, LIKE NO ONE ELSE IN THE WORLD.
HE NAMED YOU AFTER ME, YOU KNOW.
AH, NOW, NOW.
NONE OF THAT.
WE'RE GOING TO HAVE SO MUCH FUN TOGETHER.

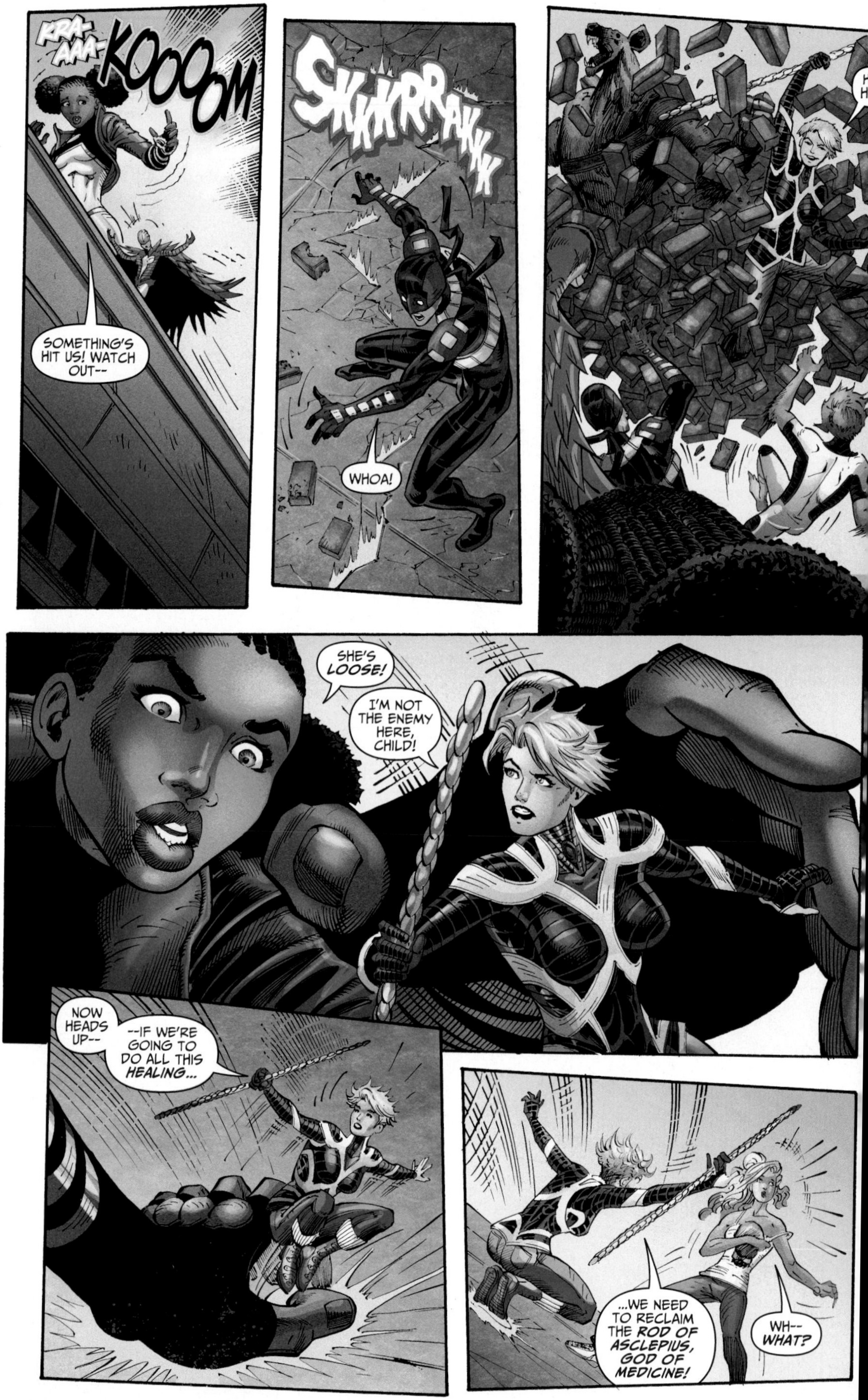
KRA-AAA-KOOOOOM
SOMETHING'S HIT US! WATCH OUT--
SKKKRRAKKK
WHOA!
SHE'S LOOSE!
I'M NOT THE ENEMY HERE, CHILD!
NOW HEADS UP--
--IF WE'RE GOING TO DO ALL THIS HEALING...
...WE NEED TO RECLAIM THE ROD OF ASCLEPIUS, GOD OF MEDICINE!
WH-- WHAT?

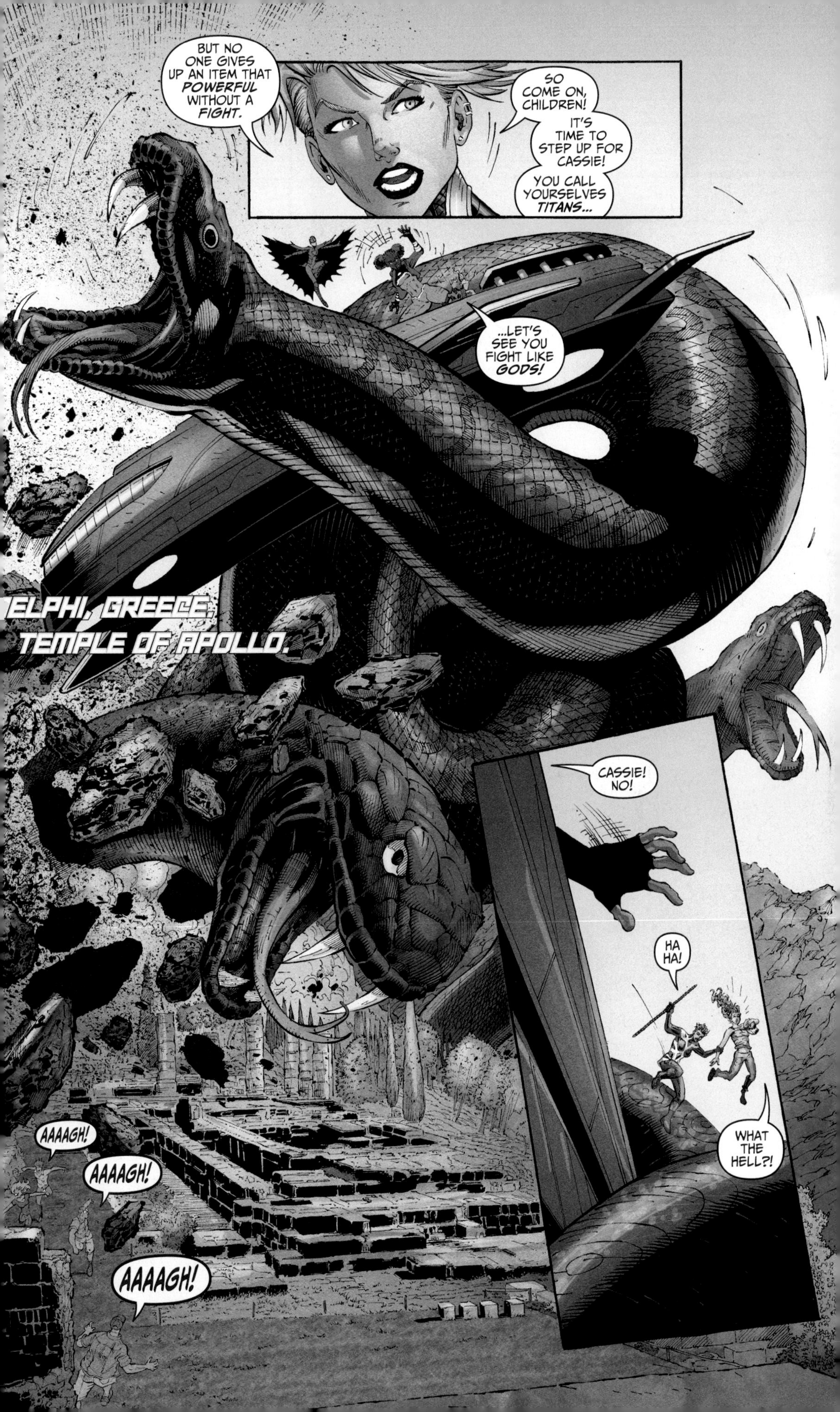

BUT NO ONE GIVES UP AN ITEM THAT POWERFUL WITHOUT A FIGHT.
SO COME ON, CHILDREN!
IT'S TIME TO STEP UP FOR CASSIE!
YOU CALL YOURSELVES TITANS...
...LET'S SEE YOU FIGHT LIKE GODS!
ELPHI, GREECE. TEMPLE OF APOLLO.
CASSIE! NO!
HA HA!
WHAT THE HELL?!
AAAAGH!
AAAAGH!
AAAAGH!

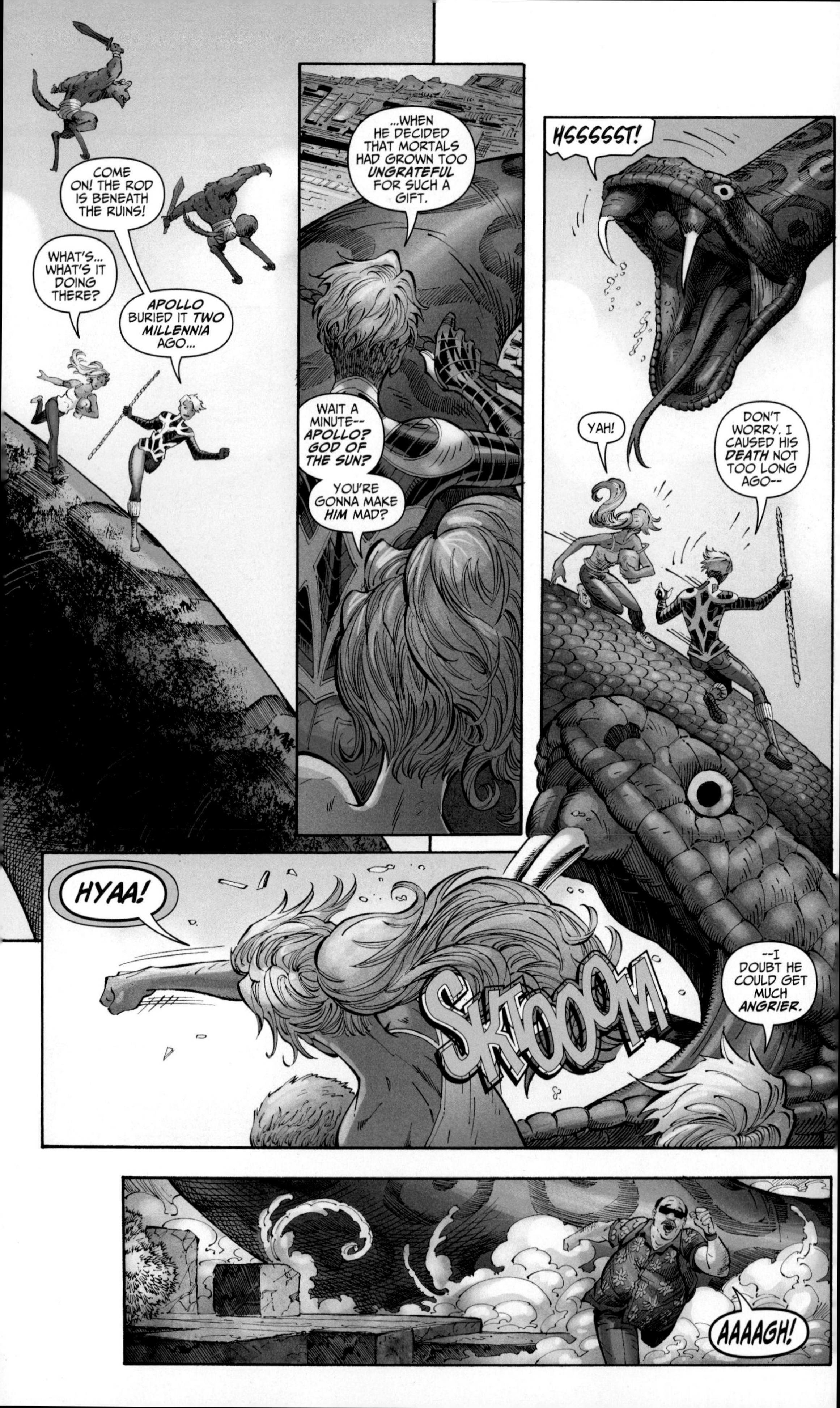
COME ON! THE ROD IS BENEATH THE RUINS!
WHAT'S... WHAT'S IT DOING THERE?
APOLLO BURIED IT TWO MILLENNIA AGO...
...WHEN HE DECIDED THAT MORTALS HAD GROWN TOO UNGRATEFUL FOR SUCH A GIFT.
WAIT A MINUTE-- APOLLO? GOD OF THE SUN?
YOU'RE GONNA MAKE HIM MAD?
HSSSSST!
YAH!
DON'T WORRY. I CAUSED HIS DEATH NOT TOO LONG AGO--
HYAA!
SKTOOOM
--I DOUBT HE COULD GET MUCH ANGRIER.
AAAAGH!

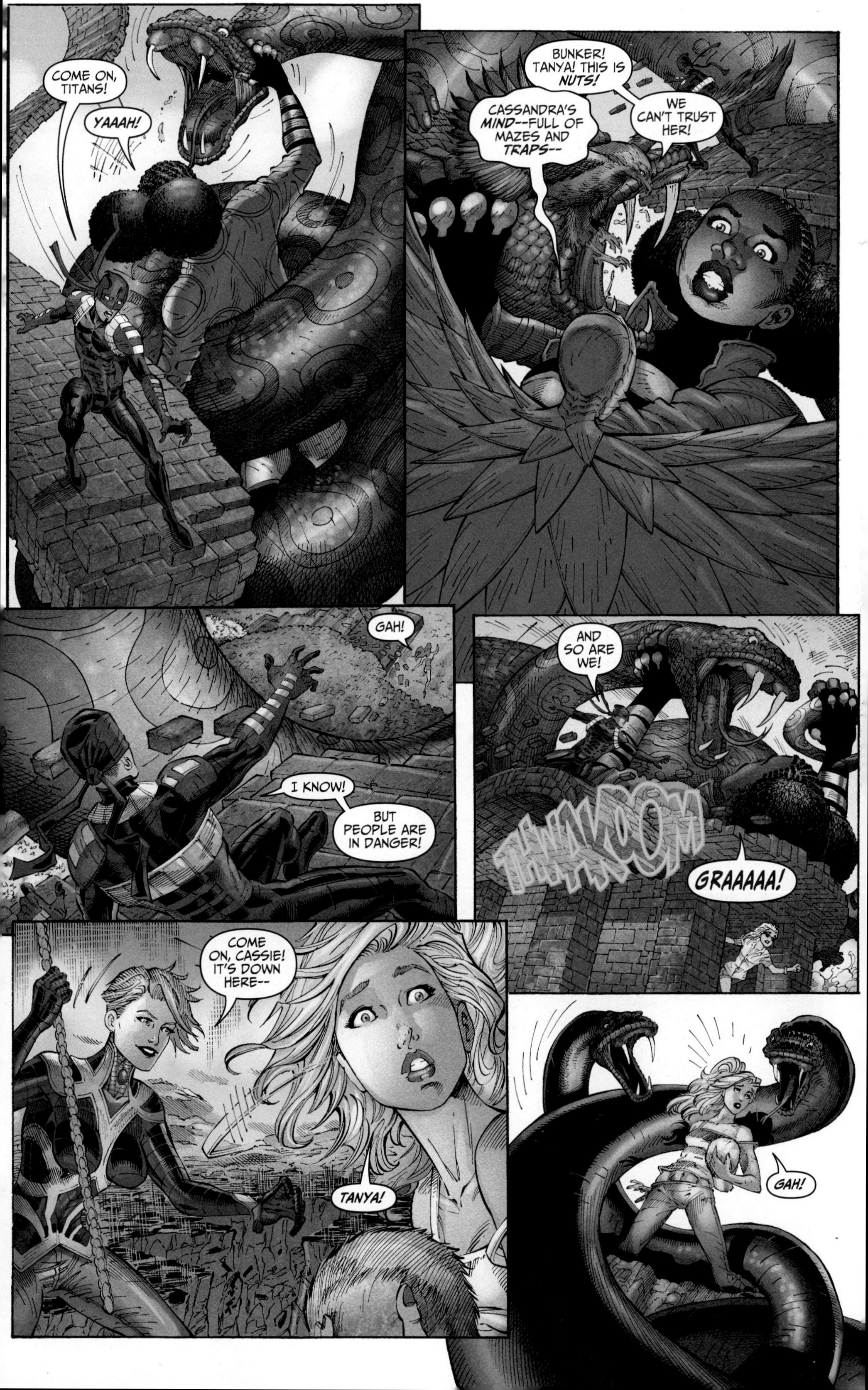
COME ON, TITANS!
YAAAH!
BUNKER! TANYA! THIS IS NUTS!
CASSANDRA'S MIND--FULL OF MAZES AND TRAPS--
WE CAN'T TRUST HER!
GAH!
I KNOW!
BUT PEOPLE ARE IN DANGER!
AND SO ARE WE!
THWOOM
GRAAAAA!
COME ON, CASSIE! IT'S DOWN HERE--
TANYA!
GAH!

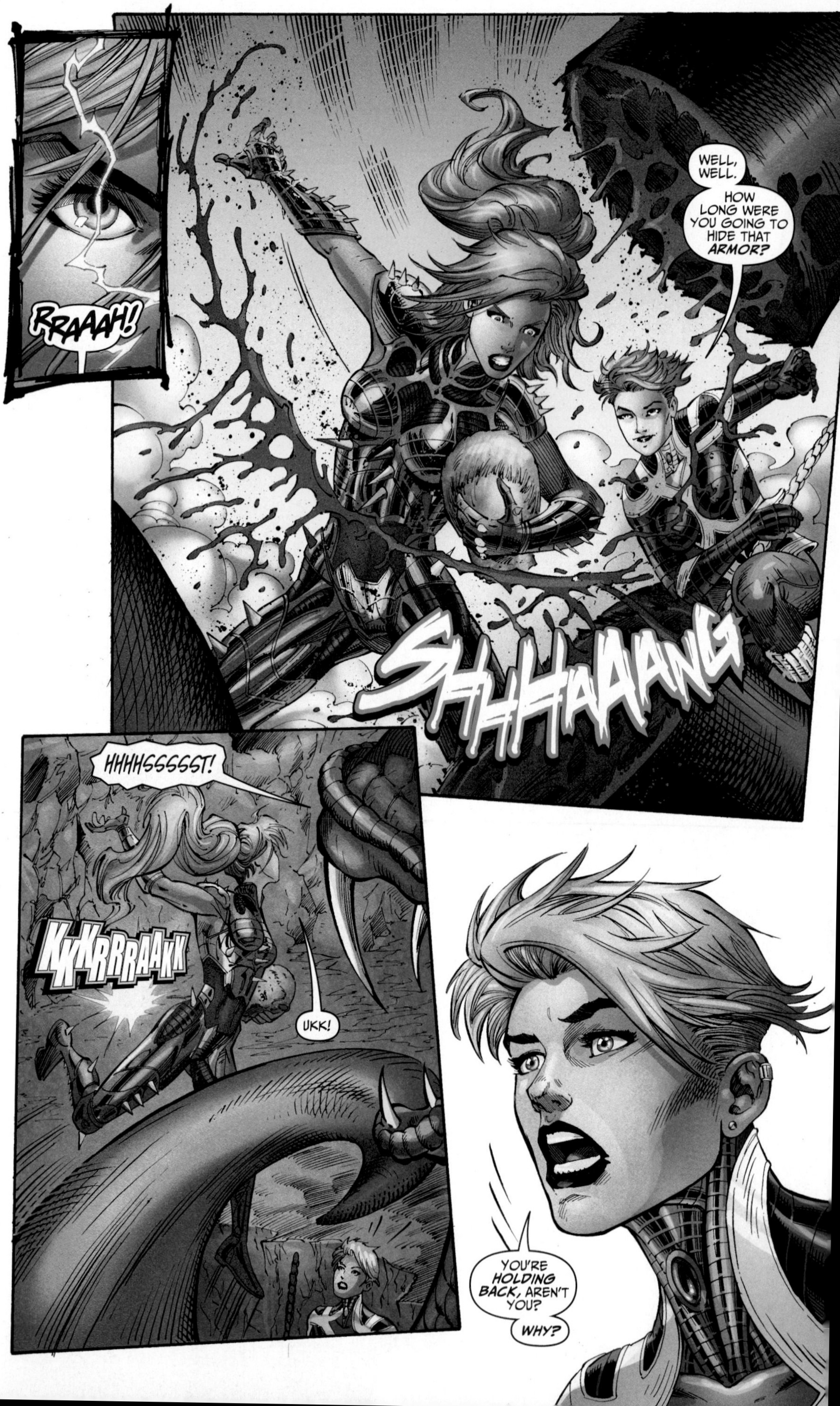

RRAAAH!
WELL, WELL.
HOW LONG WERE YOU GOING TO HIDE THAT ARMOR?
SHHHAAANG
HHHHSSSSST!
KKKRRRAAKK
UKK!
YOU'RE HOLDING BACK, AREN'T YOU?
WHY?

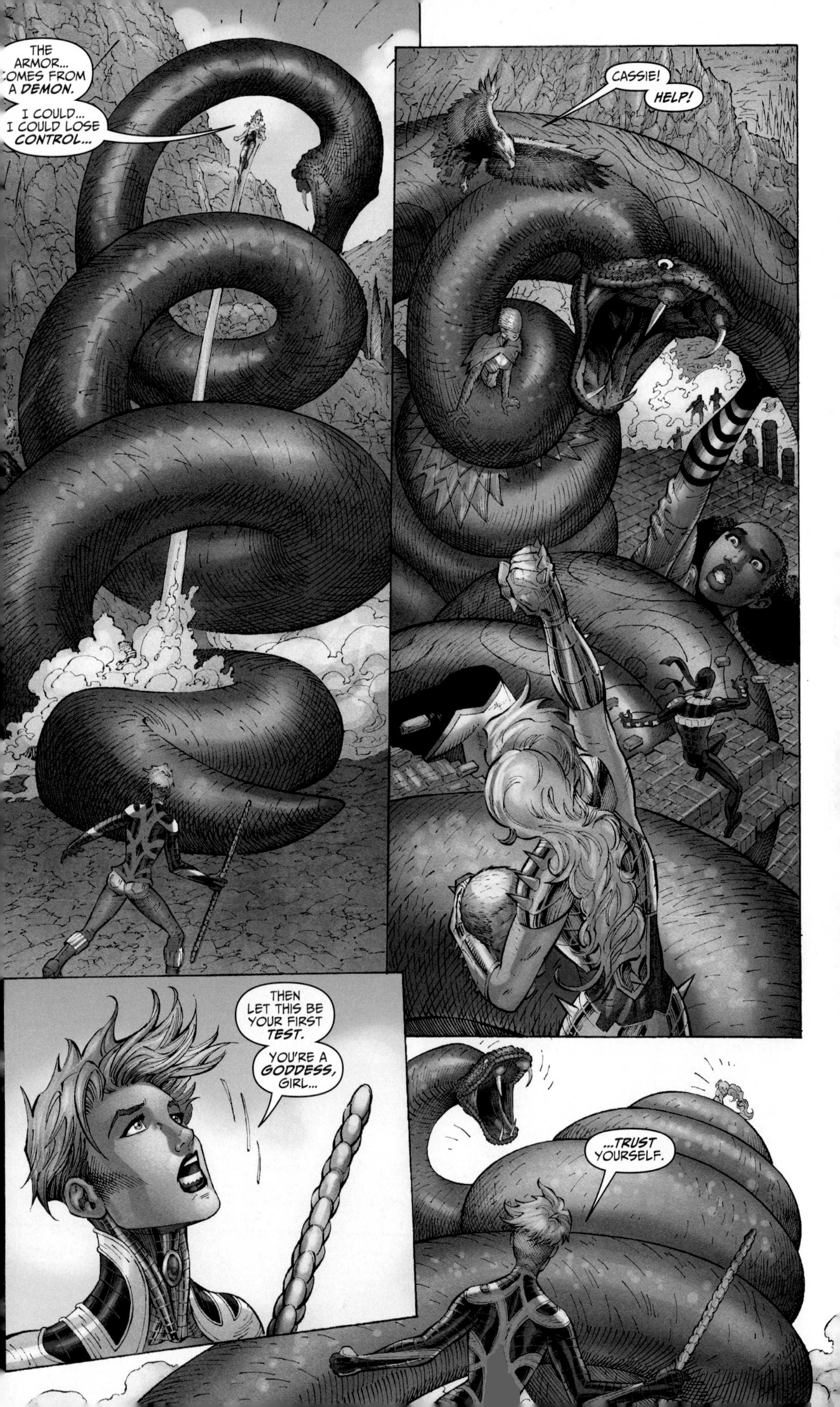

THE ARMOR... COMES FROM A DEMON.
I COULD... I COULD LOSE CONTROL...
CASSIE! HELP!
THEN LET THIS BE YOUR FIRST TEST.
YOU'RE A GODDESS, GIRL...
...TRUST YOURSELF.

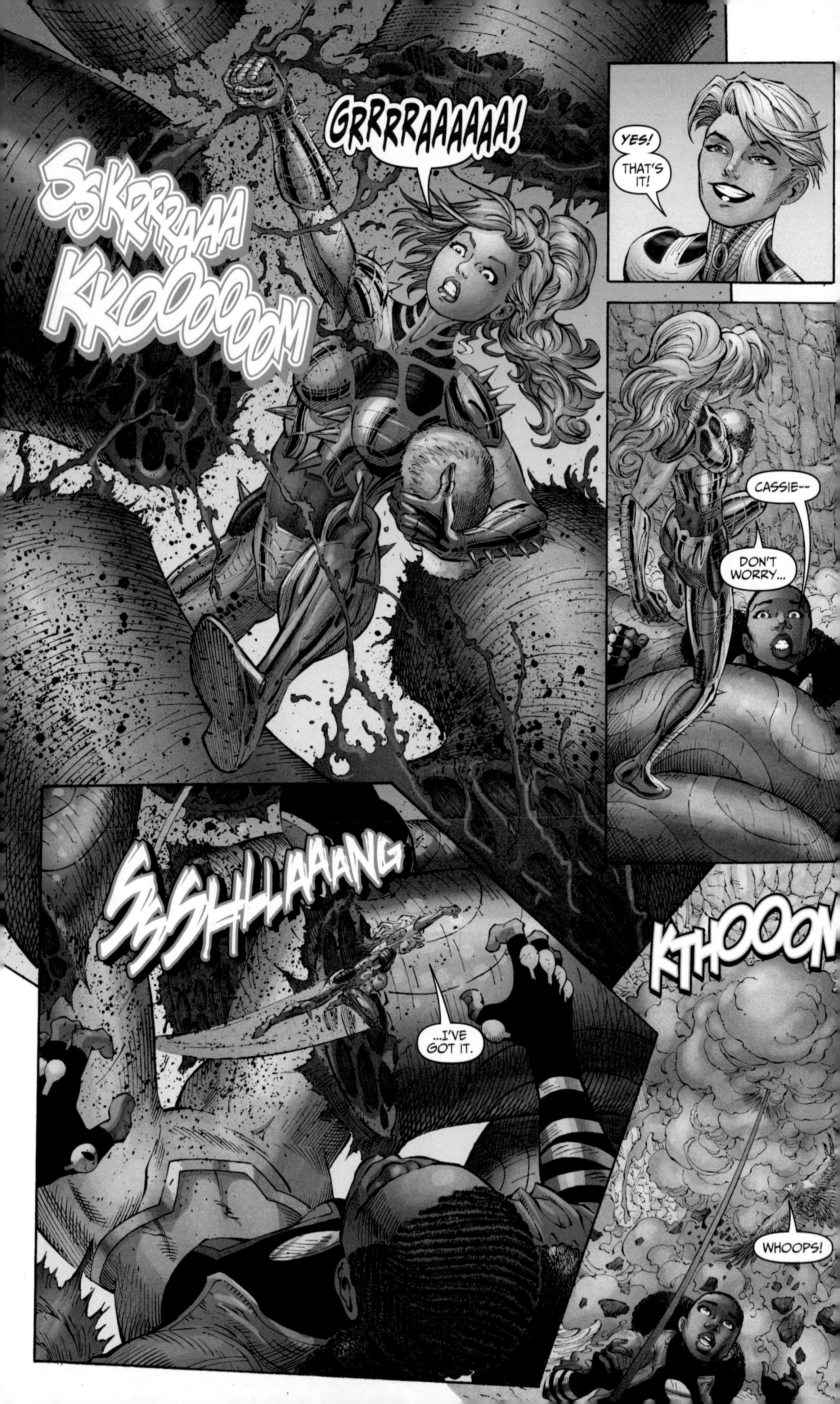
SSKRRRAAA
KKOOOOOOOM
GRRRRAAAAAA!
YES!
THAT'S IT!
CASSIE--
DON'T WORRY...
SSSHLLAAANG
...I'VE GOT IT.
KTHOOOM
WHOOPS!

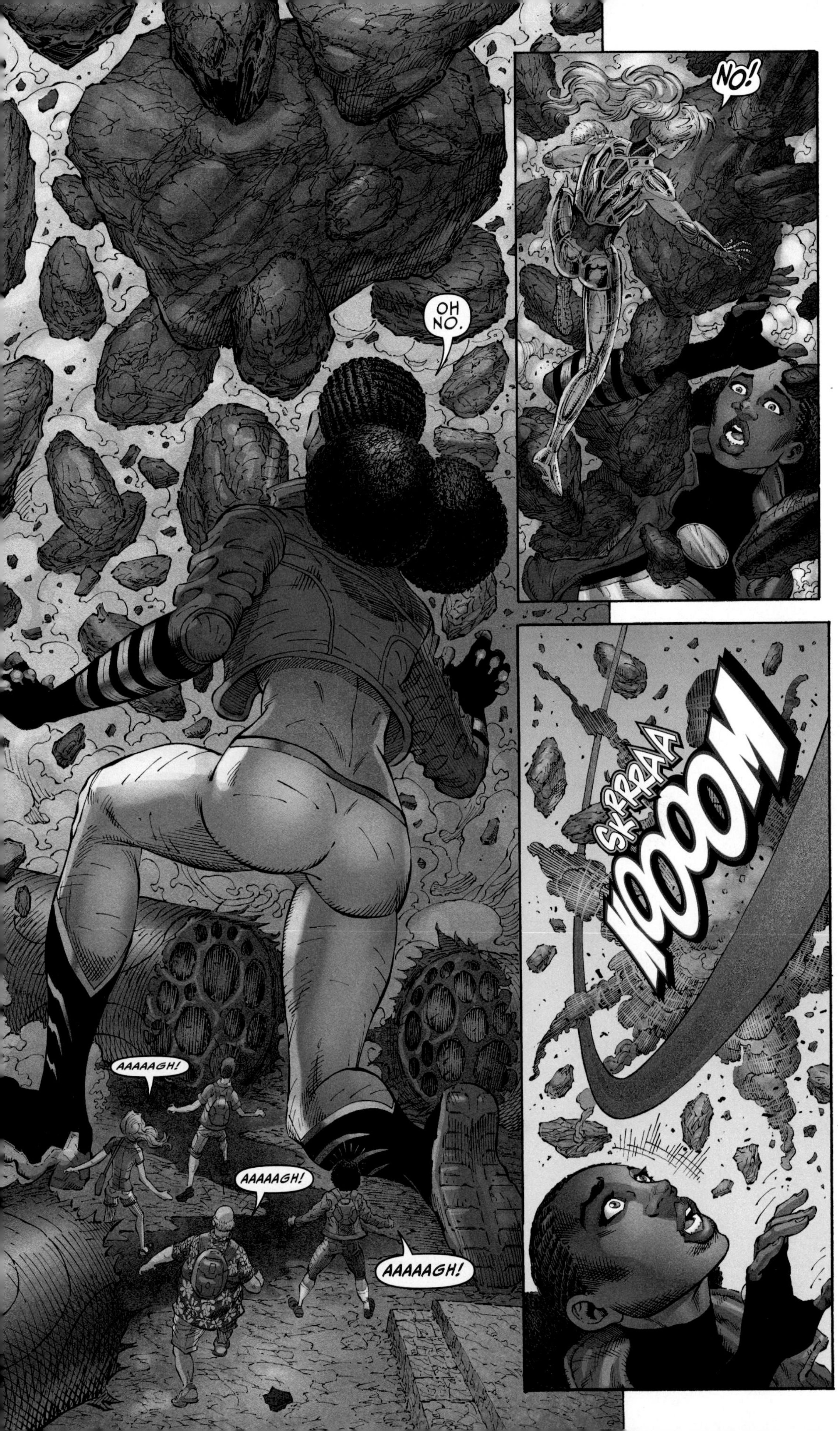
OH NO.
AAAAAGH!
AAAAAGH!
AAAAAGH!
NO!
SKRRAA
VOOOOM

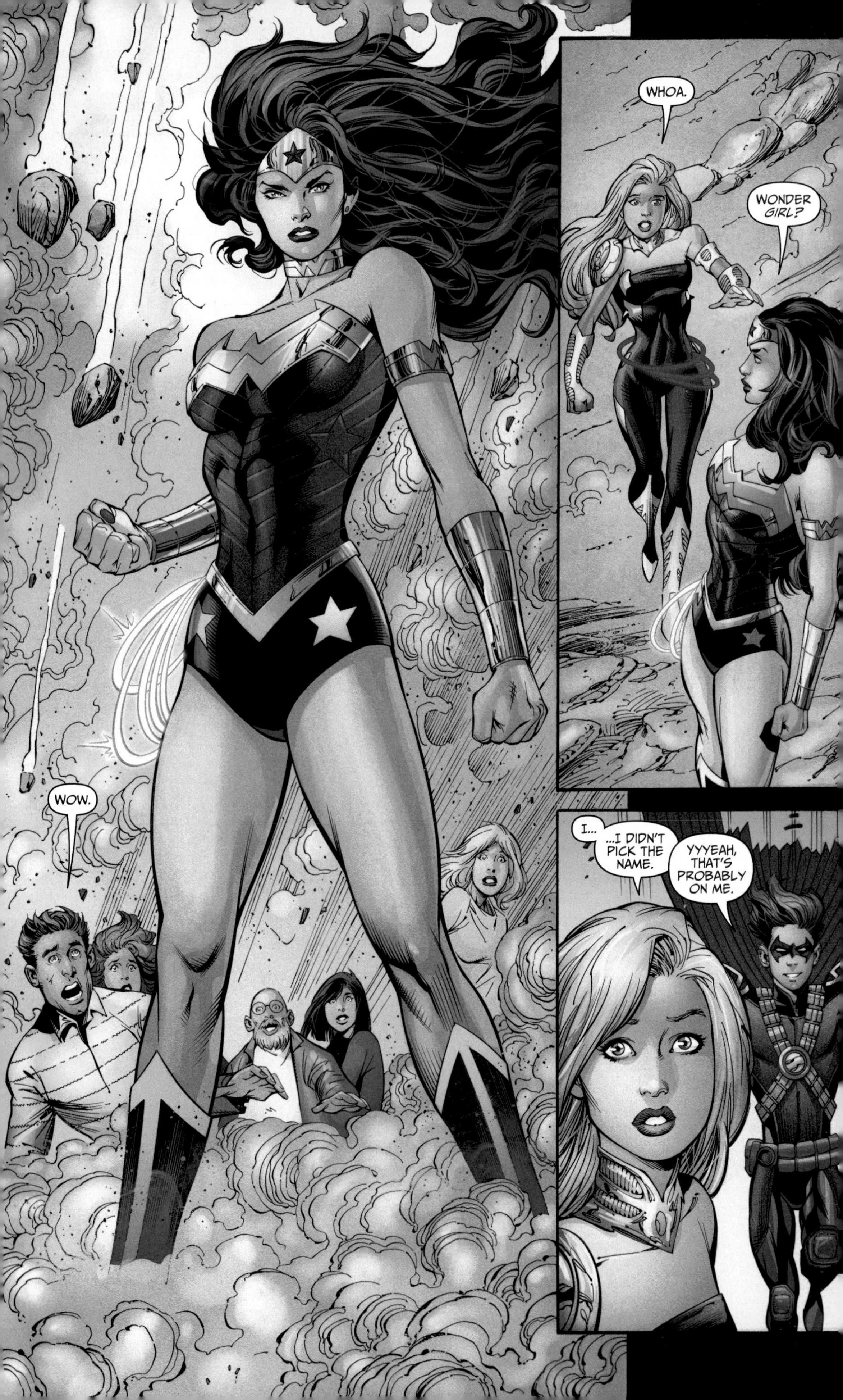
WOW.
WHOA.
WONDER GIRL?
I...
...I DIDN'T PICK THE NAME.
YYYEAH, THAT'S PROBABLY ON ME.

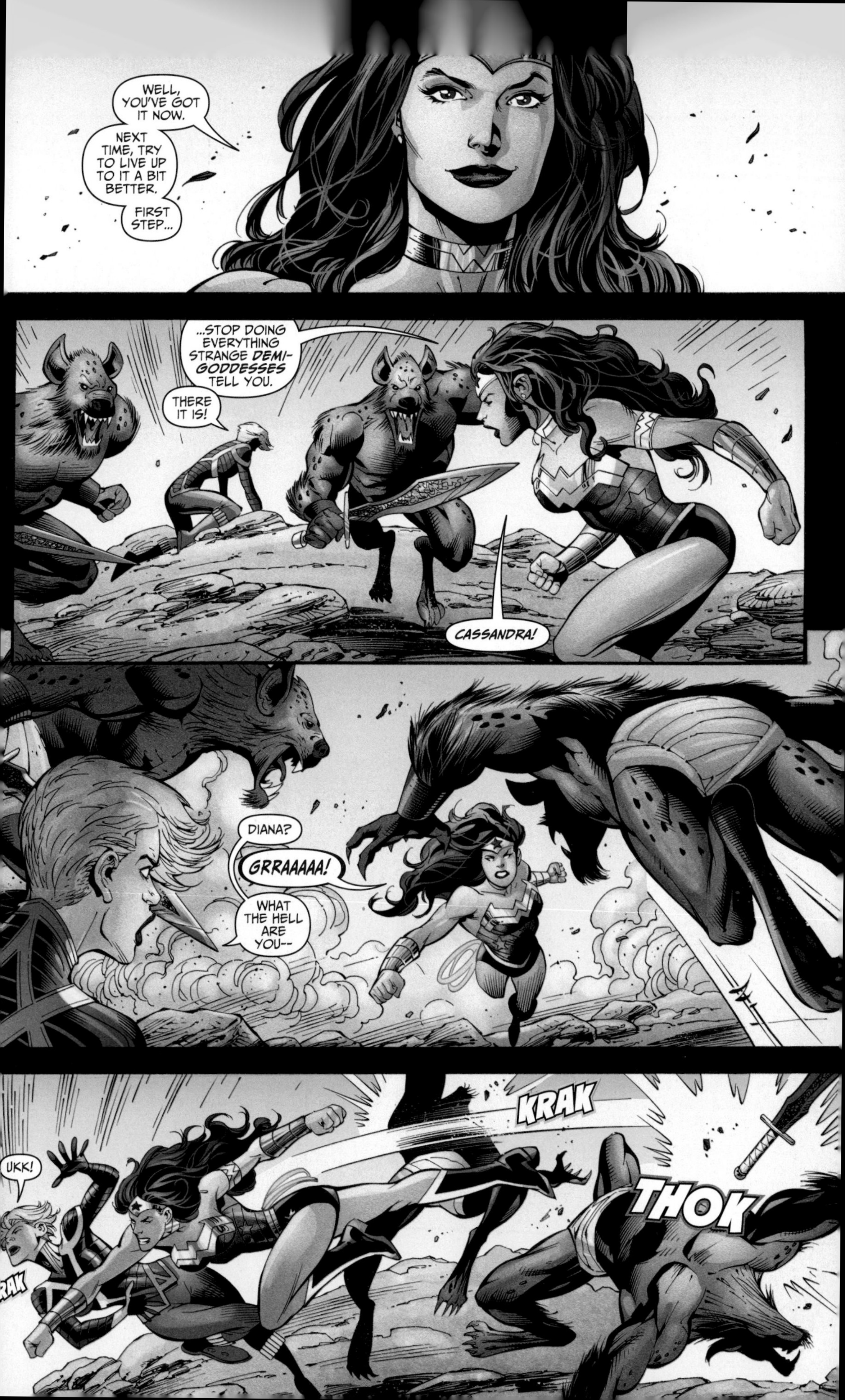

WELL, YOU'VE GOT IT NOW.
NEXT TIME, TRY TO LIVE UP TO IT A BIT BETTER.
FIRST STEP...
...STOP DOING EVERYTHING STRANGE DEMI-GODDESSES TELL YOU.
THERE IT IS!
CASSANDRA!
DIANA?
GRRAAAAA!
WHAT THE HELL ARE YOU--
KRAK
UKK!
THOK

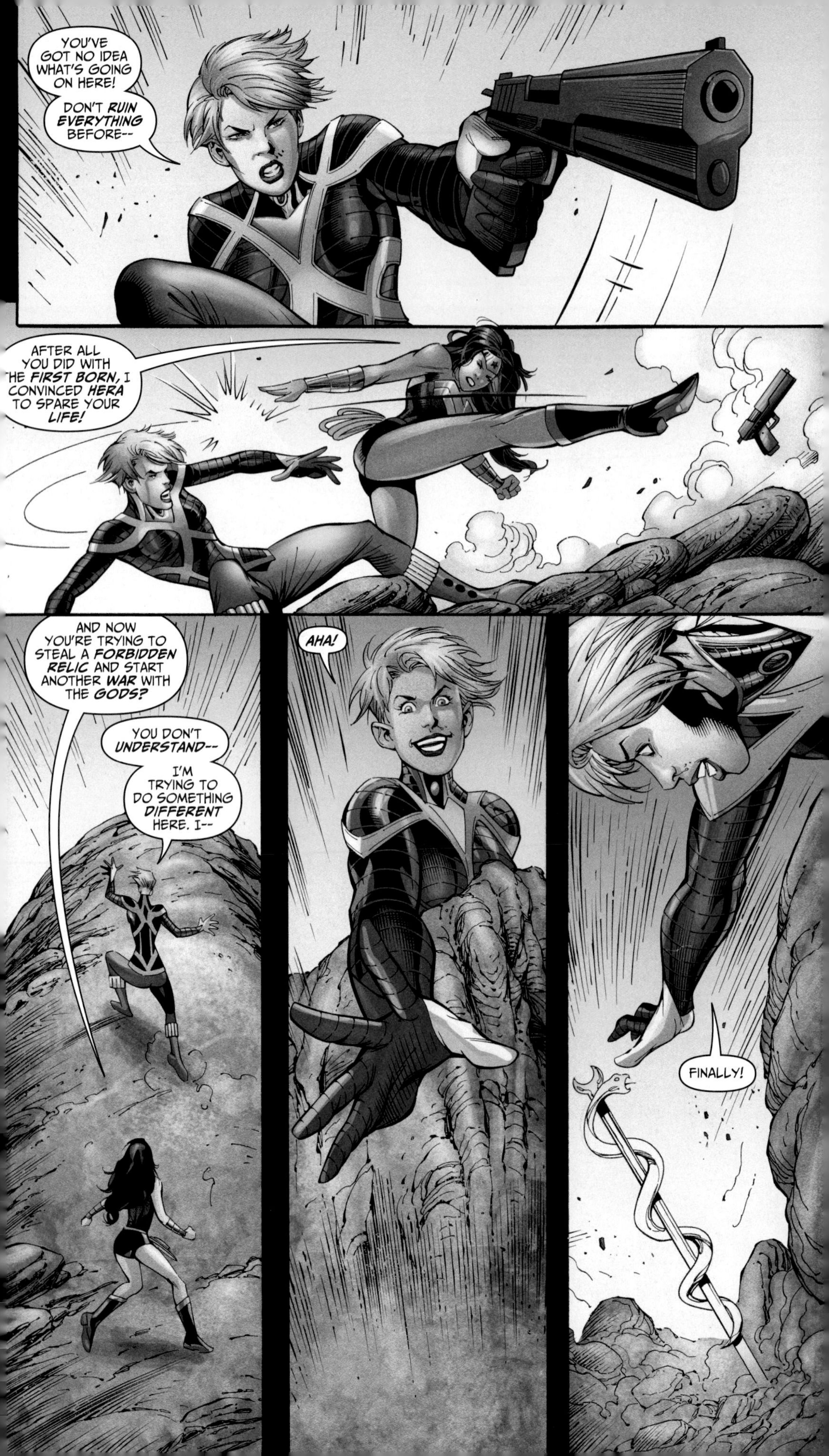
YOU'VE GOT NO IDEA WHAT'S GOING ON HERE!
DON'T RUIN EVERYTHING BEFORE--
AFTER ALL YOU DID WITH THE FIRST BORN, I CONVINCED HERA TO SPARE YOUR LIFE!
AND NOW YOU'RE TRYING TO STEAL A FORBIDDEN RELIC AND START ANOTHER WAR WITH THE GODS?
YOU DON'T UNDERSTAND--
I'M TRYING TO DO SOMETHING DIFFERENT HERE. I--
AHA!
FINALLY!

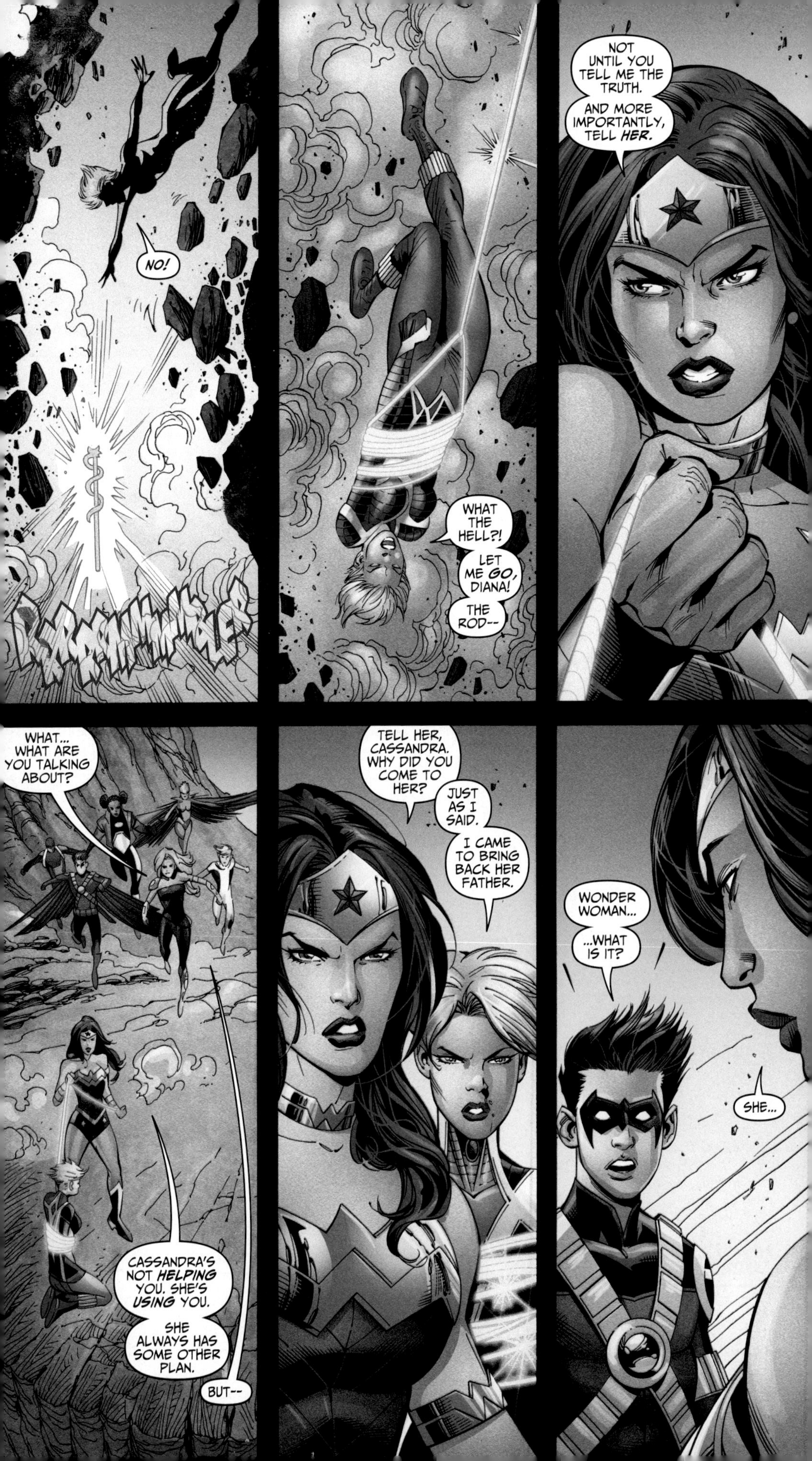
NO!
WHAT THE HELL?!
LET ME GO, DIANA!
THE ROD--
NOT UNTIL YOU TELL ME THE TRUTH.
AND MORE IMPORTANTLY, TELL HER.
WHAT... WHAT ARE YOU TALKING ABOUT?
CASSANDRA'S NOT HELPING YOU. SHE'S USING YOU.
SHE ALWAYS HAS SOME OTHER PLAN.
BUT--
TELL HER, CASSANDRA. WHY DID YOU COME TO HER?
JUST AS I SAID.
I CAME TO BRING BACK HER FATHER.
WONDER WOMAN...
...WHAT IS IT?
SHE...

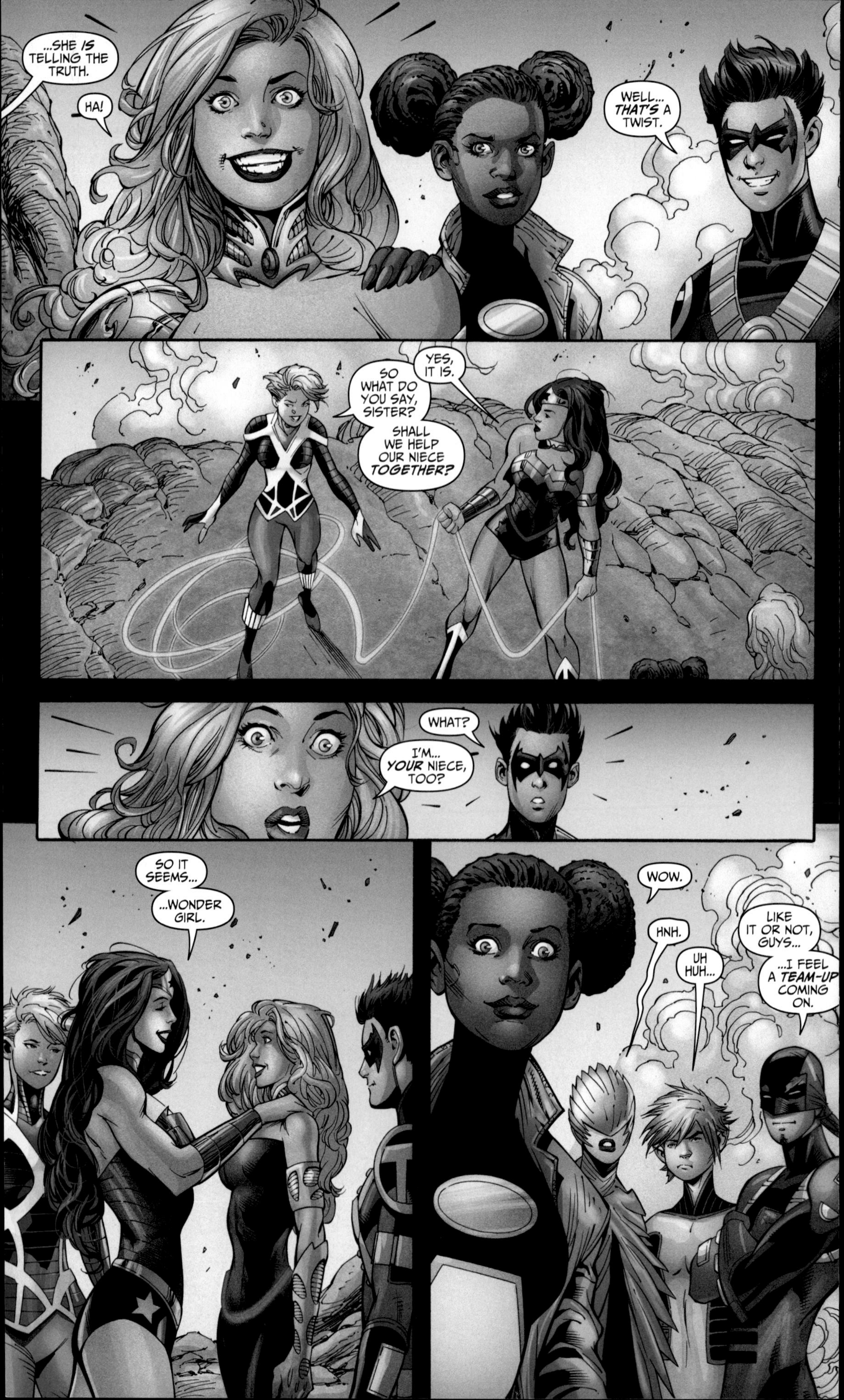

...SHE IS TELLING THE TRUTH.
HA!
WELL... THAT'S A TWIST.
YES, IT IS.
SO WHAT DO YOU SAY, SISTER?
SHALL WE HELP OUR NIECE TOGETHER?
WHAT?
I'M... YOUR NIECE, TOO?
SO IT SEEMS...
...WONDER GIRL.
WOW.
HNH.
UH HUH...
LIKE IT OR NOT, GUYS...
...I FEEL A TEAM-UP COMING ON.

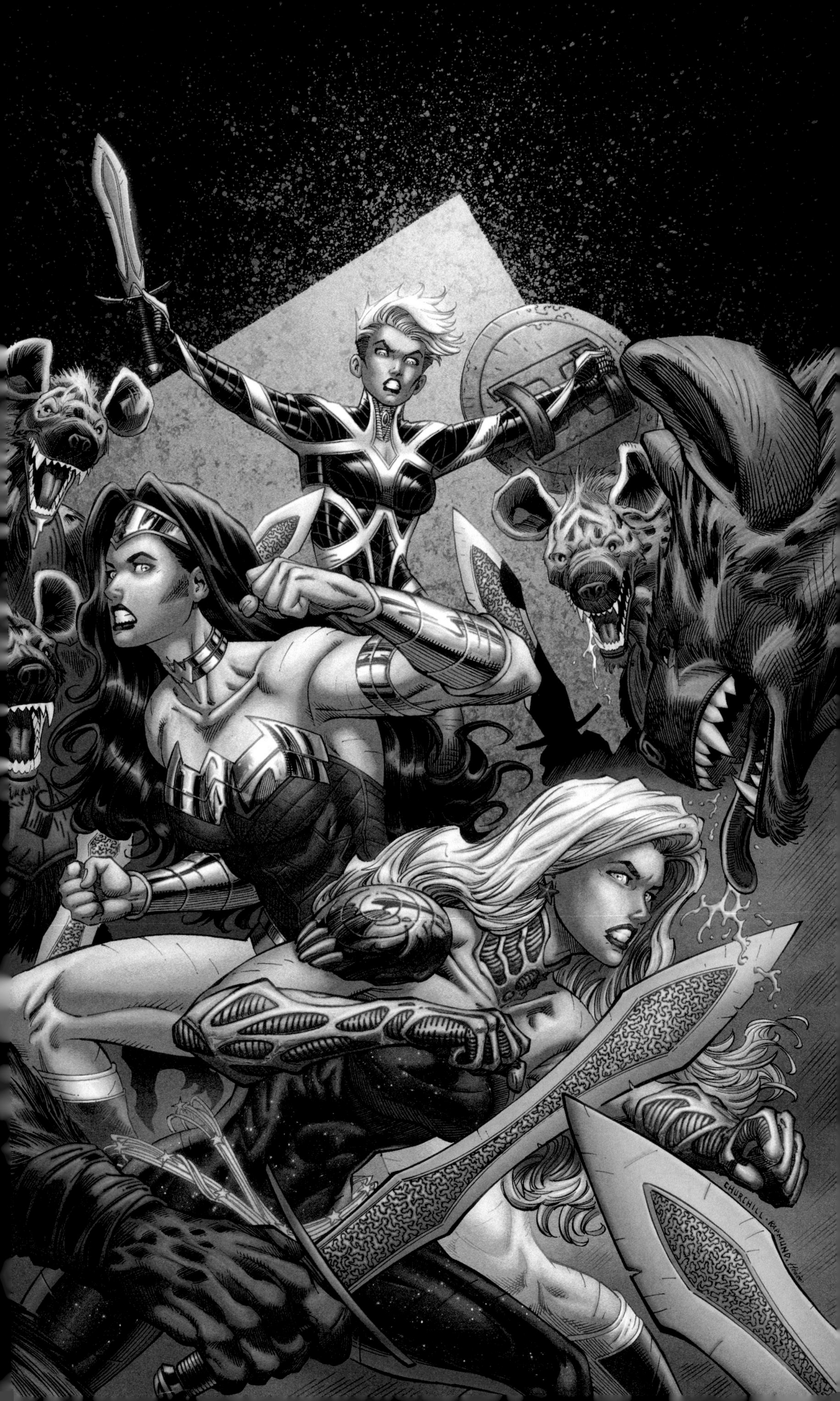

WHO IS WONDER GIRL? PART THREE

GREG PAK writer IAN CHURCHILL ALVARO MARTINEZ pencillers NORM RAPMUND RAUL FERNANDEZ inkers TONY AVIÑA colorist COREY BREEN letterer
cover art by IAN CHURCHILL & ANDREW DALHOUSE

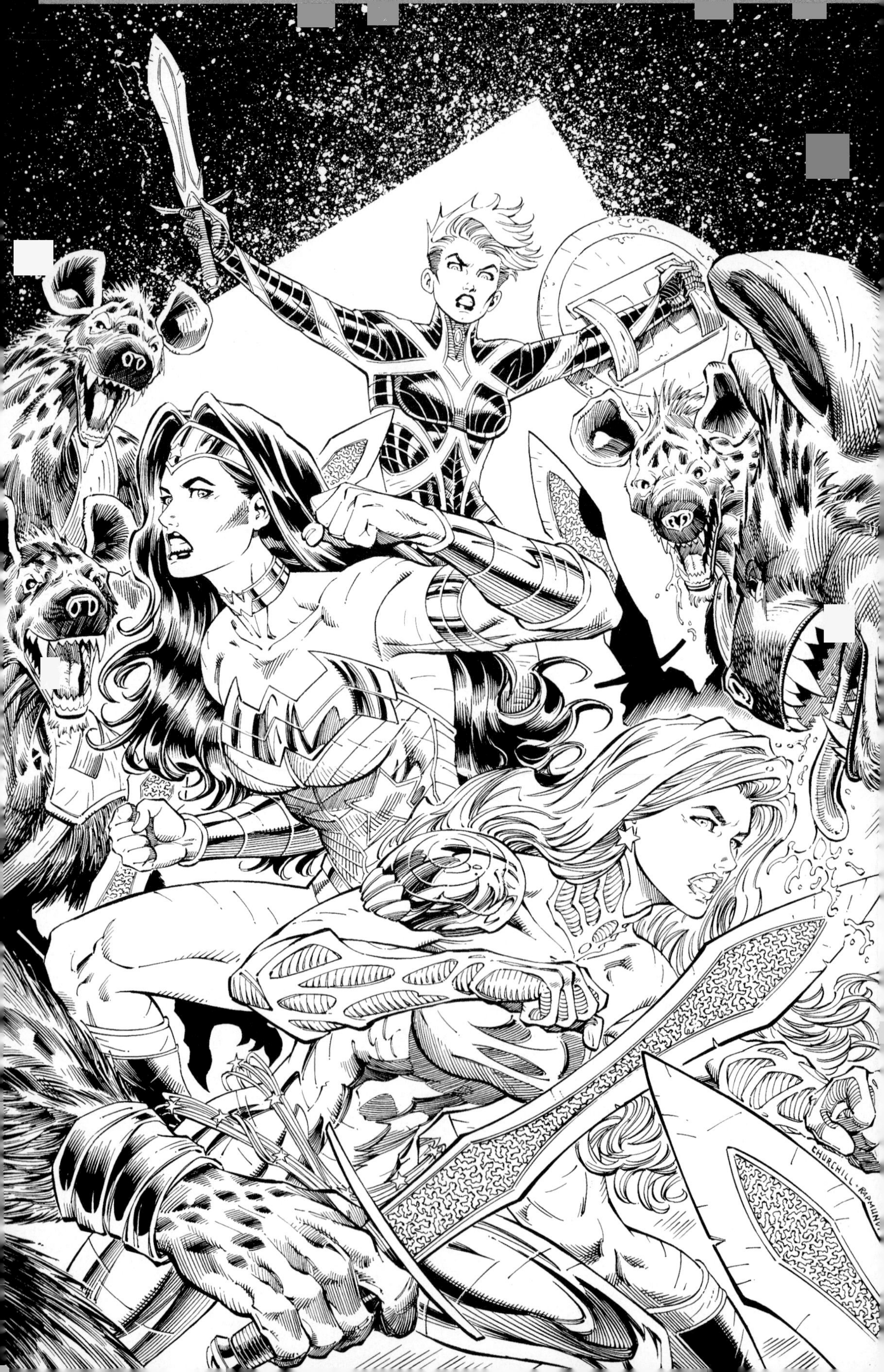

CHURCHILL - RAPMUND

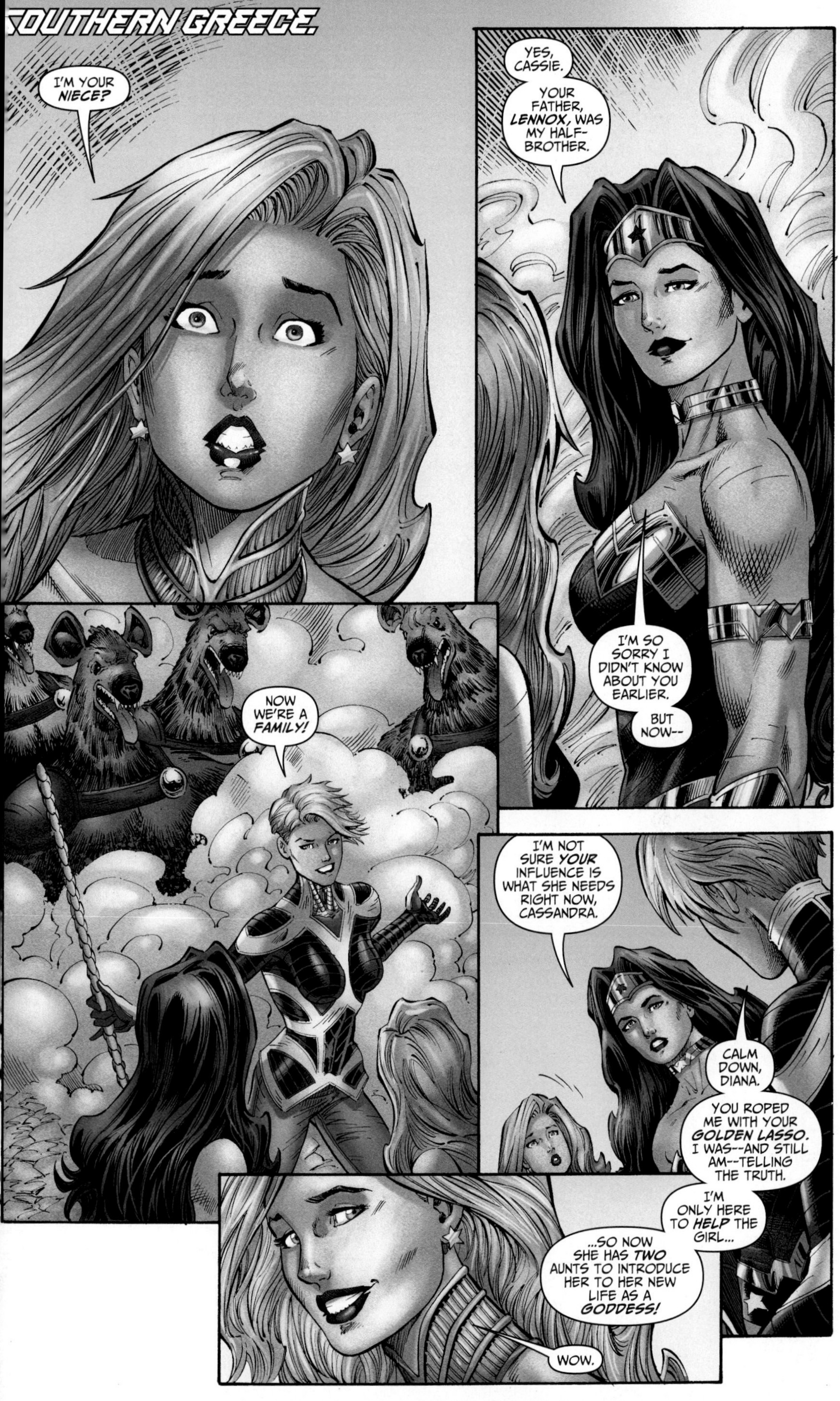

SOUTHERN GREECE.
I'M YOUR NIECE?
YES, CASSIE.
YOUR FATHER, LENNOX, WAS MY HALF-BROTHER.
I'M SO SORRY I DIDN'T KNOW ABOUT YOU EARLIER.
BUT NOW--
NOW WE'RE A FAMILY!
I'M NOT SURE YOUR INFLUENCE IS WHAT SHE NEEDS RIGHT NOW, CASSANDRA.
CALM DOWN, DIANA.
YOU ROPED ME WITH YOUR GOLDEN LASSO. I WAS--AND STILL AM--TELLING THE TRUTH.
I'M ONLY HERE TO HELP THE GIRL...
...SO NOW SHE HAS TWO AUNTS TO INTRODUCE HER TO HER NEW LIFE AS A GODDESS!
WOW.

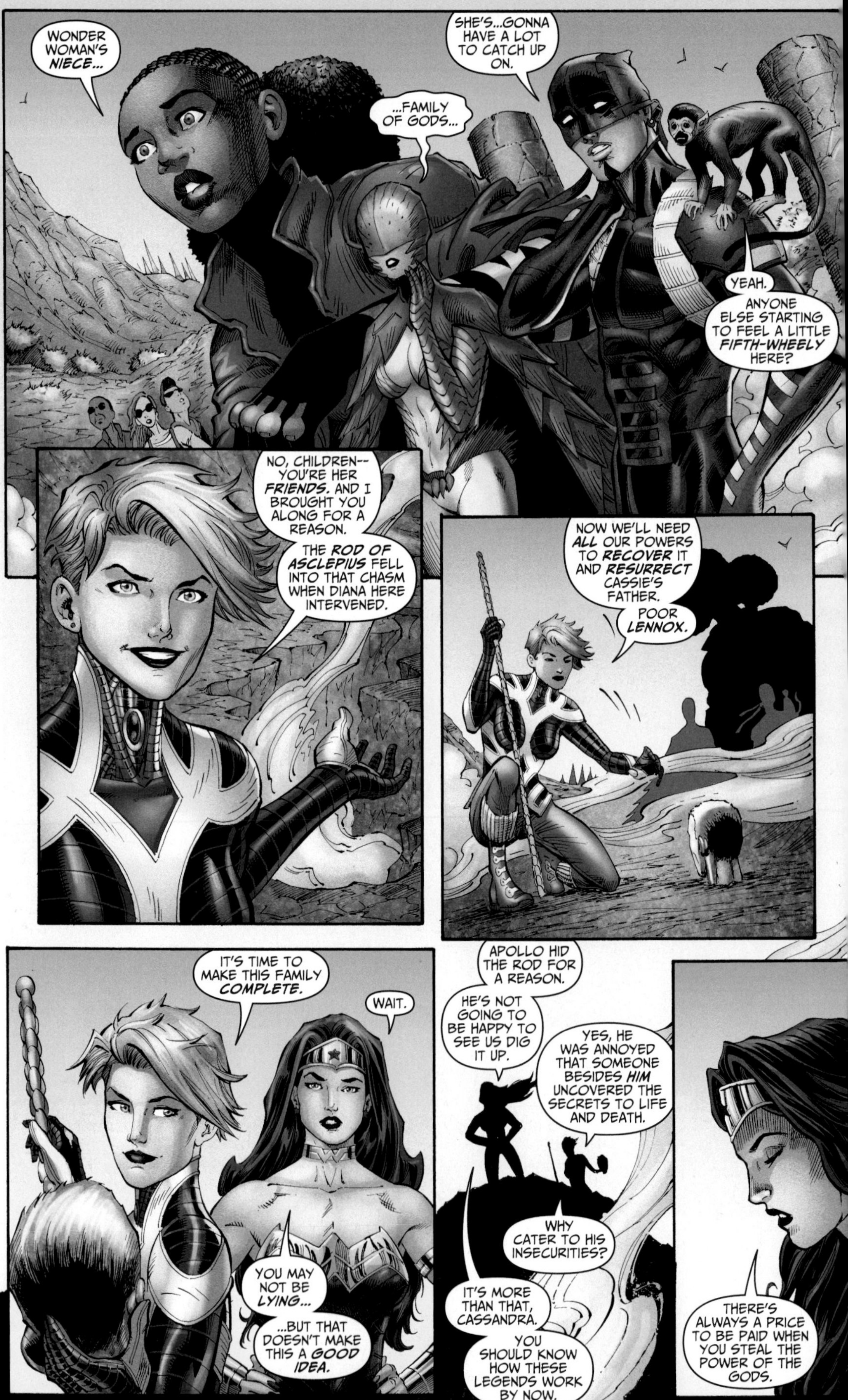

WONDER WOMAN'S NIECE...
...FAMILY OF GODS...
SHE'S...GONNA HAVE A LOT TO CATCH UP ON.
YEAH.
ANYONE ELSE STARTING TO FEEL A LITTLE FIFTH-WHEELY HERE?
NO, CHILDREN-- YOU'RE HER FRIENDS. AND I BROUGHT YOU ALONG FOR A REASON.
THE ROD OF ASCLEPIUS FELL INTO THAT CHASM WHEN DIANA HERE INTERVENED.
NOW WE'LL NEED ALL OUR POWERS TO RECOVER IT AND RESURRECT CASSIE'S FATHER.
POOR LENNOX.
IT'S TIME TO MAKE THIS FAMILY COMPLETE.
WAIT.
YOU MAY NOT BE LYING...
...BUT THAT DOESN'T MAKE THIS A GOOD IDEA.
APOLLO HID THE ROD FOR A REASON.
HE'S NOT GOING TO BE HAPPY TO SEE US DIG IT UP.
YES, HE WAS ANNOYED THAT SOMEONE BESIDES HIM UNCOVERED THE SECRETS TO LIFE AND DEATH.
WHY CATER TO HIS INSECURITIES?
IT'S MORE THAN THAT, CASSANDRA.
YOU SHOULD KNOW HOW THESE LEGENDS WORK BY NOW.
THERE'S ALWAYS A PRICE TO BE PAID WHEN YOU STEAL THE POWER OF THE GODS.

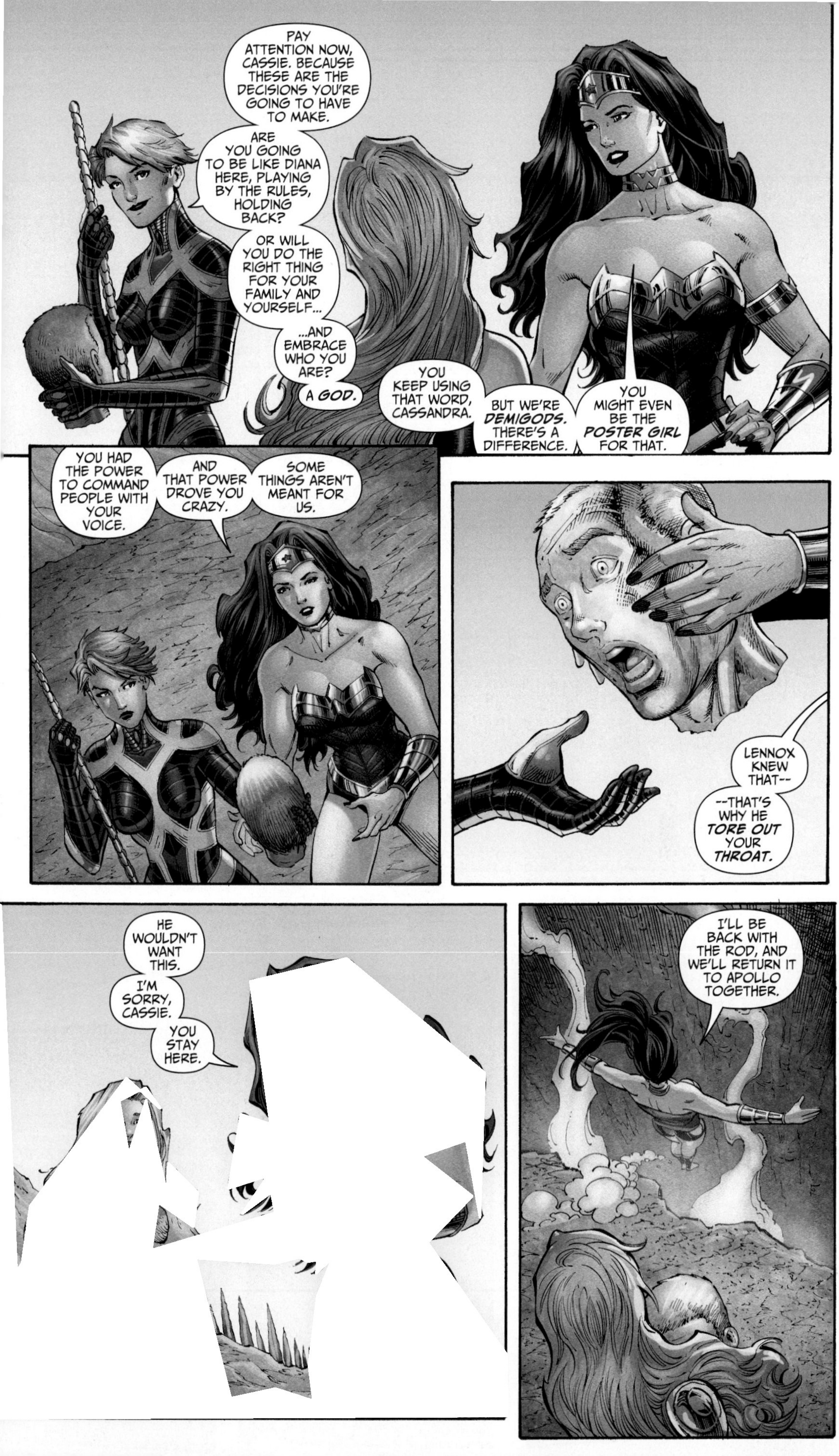
PAY ATTENTION NOW, CASSIE. BECAUSE THESE ARE THE DECISIONS YOU'RE GOING TO HAVE TO MAKE.
ARE YOU GOING TO BE LIKE DIANA HERE, PLAYING BY THE RULES, HOLDING BACK?
OR WILL YOU DO THE RIGHT THING FOR YOUR FAMILY AND YOURSELF...
...AND EMBRACE WHO YOU ARE?
A GOD.
YOU KEEP USING THAT WORD, CASSANDRA.
BUT WE'RE DEMIGODS. THERE'S A DIFFERENCE.
YOU MIGHT EVEN BE THE POSTER GIRL FOR THAT.
YOU HAD THE POWER TO COMMAND PEOPLE WITH YOUR VOICE.
AND THAT POWER DROVE YOU CRAZY.
SOME THINGS AREN'T MEANT FOR US.
LENNOX KNEW THAT--
--THAT'S WHY HE TORE OUT YOUR THROAT.
HE WOULDN'T WANT THIS.
I'M SORRY, CASSIE.
YOU STAY HERE.
I'LL BE BACK WITH THE ROD, AND WE'LL RETURN IT TO APOLLO TOGETHER.

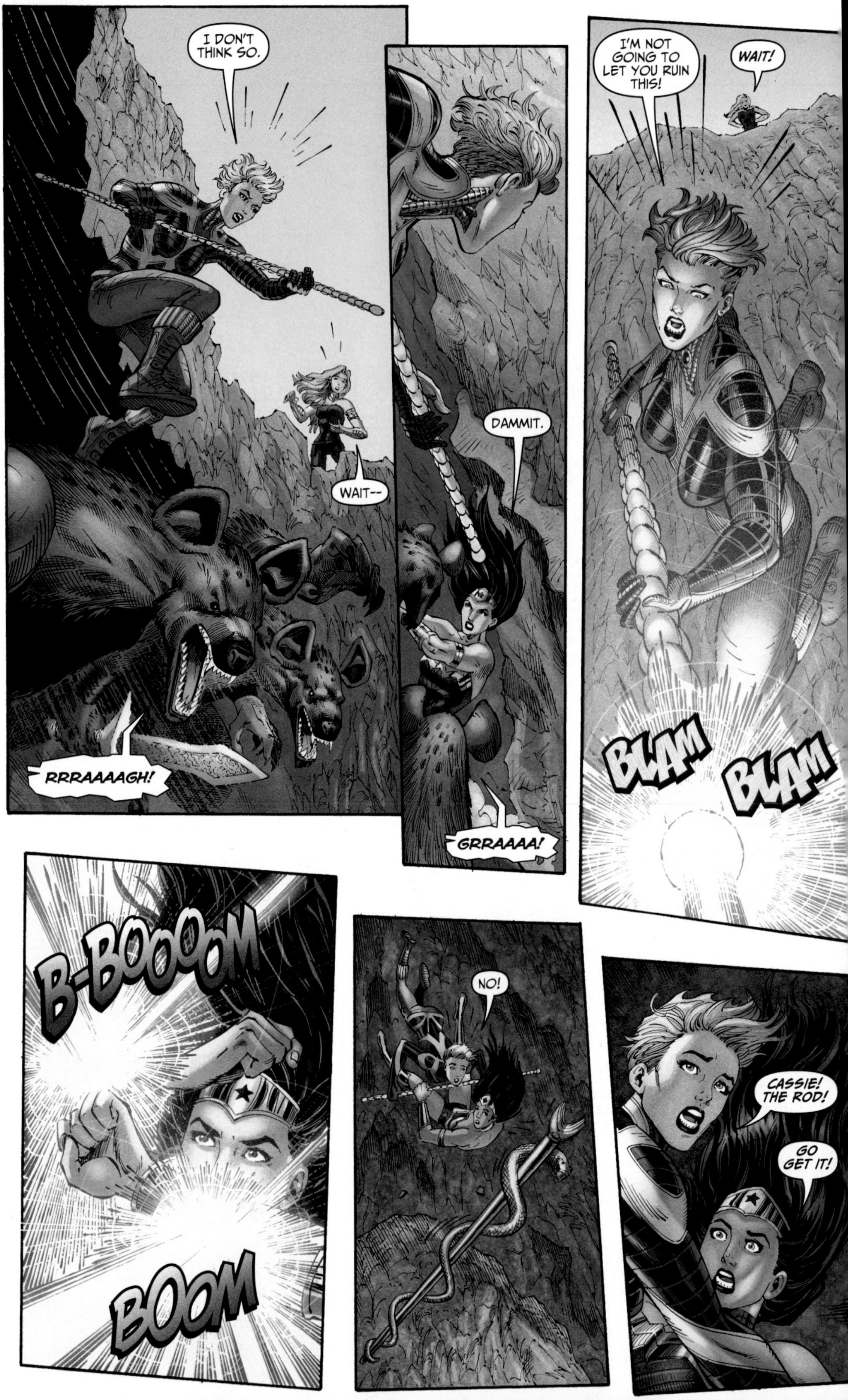
I DON'T THINK SO.
WAIT--
RRRAAAAGH!
DAMMIT.
GRRAAAA!
I'M NOT GOING TO LET YOU RUIN THIS!
WAIT!
BLAM
BLAM
B-BOOOOM
BOOM
NO!
CASSIE! THE ROD!
GO GET IT!

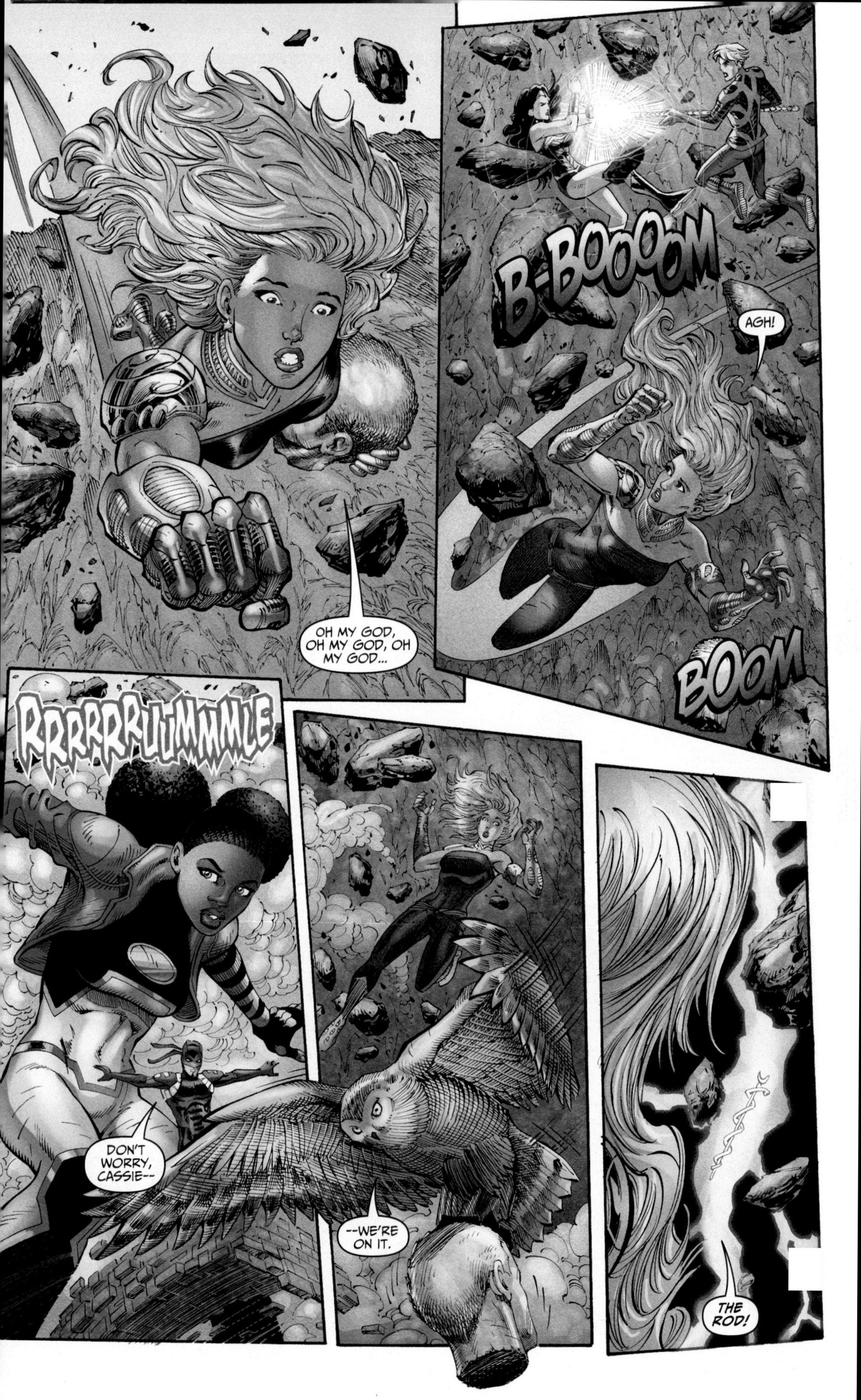
OH MY GOD, OH MY GOD, OH MY GOD...
B-BOOOOM
AGH!
BOOM
RRRRRRUMMMLE
DON'T WORRY, CASSIE--
--WE'RE ON IT.
THE ROD!

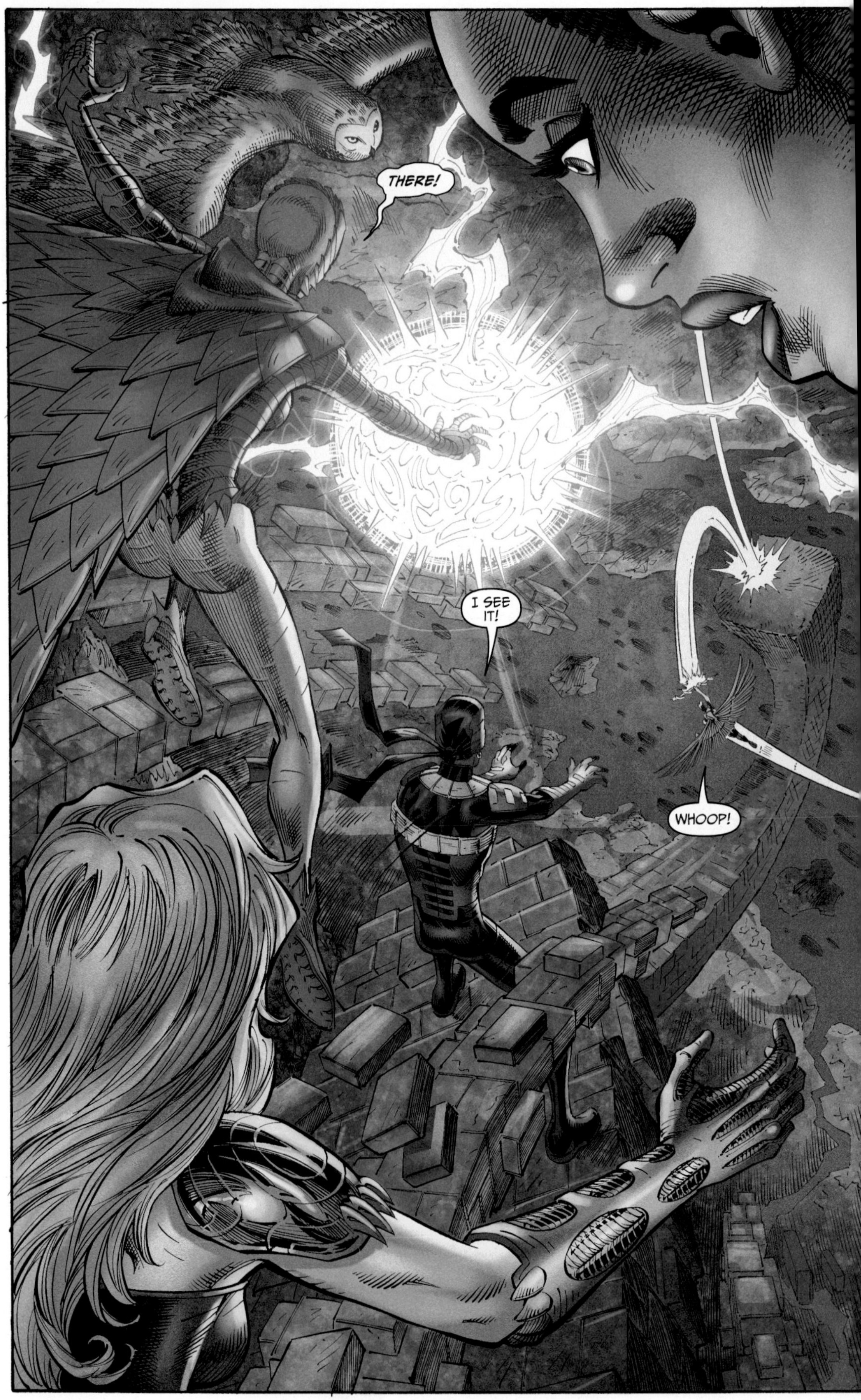
THERE!
I SEE IT!
WHOOP!

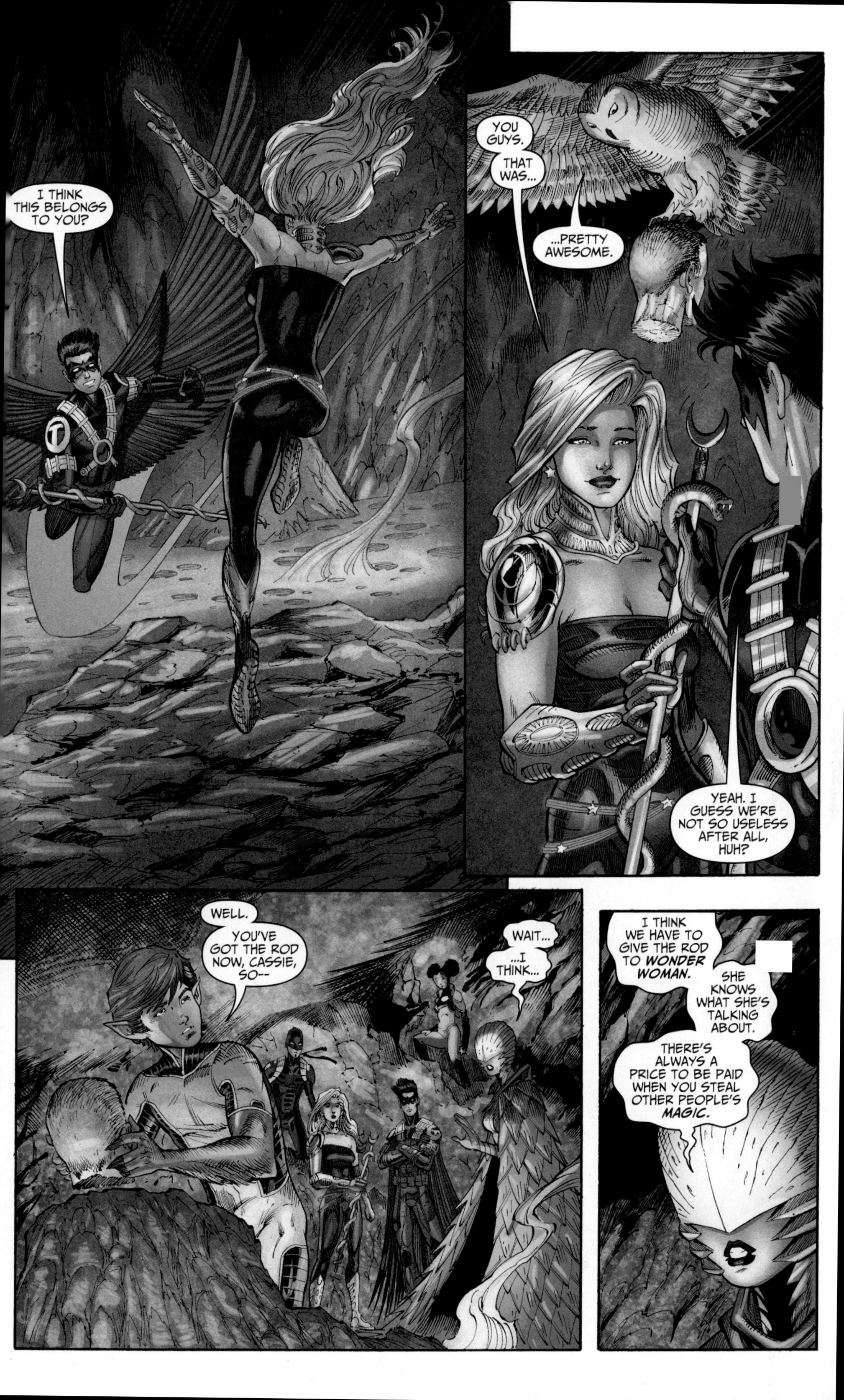
I THINK THIS BELONGS TO YOU?
YOU GUYS.
THAT WAS...
...PRETTY AWESOME.
YEAH. I GUESS WE'RE NOT SO USELESS AFTER ALL, HUH?
WELL.
YOU'VE GOT THE ROD NOW, CASSIE, SO--
WAIT...
...I THINK...
I THINK WE HAVE TO GIVE THE ROD TO WONDER WOMAN.
SHE KNOWS WHAT SHE'S TALKING ABOUT.
THERE'S ALWAYS A PRICE TO BE PAID WHEN YOU STEAL OTHER PEOPLE'S MAGIC.

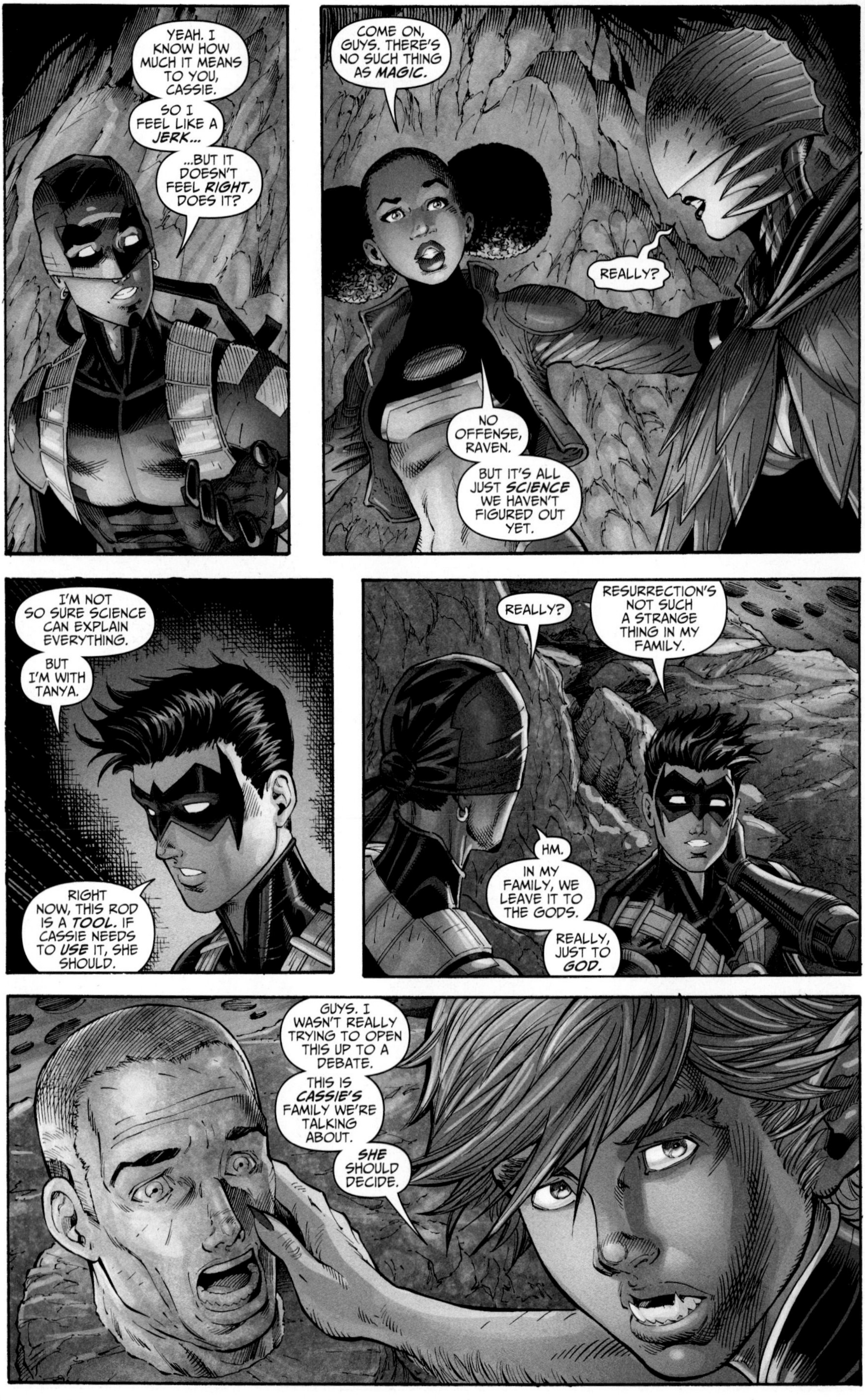
YEAH. I KNOW HOW MUCH IT MEANS TO YOU, CASSIE.
SO I FEEL LIKE A JERK...
...BUT IT DOESN'T FEEL RIGHT, DOES IT?
COME ON, GUYS. THERE'S NO SUCH THING AS MAGIC.
REALLY?
NO OFFENSE, RAVEN.
BUT IT'S ALL JUST SCIENCE WE HAVEN'T FIGURED OUT YET.
I'M NOT SO SURE SCIENCE CAN EXPLAIN EVERYTHING.
BUT I'M WITH TANYA.
RIGHT NOW, THIS ROD IS A TOOL. IF CASSIE NEEDS TO USE IT, SHE SHOULD.
REALLY?
RESURRECTION'S NOT SUCH A STRANGE THING IN MY FAMILY.
HM.
IN MY FAMILY, WE LEAVE IT TO THE GODS.
REALLY, JUST TO GOD.
GUYS. I WASN'T REALLY TRYING TO OPEN THIS UP TO A DEBATE.
THIS IS CASSIE'S FAMILY WE'RE TALKING ABOUT.
SHE SHOULD DECIDE.

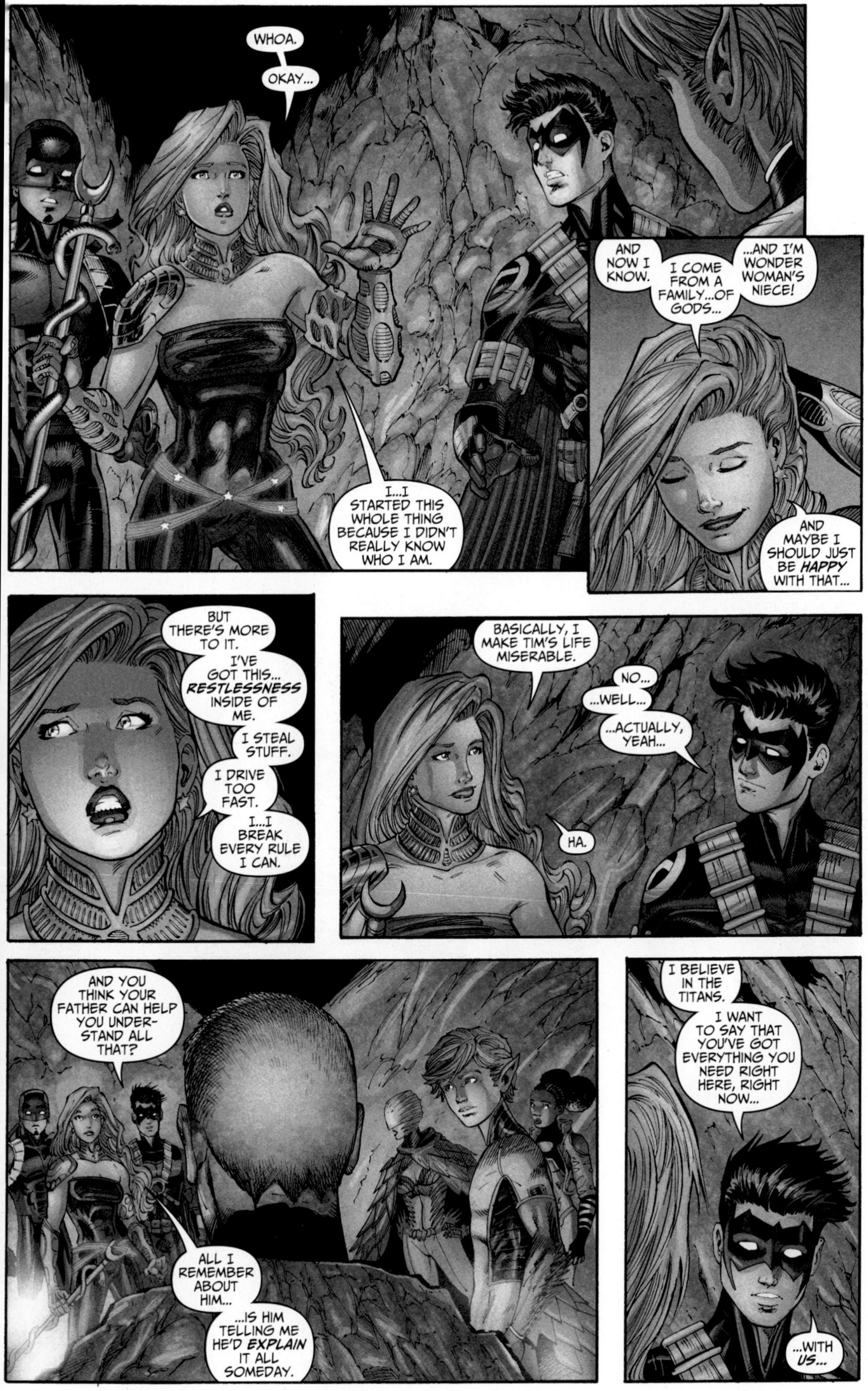

WHOA.
OKAY...
I...I STARTED THIS WHOLE THING BECAUSE I DIDN'T REALLY KNOW WHO I AM.
AND NOW I KNOW.
I COME FROM A FAMILY...OF GODS...
...AND I'M WONDER WOMAN'S NIECE!
AND MAYBE I SHOULD JUST BE *HAPPY* WITH THAT...
BUT THERE'S MORE TO IT.
I'VE GOT THIS... ***RESTLESSNESS*** INSIDE OF ME.
I STEAL STUFF.
I DRIVE TOO FAST.
I...I BREAK EVERY RULE I CAN.
BASICALLY, I MAKE TIM'S LIFE MISERABLE.
NO...
...WELL...
...ACTUALLY, YEAH...
HA.
AND YOU THINK YOUR FATHER CAN HELP YOU UNDER-STAND ALL THAT?
ALL I REMEMBER ABOUT HIM...
...IS HIM TELLING ME HE'D ***EXPLAIN*** IT ALL SOMEDAY.
I BELIEVE IN THE TITANS.
I WANT TO SAY THAT YOU'VE GOT EVERYTHING YOU NEED RIGHT HERE, RIGHT NOW...
...WITH ***US***...

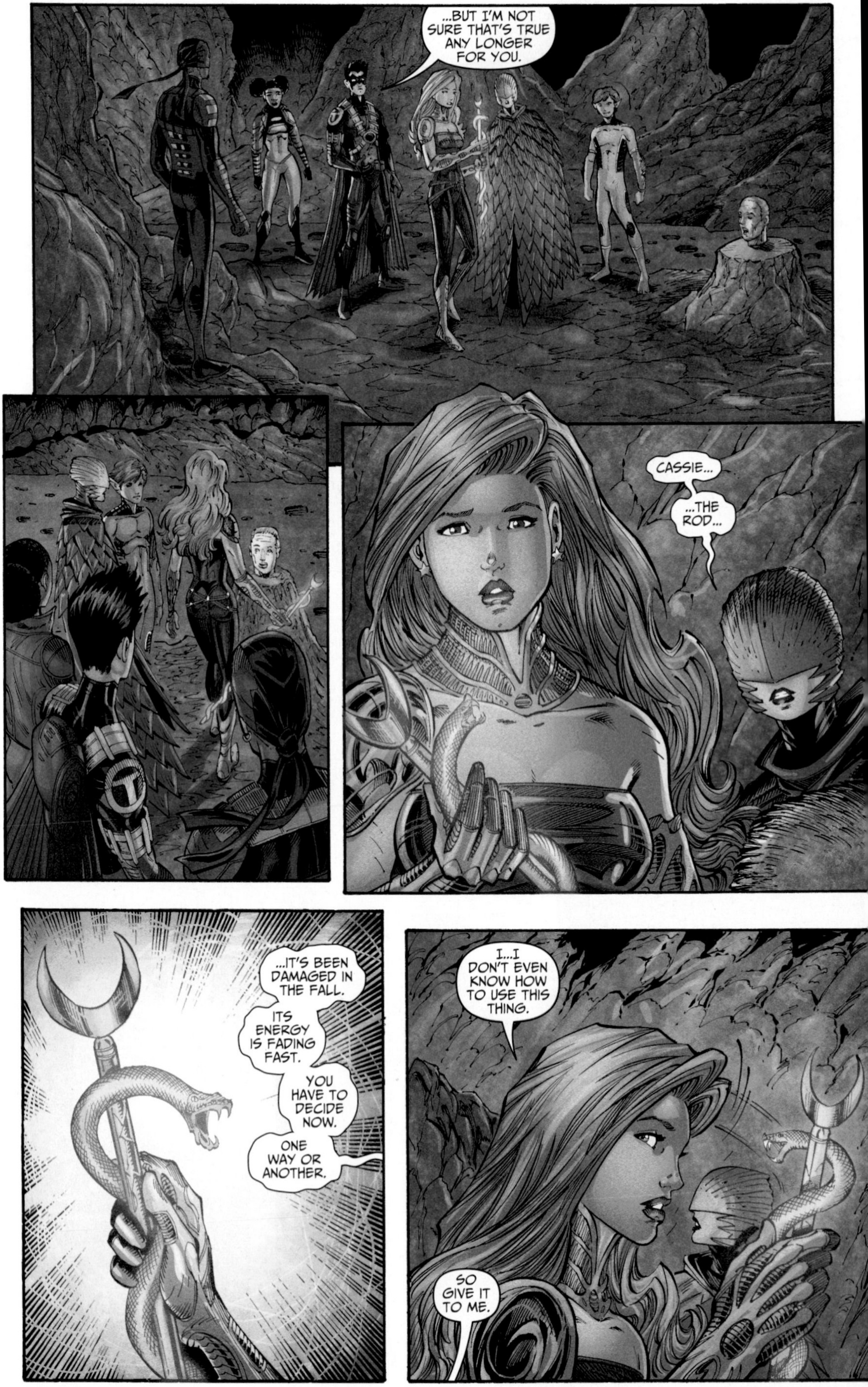
...BUT I'M NOT SURE THAT'S TRUE ANY LONGER FOR YOU.
CASSIE...
...THE ROD...
...IT'S BEEN DAMAGED IN THE FALL.
ITS ENERGY IS FADING FAST.
YOU HAVE TO DECIDE NOW.
ONE WAY OR ANOTHER.
I...I DON'T EVEN KNOW HOW TO USE THIS THING.
SO GIVE IT TO ME.

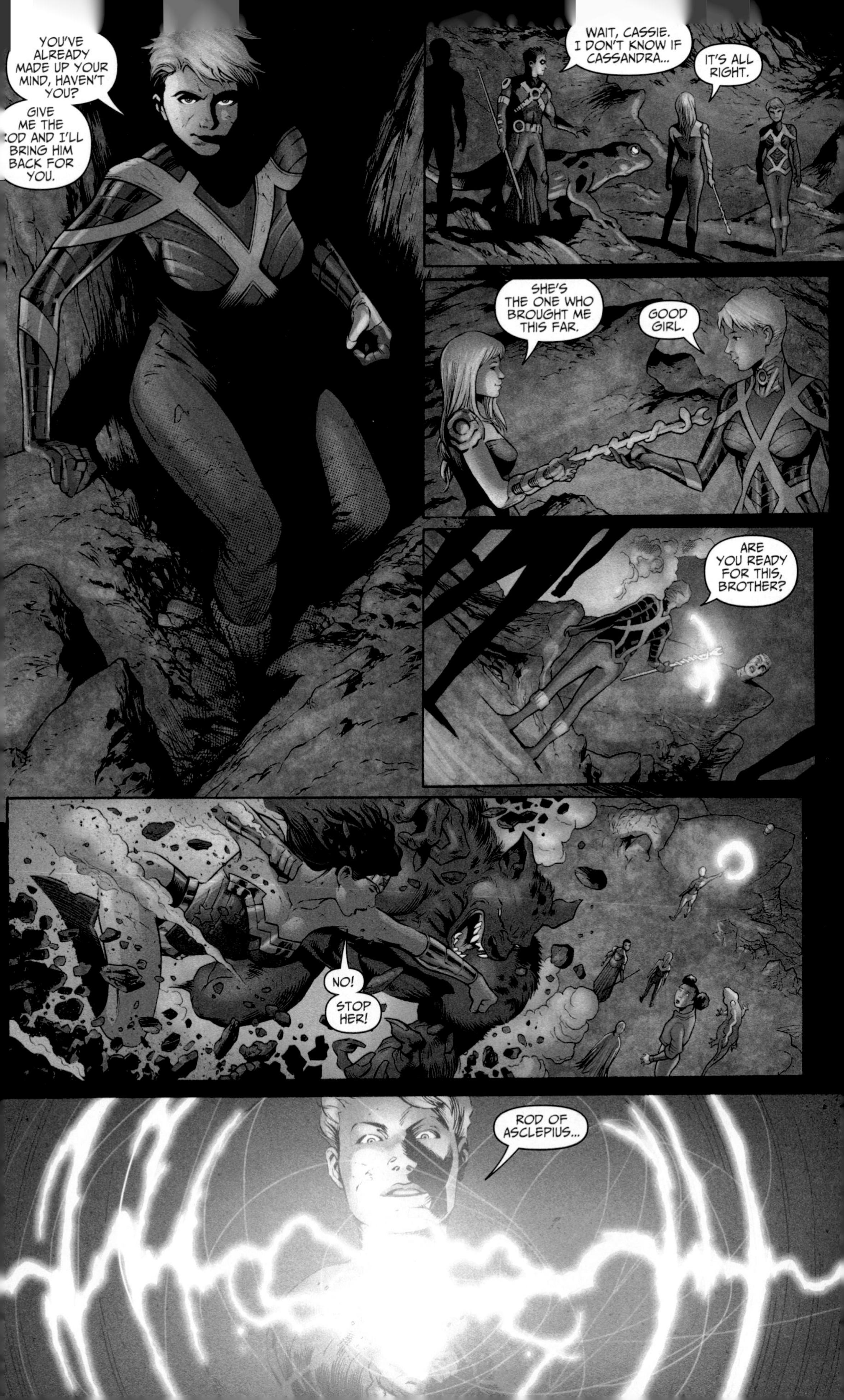
YOU'VE ALREADY MADE UP YOUR MIND, HAVEN'T YOU?
GIVE ME THE OD AND I'LL BRING HIM BACK FOR YOU.
WAIT, CASSIE. I DON'T KNOW IF CASSANDRA...
IT'S ALL RIGHT.
SHE'S THE ONE WHO BROUGHT ME THIS FAR.
GOOD GIRL.
ARE YOU READY FOR THIS, BROTHER?
NO!
STOP HER!
ROD OF ASCLEPIUS...

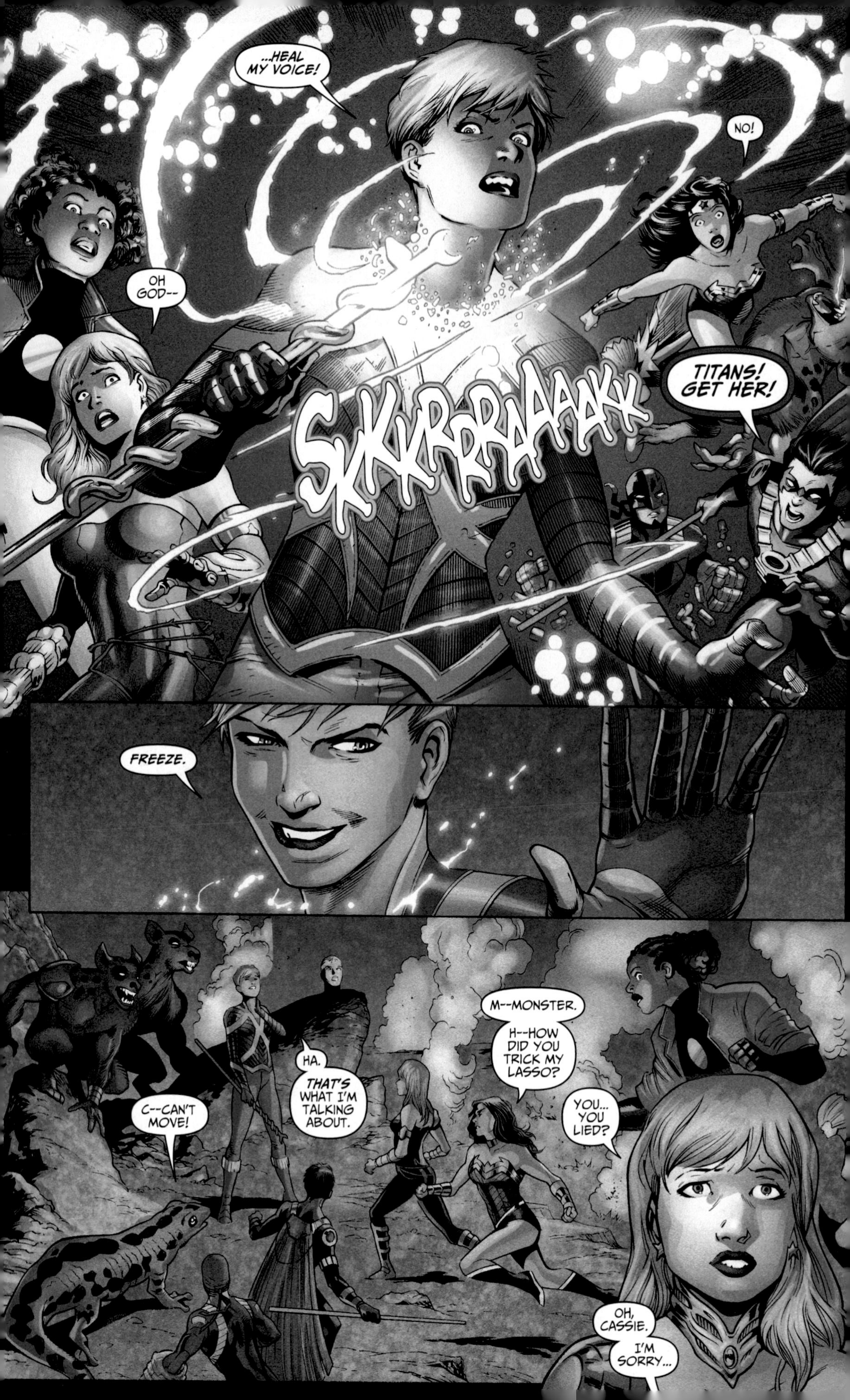
...HEAL MY VOICE!
NO!
OH GOD--
SKKRRRAAAKK
TITANS! GET HER!
FREEZE.
M--MONSTER.
H--HOW DID YOU TRICK MY LASSO?
HA.
THAT'S WHAT I'M TALKING ABOUT.
C--CAN'T MOVE!
YOU... YOU LIED?
OH, CASSIE.
I'M SORRY...

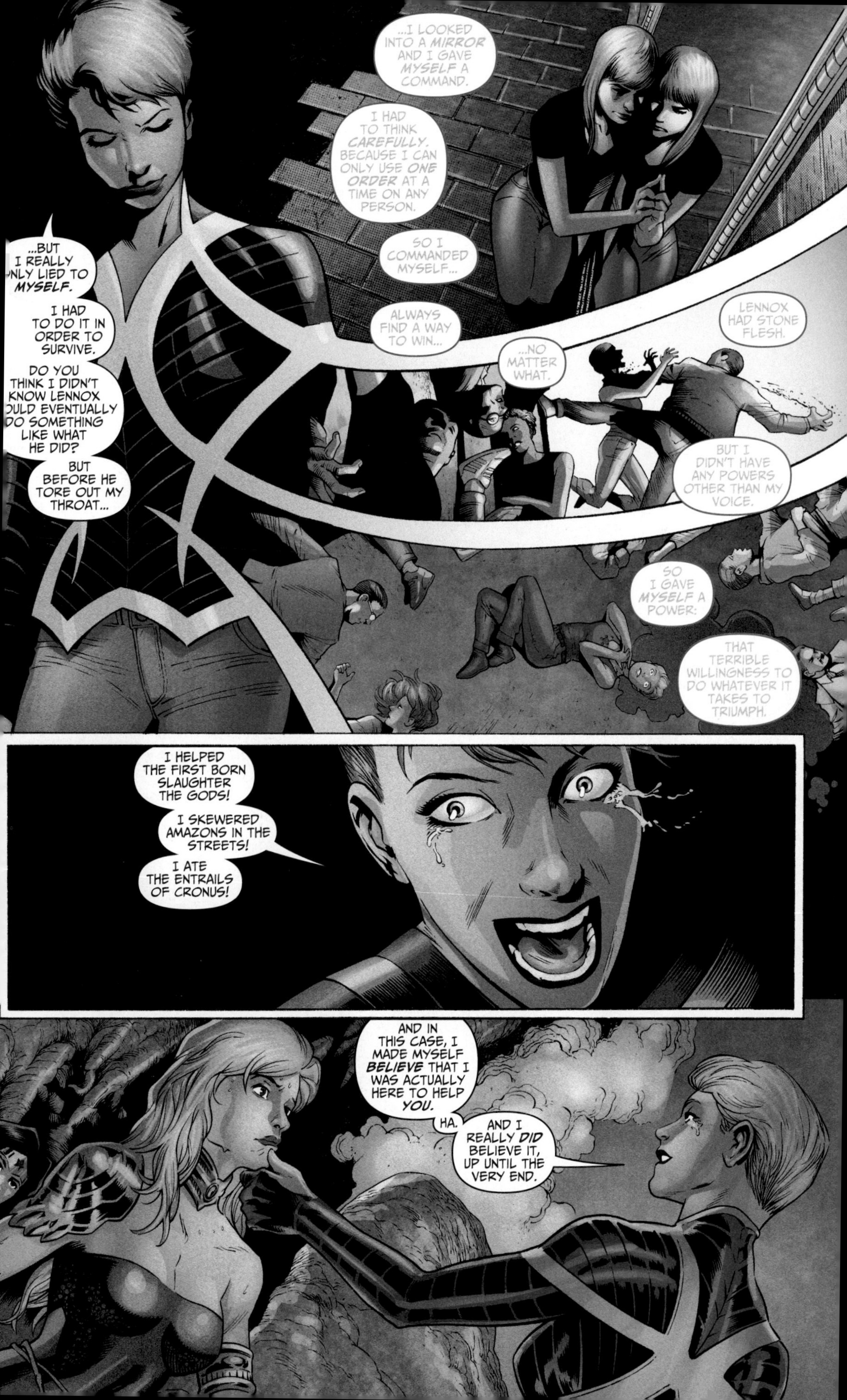
...I LOOKED INTO A MIRROR AND I GAVE MYSELF A COMMAND.
I HAD TO THINK CAREFULLY. BECAUSE I CAN ONLY USE ONE ORDER AT A TIME ON ANY PERSON.
SO I COMMANDED MYSELF...
ALWAYS FIND A WAY TO WIN...
...NO MATTER WHAT.
...BUT I REALLY ONLY LIED TO MYSELF.
I HAD TO DO IT IN ORDER TO SURVIVE.
DO YOU THINK I DIDN'T KNOW LENNOX WOULD EVENTUALLY DO SOMETHING LIKE WHAT HE DID?
BUT BEFORE HE TORE OUT MY THROAT...
LENNOX HAD STONE FLESH.
BUT I DIDN'T HAVE ANY POWERS OTHER THAN MY VOICE.
SO I GAVE MYSELF A POWER:
THAT TERRIBLE WILLINGNESS TO DO WHATEVER IT TAKES TO TRIUMPH.
I HELPED THE FIRST BORN SLAUGHTER THE GODS!
I SKEWERED AMAZONS IN THE STREETS!
I ATE THE ENTRAILS OF CRONUS!
AND IN THIS CASE, I MADE MYSELF BELIEVE THAT I WAS ACTUALLY HERE TO HELP YOU.
HA.
AND I REALLY DID BELIEVE IT, UP UNTIL THE VERY END.

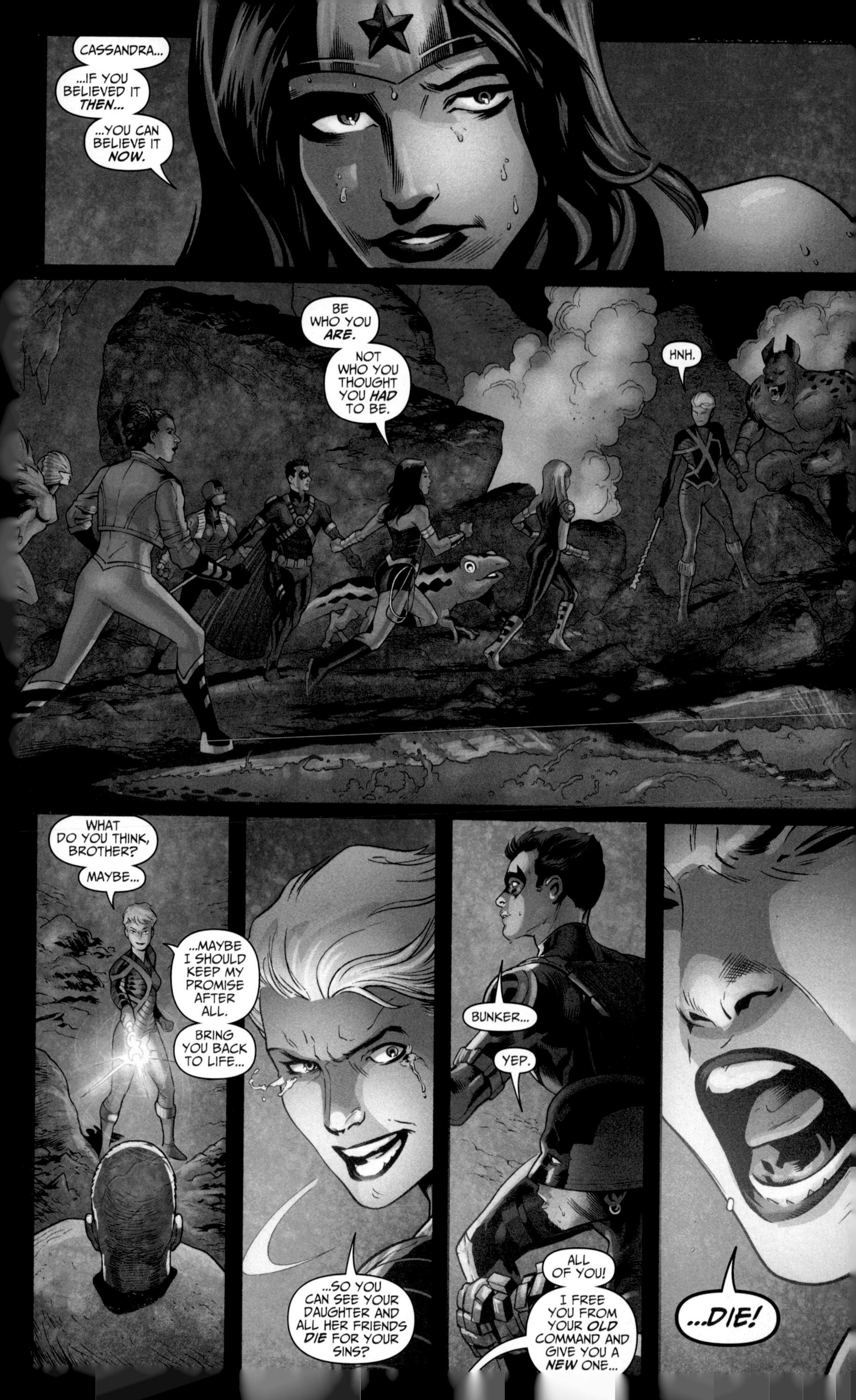

CASSANDRA...
...IF YOU BELIEVED IT THEN...
...YOU CAN BELIEVE IT NOW.
BE WHO YOU ARE.
NOT WHO YOU THOUGHT YOU HAD TO BE.
HNH.
WHAT DO YOU THINK, BROTHER?
MAYBE...
...MAYBE I SHOULD KEEP MY PROMISE AFTER ALL.
BRING YOU BACK TO LIFE...
...SO YOU CAN SEE YOUR DAUGHTER AND ALL HER FRIENDS DIE FOR YOUR SINS?
BUNKER...
YEP.
ALL OF YOU!
I FREE YOU FROM YOUR OLD COMMAND AND GIVE YOU A NEW ONE...
...DIE!

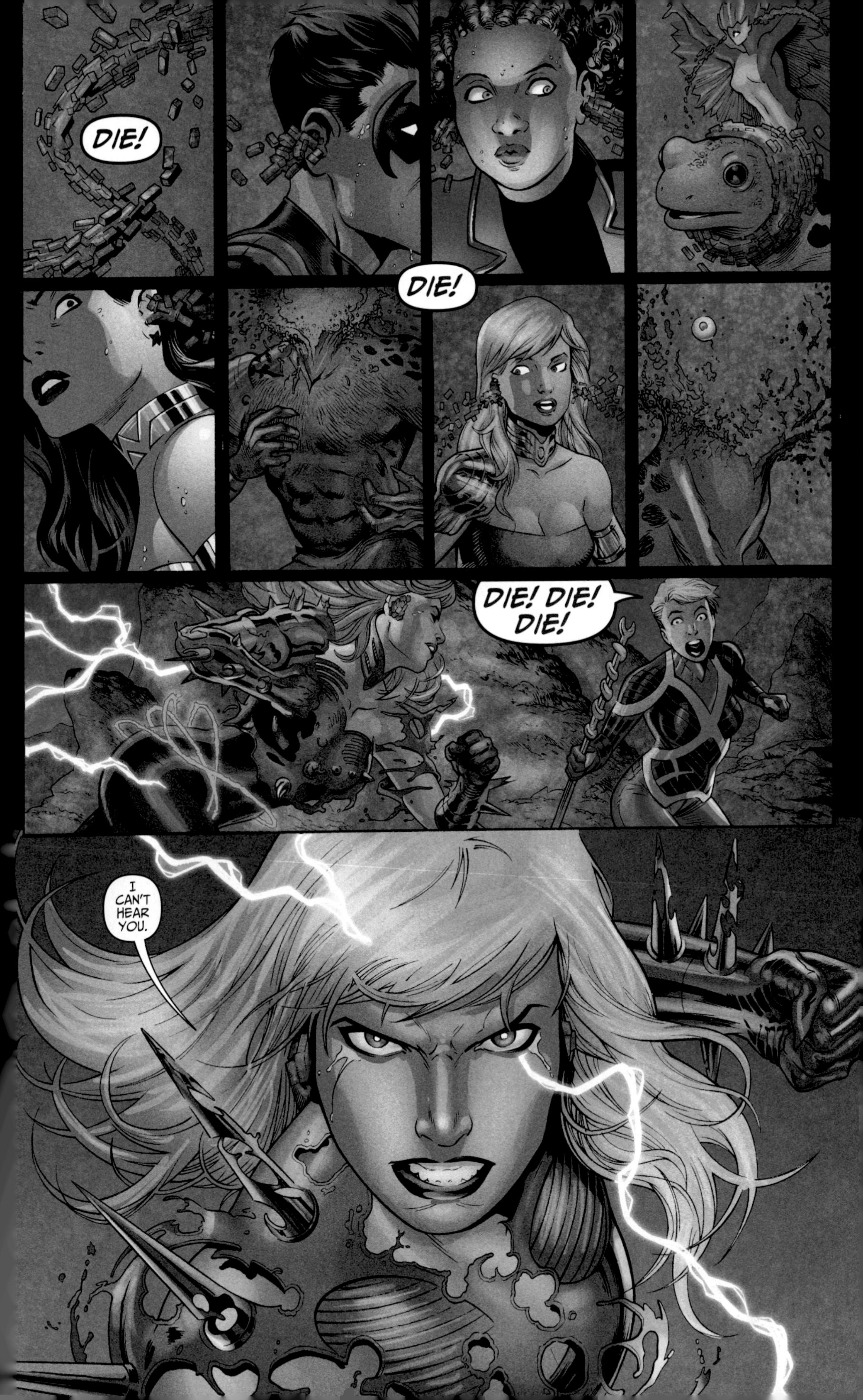
DIE!
DIE!
DIE! DIE! DIE!
I CAN'T HEAR YOU.

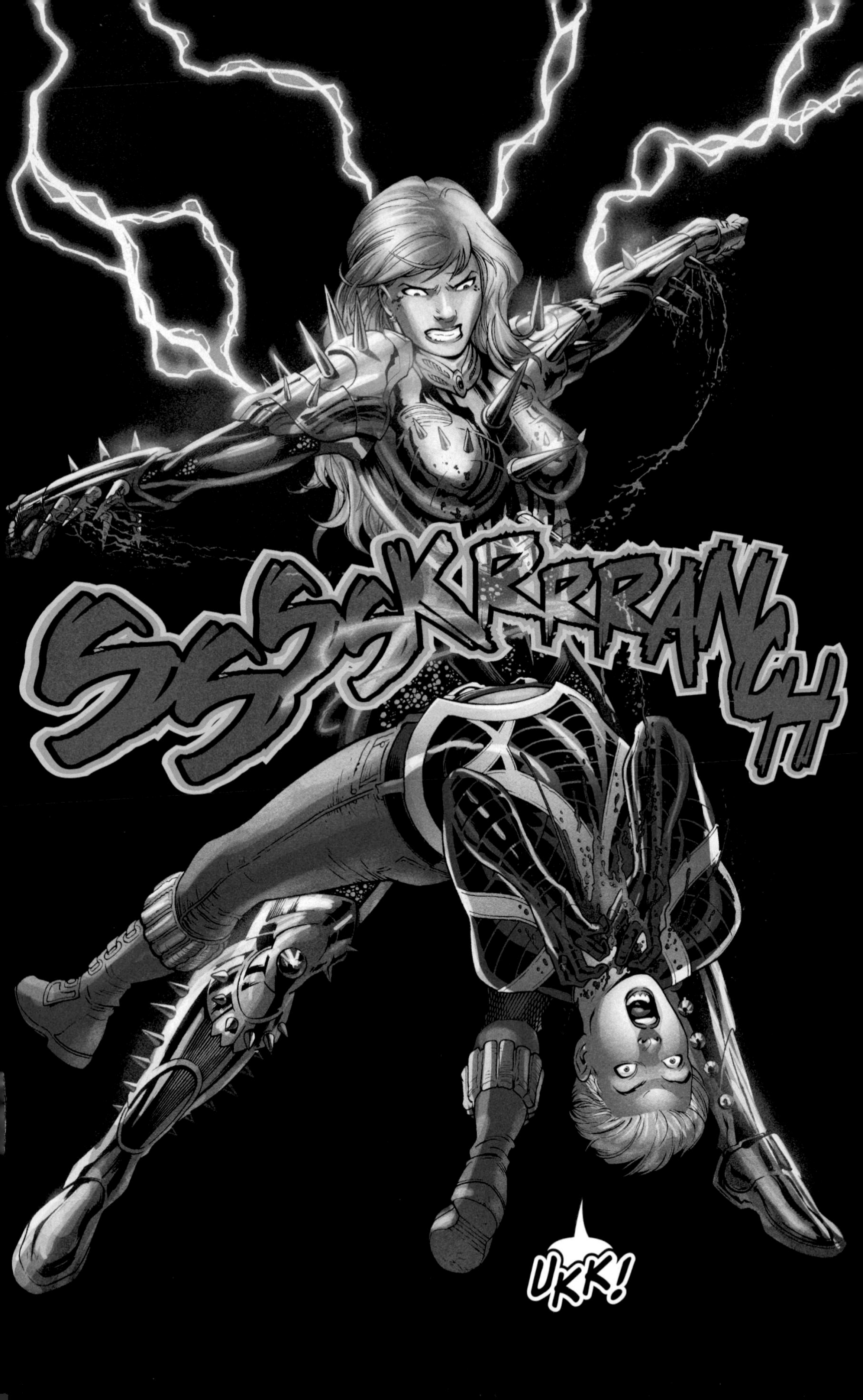
SSSKRRRANCH
UKK!

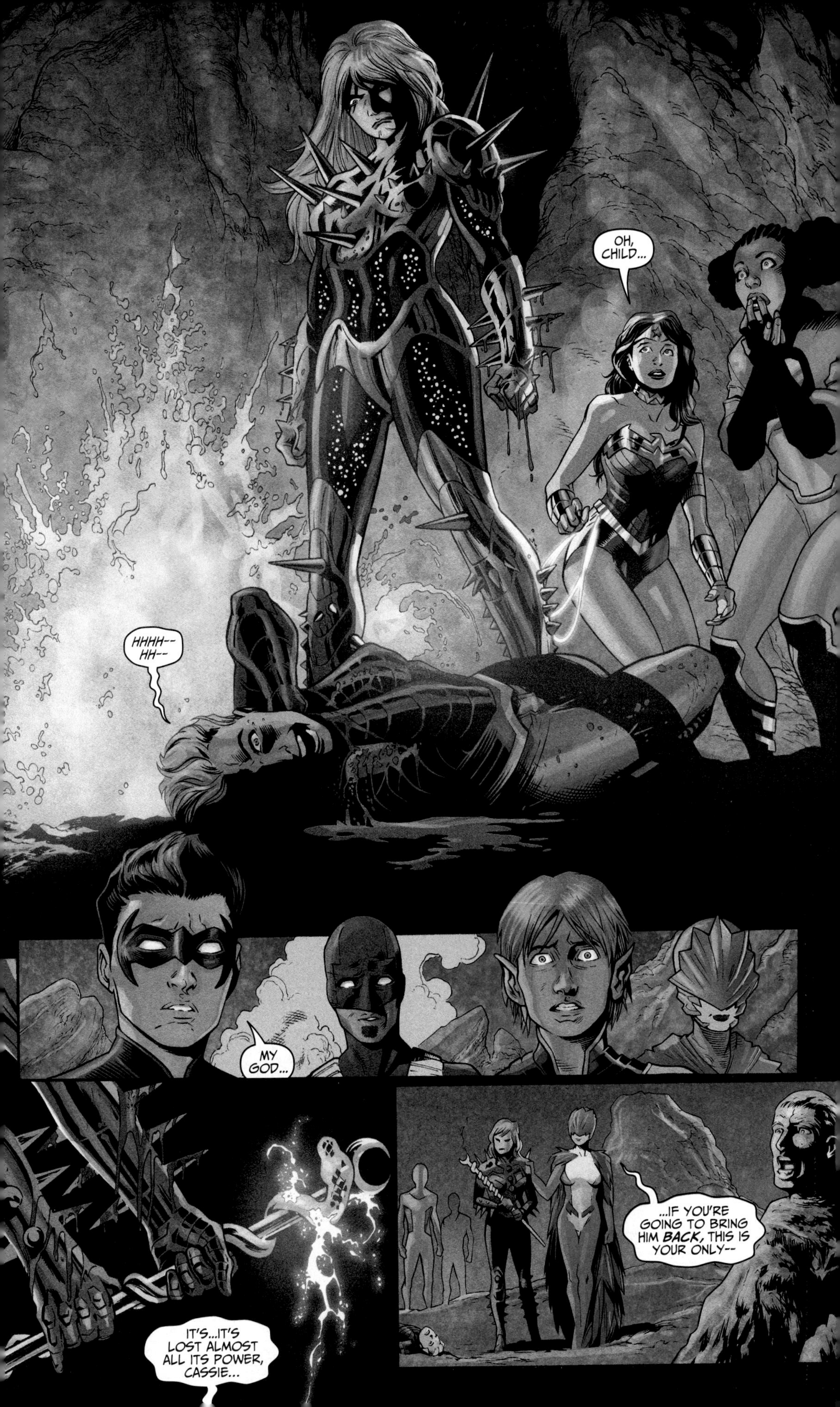
OH, CHILD...
HHHH-- HH--
MY GOD...
IT'S...IT'S LOST ALMOST ALL ITS POWER, CASSIE...
...IF YOU'RE GOING TO BRING HIM *BACK*, THIS IS YOUR ONLY--

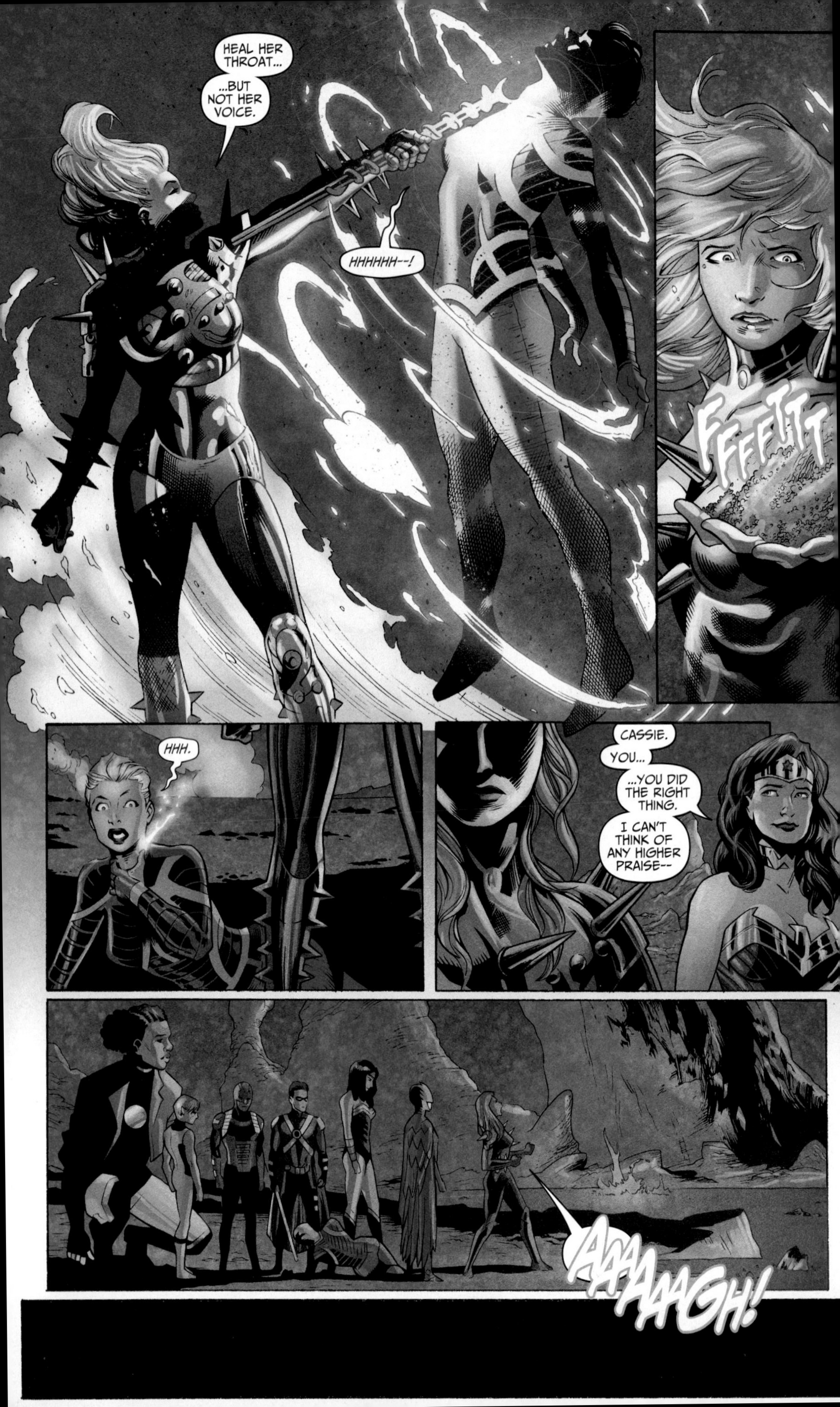
HEAL HER THROAT...
...BUT NOT HER VOICE.
HHHHHH--!
FFFTTT
HHH.
CASSIE.
YOU...
...YOU DID THE RIGHT THING.
I CAN'T THINK OF ANY HIGHER PRAISE--
AAAAAAAGH!

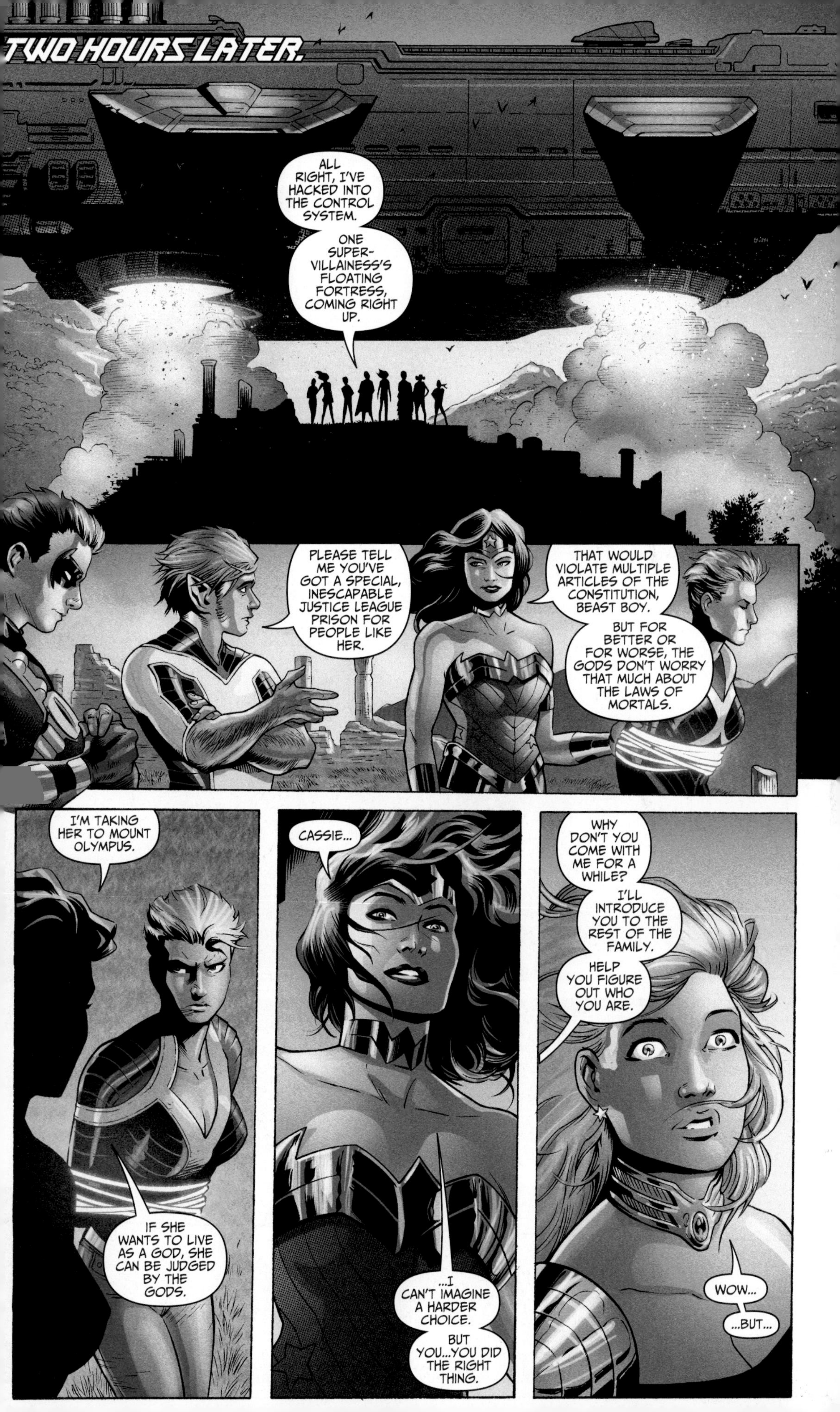
TWO HOURS LATER.
ALL RIGHT, I'VE HACKED INTO THE CONTROL SYSTEM.
ONE SUPER-VILLAINESS'S FLOATING FORTRESS, COMING RIGHT UP.
PLEASE TELL ME YOU'VE GOT A SPECIAL, INESCAPABLE JUSTICE LEAGUE PRISON FOR PEOPLE LIKE HER.
THAT WOULD VIOLATE MULTIPLE ARTICLES OF THE CONSTITUTION, BEAST BOY.
BUT FOR BETTER OR FOR WORSE, THE GODS DON'T WORRY THAT MUCH ABOUT THE LAWS OF MORTALS.
I'M TAKING HER TO MOUNT OLYMPUS.
IF SHE WANTS TO LIVE AS A GOD, SHE CAN BE JUDGED BY THE GODS.
CASSIE...
...I CAN'T IMAGINE A HARDER CHOICE.
BUT YOU...YOU DID THE RIGHT THING.
WHY DON'T YOU COME WITH ME FOR A WHILE?
I'LL INTRODUCE YOU TO THE REST OF THE FAMILY.
HELP YOU FIGURE OUT WHO YOU ARE.
WOW...
...BUT...

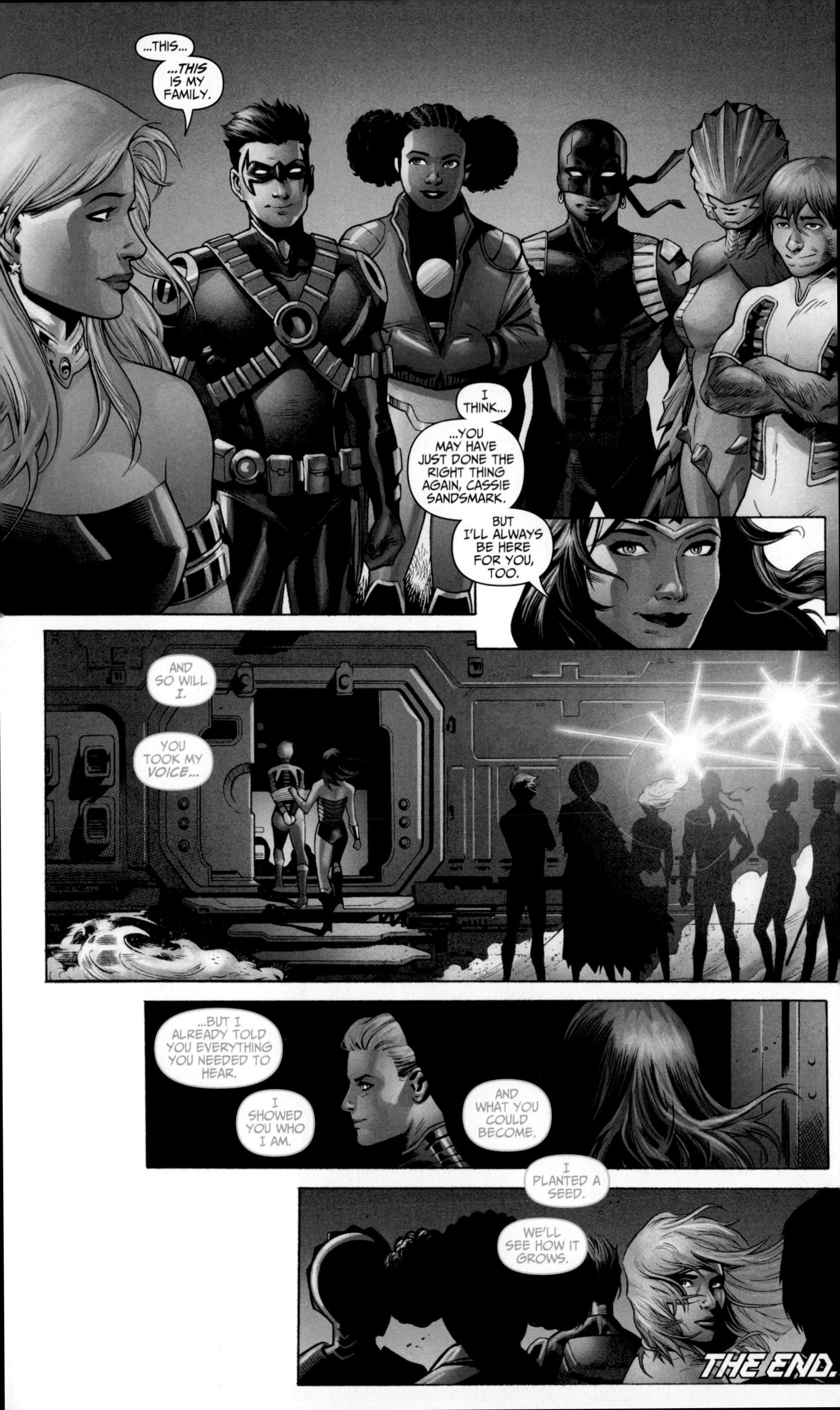

...THIS...
...THIS IS MY FAMILY.
I THINK...
...YOU MAY HAVE JUST DONE THE RIGHT THING AGAIN, CASSIE SANDSMARK.
BUT I'LL ALWAYS BE HERE FOR YOU, TOO.
AND SO WILL I.
YOU TOOK MY VOICE...
...BUT I ALREADY TOLD YOU EVERYTHING YOU NEEDED TO HEAR.
I SHOWED YOU WHO I AM.
AND WHAT YOU COULD BECOME.
I PLANTED A SEED.
WE'LL SEE HOW IT GROWS.
THE END.

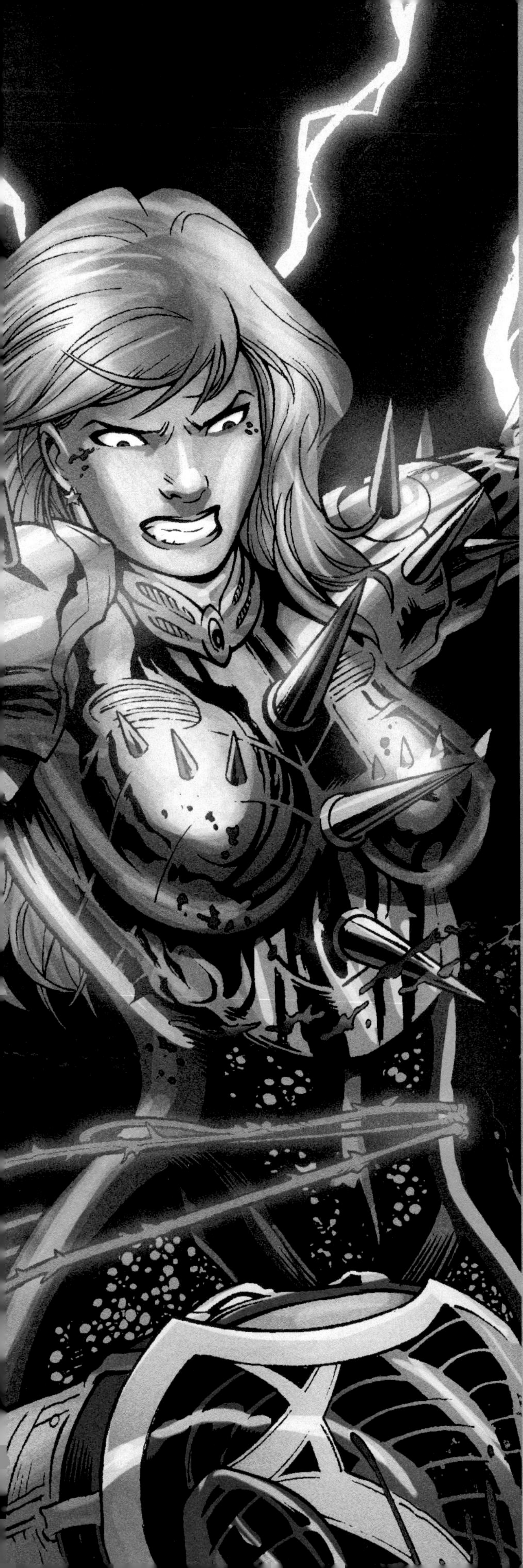

VARIANT COVER GALLERY

TEEN TITANS #14
LOONEY TUNES VARIANT COVER
BY JOE QUINONES
AND SPIKE BRANDT

TEEN TITANS #16
COLORING BOOK VARIANT COVER
BY TIMOTHY GREEN II

TEEN TITANS #17
VARIANT COVER BY
NEAL ADAMS, KEVIN NOWLAN
AND JEROMY COX

TEEN TITANS #18
BATMAN V SUPERMAN
VARIANT COVER BY PHIL JIMENEZ
AND ROMULO FAJARDO JR.

TEEN TITANS #19
VARIANT COVER BY
JOHN ROMITA JR.
AND DANNY MIKI
WITH DEAN WHITE

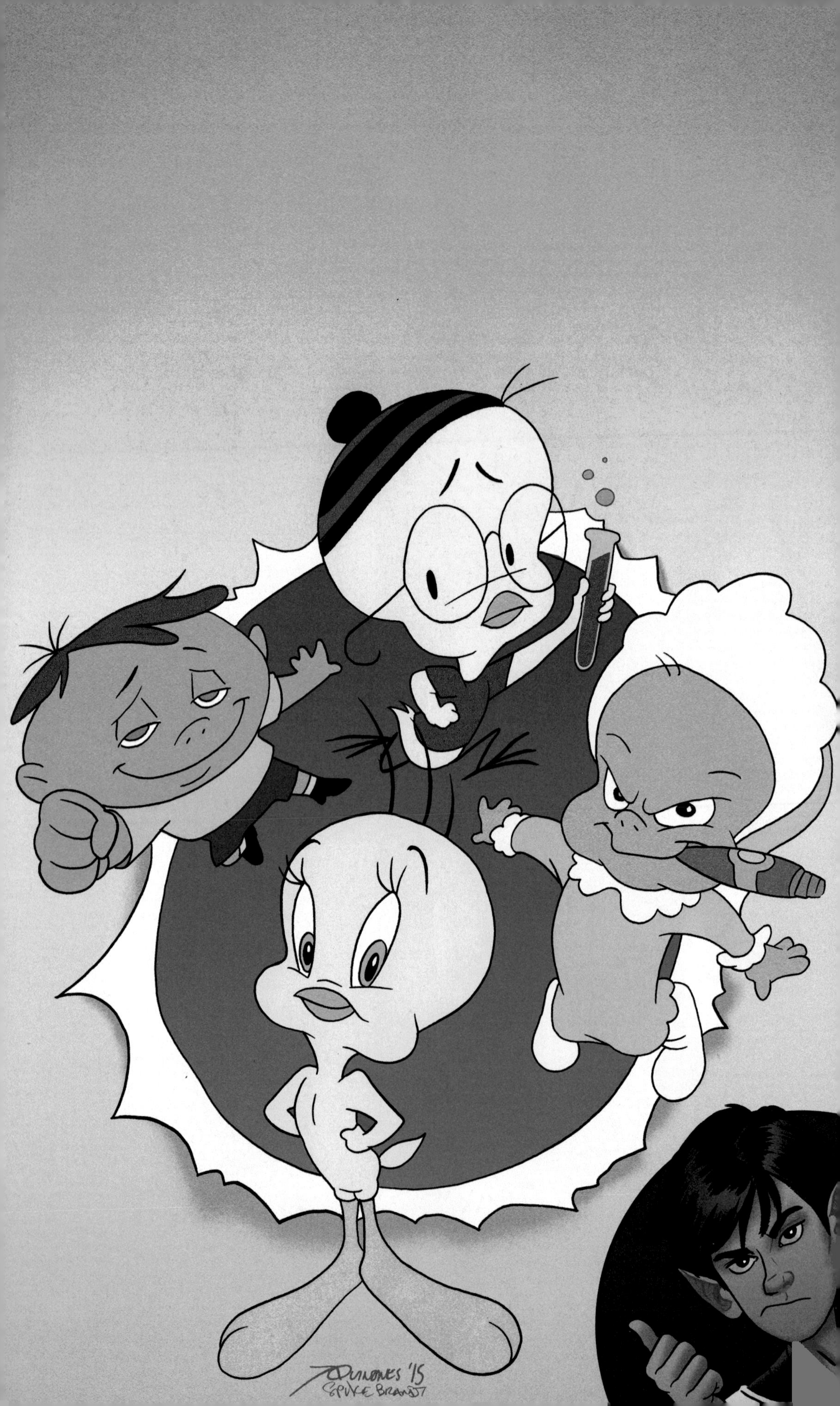
JQuinones '15
Spike Brandt

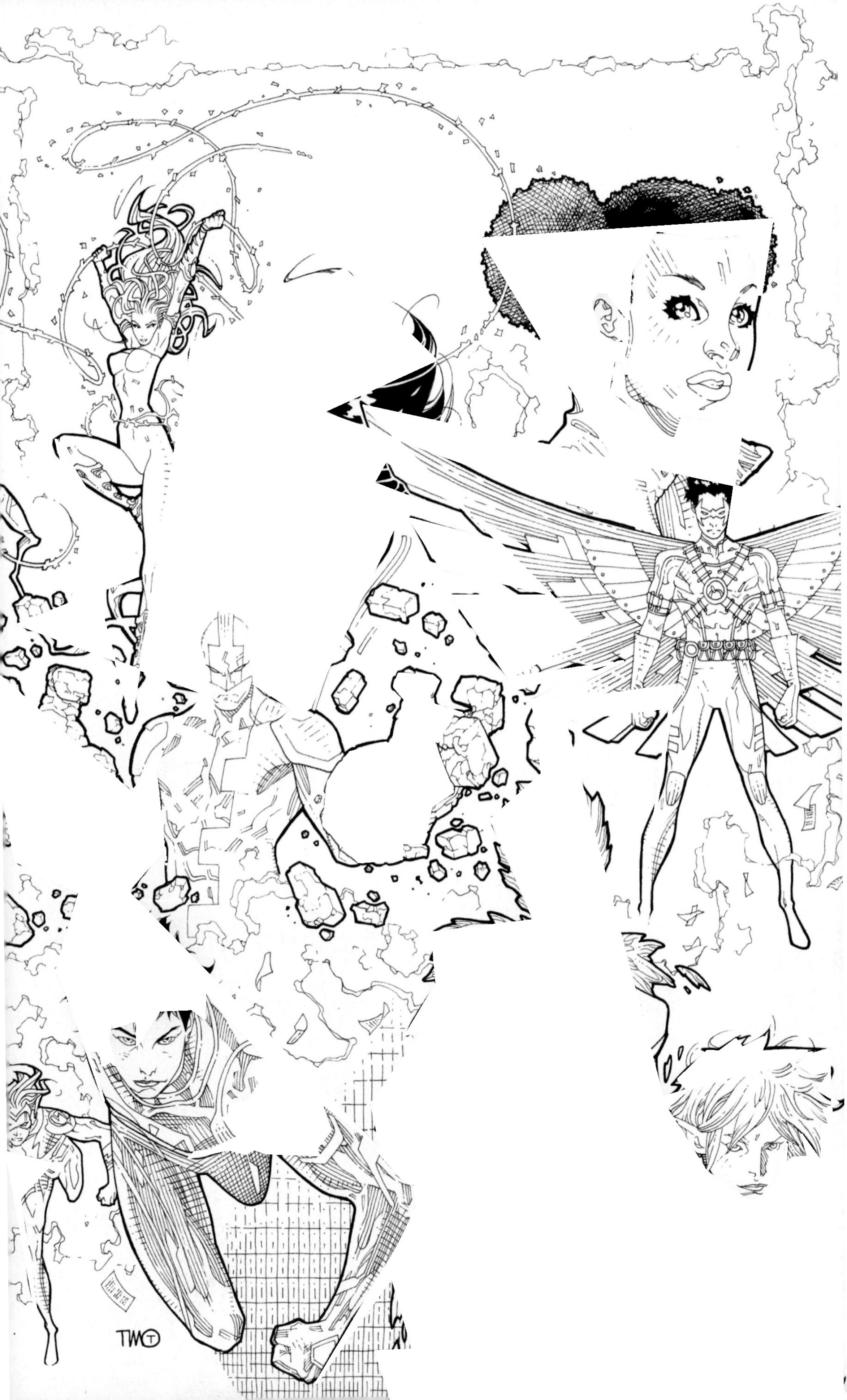

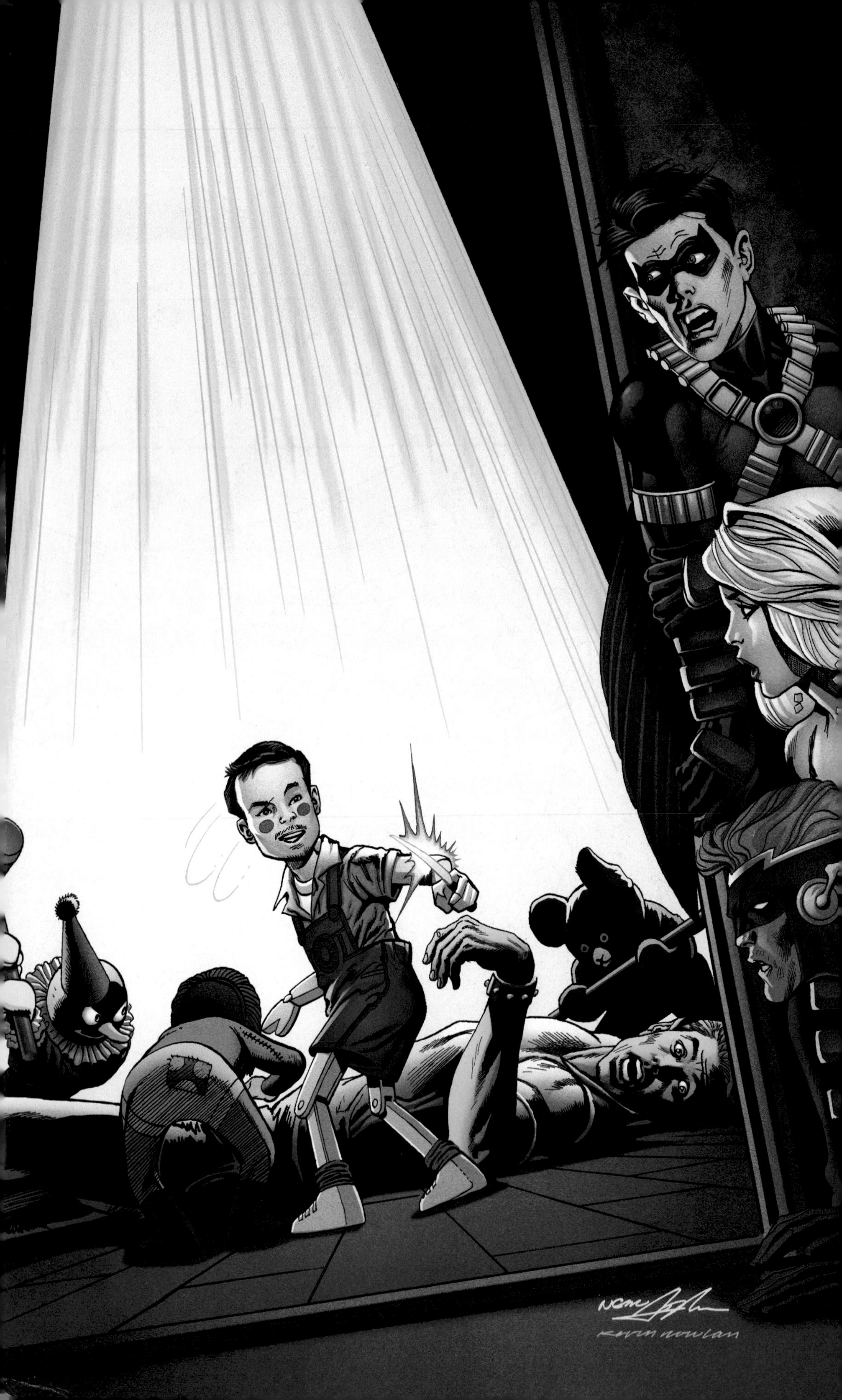
Kevin Nowlan

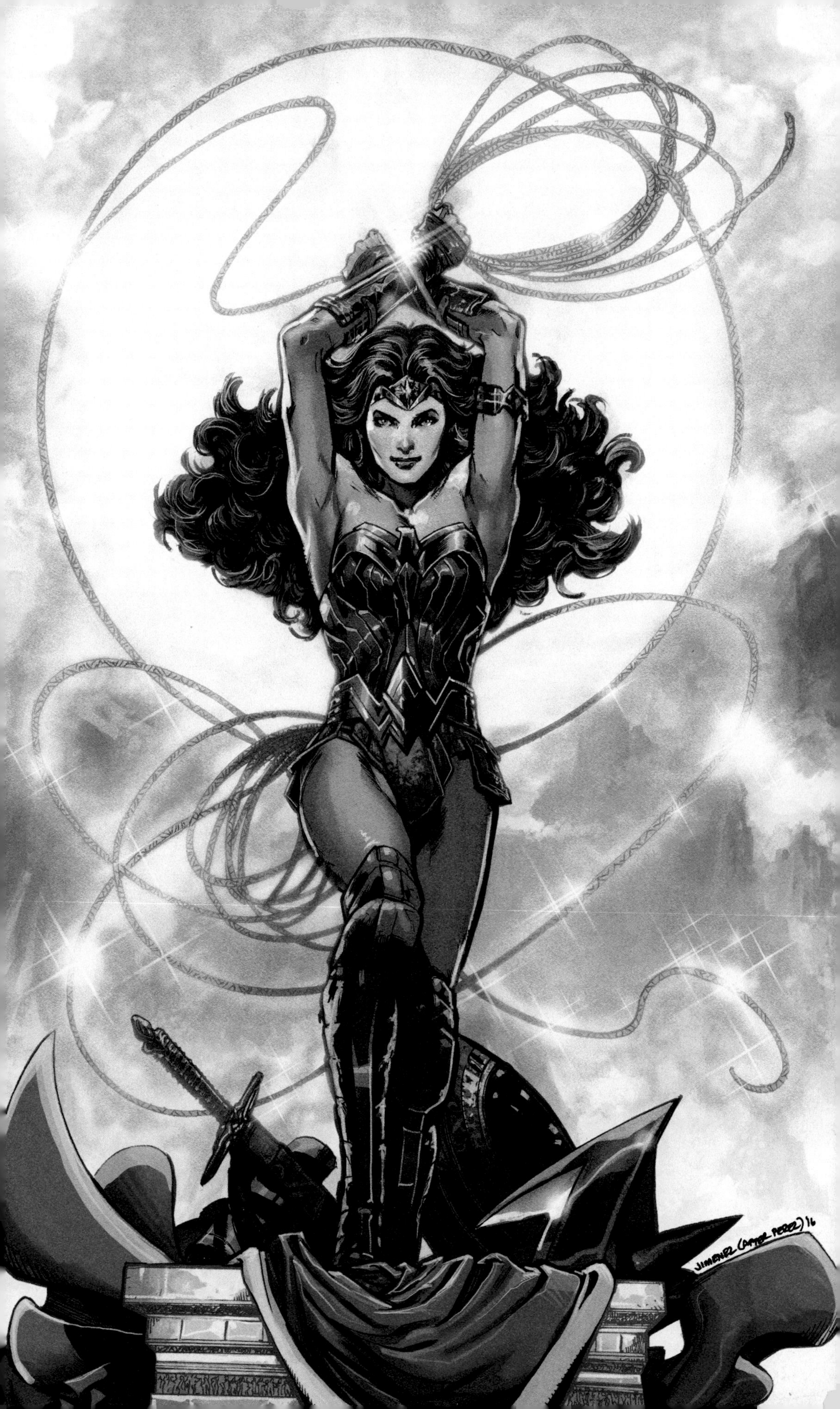
JIMENEZ (AFTER PEREZ) 16

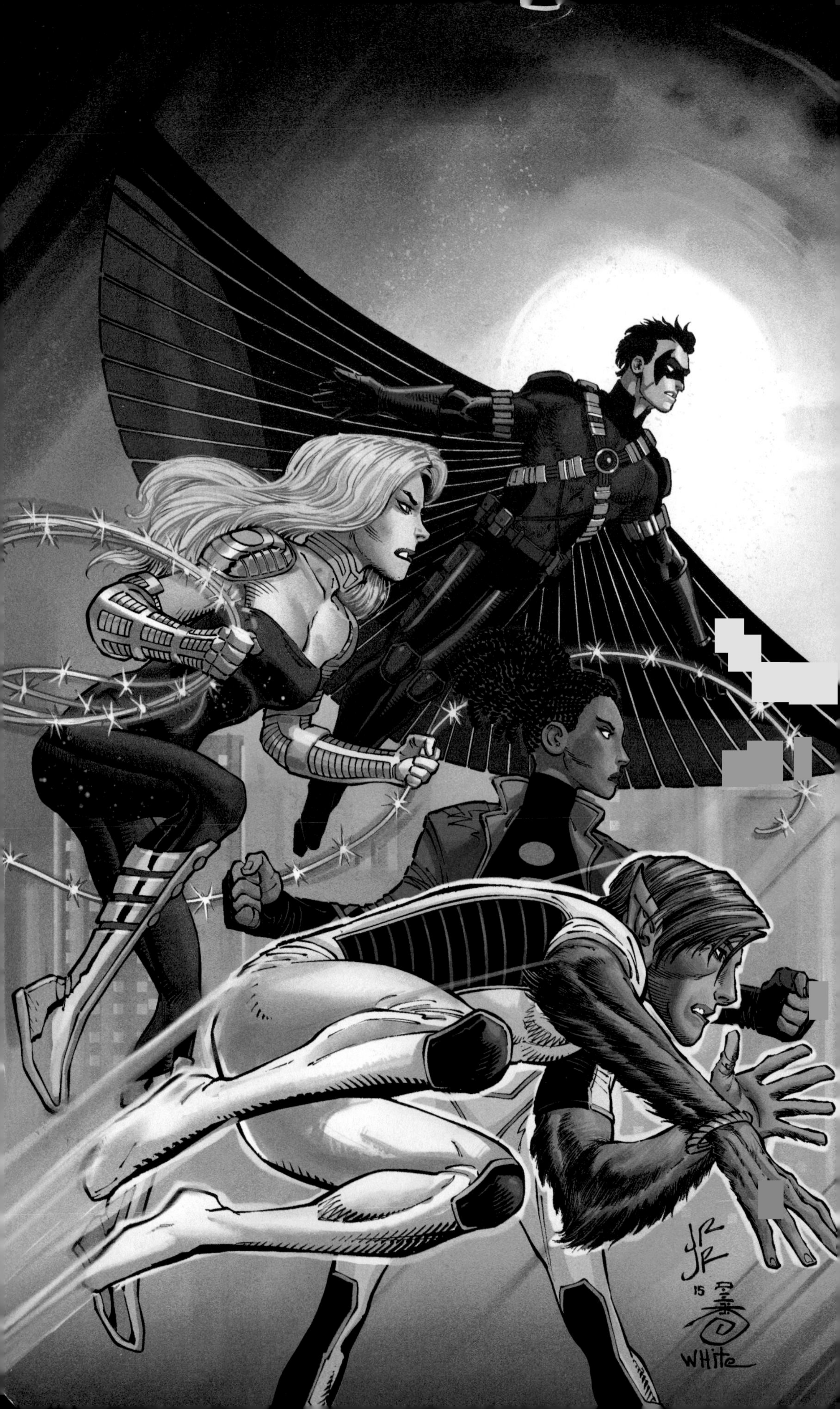